# THE VOLUNTEERS

## MEANS AND ENDS IN A NATIONAL ORGANIZATION

*Books by The Bureau of Applied Social Research, Columbia University*

*Published by The Free Press*

CONFLICT AND MOOD
by Patricia L. Kendall

MATHEMATICAL THINKING IN THE SOCIAL SCIENCES
Paul F. Lazarsfeld, Editor

PERSONAL INFLUENCE
by Elihu Katz and Paul F. Lazarsfeld

WHY FAMILIES MOVE
by Peter H. Rossi

THE FOCUSED INTERVIEW
by Robert K. Merton, Marjorie Fiske, and Patricia L. Kendall

UNION DEMOCRACY
by Seymour Martin Lipset, Martin A. Trow, and James S. Coleman

THE VOLUNTEERS
by David L. Sills

COMMUNITY CONFLICT
by James S. Coleman

THE ACADEMIC MIND
by Paul F. Lazarsfeld and Wagner Thielens, Jr.

# THE

# VOLUNTEERS

MEANS AND ENDS IN A NATIONAL ORGANIZATION

*by David L. Sills*

> Show us not the aim without the way,
> For ends and means on earth are so entangled
> That changing one, you change the other too;
> Each different path brings other ends in view.
> —Ferdinand Lassalle

*A Report of the Bureau of Applied Social Research, Columbia University*

*The Free Press, Glencoe, Illinois*

TO

*Charlotte and Malcolm Sills*
*my parents*

# PREFACE

VOLUNTARY ASSOCIATIONS of all kinds have always flourished in America, and many perceptive observers of the American scene have commented on the important role they play in American life. Alexis de Tocqueville, for example, found more than a century ago that "in no country of the world has the principle of association been more successfully used or applied to a greater multitude of objects than in America."[1] Lord Bryce was also impressed by American voluntary associations when he visited this country many years after de Tocqueville did, and concluded that they are "created, extended, and worked in the United States more quickly and effectively than in any other country."[2]*
More recently, the Editors of *Fortune,* in a book devoted to the subject, concluded that voluntary activities have "a deeper and more lasting effect upon American life, and even American policies, than do the official ones."[4]

Activities which have "a deeper and more lasting effect upon American life" than do official ones are of course worthy of serious study by anyone concerned with the preservation of a free society. But how can such a vast network of activity be studied? This book adopts what is generally called "the case study approach"; it is largely about one voluntary association, the National Foundation for Infantile Paralysis. This organization, founded by President Roosevelt in 1938, is most familiar to Americans because of its annual fund-raising campaign, the March of Dimes. But behind the March of Dimes is a vast voluntary association, the largest—in terms of both membership and annual budget—voluntary health association in America. It informs the public about infantile paralysis, supports professional education, provides financial assistance to polio victims, and dispenses millions of dollars each year in the form of research grants to scientists. The years of scientific research which recently culminated in the Salk polio vaccine, for example, were possible only because of funds provided by the American people through the March of Dimes.

This volume, however, is neither a history of the Foundation nor a

* Herbert Goldhamer first directed the attention of contemporary sociologists to these observations of de Tocqueville and Lord Bryce, in courses given at the University of Chicago.[3]

report on its contributions to scientific knowledge. Rather, it is concerned chiefly with the local organizations of the Foundation and their Volunteer members. Who are these Volunteers, and how did they initially become members of the Foundation? What do they do, and what satisfactions do they derive from their activities? What are the major rewards of volunteer participation? How do Volunteers actually perceive their organization, and what features of it do they single out as outstanding? These are some of the questions examined in this volume. Although it is essentially an institutional analysis, rather than a critique of voluntary associations generally, it constitutes in the very nature of the case one further attempt to explain the proliferation of voluntary activity in America, and to trace out some of the consequences of this activity for American society. It differs from many other attempts, however, in that explicit attention is given to the internal problems faced by voluntary associations, and to the ways—both planned and unplanned—in which voluntary associations develop solutions for these problems. More specifically, a central concern of this book is the process through which the members of a voluntary association help shape the organization's character and determine its future.

The selection of the Foundation for the purpose of studying how organizations are transformed by their members was based initially upon the fact that the Bureau of Applied Social Research of Columbia University and the American Institute of Public Opinion of Princeton, New Jersey, were provided with an opportunity to undertake a series of studies of the Foundation's local program. The writer served as project director for the Bureau studies, an experience which directed his attention to a number of fundamental problems concerning the role and nature of voluntary associations in general. These problems in turn led him to undertake further analysis of the research materials collected both by the Bureau and the Institute, and thus to the preparation of this book.

The relevance of the Foundation as the subject for an examination of the ways in which the membership of an organization influences its ultimate character stems both from its history as a voluntary association and from the fact that its local activities are directed almost entirely by Volunteer—in contrast to professional—workers. This situation contrasts sharply with that which prevails in such organizations as governmental or industrial bureaucracies, as well as in most health and welfare associations, in which the majority of day-to-day decisions are made by employed professional staff members. The far-reaching consequences of the opportunities for decision-making by Volunteers which the Foundation's ratio of Volunteer to professional workers provides are indicated throughout this volume.

For a variety of reasons social scientists have only infrequently directed their attention to the internal analysis of voluntary associations, and neither a systematic body of theory nor a standard method of analysis has as yet emerged. One study can do little to elevate the analysis of voluntary associations to a higher plane, but an accumulation of studies—each of which investigates in detail a particular set of problems, and yet which presents data of sufficient generality to make them applicable to a range of organizations—will in the long run serve the needs both of social theorists and of practical men who are seeking ways to utilize the potentialities of voluntary associations. Studies of "deviant cases," of organizations which in some way have overcome the major problems which confront voluntary associations, are particularly useful, since more can be learned from a single success than from countless failures.[5] Consider for example, a recent analysis of the International Typographical Union conducted at the Bureau of Applied Social Research by Martin Lipset, Martin Trow, and James Coleman. Since the ITU, "alone among North American labor organizations has maintained a two-party political system, much like that existing in national politics, for over half a century,"[6] it was selected by the authors as a strategic method of studying the general problems of one-party rule and oligarchy in trade unions. Similarly, since the Foundation has been so successful in maintaining a high level of interest among its members; in achieving its major goals; and, in brief, in avoiding the "organizational frustration" which is so characteristic of voluntary associations,[7] it is possible that the conclusions of this study will be of some assistance to those who attempt organizational solutions for the problems facing our society today. It is this hope which underlies the presentation of this volume.

The preparation of this book was in many ways a cooperative enterprise and it is a pleasure to cite the major contributions made by other people. I am deeply grateful to them all, but they are in no way responsible for whatever deficiencies and errors the book may contain.

The staff of the Bureau project which both gathered the data upon which much of the book is based and carried out the original analysis consisted of the following persons in addition to myself: Helmut H.

Guttenberg, Ghislaine Lovell, Rolf B. Meyersohn, Charlton R. Price, and Yole G. Sills. I have benefited greatly from the energy and intelligence which my colleagues brought to this undertaking.

Paul K. Perry and Arthur L. Keiser of the American Institute of Public Opinion were instrumental in making the data from the Institute studies of the Foundation available to the Bureau for the purpose of this re-analysis. Basil O'Connor, President of the National Foundation for Infantile Paralysis, released the data from both the Institute and my own studies to the Bureau for this purpose, and granted me full access to Foundation files. Herman Kahn, Director of the Franklin Delano Roosevelt Library at Hyde Park, made available for my use documents concerning the role played by President Roosevelt in the Foundation's early history.

The following friends and colleagues read all or major portions of the manuscript in one of its several drafts: Bernard Barber, Edmund deS. Brunner, Sigmund Diamond, Charles Y. Glock, Siegfried Kracauer, David Riesman, Natalie Rogoff, Philip Selznick, Margaret Snyder, and Sydney S. Spivack. I am indebted to them all for their criticisms and helpful suggestions. A number of Foundation staff members also reviewed the manuscript from the point of view of technical accuracy: Raymond H. Barrows, Dorothy Ducas, Melvin A. Glasser, John Gorrell, Joseph F. Nee, George P. Voss, Ruth Walrad, Hubert E. White, and Elaine Whitelaw. Although I have attempted to increase the factual accuracy of the book through incorporating their criticisms, my own interpretation of the Foundation and its activities necessarily differs in some respects from that of these staff members.

The task of typing the several drafts of the manuscript was performed with skill and patience by Richard E. Barron, Elisabeth Fontana, and Susanne Popper.

A grant from the National Foundation for Infantile Paralysis contributed substantially toward making the preparation of this book possible. Supplementary funds were obtained from grants made to the Bureau of Applied Social Research by the Ford Foundation and the Eda K. Loeb Fund.

Finally, a few totally inadequate words must be devoted to noting a number of special obligations. Paul F. Lazarsfeld has been my teacher for a number of years and was exceedingly generous of his time and wisdom during the writing of this book. Melvin A. Glasser was helpful at every stage of the project—from the pre-field work planning to the final editing of the manuscript—and his advice, based upon many years of professional experience in voluntary associations, has been most welcome. Philip Selznick's writings have had a profound impact upon my own approach to the analysis of the Foundation as a voluntary association. The frequent references in the text to his publications do not, I fear, reflect the full measure of my intellectual debt to him. Charlton R. Price played an important part both in the field research and in the original analysis of the data; since that time, he has been a constant source of ideas, criticism, and encouragement. Last, but very far from least, Yole G. Sills—in addition to her many professional contributions to the study as a staff member of the Bureau—provided during the preparation of this book an inordinate amount of understanding and forbearance.

David L. Sills

Bureau of Applied Social Research
Columbia University

# ACKNOWLEDGMENTS

THE AUTHOR wishes to thank the following publishers and copyright holders for their permission to excerpt and reprint selections:

Harper and Brothers for permission to quote from *Studies in Leadership: Leadership and Democratic Action* by Alvin W. Gouldner (ed.), 1950; *The American Red Cross: A History* by Foster Rhea Dulles, 1950; and *Communications Research: 1948–1949* by Paul F. Lazarsfeld and Frank W. Stanton (eds.), 1949.

Little, Brown and Company for permission to quote from *Sincerely, Willis Wayde* by John P. Marquand, 1955.

McGraw-Hill Book Company for permission to quote from *The Organizational Weapon: A Study of Bolshevik Strategy and Tactics* by Philip Selznik, 1952; and *Mirror for Man* by Clyde Kluckhohn, 1949.

Talcott Parsons for permission to quote from *The Theory of Social and Economic Organization* by Max Weber, translated by A. M. Henderson and Talcott Parsons; edited by Talcott Parsons, 1947.

The Ronald Press for permission to quote from *Voluntary Health Agencies: An Interpretive Study* by Selskar M. Gunn and Philip S. Platt, 1945.

The University of California Press for permission to quote from *TVA and the Grass Roots: A Study in the Sociology of Formal Organization* by Philip Selznick, 1949.

I also wish to thank officials of the following health and welfare associations for furnishing data concerning their organizations cited in this book: American Cancer Society, American Foundation for the Blind, American Heart Association, American National Red Cross, American Social Hygiene Association, National Foundation for Infantile Paralysis, National Foundation for Muscular Dystrophy, National Multiple Sclerosis Society, National Society for Crippled Children and Adults, National Tuberculosis Association, Planned Parenthood Federation of America, United Cerebral Palsy, and the United Funds and Community Councils of America (formerly the Community Chests and Councils of America).

# CONTENTS

## Conclusions

# *Appendices*

# LIST OF TABLES

# LIST OF CHARTS

# INTRODUCTION

A FUNDAMENTAL assumption of this study—an assumption which underlies many recent attempts to understand how large-scale organizations function—is that organizations are not simply collectivities of individuals but social groupings which have a reality transcending the individuals who comprise them. In his pioneering study of the principles underlying all formal organizations Chester I. Barnard made this assumption quite explicit, noting that when "the efforts of five men become coordinated in a system, that is, an organization, there is created something new in the world that is more or less different in quantity and quality from anything present in the sum of the efforts of the five men."[1]

A corollary to this assumption is that organizations are not simply instrumentalities which provide individuals with opportunities to fulfill their needs, but are also social structures with certain needs of their own. As such, the emergence, the growth, and the survival of a large-scale organization must be viewed as instances of the laws of organizational behavior—as well as those of individual or social psychology. To use the familiar expression, an organization has "a life of its own."*

It necessarily follows from these assumptions that the directives of organizational theory must be utilized in order to provide an adequate explanation for the behavior of individual members of organizations, since organizations make demands upon their members and set limits upon the range of their behavior. The adoption of this perspective does not of course mean that organizations can be examined without reference to the individuals who comprise them. In fact, a central thesis of this book is that many of the essential characteristics of organizations stem from both the social character of their membership and the satisfactions which individuals derive from participation. Furthermore, it is held that voluntary associations are particularly responsive to their membership, since their ultimate goals and their day-to-day procedures are in the very nature of the case largely determined by their members.

An organization may be defined as a rationally conceived system for coordinating the activities of a number of individuals toward some

---

* An illustration of the separate laws which govern the behavior of individuals and organizations is provided by the eternal complaint of Chiefs of Staff, Generals, and Privates alike: "I can't help it—it's the Army."

objective or purpose. Typically, the participation of individuals in organizations is segmental;—that is to say, they do not devote a major share of their time and energy to organizational activities. In these two respects—the coordinated character of the activity and the segmental participation of individuals—organizations differ markedly from such aggregates as communities and families, in which the activities of individuals are coordinated only informally, and which require a more nearly total commitment on the part of individual participants.

If we examine any organization closely, however, the "ideal" nature of this definition becomes apparent. For as Philip Selznick points out, "the individuals within the system tend to resist being treated as means. They interact as wholes, bringing to bear their own special problems and purposes; . . ."[2] In resisting manipulation and in reacting as if their segmental commitment were a total one, the individual members of an organization often determine its ultimate character. This ultimate character, or "shape" of the organization, may differ from that envisioned by its founders, since the problems and purposes of individuals do not necessarily correspond to those of the organization.

Individuals may transform organizations in a number of different ways. In order to describe the impact of these influences it is necessary to examine the social origins of individual participants, their motivations for becoming members, the gratifications they derive from membership, and their interpretation of the meaning of the organization's activities. Attention is directed to all of these topics in this inquiry, since one of its broad purposes is to trace out some of the implications of Selznick's statement that "all formal organizations are moulded by forces tangential to their rationally ordered structures and stated goals."[3] Before these topics are discussed, however, it is necessary to say a word about the nature of organizational structure itself.

### THE STRUCTURE OF NATIONAL ORGANIZATIONS

Local organizations—ranging in size and importance from such informal groupings as the Larchmont Reading Club in suburban New York to the large and powerful business and professional associations in our urban centers—are of course most numerous and in some ways most expressive of American life. In recent years, however, national organizations have shown the most spectacular growth.* A recent in-

---

* Kenneth Boulding has recently advanced the thesis that the growth of large scale organizations in recent decades is a direct reflection of changes in the technical ability to organize—consisting both of material developments and organizing skills.[4]

ventory, for example, contains the names of some 5,000 organizations which carry on activities on a nationwide basis.†[5] Since the Foundation is only one of 5,000 national organizations, it is important to describe the type of voluntary association it represents.

From a structural point of view, national organizations are of two broad types: those which have local units and those whose membership is comprised of individuals living in different parts of the country. The Foundation belongs to the former type, since it has more than 3,000 local Chapters. National organizations which have local units may in turn be subdivided into two broad categories: those which consist of a national headquarters and local branches, and those which are federations of semi-autonomous local affiliates. The Foundation, as will presently be noted, belongs to the former type.

The general existence of these two patterns of organizational structure is clearly recognized by everyone who has worked with or examined national organizations. However, no standard terminology has been developed to describe them. Since the terms "corporate-type" and "federation-type" seem to summarize the essential difference between them most succinctly, they are used throughout this discussion.

The distinction between these two types of organizational structure has many parallels. Some national states are loose federations of semi-autonomous component units while others are highly centralized. Churches may also be classified in a similar way. At one extreme are the churches which conform to the "congregational" model, in which each parish is responsible for its own affairs; at the other extreme are the "episcopal" type churches, in which ultimate sovereignty resides in the parent organization.

The absence of any standard terminology to describe these two types of national organizations is one reflection of the fact that students of large-scale organizations have confined their interests largely to organizations having a corporate structure. The categories of structural types used in industrial management or public administration texts, for example, are clearly based upon the assumption that ultimate power in an organization rests entirely in the hands of the top administrators. Even Max Weber, who is generally regarded as the instigator of the scientific study of bureaucracy (which he regarded as a pervasive form of administration characteristic of all highly-developed societies, and

† Arnold Rose reports that "in a representative sample of voluntary associations in Minneapolis and St. Paul, 59 per cent had a national affiliation, 11 per cent had a state affiliation, while 30 per cent were purely local."[6]

not confined to government or industry), selected highly centralized
governments and churches as his primary models for the discussion of
large-scale organizations.[7]

With several important exceptions, contemporary studies of large
organizations from a broadly sociological perspective—in contrast to
histories, descriptions of programs, and discussions of operational
problems—have been limited to analyses of industrial organizations
and government bureaucracies.[8] The authority structure of organizations, and the consequences for an organization of its authority structure, are of course matters which have generally interested students of
administration, but very few studies of voluntary associations have
actually directed specific attention to these problems. In the present
volume, however, an explicit attempt is made to examine the consequences for one organization—the National Foundation for Infantile
Paralysis—of its authority structure. Before this rather complex task
can be undertaken, however, it is necessary to review briefly the contributions others have made to the clarification of this problem.

Although structural differences among national organizations have
not been systematically examined by writers interested in the theory of
administration, most empirical studies of voluntary associations and
most publications in the field of social welfare record the fact that these
two structural types exist. Wayne McMillen, for example, describes
these two types of organizational structure and points out various problems which often arise in the relationship of national headquarters to
local units, but fails to mention that these problems may vary according
to the underlying structure of the organization.[9]

The *operational* problems involved in the relationship between the
national office of an organization and its local units are of course a frequent topic for discussion among professional workers engaged in community organization and social welfare. The magazine *Adult Leadership,* for example, recently devoted the major portion of one issue to a
"Workshop on Locals and their Nationals," in which a distinction was
made between local organizations which are "branches" in the sense
that "they were organized at the initiative and with the help of an
already existing national group," and local organizations which are
"roots," since "they created a national office to give them services they
needed and to make their programs and causes seen and heard throughout the country."[10]

Since *Adult Leadership* is published for use by adult educators and
others engaged in community activities—both professionals and volun-

teers—the articles included in this issue are concerned with practical measures for achieving understanding and reducing conflict between the headquarters and the local units of national organizations, rather than with an analysis of the structural arrangements of such organizations, or with the consequences which result from different types of structure. But it is interesting to note that none of the articles makes further mention of this fundamental distinction between national organizations. In fact, they are all based upon the assumption that all organizations have an identical structure. And with one possible exception, an article dealing with the resistance of members of a local unit to filling out the annual questionnaire submitted to it by its national headquarters (in which it is implied that the local unit might have the authority to disregard the questionnaire),[11] all of the articles in this special section take it for granted that national organizations have corporate rather than federation-type structures.

If we turn to empirical studies of voluntary associations, however, we find a number of discussions of the relationship of the formal structure of a particular organization to its capacity to carry out its task.[12] But comparatively few attempts have been made to extract generalizations from an examination of a number of organizations. Three efforts along these lines are worthy of examination. In the course of a theoretical analysis of the prospects for internal democracy within trade unions, Martin Lipset notes that there are two ideal-type patterns through which trade unions and other voluntary associations are created: organization "from the top down, where the group which originally starts the association organizes other individuals or branches into a larger structure," and organization "through the successive but autonomous formation of one group after another. . . ."[13] The possibilities for democracy are much greater in the second type of organization, according to Lipset, since a ready-made opposition is built into the organization. He concludes his brief discussion of structure by stating as a general hypothesis that "the greater the number of independent sources of power and status in an organization, the greater the possibility that alternative factions or parties will be established to oppose the incumbent party."[14]

A second example of an inquiry which examines the consequences for organizations of their formal structure is Ray Johns' study of national social agencies, which is chiefly concerned with the conditions under which national organizations embark upon cooperative ventures with other organizations. This analysis reveals that cooperative ability is directly related to formal structure. Organizations organized along corporate lines, Johns concludes, generally have more limited relationships with other organizations than do those which have a federation-type structure.[15]

A third, and more extensive treatment of this problem is found in David Truman's analysis of the role of "interest" or "pressure" groups in the governmental process. In contrast to most previous discussions of "pressure" groups, which concentrate upon "lobbying" activities as such, a major topic in Truman's study is the internal structure of these organizations, and the impact of structure upon activities. He compares "federated" and "unitary" forms of structure and concludes that organizations which seek to mould public opinion or influence the course of government are less effective if they have a "federated" structure, since they have difficulty in presenting a united front. Unfortunately for their own purposes, Truman notes, federated organizations establish and sanctify subcenters of power by "acknowledging in formal terms certain spheres of local or constituent autonomy, . . ."[16] He states that examples of this kind are not hard to find, but that very few careful studies of this process have been made. He cites, however, specific examples of internal dissension in such federations as the A.F. of L., the American Medical Association, the American Farm Bureau Federation, and the C.I.O.[17]

The preceding summary of previous references to the two types of structure which characterize national organizations has largely ignored the problem of historical origins. It is quite significant, however, that all of the writers cited stress the fact that historical factors usually determine a national organization's structure. McMillen, for example, notes that a federation-type structure develops when a "national organization is formed by a combination of local units. . . ."[18] The Editor of *Adult Leadership* explains to his readers that the local units of corporate-type organizations are "organized at the initiative and with the help of an already existing national group," while federations are said to have "created a national office to give them services they needed. . . ."[19] Lipset reports that "the variation in historical origins of different trade unions and other voluntary organizations may determine subsequent temporary or long-term variations in their organizational structures."[20] Johns speaks of organizations which are "federations of already established local agencies" in contrast to those which "developed a national organization before local affiliates were organized."[21] Finally, Truman notes that the problem of cohesion—which he regards as endemic to federations—"almost invariably arises where the constituent units antedate the federal body, as is usually true."[22]

It is certainly not coincidence that led all of those writers to stress the importance of historical origins in their discussions of the nature and consequences of formal structure. On the contrary, their focus upon origins is quite consistent with their descriptive purposes, since the most readily-observable and easily-documented correlates of structural types are circumstances surrounding the formation of the organizations. For this reason, an historical explanation of the Foundation's organizational structure is included in this analysis. The major focus, however, is not upon origins but upon consequences, i.e., upon the capacity of the organization to carry out the purposes for which it was established.

*National voluntary health associations.* The foundation belongs to one species of the genus "voluntary association"—it is a national voluntary health association. This classification is sometimes extended on the one hand to include primarily professional organizations, such as the American Medical Association and the American Public Health Association, and on the other to include general health and welfare organizations, particularly the American National Red Cross.[23] For present purposes, however, national voluntary health associations are defined as those national associations which 1) concentrate their efforts upon one specific disease or disorder, 2) have local affiliates or chapters throughout the country, 3) have a membership composed primarily of lay volunteers, and 4) depend upon public contributions for their financial support. In addition to excluding professional societies, general welfare organizations, and organizations which have only a national office, this definition also excludes organizational clearinghouses, such as the National Health Council, which serves as a coordinating center for all of its member health associations, or the American Foundation for the Blind, which both carries on a national program of its own and coordinates the work done by independent local agencies for the blind throughout the country.

Like national organizations generally, national voluntary health associations have either a corporate or a federation-type structure. Among the larger associations, the National Foundation for Infantile Paralysis and the American Cancer Society have corporate structures, while the National Tuberculosis Association, the American Heart Association, and the National Society for Crippled Children and Adults are best described as federations. Among the newer and smaller associations, the National Multiple Sclerosis Society and the Muscular Dystrophy Association have corporate structures, while United Cerebral Palsy is a federation.

It should be noted that the terms "corporate" and "federation" refer to patterns which seldom exist in pure form, and that not all of these organizations conform perfectly to the classification given above. More specifically, none of the federations among the major voluntary health associations conform perfectly to the definition generally found in the literature—an affiliation of previously-existing local organizations. The National Tuberculosis Association, for example, was founded in 1904 by a group of doctors and laymen and "much of the early work of the Association staff was . . . directed toward organization of state tuberculosis associations and, through them, of local associations."[24] The American Heart Association was for its first twenty-five years a professional society of physicians, which consisted of a few loosely affiliated groups. In 1948, it became a national voluntary health association, and it soon established affiliates in most of the forty-eight states.[25] United Cerebral Palsy was founded in 1949 as an affiliation of several local organizations, but most of its present affiliates have been established since then through the encouragement of the national office.[26] And the National Society for Crippled Children and Adults, which was founded as a state society in Ohio, did not acquire local affiliates until it became a national organization in 1921.[27] In spite of the fact that the initiative for the establishment of the local affiliates of these federations came from the central office, the process of organizational growth and adaptation has led to a situation in which the balance of power is located in the local organizations. For this reason they are best classified as federations.

### THE PARADOX OF DELEGATION

Although the activities of its National Headquarters are reviewed in this study, major attention is given to the Foundation's local organizations. Since authority and functions have been delegated to these organizations, it is necessary to provide a brief description of the nature of delegation itself.

Organizations are initially established when a given task cannot be executed either by one individual or by a large, undifferentiated group. The magnitude of the task of combating infantile paralysis, for example, was impressed upon President Roosevelt by his own efforts to combat it alone. "I firmly believe," he said in 1937, "that the time has now arrived when the whole attack on this plague should be led and directed, though not controlled, by one national body. And it is for this purpose that a new national foundation for infantile paralysis is being created."[28]

In creating the Foundation, President Roosevelt delegated the responsibility for combating polio to others, and the Board of Trustees of the new organization necessarily delegated responsibility to both a professional staff and to volunteers. The process of delegating authority and functions, however, necessarily involves the recognition and legitimization of individual initiative, which in turn tends to alter in some way the intentions of the delegators. For this reason, delegation is inherently paradoxical in nature. "If you want something done right, do it yourself" is the advice dictated by folk wisdom, but the complexity and size of many organizational tasks make this advice gratuitous. Organizations may thus be said to be in a state of perpetual transformation—partly, of course, in response to the external conditions which they face—but also in response to the consequences which emerge from the process of delegation.

The delegation of authority and functions may take place either *upwards* or *downwards* in an organization.* This can be demonstrated most clearly by recalling the two major circumstances under which organizations are created. Sometimes a group of people meet together and appoint or elect officers to act in the name of the organization; in such instances, delegation takes place in an *upward* direction. When, on the other hand, an organization is formed by an individual or a small group of individuals, who appoint a staff to help them carry out the task of the organization, and when this staff in turn creates committees, divisions, and branches, delegation is directed *downwards*. (As the structure of either of these types of organizations becomes more complex, and as both formal and informal rules of procedure are established, the patterns of delegation become more complicated, and

---

* Logically, authority and functions can also be delegated *laterally*. In an organization, this type of delegation typically occurs when a committee informally divides up the responsibility with which it has been entrusted. Similarly, the informal division of labor among a small work group can be viewed as lateral delegation. Alvin Gouldner, for example, reports that among gypsum miners "the informal group and its norms . . . constituted a functional equivalent for bureaucratic rules to the degree, at least, that it served to allocate concrete work responsibilities and to specify individual duties."[29] Since the present discussion is confined to the formal delegation of authority and functions, lateral delegation is not considered.

situations develop in which delegation, in effect, takes place simultaneously in both directions.)

It was noted above that national organizations have either a corporate or a federation-type formal structure. The fundamental basis for the distinction between these two types of structures is the locus of ultimate authority within the organization. In organizations having corporate structures, the national headquarters exercises supervisory powers over the component units, while in federations the affiliates retain a large measure of autonomy. In terms of delegation the fundamental difference between the two types is that organizations with corporate structures have delegated some of their authority and certain functions to their component units, while the affiliates of federations have delegated functions and authority both to their own leadership and to their national office.

Since the Foundation's formal structure is of the corporate type, the procedures by which it has delegated authority and functions downward to its local units necessarily constitute a central focus of this analysis. But upward delegation also takes place in any voluntary association. That is, the membership always authorizes some members to act in the name of the organization. In the case of the Foundation, upward delegation may be said to have taken place because the affairs of each local Chapter are administered by an Executive Committee, to which the Chapter membership has delegated authority.

If we take as a starting point for an examination of the Foundation the existence of these types of delegation, and if we embark upon this task armed with some of the conclusions which have emerged from other studies of large-scale organizations, we are immediately alerted to the fact that the process of delegation necessarily creates a set of conditions which may prevent the organization from achieving the very goals which it was established to attain. As such, the consequences of delegation may become major threats to organizational stability and continuity.

Since the Foundation has not been deflected from achieving its goal, it follows that some provisions—which may be characterized as control mechanisms—must have been developed which eliminate at least in part these consequences of delegation and which attenuate their destructive effects. The concept of "control mechanisms" is derived from a consideration of organizations as adaptive social structures constantly being altered by the very process which created them— delegation. Every organization, from this point of view, has a set of needs which must be met if it is to survive. These needs are largely met by the development of organizational features which may most conveniently be described as control mechanisms.[30]

Has the Foundation, through the incorporation of certain features in its organizational structure, in effect protected itself against the organizational forces which created it? Before this rather complex question can be approached directly a few explanatory notes are required.

First, a word is needed on the distinction between an organization's formal and informal structure. The *formal* structure of an organization is purposively established in order to provide a framework within which goals may be achieved; an organization is often deflected from achieving its goals through processes which have their origins in the *informal* structure, e.g., those patterns of behavior which emerge from the spontaneous interaction of personalities and groups within the organization.[31] But the distinction between these two structures is not quite as clear-cut as this formulation suggests. In the first place, the formal structure of an organization may fail to contain features which are needed to prevent the modification of goals—as, for example, adequate provisions for the supervision of the activities of subordinates. In the second place, the informal structure—in addition to being responsible for the nonachievement of goals—is also a necessary instrument for their achievement. For example, patterns of behavior which arise spontaneously often result in greater organizational cohesiveness through increasing the willingness of the members to perform their assigned tasks.[32] Since a major concern of this inquiry is with the control mechanisms which have kept the Foundation from being deflected from its path, both structures must be examined.

Second, it should be noted that those features of the Foundation's structure which are described in this volume as constituting control mechanisms were not necessarily created by the organization for this purpose. As will be indicated, some were explicitly planned; others were adopted because they are generally accepted principles of administration; and still others were established more or less accidentally as a response to some operational problem which was not perceived by the decision makers as being related to the broader problem of delegation. For present purposes, the extent to which the organizational planners and policy makers were aware of the usefulness of these features is irrelevant; the important point is that an examination of the

structure of the Foundation reveals that these features do in fact serve
to prevent the goals of the organization from being unduly modified.*

## THE RESEARCH APPROACH

The technical aspects of the field research are described in some
detail in the Appendices; it is necessary at this point only to provide
a general statement of the methodology employed.

Because the central problem with which this volume is concerned
is a broad one, it has not been possible to relate it to one or a few major
propositions in organizational theory. On the contrary, an explicit attempt has been made to adopt an eclectic approach. For this reason,
frequent references are made in the text to the conclusions reached in
other studies of large-scale organizations—conclusions which are used
as diagnostic criteria for the analysis of the Foundation. Stated another
way, the major features of the Foundation's formal and informal structure are discussed in this volume by noting their relevance to the
conclusions reached by other students of formal organizations. By the
same token, a number of different research procedures and analysis
techniques have been utilized in the course of this study—each selected
on the pragmatic grounds that it seemed the best way to obtain and
organize the data necessary to illuminate a particular topic.

This volume is presented as an "institutional analysis," a convenient
phrase which is actually somewhat misleading, since few investigators
attempt, and fewer succeed, to describe all relevant aspects of an organization. Each researcher starts with a particular problem, and develops a methodology which he hopes is adequate for his purposes. In
the present study, which is largely oriented toward the problem of the
influence of an organization's membership upon its fundamental character, it was of course necessary to utilize first-hand information concerning the membership, obtained through personal interviews. But
it is necessary to provide a word of explanation for the fact that the
local, rather than the national, membership of the Foundation was
examined.

* Control mechanisms which are neither intended nor recognized by participants in
an organization may be said to serve *latent functions*.[33] The methodology for verifying
the imputation of latent functions remains relatively uncodified. Ideally, such verification would involve the observation of situations in which a given mechanism was *not*
present and required functions were *not* performed. The difficulties involved in verification of this type are enormous, since it is seldom possible to approach the conditions of
a controlled experiment, i.e., to hold other factors constant. For this reason, latent
functions must be accepted largely on the basis of their "logical" character—that is,
through "mental experimentation"—and on the basis of the absence of any conflicting
evidence.

A dilemma which plagues all explanations of historical phenomena is that which derives fundamentally from the conflict between the "great man" and the "mass behavior" theories of history. In the present research this conflict is best illustrated by the responses given by Volunteers when they were asked to state what in their opinion was the "key" to the Foundation's success. This projective question elicited the expected wide range of responses. Some Volunteers attributed the Foundation's success to the appeal of the crippled child, others to the fundraising techniques utilized, etc. But a substantial number of Volunteers replied either in terms of the "great man" theory, and attributed everything to the Foundation's national leadership (particularly to President Roosevelt and Basil O'Connor), or in terms of the "mass behavior" theory, in which case they spoke of the power of billions of dimes or the concerted efforts of hundreds of thousands of Volunteers like themselves.

In this volume no attempt is made to resolve this conflict—in fact, the underlying assumption is that there is no real conflict. By focusing upon the local membership of the Foundation it has been possible not only to assess the contributions of the membership at large to the achievements of the Foundation, but also to acquire some understanding of the crucial importance of organizational structure as the link between the top leadership and the membership of an organization. And it is of utmost importance that organizational structure be examined from the "underside" of an organization, since it is only rarely that the top leadership fully appreciates or even understands the true nature of the structure which alone makes the contributions of both leaders and members possible. As Herbert Simon has noted, "in the study of organization, the operative employee must be at the focus of attention, for the succcess of the structure will be judged by his performance within it."[34]

So much for the decision to focus research attention upon the local membership of the Foundation. The decision to study the attitudes and behavior of the American public with respect to the Foundation's activities was based upon the fact that Volunteers are drawn from the public as well as upon the crucial importance to a mass organization of public support. Many special purpose associations can exist for years without the general public having any knowledge or awareness of their activities. Not so with the major voluntary health and welfare agencies, which are an integral part of the fabric of American life. Like our armed forces, our political parties and our government bureaucracy, these organizations are in a very real sense creatures of public opinion. For this reason, an attempt is made in this volume to relate the local program of the Foundation to the public which supports it and which it serves.

*The methodology of institutional analysis.* Some institutional analysis are based largely upon "inside information" of one kind or another. The researchers are generally either employees of the associations concerned or have had the opportunity, as social scientists, to witness the day-to-day operations of an organization, to interview key personnel, and to examine the organization's records. Since "inside knowledge" of an organization often has wide applicability both to other organizations and to organizational theory, these accounts form an important part of the growing literature on the functioning of large voluntary associations.

Studies based largely upon "inside knowledge," however, often have one serious drawback: the authors frequently do not make explicit the procedures through which they reached their conclusions. Accordingly, the reader must base his judgment of the validity of such accounts upon the general plausibility of the interpretations made and upon his confidence in the ability of the investigator.

Another type of institutional analysis differs from the first in the extent to which the investigators have attempted to describe the indicators from which they drew their conclusions. Since most research reports describe some of the indicators used, the assignment of individual studies to either of these classifications is necessarily somewhat arbitrary. The present study of the Foundation, however, constitutes an explicit attempt to contribute to this general research tradition.

*The description of indicators.* It is necessary to clarify what is meant by providing a description of the indicators used. The goal of most research in both the natural sciences and in experimental psychology is to report both the results and the methods used to obtain these results in such a way that another investigator can substitute new variables and thus specify the conditions under which certain conditions do and do not prevail. The subject matter of research in the social sciences, however, is often so fluid that precise replications of this kind are difficult to achieve.* In the case of the present research, for example, it is patently impossible to carry out another study of Founda-

---

* Studies of voting behavior are perhaps the closest approximations to replications of research in the social sciences. See, for example, a summary of findings from seven election studies in Berelson, et al., *Voting.*[35]

tion Volunteers at a time prior to the announcement both to the public
and to Volunteers of the efficacy of the Salk vaccine.

Although it may often be impossible in the social sciences to undertake highly controlled replication, it is usually possible for other investigators to achieve partial replication, and at the very least to use
one research project as a basis for developing an improved methodology. It is possible, that is, if the researcher has made his indicators
explicit. The issue under discussion here is not the inclusion of technical appendices describing sample selection, index construction and
the like—although these are necessary components of an explicit description of indicators—but rather the inclusion in the research report
of substantial portions of data from which conclusions have been
drawn, and of descriptions of the variables used. These may take the
form of quotations from either informants or documents, or of statistical tables, or both. No matter what form they take, it is possible for
the reader to review critically the adequacy of the conclusions which
have been drawn from the data.

*Replicability and explicitness.* In the case of the present research,
two steps have been taken in order to approach the twin goals of
replicability and explicitness. First, two research organizations—the
Bureau of Applied Social Research of Columbia University and the
American Institute of Public Opinion, Princeton, New Jersey—carried
out independent but closely related and simultaneous research projects.
The two research designs are described in Appendix A; it is sufficient
to note here that the Institute's research consisted of a nationwide
survey of the American public and a survey of Foundation Volunteers
in eight-five counties throughout the United States; the Bureau's research consisted of a survey of the general public in four cities and a
survey of Foundation Volunteers in thirty-seven counties. Since similar questionnaires were used in both surveys, there was available for
the analysis not only a larger body of data than that which is generally
available, but also two sets of independently obtained data. The Institute's research among Foundation Volunteers was conducted primarily in order to provide quantitative comparisons with the more
intensive research conducted by the Bureau, and in the interests of
brevity it is for the most part not reported in this volume. But it served
the extremely useful purpose of providing bench marks against which
to check the conclusions derived from the data obtained by the Bureau.
Much more extensive use has been made of the Institute's nationwide
survey of the general public, since the conclusions derived from a na-

tionwide survey necessarily have greater generality than those derived from research in only four cities.

A second step taken in the preparation of this volume was to present a large part of the relevant descriptive and statistical data from which conclusions have been drawn. Statistical presentations undoubtedly detract from the readability of the text; for this reason, the narrative summarizes the important conclusions drawn from them. The nontechnical reader, accordingly, can skip over the tables without missing any essential information.

The technically minded reader will note that the conclusions drawn from the statistical tables have not been subjected to tests of statistical significance. No apology is made for this omission, since in the judgment of the writer and many of his colleagues at the Bureau of Applied Social Research such tests as have been developed are not applicable to most data obtained through survey—in contradistinction to experimental—research.[36] In place of such tests of statistical significance, two criteria of validity have been utilized. First, the results presented have been judged on the basis of their *internal consistency* with other results. In the case of the Volunteer study, evidence has not been presented unless the statistical findings and those derived from the qualitative analysis of the interview materials do not conflict with one another; in the case of the general public study, the evidence was checked against that obtained from tabulations of closely related questions. Second, the results presented have been judged on the basis of their *replicability*. In the case of the Volunteer study, this involved, whenever comparable data were available, comparisons with the results of the Institute's independent study of Foundation Volunteers; in the case of the general public study, it involved comparisons between the nationwide study and the four-city study, and further comparisons of the results obtained in each of the four cities.

PLAN OF THE BOOK

Chapters I and II are devoted to expositions of two broad organizational problems—maintaining the interest of members and preserving organizational goals—which arise from the paradox of delegation, and for which the Foundation has of necessity had to develop solutions of some sort. From a methodological point of view, these two problems may be viewed as broad hypotheses requiring empirical verification. In large part, our everyday observations of organizations serve to refute the insolubility of these problems, since we know that progress toward

the achievement of organizational goals is often maintained. But common-sense observations do not necessarily indicate the specific mechanisms through which solutions to these problems have been achieved.
For this reason, these chapters are organized in such a way that specific
aspects of the problems are matched with specific aspects of the Foundation's formal and informal structure.\*

Chapters III and VI are concerned with the activities of Foundation
Volunteers. Chapter III is devoted to a problem which has until now
been largely neglected by students of voluntary associations: How are
volunteer members recruited? On the basis of interview materials, a
typology of recruits is developed; in subsequent chapters this typology
is used as a base point against which to measure changes in the orientation of Volunteers brought about by the fact of participation itself.
Chapter IV describes the Foundation's local patient care program, and
Chapter V the local organization of the March of Dimes. In both of
these chapters, the satisfactions which Volunteers derive from these
activities are described in conjunction with expositions of the activities
themselves. Chapter VI is concerned with the March of Dimes from
the point of view of its contributors, and indicates how the March of
Dimes has been so successful in obtaining contributions from a majority of the American public.

The final chapters of the book—Chapters VII through IX—present
the major conclusions of the analysis. Chapter VII demonstrates that
the images of the Foundation held by its Volunteers are an important
component of Volunteer participation; Chapter VIII summarizes the
major rewards which Volunteers obtain from their participation; and
Chapter IX indicates how the present-day experiences of Volunteers
will to a very large extent determine the Foundation's ultimate future.

Three Appendices are included. Appendix A describes the selection
and composition of the samples studied; Appendix B contains a technical description of the various indices used in the text; and Appendix
C describes the thirty-seven counties and Chapters studied.

\* It should also be noted that these two chapters contain some descriptive material
which does not necessarily illuminate the problem of how the Foundation has resolved
the paradox of delegation, but which is included in order to provide the reader with
information concerning the Foundation and its Volunteer membership basic to an
understanding of subsequent chapters.

*chapter I*

# MAINTAINING MEMBERSHIP INTEREST

## *Introduction*

DISCUSSIONS OF voluntary associations in America characteristically stress one of three major themes. First, throughout our history participation in voluntary activity has been regarded as having its origins in the fundamentally democratic nature of American society, as being an essential requirement for the survival of democracy in America, and above all as being a peculiarly *American* phenomenon.*

A second theme—more frequent in sociological analysis of voluntary associations—attempts to correct this somewhat misleading picture of American life by pointing out that participation in voluntary activities is by no means a universal phenomenon in America. Most such studies have shown that from one-third to one-half of the adult population does not belong to any voluntary associations, and that at best perhaps one-fourth of the population belongs to more than one association. Socio-economic status has uniformly been found to be the major correlate of participation. A large majority of people of higher status belong to voluntary associations, and a majority of people of lower status do not.[3]

A third theme which dominates many discussions of voluntary as-

* The assertion that voluntary associations currently play a unique role in American life cannot, however, be accepted uncritically, since there are many indications that—particularly with reference to local associations—many societies exhibit a similar proliferation of voluntary associations. This seems particularly to be the case in the Scandinavian countries, Germany, Austria, and Great Britain. However, not all countries which have a large number of voluntary associations are Western. Rural Japanese society, in particular, is characterized by many voluntary associations.[1] Nor do voluntary associations play an equally important role in all Western countries.[2]

sociations concerns the actual character of the participation of the membership. The general finding with respect to participation is that voluntary associations tend to be characterized by an active minority which actually controls the association's affairs and an inactive majority which participates only occasionally in the organization's activities and which in other ways expresses disinterest and apathy. Lord Bryce, for example, who found voluntary associations to be an important component of American democracy, nevertheless recognized the near-universality of minority rule in "all assemblies and groups and organized bodies of men. . . ."[4] More recently, Philip Selznick has described the typical voluntary association in the following terms:

Most voluntary associations . . . are skeletal in the sense that they are manned by a small core of individuals—the administration, the local sub-leaders, a few faithful meeting-goers—around whom there fluctuates a loosely bound mass of dues-payers. This type of membership has, on the whole, only a very limited relation to the organization; its agreement with it may be of the vaguest sort; it may give little or no time to the organization nor be guided by its pronouncements save, as in unions and professional groups, on very narrow issues; in short, the power implications of membership are minimal.[5]

Bernard Barber, who has perhaps devoted more explicit attention to the problem of membership apathy than any other student of voluntary associations, has cited evidence of the existence of an active minority and an inactive majority in service clubs, the American Legion, fraternal organizations, and consumer cooperatives.[6] Finally, Broom and Selznick, summarizing a large number of studies of trade unions, conclude that in most unions the majority of members have little interest in the functioning of the union, and fewer than 10 per cent attend union meetings.[7]

Concern over the problem of membership apathy and nonparticipation has stemmed largely from two sources. First, people who have a strong faith in democracy, and who believe that a precondition of democracy is active participation on the part of the citizens, have almost ritualistically deplored the existence of apathy because of its assumed negative effect upon the health of society at large. The failure of so many to vote in elections, to join voluntary associations, and to play an active role in associations to which they do belong is widely regarded as a danger signal for a democracy. As Riesman and Glazer have recently pointed out:

The discussion of apathy—and its converse, the "responsibility of the citizen"—has overflowed the boundaries of traditional political science and become the concern of the sociologist, the psychiatrist, the social psychologist, and, recently, the atomic scientists.[8]

Since one of the assumptions of this study is that voluntary associations have far-reaching implications for American society, the relevance of membership participation to the health of society at large is implicit throughout. Our present interest, however, is with another alleged consequence of membership nonparticipation: its effect upon the capacity of an organization to achieve its goals.

It must be noted at the outset that an active minority and a passive majority may exist in many organizations without interfering in any way with progress toward goals, just as widespread membership participation does not necessarily indicate an adherence to democratic practices. An inactive membership may not interfere with goal achievement particularly in organizations which serve highly specific functions for their members, and which depend for their financial support entirely upon membership dues—an automobile association or a medical payment plan are obvious examples. In organizations of this type, membership apathy may be deplored because of the fact that democratic values are violated,[9] but the organization itself is generally not adversely affected. As long as services for the membership are provided, the inactive majority will generally be satisfied.[10]

In other voluntary associations, on the other hand, membership participation is of crucial importance for the achievement of goals. This is particularly true of those organizations—like the Foundation—which are totally dependent upon their fund-raising campaigns for their financial support, in contrast to organizations which are supported by membership dues. Since the March of Dimes is a fund-raising campaign specifically geared to soliciting small contributions from millions of people, a large and active membership is necessary in order to reach these millions.

The generic problem of maintaining membership interest in voluntary associations may thus be stated in these terms: When authority and functions are delegated *upward* in an association, there is a tendency for the membership to lose interest in participating in the program of the organization, thus permitting an active minority to gain control. Two consequences may result from this process. First, the individuals to whom authority and functions have been delegated may develop interests of their own, and consequently may neglect the initial goals of the organization. Second, if some phase of the organization's program is dependent upon widespread membership participation, this process may make it impossible for the organization to achieve its goals.

In face of this problem, how has the Foundation been able to maintain a sufficiently high level of membership participation to ensure that its operational and fund-raising programs do not suffer from membership apathy? This question cannot of course be fully answered in this chapter; in fact, this entire volume is in many respects devoted to an examination of this general problem. But a beginning can be made by pointing out various features of the Foundation's formal structure which are related to the problem of membership participation.

The section which follows immediately is devoted to a general description of the Volunteer membership of the Foundation, and particularly to the Volunteers whose experiences are the main subject matter of this study. Following this description, a section is devoted to the major sources of membership apathy which students of large-scale organizations have identified. A final section describes those features of the Foundation's structure which serve to mitigate the adverse consequences of membership apathy.

## The Volunteer Membership of the Foundation

Since the Foundation is a voluntary association, it utilizes Volunteers—individuals who are not remunerated financially for their services—at all levels of the organization. Basil O'Connor, who has been President since the organization was founded, is a Volunteer, as are all members of the Board of Trustees. The medical doctors and research scientists who serve on national advisory committees are Volunteers, as were the 20,000 doctors and the 40,000 nurses who administered the Salk vaccine to children during the 1954 vaccine field trials. Each state has at least one Volunteer Advisor on Women's Activities who helps Chapter women develop year-round programs, and a Volunteer State March of Dimes Chairman, who coordinates the activities of county Campaign Directors during the annual fund-raising campaign. Finally, in each county in the United States there are two local units of the national organization. First, a local Chapter—comprised of Volunteer members—is responsible for the infantile paralysis program in the county throughout the year. Second, during the annual March of Dimes each county has a fund-raising organization which is closely related to, but administratively separate from, the Foundation Chapter in the same county.*

A word of explanation is necessary concerning the relationship of these local Chapters to the national organization. It was noted in the Introduction to this study that the Foundation has a corporate-type formal structure; that is, the primary locus of authority within the organization is in the National Headquarters. The *historical* origins of this structure are described below;† its *legal* basis stems from the fact that the Foundation is a nonprofit membership corporation, established under the laws of the State of New York. The *By-laws* define the membership of the corporation in these terms:

The Membership of the Corporation shall consist of the Board of Trustees of the Corporation, each Trustee automatically becoming a Member upon qualifying as a Trustee and ceasing to be a Member upon ceasing to be a Trustee of the Corporation.[11]

It is readily apparent that this official membership of the Foundation does not constitute the working membership. Although the Board of Trustees is currently comprised of only thirty-eight men, many thousands of Volunteers consider themselves members of the organization. The importance of this legal definition, however, is that it locates the policy-making functions of the organization in one group of people —the Board of Trustees—rather than in the membership generally.

Since the Board of Trustees obviously cannot carry on the activities of the organization by itself, it has authorized the establishment of both a National Headquarters and local Chapters. The legal position of these Chapters in the formal structure is that of *ad hoc* instrumentalities, authorized by the Board of Trustees as a means of accomplishing the objectives for which the organization was established. That is, they are component units of the organization.

It is of interest to note how this concept is explained in the various manuals prepared by the Foundation for its personnel. The *Manual for Chapters,* which provides the official framework for Chapter activities, explains the status of the local Chapters as follows:

---

* A few Chapters serve two counties, and a few counties contain more than one Chapter. There are 3,076 counties in the United States; at the time of this research there were 3,073 Chapters in the continental United States, plus Chapters in Alaska, the Canal Zone, Hawaii, Puerto Rico, and the Virgin Islands. In 1956 there were 3,086 Chapters in all.

† See pp. 45–46.

A Chapter receives its Certificate of Recognition from, is an integral part of, and is subject at all times to all rules, regulations and policies of the National Foundation.[12]

The "Orientation Manual for State Representatives" explains the legal status of Chapters:

It [the National Foundation] is the instrumentality which provides for the care and treatment of infantile paralysis victims. The Chapters are an integral part of the National Foundation. They raise the money and see that care and treatment are provided for patients, but they are not the thing which is recognized in the law as having the basic responsibility. Without the National Foundation there would be no Chapters.[13]

Finally, in more down-to-earth language, the relationship is explained to Chapter personnel:

Your Chapter is the administrative unit of the National Foundation for Infantile Paralysis responsible for carrying out locally the programs of the National Foundation.[14]

And again:

The National Foundation and its Chapters are one organization. Your Chapter is one unit within the National Foundation framework. In a sense, a Chapter is like the branch office of a large corporation; National Headquarters is its home office.[15]

A similar—but not identical—situation obtains in other voluntary health associations which have a corporate structure, although for both historical and operational reasons other organizations do not place as much emphasis upon the "unity" of the national office and the component units. The American Cancer Society, for example, is comprised of sixty Chartered Divisions, largely organized along state lines, which are required to incorporate themselves in the state in which they are located. The conditions of incorporation, however, are stipulated by the national organization. The more than 3,000 local Units are component parts of the sixty Divisions, and have a relationship to the Divisions similar in some ways to the Foundation's Chapter-National Headquarters relationship.[16] The National Multiple Sclerosis Society, to cite another example of an association with a corporate-type formal structure, permits but does not encourage its Chapters to incorporate, and requires that incorporation be under conditions set by the national office. The actual relationship of its Chapters to the national office appears to be nearly identical to that which prevails in the Foundation.[17]

The Volunteers who belong to local Chapter and March of Dimes organizations constitute, of course, the overwhelming proportion of the Foundation's membership. Accordingly, it is necessary to preface a description of them with a brief statement of the ways in which these Volunteers resemble or differ from the volunteer members of other voluntary associations.

National voluntary health associations of the type represented by the Foundation differ markedly from other types of voluntary associations with respect to the composition and nature of their membership. According to Rose, most voluntary associations are formed when "a small group of people, finding they have a certain interest (or purpose) in common, agree to meet and act together in order to satisfy that interest or achieve that purpose."[18] In the case of many voluntary associations, particularly local health and welfare associations, these people constitute the volunteer membership of the organizations, usually its "board." Since board members are often too busy to devote a great deal of time to the organization, they generally appoint a professional staff to carry out the day-to-day tasks of running the organization; since the nature of these tasks frequently requires some specialized training, this professional staff is generally composed of people trained in office management, public relations, and social work. Textbooks used in schools of social work, accordingly, generally devote some attention to the related techniques of maintaining good working relationships with volunteer boards and educating the board members in the problems faced by the professional staff. In organizations having this character, volunteers are in effect the employers of the working-level staff.

In addition to board members, another type of volunteer worker is often found in this type of health or welfare association: the part-time volunteer who assists the professional staff in such activities as home visitations, clerical work, speech-making, and fund-raising, but does not necessarily become an official member of the association. Here again, textbooks and other publications written for professional social workers place much emphasis upon the advantages of utilizing volunteer assistance for such purposes. *Adult Leadership,* a magazine devoted entirely to the problems of community organizations, recently devoted an entire issue to a "Workshop on the Volunteer," and defined a volunteer worker as: "The non-paid person who gives time to furthering the purposes of the agency or organization. He or she may be a hospital aide, agency or hospital board member, doorbell ringer in a get-out-the-vote drive, youth group leader, Sunday School teacher."[19]

A standard reference book on voluntary health associations by Selskar Gunn and Philip Platt defines volunteers as follows:

It was a "volunteer" who, seeing unattended health needs not far from his own doorstep, set out to remedy conditions. A group or society of such volunteers make up the voluntary health agency. The society sooner or later engages a professional worker, who gradually replaces the volunteers in the daily tasks except for the routine direction of boards and committees. In time, and especially in emergencies, such organizations call for help from lay volunteers.[20]

The point cannot be made too strongly that this generic definition of a "volunteer" does not adequately describe the Volunteer members of the Foundation. True, the Foundation's membership contains all the component elements: a Volunteer Board of Trustees which comprises the official membership of the association; a professional staff which carries out many of the day-to-day activities; and a corps of lay Volunteers which assists the professional staff. But when the inter-relationship of these component elements is considered, and when the role played by each is examined, the inadequacy of this definition becomes very apparent. Although the full import of this statement cannot be appreciated until the conclusion of this volume, some understanding can be achieved through a description of the Foundation's Volunteer membership. Since local Chapter and March of Dimes organizations are administratively separate, and in other ways quite different, the membership of each will be described separately.

## CHAPTER VOLUNTEERS

Many—if not most—national organizations consist of a national headquarters, forty-eight or forty-nine state organizations, and local units administratively related to the state organizations. The Foundation, on the other hand, does not have state organizations;* its organizational structure consists of the national Board of Trustees, the headquarters staff employed by the Board, and the local units. The responsibilities and activities of local Chapters are officially defined as follows:

1. Making sure that no polio patient—man, woman or child—shall go without the best available medical care for lack of funds.
2. Informing the public about the disease, methods of dealing with it, and of the activities and goals of the National Foundation.
3. Raising sufficient funds through the March of Dimes to finance adequately the National Foundation's program of research, professional education, patient care, and polio prevention.[21]

* Each state has a March of Dimes Chairman, but the organization which he directs consists solely of the county March of Dimes organizations throughout the state. Similarly, each state has a "state office," which is the headquarters of the State Representative, not an organization of Volunteers.

The specific tasks which these responsibilities entail are described in some detail throughout this volume; for the present, our interest is in the Volunteers who are entrusted with carrying out this local program.

Although there is no limit to the number of members a Chapter may have, in actual practice most Chapters are relatively small. Chapters serving counties which include large cities may have a membership of 100 or more, but Chapters of this size are comparatively rare. More often, a Chapter has ten or twelve members, and in many counties as few as five or six.

Officially, the membership of a Chapter consists of "the signers of its Certificate of Organization, the members of the Executive Committee and such persons as may be elected to membership."[22] In practice, however, the membership of the Chapter consists of the Executive Committee (which includes the Chapter officers) and a number of other people who have either been invited to join by a Chapter member or who have volunteered on their own initiative.

Regardless of the size of a Chapter, the nature of the program is such that major responsibility must be assumed either by the Chairman or by various committees. That is, there are few activities outside of one or two meetings each year—except for the March of Dimes, which will be discussed later—in which the membership as a whole can take part. Large Chapters may have four or five committees—Finance, Membership, Women's Activities, Public Information, and the like—but in most Chapters only two are needed. The Executive Committee is responsible for general Chapter administration and activities, and the Medical Advisory Committee, composed of such professionals as doctors, health officials, hospital administrators, nurses, and physical therapists, advises the Executive Committee concerning aid for polio patients.

Officially, the Chapter Executive Committee is elected by the Chapter membership at the annual meeting.[23] Since in most Chapters the Executive Committee constitutes the majority of the membership, formal elections are seldom held; a more realistic formulation is that the Executive Committee consists of those members who are informally asked to serve in this capacity for the year ahead. All other committees are appointed by the Chapter Chairman in consultation with the Executive Committee.[24] Chapter Officers—Chairman, Vice-Chairman, Treasurer and Secretary—are elected annually by the Executive Committee from its own membership.[25]

The Volunteer membership of Foundation Chapters thus differs markedly from that of the organizations described either in the special issue of *Adult Leadership** or in the Gunn and Platt study, cited above. Chapter Volunteers are for the most part neither "board members" who employ a professional worker to carry out the daily tasks of the organization nor assistants who are called in during emergencies to help out. Of course, in some respects members of the Executive Committee are the equivalent of "board members,"† and Volunteers who perform such tasks as assisting in hospitals during polio epidemics are the equivalent of the "lay volunteers" described by Gunn and Platt. But the central point is that Chapter Volunteers both make decisions and actually perform the day-to-day tasks of their organization. In large cities, of course, this becomes technically impossible, and metropolitan Chapters often engage an Executive Secretary to handle correspondence, keep records, etc. But at the time of this research only 197 Chapters (6 per cent of all Chapters) employed an Executive Secretary, and eighty-three of these were on a part-time basis. By and large, Chapter Volunteers perform the tasks which in many other voluntary associations are performed by professional personnel.‡ The import of this role of the Chapter Volunteer constitutes a recurrent theme of this study.

## MEMBERSHIP IN THE MARCH OF DIMES

Thus far only the membership of local Chapters has been considered. When March of Dimes organizations are examined, however, a totally different picture emerges. Although most Chapters have relatively few members, March of Dimes organizations even in the smallest counties are comprised of forty to fifty Volunteers, and in counties containing large cities, many thousand Volunteers participate actively in the March of Dimes each year.

March of Dimes organizations are discussed separately from local Chapters because they are separate and distinct organizations; fundraising, as indicated earlier, is a Chapter *activity,* but is technically directed by National Headquarters, not by the Chapter.

* See p. 25.
† In fact, many Volunteers refer to the Executive Committee as "The Board," presumably because of the greater prestige associated with this term.
‡ Arnold Rose, for example, reports that his study of voluntary associations in Minneapolis and St. Paul revealed that about half of the associations had at least one paid employee.[26] Foundation Chapters in cities of this size generally employ one Executive Secretary.

In actual practice this means two things. First, the dates of the campaign are set by National Headquarters, which also furnishes local communities with campaign material and a manual containing instructions and suggestions. Since it is a nationwide campaign, a great deal of the publicity is initiated by the the national office. Second, the March of Dimes Campaign Director in each county is officially appointed not by the local Chapter, but by the State March of Dimes Chairman, who is in turn appointed by National Headquarters.[27] The Chapter Chairman, of course, is generally consulted, and in most instances he actually nominates the Campaign Director. In fact, in some small Chapters, the Chapter Chairman *is* the Campaign Director. The two organizations are, however, administratively separate.

The actual organization of the March of Dimes campaign varies somewhat according to the size of the county. In every county, however, the Campaign Director appoints a number of deputies, as well as a community Chairman for each city or town lying within the county limits. Each of these Chairmen, in turn, appoints deputies to handle specific aspects of the campaign. This amount of specialization, coupled with the fact that each Campaign Director creates a staff of his own, leads to the development of a large organization even in counties with a relatively small population. Thus, although local Chapters have on their rolls only an estimated 80,000 Volunteers, some 3,000,000 Americans play some part in the annual March of Dimes.*

The vast majority of March of Dimes Volunteers are individuals whose participation is confined to a few hours each January. But each local March of Dimes organization is staffed by Volunteers who have positions of major responsibility, and who actually manage the campaign. Again, in large cities one or more full-time employees are usually hired for the duration of the March of Dimes, but their official role is to assist the Volunteer leaders, not to run the campaign.

### THE VOLUNTEERS STUDIED

The description of the Foundation's Volunteer membership has been confined thus far to an overview of the entire organization. In order to obtain first-hand information concerning Volunteers and their activities, intensive interviews were held with 129 Chapter and 105

---

* Precise membership statistics are impossible to obtain, since only the names of Chapter and March of Dimes officers are reported to National Headquarters, and local organizations themselves do not for the most part maintain complete membership rosters. These figures represent the best estimate of National Headquarters personnel.

March of Dimes Volunteers residing in thirty-seven counties through-out the United States.*

It should be noted that these 234 Volunteers do not constitute a representative sample of *all* Foundation Volunteers. No attempt was made to interview a true cross-section of Volunteers, since a sample of this kind would be composed largely of rural people who do not occupy positions of responsibility, and who are in other ways less involved in, and informed about, Foundation activities. The sample over-represents Volunteer leaders. All but 13 per cent of the Chapter Volunteers are either Chapter officers or members of the Executive Committee, and all but 23 per cent of the March of Dimes Volunteers interviewed are either Campaign Directors or Chairmen of one phase of the March of Dimes campaign.

Since nine out of every ten Chapter Volunteers also take part in the March of Dimes, the distinction between the two groups is from one point of view artificial. That is, most Chapter Volunteers also serve as March of Dimes Volunteers during the annual fund-raising campaign. Nevertheless, the fact that the two organizations are officially separate is of far-reaching significance for the Foundation. In order to demonstrate why this is the case, and in order to make comparisons between the two organizations, it is necessary to maintain this distinction. Chapter Volunteers, accordingly, are those Volunteers who were interviewed who participate in Foundation activities on a year-round basis, regardless of the fact that they may also take part in the March of Dimes. March of Dimes Volunteers, on the other hand, are Volunteers who are active members of the Foundation only during the annual fund-raising campaign.

The fact that the sample of Volunteers upon which this analysis is based is composed largely of Volunteer leaders should be kept in mind when the characteristics of the total group are described.† When

---

* See Appendix A for a description of the procedures followed in selecting these thirty-seven counties and 234 Volunteers, and for more detailed statistical information concerning Volunteers than that presented in this chapter. Appendix A also describes the selection and composition of a sample of Volunteers interviewed by the American Institute of Public Opinion. Since the Institute's interviews with Volunteers were held primarily to obtain quantitative data for comparison with the more qualitative interviews conducted by Columbia University researchers, they are referred to in the text only when they shed light upon or differ substantially from the interviews conducted in the thirty-seven selected counties.

† One further characteristic of the sample should be mentioned: it is composed entirely of *lay* Volunteers. Although all Chapters have a Medical Advisory Committee composed of doctors and other professional people, these Volunteers were not included in the study, since the focus of the research was upon the lay membership of the Foundation.

comparisons are made between different types of Volunteers (e.g., comparisons between Chapter Chairmen and County Campaign Directors), the data presented have a much greater generality.

An important difference between the two groups is the average length of time Volunteers have been affiliated with the Foundation. Nearly one out of five Chapter Volunteers has been active since the early years of the Foundation or since before the Foundation was established, as a member of a local Committee for the Celebration of the President's Birthday. However, only one out of every twenty March of Dimes Volunteers is an old-timer.

Partly as a result of this higher turnover rate, March of Dimes Volunteers are somewhat younger than Chapter Volunteers; 59 per cent are under forty years of age, in contrast to only 39 per cent of Chapter Volunteers. Accordingly, they are more likely to be parents of young or adolescent children (71 per cent versus 63 per cent).

Men and women are about equally represented in both groups, as are Republicans and Democrats; and both groups—like the American public at large—are predominantly (80 per cent) Protestant in their religious affiliation.

Both Chapter and March of Dimes Volunteers participate widely in other community organizations: seven out of every ten belong to at least three organizations other than the Foundation, and many belong to six or more. Some reported this activity with pride, and others took occasion to complain about the demands constantly made upon their time. But organized community activity is clearly a major part of the lives of Foundation Volunteers. Volunteers recognize this themselves and those who are not active in other community organizations realize that they are the exception to the rule. Witness the plaintive tone in this comment of an atypical March of Dimes Volunteer in College Town:*

(*Are you active in other community organizations?*)No. . . . I've no time for anything else. I avoid the P.T.A. like the plague. I'm a member of the A.A.U.W., but I never go. (*Do you belong to any service organizations, church organizations, or any others?*) No. I'm anti-social. I imagine I don't fit into the pattern. Maybe I'm a little queer, but I can't help it.

Foundation Volunteers have generally been residents of their communities for many years; more than two-thirds of both groups have lived in their present communities for ten years or more, and nearly half were either born where they now live or came to live there when they were children.

* See Appendix C for descriptions of the communities studied.

An important characteristic of Foundation Volunteers is their middle-class (rather than upper-middle or upper-class) status; they are only rarely (and chiefly in the South) people of high social status in their communities. Occupationally, they (or their husbands) are for the most part small businessmen, lawyers, insurance agents, school superintendents, teachers, and the like—people whose status in the community is largely the result of their own efforts rather than inherited from their family's social position.

This last characteristic of Foundation Volunteers requires some additional comment. The predominantly middle-class composition of Volunteers is easily documented in a general way by noting their occupations. But other measures of social position are available. Since all interviews were conducted by four members of the project staff, who wrote lengthy descriptions of each Volunteer interviewed, considerably more information is available concerning Volunteers than is normally the case with respondents in survey research. Furthermore, the conversational nature of the interviews, as well as the initial question asked each Volunteer—"Before we talk about Chapter (March of Dimes) affairs, can you tell me a little about yourself?"—made it possible to obtain a wealth of information about social origins and living patterns. A difficult question to answer, however, is whether or not the Foundation's membership differs substantially in this respect from that of other voluntary health and welfare associations. According to many Volunteers it does, but most of the comparisons made were with the Community Chest, the Red Cross, and the Y.M.C.A., not with such voluntary health associations as the American Heart Association or the American Cancer Society.* In the absence of any data concerning the volunteer membership of these organizations, it is impossible to determine the extent to which the Foundation is different in this respect. For present purposes, the important point to be made is that most Foundation Volunteers consider their organization to be unique because of the middle-class composition of its Volunteer personnel.

## Sources of Membership Apathy

Now that the local organizations of the Foundation have been described, and the major characteristics of their Volunteers reviewed, it is possible to turn to a review of the major sources of membership

* The long-standing practice in the Red Cross of recruiting volunteers from among the social elite has been noted by its official historian.[28]

apathy which students of voluntary associations have observed. These sources are described in some detail in this section, since in the section which follows they are used as diagnostic criteria for an examination of the structural sources of membership participation in Foundation activities.

The classic statement of the difficulty of achieving full membership participation in the affairs of a voluntary association has been provided by Robert Michels, who defined his now-famous "iron law of oligarchy" in these terms:

Organization implies the tendency to oligarchy. In every organization, whether it be a political party, a professional union, or any other association of the kind, the aristocratic tendency manifests itself very clearly. *The mechanism of the organization,* while conferring a solidarity of structure, *induces serious changes in the organized mass,* completely inverting the respective position of the leaders and the led. *As a result of organization,* every party or professional union becomes divided into a minority of directors and a majority of directed.[29]

What, specifically, is there about organization which implies the tendency toward minority rule? Michels is vague on this point, and cites only the numbers of people involved and the "technical indispensability of leadership"[30] as sources which stem from the fact of organization itself, since his major interest was in the psychological rather than the organizational origins of oligarchy. But by drawing both upon the work of Michels and that of contemporary students of voluntary associations it is possible to identify more specifically some of the structural sources of membership apathy and nonparticipation. The following sources will be discussed in this section: size, functional specialization, membership heterogeneity, and multi-group membership.

### SIZE

The problems brought about by the size of an organization have often been cited as responsible for the phenomenon of membership apathy. Michels, for example, directed his analysis primarily at the problems of large organizations; specifically, he suggested that the "iron law of oligarchy" holds true only for organizations having a membership of 1,000–10,000.[31] David Truman also mentions size as an important determinant, largely, he feels, because "those at the upper reaches of a large organization develops a remoteness from the rank and file. . . ."[32] Finally, John Tsouderos, on the basis of his investigation of organizational change in ten voluntary associations, observes that as organizations grow larger there is a marked decline in the extent of membership participation.[33]

## FUNCTIONAL SPECIALIZATION

Closely related to the problems emergent from size alone are those which stem from the fact that in large organizations specific tasks must be allocated to individual members. Bernard Barber, for example, has noted that "the internal structure of the voluntary association itself, that is, . . . its formal organization and division of functions among members, makes it possible for a minority to achieve the interests of the association with the majority participating very little or not at all."[34] And Tsouderos also found that specialization of function, or "overbureaucratization," is itself sufficient to make many members disaffected and apathetic. He noted this to be true particularly among people who had joined the organization at an early stage, when informality was the keynote. When more formal procedures and greater specialization of function are introduced, they often become alienated.[35]

Why do organizations often find it necessary to make a distinction between individuals who have specialized functions and the main body of the membership? The technical difficulties of coordinating the activities of a large number of key participants is certainly one major reason. But it is also necessary to take into consideration the essential qualifications which leaders must have.

To be effective, a leader must first of all be able to devote more *time* to organizational activities than is expected of the rank-and-file. Since voluntary associations are for most people a leisure time activity, time is a major factor in determining the extent of their participation. Oliver Garceau, for example, has pointed out that one of the factors which enables an active minority to retain a great deal of control over the policies of the American Medical Association is that doctors in a position of leadership must have "some margin of wealth and leisure . . ." in order to attend conventions and serve on committees.[36] Since most doctors do not have a margin of either wealth or leisure, they are in this sense disqualified for leadership positions.

Another qualification for leadership is *temperament*. Some people, for a variety of reasons, have a strong need for the satisfactions deriving from positions of leadership. "There are always men," says Selznick, "who *want* to be officials."[37] Particularly in those voluntary associations whose leaders are not automatically accorded deference by the public, such people are often actively sought out by the membership; to attribute their rise to a position of importance within the organization, and their maintenance of this position over a period of time, solely to the apathy of the membership is certainly an oversimplification.

Finally, leadership often requires particular *skills*. In order to deal with the leadership of other organizations, with business leaders and with government officials, to cite only the most obvious examples, certain social skills are necessary. Further, many voluntary associations need people among the top leadership who are familiar with the law. And perhaps of greatest importance, all organizations require leaders who have managerial skills. Sometimes organizations recruit leaders who have had previous experience in managing the affairs of other organizations; sometimes leaders develop these skills within the organization itself. For present purposes, however, the important point is that all members of an association are generally not equally qualified in this way to occupy a position of authority.[38]

## MEMBERSHIP HETEROGENEITY

The emergence of a heterogeneous membership in an organization is of course largely an outgrowth of increasing size and functional specialization. The more people there are in an organization, and the greater the number of specialized skills required for specific jobs, the greater the probability that an organization will incorporate into its membership people who come from dissimilar backgrounds and who hold dissimilar views. Heterogeneity in turn decreases the likelihood of consensus, and when there is an absence of consensus within an organization it is generally easier for an active minority—if it is so motivated—to gain control. Selznick has noted that groups which have "no firm values of their own become the instruments of the values of others"—that is, become vulnerable to Communist infiltration.[39] And in a discussion of organizations generally, Reinhard Bendix has made use of this principle to point out the inadequacy of the "iron law of oligarchy":

It is . . . misleading to assume that a ruling clique can deliberately prevent the "success" of an organization, while everybody else agrees on the methods and desirability of achieving it. Rather, an organized minority can maintain its power and it can make *its* idea of success prevail, as long as disagreement is widespread both with regard to the meaning of "success" and to the methods by which it is to be achieved.[40]

An absence of consensus not only makes it easier for an active minority to gain control—it also fosters membership nonparticipation. Barber, for example, has shown that the amount of voluntary participation that occurs in the United States is much greater in time of war than in time of peace, since "in time of war there is a relative clarification and sharpening of the hierarchy of values which is an essential constituent of any social system."[41] And with reference to particular voluntary associations, Herbert Simon has cited the fact that "the various participants may have conflicting interpretations of the organization's objective, . . ." as a factor which contributes to membership apathy.[42]

## MULTI-GROUP MEMBERSHIP

The sources of membership apathy discussed above all relate to various structural characteristics of voluntary associations. But it is necessary to consider some sources of apathy which stem from certain characteristics of the membership itself as well. David Truman has called this factor "crucial," and in the course of attacking the uncritical use of such terms as "mass apathy" by Michels and others has asserted that "it is not an exaggeration to say that what one regards as the verified facts in this area will determine the adequacy of one's theory of the political process."[43]

Mass apathy is the explanation for membership nonparticipation most frequently advanced by those who have approached the problem from an "activist" position. "Apathy is everywhere," they seem to say, "because people are apathetic!"[44] Since this formulation confuses the diagnosis with the disorder, it can contribute little to the present discussion. But it does call attention to the fact that some characteristics of individual members do contribute to the phenomenon. Participants in voluntary associations, in other words, are influenced by the social structure to which they belong, as well as by the structural characteristics of the associations themselves. Two characteristics of the social structure which have been specifically mentioned in this connection are the prior obligations which individuals have to their job and their family and the pressures which result from membership in several associations.

*Obligations to job and family.* Many people do not belong to voluntary associations, but practically everyone "belongs" to either a job or a family. According to Barber, the major characteristic of American society which is responsible for the growth of voluntary associations—

the segregation of "a large number of specific interests from kinship and occupational ties, with which they are usually fused in other societies, . . ."—is also responsible for the phenomenon of the inactive majority, since "American social structure does more than segregate these other interests from family and job obligations. *It defines them as being of less importance. . . ."*[45] It is only the unusual person, according to Barber, who is motivated to participate actively in the affairs of an association. He may find his occupation unsatisfying, or his feelings of family obligation may be minimal; more likely, he may have unusual resources of energy and talent. In any event, the nature of our social structure is such that only a relatively few people are able to escape the demands of job and family.

*Membership in several associations.* Another set of prior obligations which is conducive to inactivity in an organization is the proclivity of those people who do join associations to join several, rather than just one. Since participation in voluntary associations is generally a leisure-time pursuit, there are definite limits upon the amount of time people can devote even to one organization. People who belong to several associations, accordingly, must almost invariably be relatively inactive in some of them. Furthermore, as both Kenneth Boulding and David Truman have noted, membership in several associations may lead to moral dilemmas and internal conflict, since many of the objectives for which voluntary associations are established are at cross-purposes with each other.[46] And when individuals are under cross-pressures from conflicting groups, the possibility exists that they will resolve their dilemma by withdrawing from active participation.[47]

## The Foundation and the Problem of Membership Interest

Since the Volunteers studied in this research are for the most part leaders in their local organizations, their active participation in Foundation activities cannot in itself be accepted as evidence of the fact that the Foundation has "solved" the near-universal problem of maintaining full membership participation. In fact, as most of the writers cited earlier in this chapter have suggested, the problem is inherently insoluble, since the structural characteristics both of individual organizations and of society at large are of such a nature as to establish what Barber has termed a "socially structured pull" away from full membership participation.[48]

There is of course an important countervailing force in our society —the high valuation placed upon full membership participation in a democracy. But the mere existence of a given value in a society can seldom if ever by and of itself ensure that the behavior required by the value will actually take place. Consider, for example, the amount of individual behavior which is at variance with such values as "honesty is the best policy," marital fidelity, the "brotherhood of man," etc.

To say that the Foundation has not "solved" the problem of maintaining full membership participation, however, is not to say that its membership is characterized by apathy. On the contrary, it will be demonstrated below that to a very large extent the Foundation's structure has made it possible for it to *circumvent* the problem in such a way as to make it possible for it to be both a mass organization and one which has not been deflected from the achievement of its major goals. Following the outline of the previous section—in which the diagnostic criteria to be used were described—those structural characteristics of the Foundation which bear most directly upon each of four sources of membership apathy are described below.

### SIZE

Since by any criteria the Foundation is a large organization, the relevance of its size to membership participation must be considered. As mentioned previously, Chapters differ fundamentally from March of Dimes organizations in their membership characteristics, so these two types of local units will be discussed separately.

*Chapters.* The Foundation has a large membership, but the Chapter system means that it is a large organization divided into over 3,000 small ones. Although each Chapter is officially a component unit of the national organization, individual Volunteers are officially members not of the Foundation itself, but of a local Chapter.

Most Chapters are small, and most members have definite assignments. Each member of the Executive Committee, for example, generally attends a monthly meeting at which decisions are made concerning Chapter activities, and many Chapter functions are carried out without the formality of meetings.

There is, nevertheless, considerable variation in the extent to which Chapter members actively participate in Chapter activities. In many Chapters, the Chairman is by far the most active member. He often takes pride in the fact that he is known locally as "Mr. Polio," and he spends an average of perhaps ten or fifteen hours a week throughout the year living up to his reputation. In other Chapters, four or five individuals may share the major burden of responsibility; in still others, as many as thirty or forty Volunteers are active throughout the year.

These variations, however, do not necessarily mean that membership apathy exists in some Chapters and not in others. Even in Chapters dominated by a "Mr. Polio," the other members generally have definite responsibilities which they must carry out. And in Chapters which have a comparatively large membership, one of two situations generally prevails. If the community is a large one, there is a sufficient number of tasks connected with the patient care program to keep the membership busy; if the community is small, and there are only a few polio patients being assisted by the Chapter, the responsibilities of Volunteers who are not Officers are specifically defined as limited to attending the annual meeting. That is, the problem of membership nonparticipation in Chapters is explicitly circumvented by a 'careful definition of the responsibilities of membership. The *Chapter Reference Book,* for example, discusses membership participation in these terms:

The size of your Chapter should be determined by the number of persons required to carry out successfully your responsibilities for patient assistance, community education and fund raising. . . . Just as unused muscles weaken, so do unused volunteers. . . . Every member should be assigned to a committee which will provide him with the satisfaction of active participation.[49]

*March of Dimes organizations.* In contrast to local Chapters, which are small organizations characterized by informal procedures and face-to-face interaction, March of Dimes organizations are large and comparatively "bureaucratic" in their procedures. That is, individuals are generally assigned highly specific tasks for which they are responsible, and face-to-face interaction between members of different components of the organization is often infrequent. In addition to the Campaign Director and his immediate staff, a Chairman is generally appointed for every city or town in the county. In many cases, the Campaign Director has only telephone contact with his subordinate Chairmen, and interaction among Volunteers on lower echelons in different communities is even more infrequent.

Another distinguishing characteristic of March of Dimes organizations is that their members devote unequal amounts of time to fund-raising activities. The top leadership of course spends a great deal of time on the campaign during the months of December and particularly January; in fact, many Volunteers practically suspend their business and professional work for weeks on end. But most March of Dimes

Volunteers devote a total of less than ten hours during the year to the organization, and the largest single group of Volunteers—the Marching Mothers of the Mothers' March on Polio—spend only a few hours each.*

On the surface, accordingly, a March of Dimes organization would seem to be vulnerable to membership apathy. It is large, it requires an active leadership, and there is relatively little for most members to do. But note another crucially important characteristic of the organization: it is in effect reconstituted and then dissolved each year. That is, Volunteers are mobilized when they are needed; they are assigned highly specific tasks; and when the campaign is over the organization is dispersed. The problem of membership apathy in a March of Dimes organization, in other words, is circumvented by not enlisting a large, permanent membership.

The relatively transitory nature of the membership of the March of Dimes is demonstrated not only by the fact that Volunteers are dispersed after the campaign is over, but also by the fact that, as reported earlier, March of Dimes Volunteers generally remain members of the organization for a fewer number of years than do Chapter Volunteers. There are a number of reasons for this briefer period of participation of March of Dimes Volunteers. Some relate to operational procedures which have been widely adopted. For example, many Chapters make use of the March of Dimes campaign as an opportunity to recruit new Chapter members. In fact, 46 per cent of the Chapter Volunteers interviewed were first active in the March of Dimes. This pattern of recruitment necessarily results in the average Chapter Volunteer having been a member of the Foundation longer than the average March of Dimes Volunteer.

Another procedure which explains the briefer participation on the part of March of Dimes Volunteers is the practice of asking other community organizations to take responsibility for some phase of the campaign. Since these arrangements with other organizations are often made on a year-to-year basis, the Volunteer composition of the March of Dimes necessarily undergoes some rotation every year, as new organizations agree to cooperate, and others drop out. Furthermore, even if the cooperating organizations continue to participate for several years, the normal leadership and membership changes in the organizations will be reflected in the March of Dimes membership.

A third reason for the higher turnover among March of Dimes

* See p. 152.

Volunteers is the widespread feeling among both Chapter and March of Dimes leaders that "new faces" (and "new names" in the newspaper) are an asset to the fund-raising campaign. Accordingly, many March of Dimes Volunteers are simply not asked to participate another year, while Chapter Volunteers can continue as long as their interest persists. Furthermore, March of Dimes positions are often "given" to younger businessmen and lawyers who are anxious to "establish themselves" in the community. After one or two years of activity, these Volunteers either join the Chapter as year-round participants or drop out completely.

But perhaps the most important reason for the longer tenure of Chapter Volunteers is the structural difference between the two organizations. Since the Chapter is a more truly local organization, with greater autonomy over the selection of its top leadership, its Officers are rotated among the members of the semi-permanent Executive Committee. The March of Dimes, on the other hand, is officially directed by National Headquarters, and it is fairly general practice to appoint a different Campaign Director every year or so. Although the new Director generally makes extensive use of Chapter members in building his campaign organization, the large number of Volunteers needed, and the fact that the Director himself is often a new recruit, inevitably leads to the recruitment of March of Dimes Volunteers who are not year-round members of the Foundation. The net result of the high rate of turnover among Campaign Directors, accordingly, is a relatively high rate of turnover among the entire membership of the March of Dimes.

The membership of the March of Dimes thus has two characteristics which are not generally found in voluntary associations, and which go far toward explaining why it is able to function efficiently as a mass organization. First, it is a temporary organization, mobilized only for one specific purpose and then dissolved. Second, it has a high rate of membership turnover, which makes it possible for a large proportion of the membership to have the enthusiasm which generally characterizes new members of organizations, but which often wanes with the years. If March of Dimes Volunteers maintain their enthusiasm, it is possible for them to transfer to the Chapter; if they do not, there are no pressures which serve to incorporate them into the Chapter membership. After the campaign is over, accordingly, most March of Dimes Volunteers simply take up other spare-time pursuits, and for the most part do not think of themselves as members of the Foundation until the next year's campaign. When that time comes, their enthusiasm is either re-kindled or they simply do not participate; in either event, they do not constitute a large group of inactive members.*

In summary, the factor of size has not led to membership apathy in the Foundation for three reasons. First, the large year-round membership of the organization is distributed among the local Chapters, which are themselves relatively small organizations. Second, the committee system of conducting the affairs of the Chapter ensures that each member will generally have some definite assignment to carry out, thus mitigating against the possibility that apathy will result from inactivity. Third, the one large local organization of the Foundation, the March of Dimes, is mobilized only for the specific purpose of carrying out its fund-raising function, and then is dissolved. All three of these structural features make it possible for the vast majority of the Volunteer membership to be affiliated with the Foundation only at such times as its services are actually needed.

These structural features of the Foundation are not unrelated to the problems faced by other voluntary associations. Consider for example the historically-decisive controversy which developed in an organization having a totally different character from that of the Foundation: the pre-Revolution Russian Social Democratic Party. The Bolshevik-Menshevik split at the Party's Second Congress in 1903 was over the issue of an "élite" versus a "mass" party. The Lenin (Bolshevik) faction maintained that a small élite should direct larger spontaneous groups which would exist alongside and outside the Party; the Martov-Axelrod (Menshevik) faction, on the other hand, favored a wide basis of membership which would admit to the party all who sympathized with its program.[50]

It is noteworthy that it was the Menshevik position which was generally adopted by Western European Social Democratic Parties, and that it was membership apathy and nonparticipation in these parties which Michels used as primary data for his analysis of oligarchic rule in voluntary associations. The relative ease with which Hitler was able to neutralize the German Social Democratic Party, and with which the Communists were able to eliminate Social Democratic opposition in such countries as Czechoslovakia after World War II, must in part at

---

* Although a considerable number return for the next year's campaign, the March of Dimes is not fully dependent upon previous members. One issue about which the Volunteers interviewed were most unanimous is the ease with which it is possible to recruit new Volunteers for the duration of the March of Dimes.

least be attributed to the fact that these parties were characterized by a few active leaders and a large, inactive membership.

## A NOTE ON HISTORICAL ORIGINS

These fundamental differences between the structure and size of Chapters and March of Dimes organizations are of such basic importance for an understanding of the current program of the Foundation that it is necessary to interject at this point in the discussion a note on their historical origins. This brief historical review will clarify the nature of these differences as well as provide information necessary for an understanding of much of the discussion which follows.*

As is the case with many of the organizational features of the Foundation, both the separation of Chapter and March of Dimes activities and the concomitant development of two separate but closely related groups of Volunteers were not deliberately planned, but came about as unanticipated consequences of decisions made with other ends in view. In fact, these decisions were not made by the Foundation at all, but by the leaders of the Georgia Warm Springs Foundation.

The Georgia Warm Springs Foundation was initially a private philanthropy, established by Franklin D. Roosevelt in 1927. In its early years, the treatment center at Georgia Warm Springs was supported financially by Roosevelt himself and by some of his friends. The Depression made large gifts increasingly difficult to obtain, however, and donations declined from a peak of $368,991 in 1929 to $30,331 in 1932.[51] The Georgia Warm Springs Foundation, like much of America, was nearly bankrupt.

*The first mass fund-raising.* In 1933, two decisions were made which were to have far-reaching consequences for the then unborn National Foundation for Infantile Paralysis. First, in order to raise the necessary funds to replace the old Meriwether Inn—the main building at Warm Springs, and, according to Roosevelt, "our principal handicap"—[52] a decision was made to abandon an earlier plan to seek large gifts from wealthy Georgians and to embark instead upon a mass fund-raising campaign. As a result, over 60,000 gifts, ranging from a dime to $500, from farm produce to hand-made articles, were con-

---

* The source materials upon which this historical note is based were for the most part supplied by the Historical Division of the National Foundation for Infantile Paralysis, which is preparing a series of monographic studies for eventual use in the preparation of a definitive history of the Foundation. The present interpretation of these events, however, is the responsibility of the author, who gratefully acknowledges the assistance and advice furnished by the Historical Division.

tributed by the people of Georgia for the construction of a new building named Georgia Hall. As the anonymous author of a history of
Georgia Hall phrased it, this building was "a gift great in itself . . . but
greater because it unlocked the door for the future development of a
crusade on a nation-wide scale."[53]

*The President's Birthday Ball.* The second far-reaching decision
made by the Georgia Warm Springs Foundation in 1933 was to embark
upon a nationwide fund-raising campaign—a decision which was of
course an outgrowth of Roosevelt's election to the Presidency the previous November. On Thanksgiving weekend a group of people interested in Georgia Warm Springs met there to discuss fund-raising possibilities. Here is one participant's report of the most important conver-
sation of the weekend:

Col. Doherty insisted that it should not be a long campaign, that it should
be some particular event connected with some particular day, the kind of
thing that could be repeated from year-to-year. "Give the people some sort
of entertainment, a party, so that it will not be a matter of passing the hat,"
Col. Doherty said.
"The President's Birthday!" someone exclaimed, "Why not a President's
Birthday Ball?"
To save me, I can't say now which one of us four men made the suggestion.
I just don't remember. We were all so pleased by the idea we paid little
attention to who made it.[54]

A few moments later another important decision was made, as the
question was discussed as to who—on such short notice—could organize Birthday Balls throughout the country. "I've got it!" said Keith
Morgan. "The Postmasters. They just got jobs after ten Republican
years. They ought to be glad to do something for the boss."[55]

Keith Morgan was right, and Birthday Balls and similar celebrations were quickly organized in thousands of communities throughout
America, many of them by postmasters. This first venture into a nationwide, publicly supported fund-raising campaign turned out to be
more successful than anyone had dared hope. Basil O'Connor, for example, had thought "the entire stunt might not even hit the first $100,-
000" and was "actually shaken" when he learned that the event had
been a huge success.[56] For so many Americans turned out on the evening of January 30, 1934—either to honor the President, to help fight
infantile paralysis, or just to dance—that $1,016,444 was raised, after
expenses.[57]

The unanticipated success of the first President's Birthday Ball con-

fronted the Georgia Warm Springs Foundation with something of a
dilemma. Although part of the proceeds could have been used to repay
Roosevelt and others for what they had personally advanced to the
Foundation, Roosevelt—in accepting the check for the Foundation—
vetoed this suggestion, saying that "of course no part of this fund will
be used to repay any advances made the Foundation by any of its
officers or trustees."[58] Another solution would have been to establish
a permanent endowment fund, the proceeds of which would have contributed to the support of Georgia Warm Springs. The Trustees, however, believed that they now had a mandate to launch a nationwide
program to combat infantile paralysis, a program envisioned nearly
three years before by Roosevelt when he proposed "one vast national
crusade against infantile paralysis."[59] Accordingly, the Certificate of
Incorporation was amended to extend the territory in which the Georgia
Warm Springs Foundation would carry out its activities. Instead of
being confined to the states of New York and Georgia, it now became
empowered to operate in "the United States of America, its possessions
and dependencies, but the operation of the corporation shall not be
limited to such territory."[60] Furthermore, the proceeds from the 1934
celebrations were used both to support Georgia Warm Springs and to
launch a nationwide program for combatting infantile paralysis. In the
three subsequent years, 1935 through 1937, the local Committees for
the Celebration of the President's Birthday were authorized to retain
for use in their own communities 70 per cent of the proceeds from the
Birthday Balls—the remaining 30 per cent going, in 1935, to the newly-
created President's Birthday Ball Commission for Infantile Paralysis
Research, and, in 1936 and 1937, to the Georgia Warm Springs Foundation.[61]

*Origins of the patient care program.* Local communities made use
of their portion of the proceeds from the Birthday Balls in a number
of ways, including providing financial assistance to polio patients. The
local patient care program thus emerged accidentally, as the result of a
"too successful" fund-raising idea. Accordingly, when plans for establishing a new National Foundation for Infantile Paralysis were being
made in the latter part of 1937 the planners had to decide not only
how to insure continuity to the Georgia Warm Springs Foundation, but
also how to convert the already-established fund-raising and patient
care programs to the uses of the new organization. President Roosevelt asked Basil O'Connor, who was then Treasurer of the Georgia
Warm Springs Foundation, to take charge of the 1938 Birthday Ball,

and to decide how the funds should best be utilized.[62] In his reply to the President, O'Connor reviewed the previous Birthday Balls, and said:

Any funds raised from the celebration of your birthday in 1938 are to be administered by the new Foundation. The efforts of that new Foundation are not to be confined to research or after-treatment or any one phase of the disease, but are to attack the problem from every angle and as a whole. With this thought in mind . . . it is unhesitatingly recommended that all funds raised in the communities . . . be sent in their entirety to the committee . . . to be given to the new National Foundation to be administered by it for the good of the cause locally or nationally.[63]

Early in November, 1937, an announcement was made to the press that President Roosevelt had "given his birthday to the new National Foundation for Infantile Paralysis," and the new plan for the centralized administration of the funds was explained.[64] The Foundation was thus launched as a truly national organization with no mention made of local affiliates or branches.

It is easy to say in retrospect that it should have been possible to predict an unfavorable reaction to this announcement that henceforth local communities would retain none of the proceeds of the Birthday Balls. But to Basil O'Connor and his associates, who were entering into the unknown field of a large-scale, publicly supported attack upon a still mysterious disease, it must have seemed perfectly sensible to want to have control over the expenditure of the available funds.* In any event, protests did come in from local communities shortly after the announcement was made.[66]

*Origins of local Chapters.* The reaction of the national leadership to these protests from the local Committees proved to have far-reaching effects. In a report to the Board of Trustees on November 30, 1938, Basil O'Connor reviewed his reasoning in having previously recommended the centralized control of the Foundation's funds, and noted that a large number of "requests for financial assistance from local communities" had been received. "I think the experience of this last year indicates clearly that the time has now come," his report went on to say, "when the so-called local situation can be properly handled only by the National Foundation taking a certain amount of activity in it, otherwise the localities will be unable to finance their requirements."

---

* The only major voluntary health association which predates the Foundation is the National Tuberculosis Association, which has always had less of a commitment to a research program than the Foundation has had since the creation of the President's Birthday Ball Commission for Infantile Paralysis Research in 1934.[65]

Therefore, he recommended that "in each year a certain percentage of the money raised . . . be left in the localities where raised throughout the country on a county basis where practical . . ." and that "the Foundation organize in each county . . . a chapter or unit to administer the funds left in the particular county, the method of organization and the personnel of said chapters or units, and the method of administering its funds to be worked out by the committee of Trustees. . . ."[67]

This plan to establish local chapters was approved by the Trustees, and O'Connor was given approval to appoint a committee of three trustees to prepare a *Manual for Chapters*.[68]

Most of O'Connor's report to the Trustees was included in a radio broadcast he made that same day. But he stressed to the public even more strongly than he had to the Trustees that the plan to establish Chapters was the result of local pressures. "The National Foundation does not seek this," he said, "the local situation requires it."[69]

November, 1938, like the November five years before when the Birthday Balls were first planned, was thus a crucial month in the Foundation's history, since a program of locally-administered assistance to polio patients was established and local organizations were authorized to administer it for the first time.

Most Chapters were initially organized by the local Chairman of the Committee for the Celebration of the President's Birthday, but the Committees as such did not go out of existence. Instead, the newly-formed Chapters were assigned responsibility for the patient care program, and the Committees—which gradually evolved into March of Dimes organizations—remained as the fund-raising units of the Foundation.

This brief historical review has demonstrated that the current structural differences between Chapter and March of Dimes organizations were not explicitly planned, but developed as unanticipated consequences of decisions made in order to solve pressing problems. March of Dimes organizations had their origin in the local Committees for the Celebration of the President's Birthday, which were established in order to raise the funds necessary for the continued existence of the Georgia Warm Springs Foundation; local Chapters were established in order to administer a patient care program which had evolved in an unplanned fashion as a result of the decision to permit the local Committees to retain part of the proceeds from the second and the two subsequent Birthday Balls. Before continuing with the discussion of the Foundation today, however, it is necessary to note the impact of these decisions upon the Volunteer personnel of the Foundation.

*Origins of middle-class Volunteers.* It is virtually impossible to describe accurately the political composition of the early membership of
Foundation Chapters, since the only comprehensive records which are
available include only the names and the occupations of the people involved. It is known that many of the Committees for the Celebration of
the President's Birthday were originally headed, following Keith Morgan's suggestion, by postmasters—who, because of the political ap-
pointment system then in effect, were in most cases Democrats—and by
local Democratic leaders. In fact, thirty-four Volunteers in thirteen
of the thirty-seven Chapters studied intensively during this research
spontaneously mentioned that their Chapter originally had had close
relationships with the local Democratic Party. Furthermore, the Volunteers interviewed during this research by the American Institute of
Public Opinion were asked specifically to relate what they knew of the
origins of their Chapter: In fifty-nine out of eighty-five Chapters, one
or more Volunteers reported that the original members had largely
been Democrats.*

Not all of these original Volunteers were Democrats, however, and
some were even active in Republican Party activities. By and large they
were businessmen, professionals, and persons of *civic* prominence for
one reason or another; in most cases, however, they were not persons
of *social* prominence in the community. When the original Chairman
were asked to organize local Chapters they naturally turned to people
who had worked with them in the past, either on the Birthday Ball or
on some other activity. As a result, the early Chapters included members who were not necessarily active in Democratic Party activities, but
very seldom people of high social status in the community.

The decision to ask postmasters and persons of civic prominence
to head the first Birthday Balls thus had far-reaching consequences for
the Foundation. For it established the tradition that Foundation Volunteers are recruited from what might be best described as the "functioning" or "Main Street" segment of the community, rather than from the
ranks of the socially prominent. It is this characteristic of Foundation
Volunteers, rather than Democratic Party affiliation, which has remained most unchanged with the passing years. As noted earlier, Volunteers—regardless of political affiliation—generally think of themselves as members of the middle class, and consider the Foundation to
be unique among health and welfare associations because of the middle-
class composition of its personnel.†

* See Appendix A for a description of this phase of the field work.
† See p. 31.

## FUNCTIONAL SPECIALIZATION

A number of structural characteristics of the Foundation which serve either to circumvent or attenuate the membership apathy which often results from functional specialization were mentioned earlier in this chapter. For example, Foundation Chapters are small, and in the March of Dimes the practice of assigning Chairmen to geographical areas serves to mitigate overspecialization. But it is also necessary to comment upon another aspect of voluntary associations which traditionally leads to membership nonparticipation and apathy: the special qualifications which leaders must have.

It was noted above that three qualifications for leadership—time, temperament, and skill—impose *a priori* limitations upon the proportion of the membership of any organization which is eligible for positions of major responsibility. The Foundation is no exception to this generalization; like most organizations, it is aware of the possibility of a stagnation of leadership and urges its membership to seek constantly to augment its ranks. "Don't make the mistake of restricting your membership to the same loyal few, year after year,"[70] Volunteers are told. And again:

It is highly desirable to rotate the office of Chairman among Executive Committee members from year to year. *Don't ask the same individual to be Chairman for more than two years, nor to run for Chairman again until he has been out of office at least one year.* Experience has shown that a more informed point of view results, and Chapter activities are conducted with more vitality, when there is a new Chairman every two years.[71]

Since the office of Chairman is the most crucial one in the Chapter, it is interesting to note the qualifications for office which are suggested to Chapters by National Headquarters:

The Chairman . . . must be . . . a person of poise and administrative ability, with a deep interest in people, public health and human welfare. Try to select an individual who has proved himself interested in civic, philanthropic and health activities. . . . There are no professional qualifications. The Chairman might be a businessman, an attorney, an educator, or a housewife. . . . *Physicians and public health officers should not be asked to serve as Chairman.* . . . The Chairman should not be so identified with any political organization as to create distrust on the part of members of rival political organizations. He should be without prejudice against race, color, creed, or class.[72]

In short, a Chairman should be a public-spirited layman who is not distrusted in any way by the public; no particular skills are required for the position.* In all these respects save one, local Chapters do not differ substantially from many other voluntary health associations. An important exception, however, is that the Chairman must be a layman. In the case of many other voluntary health associations, on the other hand, the Chairman may be, and often is, a physician. Here again, historical origins had a decisive role. The individuals who founded the Foundation—President Roosevelt and his associates—were all laymen, and the first Chapter Volunteers were primarily laymen. The National Tuberculosis Association, on the other hand, was established largely upon the initiative of doctors;[73] and the American Heart Association and the American Cancer Society were both established in the post-World War II years as reorganizations of already-existing professional societies.[74]

Public-spirited laymen, however, are not trained to cope with many of the technical problems which arise in voluntary health associations, and in larger communities the work load invariably becomes too great for Volunteers to handle during evenings and weekdays. The twin demands of technical competence and available time characteristically require that a professional staff be hired in most voluntary associations. And it is precisely this step which often generates the problem of membership apathy. When a staff is employed, even the volunteer officers who are officially in control of the organization tend to leave the actual conduct of the program in the hands of people who are trained for this purpose, and who are paid. It is accordingly of some interest to observe how these problems are met in the Foundation.

Let us first consider the problem of technical competence. The easiest way for a Chapter to ensure that its program is competently carried out would be to elect a doctor or a hospital administrator as one of its Officers, or as a member of the Executive Committee. However, this is specifically prohibited by National Headquarters.† Nor can a Chapter pay the salary of a nurse or physical therapist.[75] The reason given to Volunteers for these prohibitions is that part of a Chapter's function is to pay bills submitted to individuals by doctors and hospitals, and no one should be placed in the position of having

---

* The only qualification for office officially prescribed in the *Manual for Chapters* or in the Chapter *By-laws* is that the Chairman must be a member of the Executive Committee. The qualifications for Vice-Chairman are the same as those for Chairman, and those for Treasurer and Secretary are the self-evident ones expected in all organizations: a sense of responsibility, attention to detail, etc.

†In actual practice, several Chapters have Officers who are doctors. Such occasional deviations from official regulations are condoned by National Headquarters personnel, who take pride in pointing out the "flexibility" permitted Volunteers in the interpretation of rules.

to approve his own bills.[76] In short, the prohibition avoids the emergence of role conflict situations. But it also serves an important unintended or latent function: it makes it necessary for lay Volunteers to maintain close contact with Chapter affairs, for they must pass approval on bills, prepare checks, maintain records, etc. Professional training is of course utilized by the Chapter through the establishment of a Medical Advisory Committee, which furnishes professional and technical guidance. But it is of the utmost significance that this is an *advisory* committee; final responsibility rests in the hands of the Chapter Officers and the Executive Committee.

Since members of the Medical Advisory Committee are Volunteers, not employees of the Foundation, the amount of time they can give to Chapter activities is necessarily limited; since they are not Chapter Officers, they cannot act in the name of the Foundation. Furthermore, some form of liaison between National Headquarters and Chapters is necessary. Various techniques for establishing communication and facilitating administration are utilized: general manuals and bulletins covering specific topics, visits to Chapters by National Headquarters staff personnel, regional meetings of Chapter Chairmen, news bulletins, and the like. But the most direct link between headquarters and Chapters is the State Representative, a paid employee of the national office responsible for all the Chapters located in the state to which he is assigned.[77]

Broadly speaking, a State Representative has two functions: furnishing guidance to Chapters in the conduct of their programs and ensuring that Chapters adhere to Foundation policy. Although the various manuals provided by the Foundation for Chapter reference are very explicit, there are always special and emergency problems which require professional assistance. A problem which a Chapter may face only once or twice a year, for example, is merely routine for a professional employee who is responsible for twenty or thirty Chapters. Furthermore, in order for the facilities of National Headquarters to be available to Chapters, it is necessary that someone within a reasonable distance be empowered to act in the name of the national office.

The State Representative thus plays a very crucial role in ensuring that Chapter affairs are not mismanaged. His surveillance ensures that Chapters fulfill their major responsibilities, and his guidance makes it possible for lay Volunteers to perform the technical tasks of running a Chapter. In this connection, it is very significant that these roles are performed by an individual who is a professional employee of National

Headquarters, not of local Chapters, and who has many Chapters under his jurisdiction, not just one. For if he were a Chapter employee, there would be an inevitable tendency for Chapter Volunteers to withdraw from active participation by delegating authority to him; and if he were assigned to only one Chapter, his immediate availability would result in his assuming increasing responsibility for the conduct of Chapter affairs. Under the present arrangement, it is impossible for Volunteers to delegate authority to the State Representative since he is not a Chapter employee, yet his training and technical competence are available to Chapters—but not so readily available as to make it possible for Chapter Officers to avoid assuming major responsibility themselves.

The problem of managing an excessive Chapter work load is handled quite differently. Chapters located in populous counties or faced with an emergency such as a polio epidemic are permitted to hire clerical and secretarial assistance, and Chapters serving large cities may hire an Executive Secretary. This position is purely administrative, and Chapters are reminded by National Headquarters that "the Executive Committee is responsible for the operation of the Chapter; the Executive Secretary is merely the agent of the Chapter."[78] As in the case of technical and professional assistance, the provisions made for administrative assistance are such that Volunteers cannot escape responsibility for the conduct of Chapter affairs.*

To recapitulate: The following structural characteristics of the Foundation serve to mitigate against the emergence of membership nonparticipation stemming from the special qualifications required of leaders. First, Chapters are explicitly prohibited from electing a physician or a public health official as Chairman, and from hiring any member of the medical profession to assist with Chapter activities. Instead, Chapters are directed to create a Medical Advisory Committee to furnish technical and professional guidance. As a result, the lay Officers of the Chapter must of necessity maintain an active interest in its affairs, since they are the responsible agents of the Foundation.

Second, the State Representative, a National Headquarters employee who furnishes Chapters with professional guidance, is not in a position to assume responsibilities which are assigned to Chapters, since he is not in the employ of local Chapters and has too many Chapters under his jurisdiction to give undue attention to any one. Here

---

* In a few of the Chapters studied in this research, the researchers noted that the Executive Secretary seemed to be given "excessive" responsibility, but in most Chapters this National Headquarters directive was being carried out.

again, the lay Officers must remain active if the Chapter program is to be carried out.

Third, Chapters are permitted to hire clerical and secretarial assistance—and, in the case of Chapters located in large cities, an Executive Secretary—but final responsibility for the conduct of Chapter affairs rests in the hands of Chapter Volunteers. All three of these features, then, prohibit professionally trained people from managing the program of the Chapter, yet make professional guidance available when it is needed.

## MEMBERSHIP HETEROGENEITY

The membership of an organization may be said to be heterogeneous if either one of two situations prevails. First, there may be an absence of consensus among the members concerning the organization's objectives and the nature of the program which should be carried out in order to further these objectives. Second, members may come from different social backgrounds, and have few interests in common. Since these factors are fundamentally different from each other, they must be discussed separately.

*Consensus concerning objectives and program.* A characteristic of the Foundation's objectives which sets them apart from those of such voluntary associations as fraternal orders, service organizations, women's clubs, and veterans' groups is that they are highly specific in nature. Here are the Foundation's four major objectives, as set forth in its original *Certificate of Incorporation:*

1. To direct, unify, stimulate, coordinate and further the knowledge of, and the work being done on any and all phases of infantile paralysis, including study and research into the cause, nature and methods of prevention of the disease and the prevention of harmful after-effects of the disease.

2. To arrange for, and to direct, unify, stimulate, coordinate and further the work being done on the treatment in lawfully established institutions conducted by others of persons afflicted with infantile paralysis and/or suffering from its after-effects.

3. To make voluntary contributions or grants of money from funds of the corporation at any time and from time to time to individuals who are disabled or handicapped in whole or in part as a result of infantile paralysis or any disease or cause whatsoever or to lawfully established agencies for the benefit of such persons or for the purpose of prevention, diagnosis, treatment, alleviation or after-treatment of infantile paralysis.

4. To do any and all things necessary and incidental to the carrying out of these purposes.[79]

This statement of objectives has several interesting characteristics. First, the initial two paragraphs contain the words "direct," "unify" and "coordinate"—evidence that an original goal was to eliminate the waste and duplication of effort which so often characterize attacks upon social or health problems. Even though the formal structure of the organization had not been developed at the time these objectives were formulated, it is clear from this wording that a corporate-type formal structure would be required, and was envisioned by the original leadership. Second, the specificity of the objectives is matched by the comprehensiveness of the program to be adopted in carrying them out. The fourth paragraph makes this intention quite clear: "To do any and all things necessary and incidental to the carrying out of these purposes." Third, the objectives are inherently noncontroversial in nature; practically no one in our society will deny the importance of preventing disease, the value of the scientific approach to disease control, or the humanity of making grants of money to individuals who are disabled or handicapped.

Although practically everyone in our society does share the values implicit in these objectives, people who for some reason do not feel that polio patients should be helped in this way, or do not think that it is important that people be informed concerning polio, or do not believe in fund-raising campaigns simply do not become Volunteers. Since all three of these are culturally approved activities, Volunteers are not required to adopt new attitudes upon becoming members. The justification for the program is rooted in the cultural system itself; Volunteers are merely people who have elected to take action to further culturally approved values.

Fund-raising, however, is not without its controversial aspects, since many American communities have Community Chests or similar organizations which seek to combine a number of fund-raising activities into one united campaign. In order to demonstrate that an absence of consensus among the membership generally does not arise over this issue, it is necessary to provide a word of explanation concerning the Foundation's policy with respect to federated or united fund-raising.

Federated fund-raising is a relatively new development in American philanthropy. Although a federated campaign was held in Denver as early as 1887, "the first real community chest is considered to be the Federation of Charities and Philanthropy organized in Cleveland in 1913."[80] The growth of the movement was comparatively slow at first. When the Foundation was established in 1938, for example, there were only 475 Community Chest campaigns held throughout the United States.[81] By 1955, however, Community Chest organizations held campaigns in some 1,900 American communities.* [82]

Although in its early years the Foundation permitted its local organizations to participate in federated fund-raising, it exercised strict control, requiring that any agreements entered into by Chapters with Community Chests had to receive the prior approval of the Board of Trustees.[84] With the advent of World War II, however, and the emergence of War Chests throughout the country, an even stricter policy was enacted. Participation in War Chests was absolutely prohibited, on the grounds that the fight against infantile paralysis was purely a health problem, not a war activity, and to participate in a War Chest would be to obtain money under false pretenses. This policy was soon extended to cover all federated campaigns, and the 1944 (as well as the current) *Manual for Chapters* contained an absolute prohibition against participation in Community Chests of any kind.[85]

There are a number of reasons for this policy. The Foundation feels (1) that contributors to a fund-raising campaign have the right to know where their money is going; (2) that the Foundation has neither a legal nor a moral right to delegate its fund-raising functions to another organization; (3) that individual campaigns serve to educate and inform the public concerning health and welfare problems; (4) that the Foundation has a responsibility to its Volunteers to enable them to remain active; (5) that the epidemic nature of polio makes budgeting for the patient care program impossible; and (6) that more money is raised by conducting its own campaign.[86] Supporters of federated campaigns, on the other hand, advance arguments such as these:

Experience shows that federated fund raising saves millions of dollars in campaign costs while raising the money. It assures fair distribution of funds through annual budget reviews of each participating service. Planning of services to eliminate duplications guarantees the most effective use of contributed funds. The united way saves volunteer time and energy and helps the contributor to give systematically and intelligently to an all round program of service. It frees givers and campaign workers from the annoyance of separate, repeated and competitive appeals, from tag days, benefits and other costly money raising devices and protects them from "charity rackets."[87]

* A technical distinction is currently made between the terms "Community Chest" (in which only local organizations participate), "United Fund" (in which local organizations plus the Red Cross participate) and "Extended Federation Campaign" (in which local organizations plus one or more national voluntary health associations participate). For present purposes, however, considerable confusion is avoided by referring to all joint or federated fund-raising campaigns as Community Chests.[83]

Since the March of Dimes campaign has such widespread public appeal, most local Community Chest organizations apply as much pressure as possible upon the Foundation Chapter in their community in order to persuade it to join; since Chapters are forbidden by National Headquarters to do so, considerable conflict has resulted. In fact, the conflict has become such a joined battle, both locally and nationally, that emotionally charged statements have become the rule in many public discussions. The Foundation, for example, speaks of Community Chests as "catch-all-drives" and "super-chests"; it refers to "the negative philosophy which seeks to bury the identity of health agencies and blunt the stimulating impact of individual drives"; it states that joining such a campaign would force its Volunteers to become "faceless, voiceless contributors to a conglomerate group of charities"; and it asserts that it rejects a "philosophy which would turn all philanthropy into an assembly line project."[88] An unofficial spokesman for the Community Chest, on the other hand, has recently stated that organizations such as the Foundation "have engaged in independent, high-powered fund raising, completely unrelated to federated community efforts," and has charged that:

These independent campaigns have challenged the basic philosophy of modern private welfare financing. The objective of the community chest has been to relieve the contributor of numerous competitive appeals, by a single annual welfare drive.[89]

It is of some interest that the other three major voluntary health associations, stimulated in part by the success of the Foundation's policy of nonparticipation in federated campaigns and in part by the success achieved by their own nonparticipating local units, have recently adopted policies of either discouraging or prohibiting such participation. The National Tuberculosis Association and the American Heart Association now forbid their units to participate in federated campaigns, except for those units which are already committed, and the American Cancer Society has adopted a policy of requiring its units to withdraw from such participation unless their growth keeps pace with that of the Society as a whole.[90]

If the Foundation had a policy of discouraging participation, but permitting local option, Volunteers would be placed in a classic "cross-pressure" situation. Their loyalty to the Foundation would incline them to vote against participation, and the pressures invoked by many of their business and professional associates would incline them to vote for it. But since local option is not permitted, people who sympathize with the Community Chest position generally do not become Volunteers, or withdraw from participation in the organization if their views change. In fact, several Volunteers interviewed in the course of this research recounted instances of other Volunteers resigning from their Chapter or March of Dimes organization because of the conflict in loyalties entailed in membership in, or loyalty toward, both the Foundation and the Community Chest. Furthermore, several other Volunteers reported that they themselves were in disagreement with the policy, but remained Volunteers because of the uses to which the funds raised are put. By and large, however, being a Volunteer implies agreement with the Foundation's philosophy concerning federated fundraising.*

*Similarity of social backgrounds.* The problem of divergent social backgrounds presents a somewhat different problem. Any community organization which seeks either to provide services to the community or raise funds from the public faces a dilemma with respect to the character of its membership. On the one hand, membership participation is more easily obtained when members "speak the same language," that is, come from a similar stratum of the population, have many mutual friends, share the same values, etc. On the other hand, public support is more easily obtained if the organization is broadly representative of many strata in the community, and includes individuals with differing points of view. In order to satisfy the demands both of its own membership and that of the public, a voluntary association must both provide opportunities for "primary relationships" to develop among its members *and* ensure that the organization does not come to be dominated by any one clique.

From the point of view of the organization, the major problem is to ensure heterogeneity, since there is a natural tendency for people who share similar values to associate with each other without any official encouragement; furthermore, once a primary group is established, there is a tendency for even greater homogeneity to develop. As Elihu Katz and Paul Lazarsfeld have recently pointed out, "interdependent individuals demand conformity of each other."[91]

The Foundation encourages its Chapters to make their membership as representative of the community as possible:

* Agreement with the Foundation's policy does not, of course, prevent Volunteers from serving as volunteer fund-raisers for the Community Chest. In fact, nearly half of all March of Dimes Volunteers also participate in a Community Chest campaign. See p. 61.

Avoid loading your Chapter with members of one civic club, one city, one profession, or one income level. Your Chapter should draw its members from the various professions, occupations, religious and racial groups, economic levels and organizations within your county.[92]

Similarly, it insists that Chapters be regarded as open-membership organizations. *"Membership in our organization,"* Volunteers are told, *"should be open to anyone genuinely interested in working for our cause."*[93] How then, does Chapter membership remain sufficiently homogeneous so that members will be motivated to participate actively with others whom they feel have like interests?

This seems to come about in several ways. First, most Chapters, as indicated earlier, are relatively small. This means that it is possible for people from diverse backgrounds to get to know and understand each other more readily than is the case in larger organizations. Second, although membership in local Chapters is officially open to everyone who is interested, in actual practice relatively few people join on their own initiative.* Thus, even though Chapters may seek to make their membership broadly representative of the community, it is still possible for them to maintain some degree of control over the actual individuals who become members, and thus insure a measure of homogeneity. Finally, since Chapter meetings are held only once or twice a year, and most Chapter business is conducted either over the telephone or in small committee meetings, there are few opportunities for conflicts to arise as a result of what membership heterogeneity does exist.

In actual practice, the membership of most Chapters is quite homogeneous. This may be demonstrated by showing the extent of social class, occupational, and political homogeneity among the thirty-seven Chapters studied.

In eighteen of the Chapters studied, a majority of Volunteers are members of the middle class (as rated by the interviewers), in nine a majority are of the upper class, and in ten Chapters neither class is represented by a clear majority.

In nineteen of the Chapters, a majority of Volunteers are members of the "business community"—businessmen, accountants, insurance agents, and the like. In five Chapters, a majority are professionals or municipal and governmental employees—lawyers, teachers, postmasters, etc. And in thirteen Chapters, neither occupational group predominates.

---

* Only 10 per cent of the Volunteers studied in this research joined on their own initiative. See Chapter III for a more extensive discussion of Volunteer recruitment.

In terms of political preferences, in fourteen Chapters a majority of Volunteers are Democrats; in thirteen Chapters a majority are Republicans; and in ten Chapters partisans of neither political party have a clear majority.

When all three of these characteristics are considered simultaneously, an even more striking picture of Chapter homogeneity emerges. In eleven Chapters, the membership is homogeneous with respect to all three characteristics;* in twenty-one Chapters, the membership is homogeneous with respect to two characteristics; and in three Chapters, with respect to only one. Only two of the Chapters studied, then, are truly heterogeneous as far as social class, occupation, and political preferences are concerned. Interestingly enough, in both of these Chapters the Chairman is by far the most active Volunteer; that is, the other members are less active than in the other Chapters studied.

Although Chapter homogeneity is striking as measured by these indices, it should be remembered that the criterion of a majority was used to indicate homogeneity. In none of the Chapters studied are *all* Volunteers members of the same class, the same occupational group, or holders of the same political views (except of course in some Southern Chapters with respect to political preference). The typical Foundation Chapter is sufficiently homogeneous to ensure that its members will "speak the same language," but not so homogeneous as to make it appear to outsiders that it is dominated by any one group in the community.

It is of interest also that Chapter heterogeneity-homogeneity was not found to be systematically related to Chapter performance, as measured by the extent to which Chapter members work as a "functionally cohesive" group, a performance rating given to the Chapter by the State Representative, and the extent to which the funds raised during the most recent March of Dimes were obtained through only one activity—the Mothers' March on Polio.†

## MULTI-GROUP MEMBERSHIP

It will be recalled that the obligations which individuals feel toward their job and family, on the one hand, and toward other voluntary associations to which they belong, on the other, have been cited by students of voluntary associations as conducive to membership apathy and

* That is, a majority of the Volunteers comes from the same social class, the same occupational group, and the same political party.

† See Appendix B for a description of these indices, and Appendix C for a presentation of the data upon which this discussion of Chapter homogeneity is based.

nonparticipation. The relationship of each of these group membership obligations to participation in the Foundation is discussed below.

*Obligations to job and family.* Barber's sociological analysis of the problem of membership apathy led him to conclude that socially structured role obligations to the job and to the family are culturally defined in our society as taking precedence over obligations to voluntary associations; only in times of such national emergencies as war, he concluded, is anything like "mass activism" possible. This conclusion applies only to the *rate* of participation in voluntary associations, and it was pointed out that there are always individuals who either can devote less attention to fulfilling these obligations or who have the energy and talent to fulfill many obligations simultaneously.

In one sense, the Foundation does not compete with the prior obligations of job and family. As is the case with the problems attendant upon organization size, it circumvents them. This is accomplished in two ways. First, the Foundation recruits the majority of its Volunteers from that portion of the public which has already demonstrated that its interests are broader than job and family; that is, people who are already members of several other community organizations. *"Don't be afraid to approach busy people,"* the national office counsels local Chapters. And again, "If you want to get a job done, get a busy man to do it—the others haven't time."[94] In this respect, the character of the Foundation's membership confirms the thesis that most people are unable to devote much time and energy to activities other than those which concern them directly. By making full use of people who do have the necessary time and energy, the Foundation precludes the possibility of acquiring an inactive and passive membership.

Second, the nature of the Foundation's program is such that many Volunteers actually define it as the *fulfillment* of an obligation to their family. Since most Volunteers are parents, and since parents are more concerned than any other group in American society about the threat of polio, it is apparent that participation as a Volunteer can be regarded as an activity which serves to protect one's own family. But Foundation activity does more than provide an outlet for the natural desire of many parents to help combat polio; it also permits them to participate in a program which may benefit them personally—the patient care program.

*Membership in several associations.* Obligations to job and family are not the only ones with which voluntary associations must compete. Since voluntary associations draw their membership largely from peo-

ple who are also members of other organizations, the problem of divided loyalties may arise. It will be recalled from the earlier discussion
that the major problem which emerges from the fact that people may
belong to several organizations is that a conflict between the goals or
values of two organizations to which they may belong tends to foster
inactivity in one or both organizations. Since a majority of Foundation
Volunteers do belong to several organizations, it is pertinent to examine
what possibilities exist for inactive participation to result from their
multiple memberships.

Although Foundation Volunteers belong to many community organizations, their interests are widely scattered. Fewer than half belong
to any one *category* of organizations; accordingly, even fewer belong
to any one other *organization*. Table 1 presents the percentage of Volunteers who belong to each major type of community organization.

## Table 1—Participation in Other Community Organizations

| Community Organizations | PER CENT WHO BELONG | |
|---|---|---|
| | Chapter Volunteers | March of Dimes Volunteers |
| Church-related | 43 | 51 |
| Social, recreational | 43 | 37 |
| Professional, trade | 41 | 39 |
| Service (e.g., Lions Club) | 40 | 41 |
| Youth (e.g., Boy Scouts) | 38 | 24 |
| Health and welfare | 38 | 24 |
| Political, civic | 25 | 23 |
| Fraternal (e.g., Masons) | 17 | 23 |
| Patriotic, veterans | 11 | 14 |
| None except Foundation | 4 | 2 |
| N | (129)* | (105)* |

* The numbers in parentheses in the tables throughout this volume indicate the number of
cases upon which percentages are based.

Although Chapter Volunteers are somewhat more likely than
March of Dimes Volunteers to belong to organizations which in a general way are comparable to the Foundation—youth, health and welfare groups—only 38 per cent belong to organizations in each of these
categories. Furthermore, there is little possibility for the emergence of
a conflict of interests, since no community organizations have programs
or philosophies which in any way are incompatible with the patient
care program. In fact, the national office urges Chapters to recruit members of other organizations which serve the youth and the health needs
of the community.[95] More specifically, it cites seven national health
and welfare organizations, and sixteen national youth organizations,
with which Volunteers are urged to cooperate. "There is no basis for

any feeling of 'rivalry' between other organizations caring for the crippled and your Chapter," Volunteers are told. "On the contrary, the utmost cooperation between you will serve your Chapter and the other organizations equally well. Make every effort to work out satisfactory relationships with them."[96]

Participation in several fund-raising organizations is potentially more likely to lead to conflict-of-interest situations than is participation in the actual programs of other youth, health and welfare organizations, since organizations which depend upon public financial support are in the very nature of the case somewhat in competition with each other.

More than two-thirds of all Chapter Volunteers, and 99 per cent of all March of Dimes Volunteers, actually do take part in other fund-raising activities. However, as is the case with their participation in community organizations generally, Volunteers participate in a wide variety of fund-raising activities, with only a relatively small proportion taking part in any one campaign. Two exceptions to this statement are the American Red Cross and the Community Chest. Thirty-six per cent of all Chapters Volunteers and 51 per cent of all March of Dimes Volunteers have recently worked on a Red Cross Drive, and 34 per cent of all Chapter Volunteers and 44 per cent of all March of Dimes Volunteers have recently worked for the Community Chest campaign. The amount of multi-group membership represented by these percentages reflects the fact that in most American communities the March of Dimes, the Red Cross Drive, and the Community Chest campaign are the largest annual mass fund-raising campaigns, both in terms of funds raised and in the number of volunteer workers employed.

Since Red Cross funds are used for general welfare purposes, there is no conflict of interest involved. A Volunteer can take part both in the March of Dimes and the Red Cross Drive without feeling that he is working at cross-purposes, particularly since these two campaigns are held two months apart. The Community Chest represents something of a special case, since in most communities there is some conflict between it and the various national voluntary health associations, including the Foundation, which specifically prohibit their local units from taking part in any joint or federated campaigns. This prohibition of course applies to Chapters, not to individuals. In fact, Community Chest volunteers have a very good reason for taking part in the March of Dimes. Since local polio activities cannot be financed through the Community Chest, the March of Dimes provides the only opportunity for funds to be raised to support a polio program in the community.

## chapter II

# PRESERVING ORGANIZATIONAL GOALS

## Introduction

THE PROBLEM of maintaining membership interest, a problem common to all voluntary associations, was described in the previous chapter as stemming primarily from the process of delegating authority and functions *upwards* in an organization. A number of the Foundation's structural features which serve to alleviate this problem were indicated—of which the most important is undoubtedly the administrative separation of Chapter and March of Dimes organizations. The problem of preserving organizational goals, on the other hand, stems from the process of *downward* delegation, and is met in quite different ways.

The generic problem of goal preservation may be stated as follows: In order to accomplish their goals, organizations establish a set of procedures or means. In the course of following these procedures, however, the subordinates or members to whom authority and functions have been delegated often come to regard them as ends in themselves, rather than as means toward the achievement of organizations goals. As a result of this process, the actual activities of the organization become centered around the proper functioning of organization procedures, rather than upon the achievement of the initial goals.

This phenomenon of goal displacement is perhaps the most frequently noted pathological aspect of large-scale organizations. Philip Selznick, for example, calls it "the organizational paradox," and notes that because of this phenomenon organizational frustration is a persistent characteristic of our times.[1]

Practically every serious observer of large-scale organizations has noted instances of this tendency. Robert Michels, for example, in summarizing the tendencies toward oligarchy in socialist and labor organizations, noted that "from a means, organization becomes an end. . . . Henceforward the sole preoccupation is to avoid anything which may clog the machinery."[2] Walter Sharp's analysis of the French Civil Service led him to conclude that any bureaucracy faces "the constant danger that these routine operations will become sterilizing ends in themselves rather than the effective means to desirable ends."[3] Alvin Gouldner notes that a basic difference between two bureaucratic patterns he found in an industrial organization is that in "representative bureaucracies" obedience is given to the rules because this would lead "to desirable consequences *beyond themselves,*" while in "punishment-centered bureaucracies" the rule is treated "as an end in itself."[4] And Robert Merton, in his discussion of bureaucratic structure and personality, states that "adherence to the rules, originally conceived as a means, becomes transformed into an end-in-itself; there occurs the familiar process of *displacement of goals.* . . ."[5]

Arthur Davis has reported many instances of this phenomenon in the Navy Officer Corps in World War II. For example, he observed that the rule that communications in the Navy must follow the chain of command means that very simple messages sent from one officer to another often require the attention of eight to twelve persons over a ten-day period and that heavy-bomber crews on submarine patrol, in order to avoid being criticized by their superiors for errors in bombing missions, would often fly their patrols exactly as they were charted, even if this meant ignoring a suspicious object a few miles abeam. In short, he concluded, there is a "disfunctional tendency of formal organizations to overemphasize their main instrumental devices. . . ."[6] S. D. Clark's study of the Salvation Army in Canada revealed that as the Army grew its leaders devoted increasing attention to the problems of maintaining the organization. They spent a disproportionate share of their energies on problems of administration and finance, for example, and even gave up evangelical work in areas where there was insufficient support for a strong local organization.[7] Finally, Philip Selznick, who has devoted more explicit attention to this phenomenon than any other student of large-scale organizations, has formulated the problem as follows:

Running an organization, as a specialized and essential activity, generates problems which have no necessary (and often an opposed) relationship to the professed or "original" goals of the organization. The day-to-day behavior of the group becomes centered around specific problems and proximate goals which have primarily an internal relevance. Then, since these activities come to consume an increasing proportion of the time and thoughts of the participants, they are—from the point of view of actual behavior—*substituted* for the professed goals.[8]

This brief review of the attention which has been given to the problem of preserving organizational goals is perhaps sufficient to suggest its near-universality. In fact, the problem is mentioned so often, and the deleterious effects of goal displacement have been so frequently described, that the question inevitably arises as to how large-scale organizations are able to make progress toward their professed goals. The answer to this question of course is that organizations develop mechanisms of various kinds for minimizing the displacement of their goals. Before those mechanisms which the Foundation has developed are described, however, it is necessary to identify those specific sources of goal displacement which students of large-scale organizations have most frequently observed.

## Sources of Goal Displacement

The ultimate source of goal displacement is the process of delegation itself, since the individuals whose actions modify the goals of an organization are generally those to whom authority and functions have been delegated. The general process of goal displacement, in other words, takes place as a result of the actions of delegates coming to have an increasing *internal* relevance, rather than a direct relationship to the ultimate goals of the organization.[9] In more specific terms, the process may be observed by noting the actions of delegates which relate to (1) their status within the organization, (2) their interpretation of organizational rules, (3) their execution of organizational procedures, (4) their relationships with other participants, and (5) their relationships with the general public. Accordingly, the following discussion will focus upon each of these behavioral areas in turn. The major findings of previous research are summarized, and those aspects of the Foundation's formal structure which serve to preserve its goals are described.

### STATUS WITHIN THE ORGANIZATION

Discussions of large-scale organizations generally take it for granted that all the participants are employees of the organization. Max Weber, for example, included among the characteristics of an administrative staff the requirements that members be "remunerated by fixed salaries in money"; that "the office is treated as the sole, or at least the primary, occupation of the incumbent"; and that the office "constitutes a career ... (with) a system of 'promotion' according to seniority or to achievement, or both."[10]

Most large-scale organizations meet Weber's requirements with respect to the character of their personnel. Accordingly, most discussions of the problem of goal displacement locate as one source of the phenomenon the desire of the employee to maintain his position and advance his career. According to Selznick, "[the employee's] interest in the ultimate purpose of the organization, or in the 'common good,' becomes subordinate to his preoccupation with the problems involved in the *maintenance* of his post."[11] And in his analysis of the prospects for democracy in trade unions, Martin Lipset has pointed out that a democratic turnover in office would demand "the institutionalization of movement from high to low status. . . ." Since this in turn would involve "the institutionalization of a major deviation from the dominant value of achievement," Lipset concludes that "the functional requirements for democracy cannot be met most of the time in most unions."[12] In order to maintain their high status and high salaried positions within the union, leaders often strive to minimize rather than maximize the effect of the democratic process.[13]

### THE INTERPRETATION OF ORGANIZATIONAL RULES

A fundamental characteristic of large-scale organizations is that the behavior of their membership is governed by a set of rules, rather than by traditions or by "devotion to the specific and exceptional sanctity, heroism or exemplary character of an individual person. . . ."[14] Rules are of course necessary for the efficient day-to-day conduct of an organization. If every question had to be decided on its own merits, as happens quite frequently, for example, in such informal groupings as families or friendship cliques, an organization would be able to devote little attention to the conduct of its program.[15]

The rules which govern an organization, however, can also serve as a source of goal displacement. The underlying reason for this phenomenon is that the sentiments which are developed to buttress the rules are often more intense than is technically necessary. Strong sentiments surrounding obedience to rules are often necessary to protect the organization from the minority of irresponsible members, but these sentiments may cause other members of the organization to concentrate upon the details of behavior involved in abiding by the rules, rather than upon the aims of the organization. This phenomenon has been noted by most students of formal organizations; it has been described most fully by Merton (whose formulation of the problem has been followed here)[16] and by Peter Blau, who observed among some of the government employees he studied a tendency for the objectives of rules to be displaced by the techniques designed to achieve them.[17]

## THE EXECUTION OF ORGANIZATIONAL PROCEDURES

Without an organization a goal is merely a desired state of affairs; an organizational structure creates the conditions which allow concrete steps to be taken toward the realization of a goal. But the paradoxical fact is that the procedures involved in running an organization may come to assume greater importance than the initial goals themselves. As Selznick has noted, in a passage cited earlier, these procedures come to be "*substituted* for the professed goals."

The substitution of proximate goals for professed goals is a phenomenon which can occur in a number of ways. Merton has noted that it may occur through a process which he calls *sanctification:*

Through sentiment-formation, emotional dependence upon bureaucratic symbols and status, and affective involvement in spheres of competence and authority, there develop prerogatives involving attitudes of moral legitimacy which are established as values in their own right, and are no longer viewed as merely technical means for expediting administration.[18]

Davis, in his study of the Navy Officer Corps, notes the adverse impact of *ceremonialism* upon the manifest goals of the Navy. Ritual, which is particularly prevalent in the Navy, helps to maintain morale, but it also "may become an end in itself at the expense of the organization's capacity to perform efficiently its manifest functions."[19] Marshall Dimock has observed that *traditionalism* serves to impede an organization from selecting the most expedient procedures for achieving its goals:

The older an institution becomes, the more settled its mould and procedures are likely to be. Traditions are hallowed. Ways of doing things take on a reverence which defies successful change, even when they may have been quite accidental in the first place or when better methods have been discovered. Institutions are conservative in the extreme.[20]

Numerous students of organizations have found that *red tape,* particularly as it involves obtaining approval or transmitting a communication through a chain of command, very often becomes an end in itself. Finally, Selznick has noted that *routinization* also often results in the displacement of goals; he suggests that the actual performance of the activities of an organization may become so routine that the underlying purposes of the activities tend to become obscured.[21]

### RELATIONSHIPS WITH OTHER PARTICIPANTS

The formal structure of an organization generally does not explicitly provide for the emergence of informal groupings among its participants, yet both everyday experience and systematic research furnish incontrovertible evidence that such groupings are inevitably developed. In fact, there is increasing official awareness of the fact that informal groups within an organization are necessary for the effective operation of the formal structure itself.* Selznick has summarized this necessity as follows:

The informal structure will be at once indispensable to and consequential for the formal system of delegation and control itself. Wherever command over the response of individuals is desired, some approach in terms of the spontaneous organization of loyalty and interest will be necessary. In practice this means that the informal structure will be useful to the leadership and effective as a means of communication and persuasion. At the same time, it can be anticipated that some price will be paid in the shape of distribution of power or adjustment of policy.[23]

The present concern is of course with what Selznick calls the "price . . . paid in . . . adjustment of policy," that is, with the role primary groupings may play in the displacement of goals. Perhaps the best known study which demonstrates the existence of this possibility is the Roethlisberger and Dickson research into worker productivity. They found that the day-to-day practices of workers resulted in the emergence of an informal structure, which, among its other effects, led to the development of productivity norms. Since the professed goal of the organization was to maximize productivity, the restriction of output encouraged by these norms may be said to represent a displacement of goals.[24]

A second source of goal displacement generated by the informal structure is the sense of a common destiny which so often develops among fellow participants in a large-scale organization. Merton has

---

* A dramatic example of this increasing awareness is the recent attempt of the U.S. Army to encourage the emergency of informal groupings by establishing four-man teams which remain intact from basic training through assignment to an overseas unit.[22]

noted that these sentiments may lead the participants "to defend their
entrenched interests rather than to assist their clientele. . . ,"[25] and
Davis has gone so far as to suggest that the inability of the Navy to perform properly at Pearl Harbor in 1941 was in part attributable to the
"insulation of officers preoccupied with professional routine and Navy
social life. . . ."[26]

The most extensive analysis to date of the effect of informal groupings upon the goals of an organization is Selznick's study of the T.V.A.
One of his major findings concerns the consequences which resulted
from the delegation of certain phases of the T.V.A.'s agricultural program to local organizations already existing in the T.V.A.'s area of
operations. In order to make the program effective, these organizations
were informally "co-opted" into the policy-making apparatus of the
T.V.A. itself, and under the pressure of these "co-opted" organizations,
the T.V.A. was deflected from the achievement of some of its primary
goals.[27]

## RELATIONSHIPS WITH THE PUBLIC

All large-scale organizations which seek in any way to influence
the behavior of outsiders, or which provide services for outsiders, must
of necessity establish contact with members of the public. This is of
course the most frequently delegated function, and one which is generally delegated to individuals on the lowest level of the organization.
Post-office clerks, sales personnel, social workers, and campaign solicitors are ready examples of these types of positions.

Students of formal organizations have noted three characteristic
problems which emerge from these interpersonal relationships and
which may lead to the displacement of goals. First, there are problems
which emerge from the *status* of the organizational member vis à vis
the status of the people with whom he comes in contact. Merton has
noted that—particularly in government organizations—the status of
the official within the organization may not be commensurate with his
status in relationship to the public. This situation may lead to an actually or apparently domineering attitude which interferes with the performance of his job.[28]

Second, problems may emerge from the fact that *impersonality* is
usually supposed to govern relationships with the public. A bureaucratic organization, according to Weber, is governed by "a consistent
system of abstract rules. . . ," and the activities of individual members
"consist in the application of these rules to particular cases. . . ."[29] In

applying these rules, the members should eliminate from their job "love, hatred and all purely personal, irrational, and emotional elements which escape calculation."[30] The need for impersonality in many situations is readily apparent, since the organizational member who comes into contact with the public is expected to act in the name of the organization, not on his own behalf. The possibility exists, however, that the minimization of personal relations and the resort to categorization may result in the disregard of the peculiarities of individual situations. If one of the purposes of the organization is to cope with peculiar cases, impersonality may lead to the displacement of goals.[31]

A third source of difficulty arising from relationships with the public is the violation of impersonalization, called *particularism*. Peter Blau, for example, in his study of two government agencies, noted that "some officials lost sight of the generic objective of raising the standard of living of American workers in the course of dealing with particular underpaid (or unemployed) individuals. . . . Although this particularistic orientation enhanced work satisfaction, it . . . created resistance in those situations where the interest of individual employees had to be set aside in the interest of the generic objectives of the agency. . . ."[32]

## The Foundation
## and the Problem of Goal Displacement

If we examine the record of achievement of the Foundation it is quite apparent that the organization has not been deflected from achieving its major goals. In fact, in the nearly two decades since its establishment it has sponsored research which has vastly increased medical knowledge of infantile paralysis; it has brought about revolutionary changes in the methods of treating victims of infantile paralysis; it has introduced a completely new concept of how payment for medical and hospital bills may be shared by all the members of a community; it has sponsored the development of the Salk polio vaccine; and it is now on the threshold of achieving its major purpose—the elimination of epidemic infantile paralysis. It follows from this record of achievement that some provisions must have been incorporated into its formal structure which have served to minimize the displacement of its goals. This section is devoted to a description of those provisions which have served to mitigate the adverse effect of each of the sources of goal displacement previously described.

## STATUS WITHIN THE ORGANIZATION

Voluntary associations are inherently better protected than are other organizations against being deflected from their goals by the career interests of their members since the vast majority of their membership consists of unpaid volunteers for whom the activity is not their primary occupation. But a largely volunteer membership by no means provides complete immunity. In the first place, all large-scale voluntary associations employ some full-time professionals who carry out part of the day-to-day activity of the organization; in the second place, a volunteer member may be as interested as an employee in maintaining his position in the organization, and may accordingly orient his activities toward that end.

The formal structure of the Foundation provides several safeguards against the dangers inherent in the vested interests of individuals in maintaining their positions. In the first place, the ratio of professional employees to volunteer members is very low. The entire organization has fewer than 800 full-time employees, while more than 12,000 Volunteers are officers in local Chapters and many more Volunteers participate either in Chapter activities or in the March of Dimes. This reliance upon the volunteer membership for the performance of many functions is made feasible in two ways. First, unlike the situation which prevails in many national voluntary associations, there are no state societies which occupy an intermediate position between National Headquarters and local Chapters.* Since a state organization might require a minimum of perhaps ten or fifteen full-time employees, 400 to 600 positions are unnecessary. Second, the day-to-day program of the organization itself is such that it is possible for it to be performed for the most part by a few part-time Volunteers. This contrasts sharply with the situation which prevails in trade unions, for example, in which even the smallest local usually requires one or more employees to carry out the day-to-day responsibilities of the organization.

Another feature of the Foundation's formal structure which counterbalances the problems which arise from the desire of individuals to maintain their positions is the relative absence of status rewards associated with holding office. The professional employees have few

* As noted earlier, the Foundation's state offices are the headquarters of the State Representatives, not state organizations.

opportunities to become widely-known outside of the organization and profession itself, and the officers of local Chapters generally do not hold widely-coveted positions in the community. Furthermore, there are few opportunities for Volunteers to advance upward in the Foundation hierarchy. Paid personnel, for example, are only rarely ex-Volunteers, and the absence of state societies means that there are no higher positions within the Foundation toward which Volunteers can aspire. This situation contrasts sharply with that which prevails in organizations such as trade unions or the American Legion, where there is generally active competition for the position of local President or Post Commander, and active competition among these officers for state or national positions.

### THE INTERPRETATION OF ORGANIZATIONAL RULES

The rules which govern any organization are of two broad types. *Structural* rules specify how the organization is to be established, and include such items as qualifications for membership, the offices and committees which are authorized, and specific details concerning the delegation of authority and function. *Procedural* rules, on the other hand, specify how the activities of the organization are to be carried out, and consist largely of "do's" and "don't's."

The rules which govern both the structure and the procedures of the Foundation's local Chapters are codified in the *Manual for Chapters,* which includes the *By-laws* of Chapters. Since Chapters are conceived as administrative units of the national organization, the *Manual* and the *By-laws* apply to all Chapters; they are established by the Board of Trustees and may not be changed except by the Board.[33]

Upon first inspection, the *Manual* and the *By-laws* seem very similar to those of any organization. They include such details as the name of the organization, its purpose, its qualifications for membership, its major activities, its financial procedures, and the like. But if an examination is made of those provisions of the rules which relate to the major activities of the local Chapter—granting financial aid to polio patients and raising funds through the annual March of Dimes—a significant fact emerges: practically none of the rules applies to these activities. This is particularly surprising with respect to the patient care program, since as any one who has had first-hand familiarity with assistance programs of any kind knows all too well, rules concerning such details as eligibility requirements are often worded in such a way that only an expert at finding "loop-holes" can make the program truly effective. But the *Manual* has nothing to say concerning eligibility for financial aid, and stipulates only one prohibition: grants or expenditures in the aggregate amount of $2,000 or more cannot be made in one year for the benefit of any one person or institution without the written consent of National Headquarters. There are of course a number of absolute prohibitions upon expenses. A Chapter cannot, for example, purchase or erect hospitals or clinics, support research, or contribute to the educational expenses of polio patients. But the types of rules which lead to "over-interpretation" in any organization are seldom those which establish absolute prohibitions, but rather those which apply to judgments made in individual cases. Since the rules which govern the patient care program are not of this character, there is little opportunity for Volunteers to subvert the aims of the program by focusing undue attention upon legalisms.*

Very much the same situation holds with respect to the conduct of the March of Dimes. The broad outlines of the campaign are stipulated in the *Manual:* it is to be held in January, and it must be supported by each Chapter. But there is only one prohibition: no Chapter can engage in any fund-raising activity, either alone or in conjunction with another organization, other than the March of Dimes. Here again, it is difficult for Volunteers to displace the goals of the campaign by paying too strict attention to legalities.

### THE EXECUTION OF ORGANIZATIONAL PROCEDURES

An examination of the Foundation's formal structure reveals a number of implicit safeguards against the displacement of goals through undue emphasis upon procedures designed to achieve them. Perhaps of greatest importance is the division of responsibilities between National Headquarters and local Chapters. As described earlier, Chapters are responsible for granting financial assistance to polio victims in their area of responsibility, or informing the public about polio and the steps being taken to combat it, and for assisting to raise funds during the annual March of Dimes. Similarly, the responsibilities and activities of National Headquarters are described to Chapter Volunteers in specific terms:

* The functioning of the patient care program is discussed more fully in Chapter IV. The existence of only a few rules governing the patient care program does not mean that Chapters are not provided with suggestions concerning how it may most effectively be carried out; in fact, an entire manual is devoted to this subject.[34]

1. It is currently engaged in support of research projects of great variety, nationally planned and coordinated. . . .

2. It investigates new methods of treatment offering promise, and facilitates their use when advisable.

3. It undertakes the training of physicians, nurses, physical therapists, health educators, medical social workers, medical record librarians and other professional workers. . . .

4. It aids schools, colleges and universities to expand their technical educational programs.

5. It engages in a widespread information program to the public, designed to present the facts about infantile paralysis, insure proper care and aid in dissipating panic.

6. It disseminates information to physicians, health departments, welfare agencies, to aid them in programs in the care and rehabilitation of infantile paralysis patients.[35]

The most crucial aspect of this division of labor is that the sponsorship of scientific research—clearly the most directly goal-related activity of the Foundation—is confined to National Headquarters, while Chapters have major responsibility for patient care and fundraising. This centralization of the function of sponsoring research serves of course the manifest function of making it possible to coordinate the research activities of hundreds of scientists more effectively. But the prohibition of Chapter sponsorship of research also serves an important unintended or latent function: it precludes the possibility that Chapters might neglect the research program in favor of the more immediately rewarding patient care program. Stated differently, it ensures that the ultimate goal (elimination of polio) will not be displaced by a proximate goal (caring for polio patients).

It is very significant in this connection that those national voluntary health associations which have corporate-type formal structures generally devote a much larger percentage of their budgets to research than do those with federation-type structures, expenditures which are for the most part made possible by the fact that the national headquarters of these organizations receive a larger share of the annual fund-raising proceeds.[36] The local units of voluntary health associations are generally reluctant, even when they are empowered to do so, to allocate funds for research, since other types of expenditures provide a more immediate return in terms of public response and personal satisfactions.

Since patient care is a proximate goal, and since the division of responsibility in the Foundation between National Headquarters and local Chapters ensures that patient care activities will not come to stand in the way of progress toward the ultimate goal, Volunteer attention to the needs of polio patients serves only the worthwhile function of making the program more effective; it does not, in short, serve as a possible source of goal displacement. Fund-raising, on the other hand, could easily become an end in itself, a development which would eventually react unfavorably upon the success of the fund-raising program. This possibility is clearly recognized by the Foundation; hence the oft-repeated admonition to Volunteers: "The National Foundation raises money to exist; it does not exist to raise money." But fund-raising is an activity which has such immediate and tangible rewards that some mechanism more effective than a verbal admonition is patently necessary to prevent local Chapters from focusing undue attention upon their fund-raising responsibilities. This mechanism is provided by the device of making fund-raising a Chapter *activity,* but one which is under the actual *direction* of National Headquarters.*

Other features of the formal structure also serve to prevent a disproportionate emphasis upon procedures. *Sanctification* and *ceremonialism* are minimized by the fact that local Chapters are organized in such a way that Volunteers have few opportunities to devote attention to organization-related activities, at the expense of those which are goal-related. The headquarters for the Chapter is generally the business office or home of the Chairman; even in the case of large Chapters, the headquarters is simply a rented or donated small office. There is, in other words, no meeting place for the Chapter which can be invested with ceremonial sentiments. There are no initiation rites or investiture ceremonies and no uniforms or badges. With the exception of one or two meetings each year, the business of most Chapters is conducted over the phone and at small committee meetings over the lunch table or in the living room of one of the committee members. Similarly, the rigidities of *traditionalism* and *routinization* are largely avoided because the Foundation is a young organization, because the patient care and fund-raising programs are largely seasonal in nature, and, in the case of fund-raising, because the March of Dimes organization is reconstituted each year. There is, moreover, a strong tradition of informality which pervades all levels of the Foundation. As is the case with virtually every major feature of the Foundation, this tradition has its roots in the Georgia Warm Springs Foundation, which has since its inception prided itself upon its friendly and almost "family" atmosphere. This in turn had its origins in the personality of President

* See pp. 27–28.

Roosevelt, who took pride in being the self-styled "Vice President in Charge of Picnics" at Georgia Warm Springs.[37]

## RELATIONSHIPS WITH OTHER PARTICIPANTS

It was noted above that there are three quite different situations in which the relationships among participants may lead to the displacement of goals: the development of group norms which are incompatible with the organization's goal, the development of a sense of common destiny among participants, and the informal co-optation into the policy-making apparatus of outside groups which exert an adverse influence over the achievement of the original goals.

Consider first the emergence of group norms concerning how many polio patients should be helped, and how much assistance should be given. Every person residing in a Chapter's area of responsibility who contracts polio, and for whom the full payment of medical and hospital bills would constitute a major hardship, is eligible for aid. Since Chapter funds are limited, there is a natural desire of Volunteers to give aid only when it is actually needed. On the other hand, Chapter funds are intended precisely for this purpose, so there is nothing to be gained by withholding aid when it is needed. Accordingly, the scope of the patient care program within any one Chapter is governed in part by the incidence of polio and in part by the amount of funds available; since both polio incidence and March of Dimes success varies from year to year, the likelihood that a norm will emerge concerning how extensive the program should be is very slight.

The fund-raising program presents a somewhat different situation, since the possibility exists that a group norm might develop concerning how much money should be raised. Such a norm would violate Foundation policy, which is not to set quotas but to raise as much money as possible, since the needs of patients and the requirements of the research program have usually been in excess of the funds available.

Two mechanisms seem to prevent the emergence of such a norm. First, since the local Chapter receives for its own use only 50 per cent of all the funds it raises, which is often insufficient for local needs, and since the expenditure of these funds for patients is a source of satisfaction to individual Volunteers, the development of a quota would be against the better interests of the Chapter members. Second, as already noted, the March of Dimes is technically directed by National Headquarters, not by the local Chapters, and the national office technically appoints the local Campaign Director, who in many cases is not a member of the Chapter. This provision of the formal structure, which means that the Chapter supports but does not direct the March of Dimes, serves to minimize the possibility that Chapter members might be able—even if they so desired—to exert an influence over the amount of funds raised.

The major structural feature of the Foundation which mitigates against adherence to career interests is of course the over-whelmingly volunteer character of its personnel. Volunteers for the most part belong to many organizations, and their participation in Foundation activity is only part-time; accordingly, it is easier for them to maintain a goal orientation than it is for full-time employees of an organization whose career interests are inextricably bound up with the future of the organization itself.

Finally, the Foundation's structure precludes the possibility that outside groups will come to exert an untoward influence over its activities. An explicit feature of Foundation policy, it should be noted, is for Chapters to work in close cooperation with other community organizations—both official and private agencies concerned with health and welfare problems and voluntary associations which carry on a more general program. The purpose of this cooperation is three-fold. It avoids duplication of effort with respect to patient aid, it increases community recognition of the Chapter, and it enlists support for the March of Dimes. However, Chapters are not permitted to be sponsored by any other agency, nor are they permitted to delegate responsibility for the conduct of the entire fund-raising campaign. Rather, community organizations are informally asked to take over one specific phase of the campaign. The Parent-Teachers Association, for example, is often given major responsibility for the Mothers' March on Polio, and the Lions Club may take charge of Street Solicitation. Because responsibility is delegated piece-meal, as it were, rather than *en bloc,* the chances are slight that any cooperating organization could exert any influence over the policy of the March of Dimes.

### RELATIONSHIPS WITH THE PUBLIC

The provisions of the Foundation's formal structure which mitigate against relationships with the public, leading to a displacement of goals, may be stated very briefly. First, the character of local Chapter activities is such that Volunteers are never placed in a position of authority over members of the public. The patient care program involves a situation of helpfulness, not authority; the information program brings the Volunteer to the public as an expert on the problems of polio; and the fund-raising program puts him in the position of petitioner. In none of these situations is there any discrepancy between the Volunteer's role in the organization and his role with respect to the general public.

The patient care program involves making decisions with regard to individual cases, which is precisely the situation in which the adverse effects of both impersonalization and particularism are likely to take place. Two aspects of this situation, however, serve to reduce the possibility that these adverse effects will take place. First, since there are no rigid criteria on which the merits of individual cases are supposed to be judged, and since the number of cases concerning which decisions are to be made is small, it is possible for Volunteers to treat each case "on its own merits." Second, particularism is minimized by the fact that the relationship with patients is mediated through the medical profession. Since physicians are explicitly trained to strike a balance between impersonalization and particularism in their relationships with patients—an attitude of "detached concern" is considered the ideal*— Volunteers generally find it possible to adjust their own attitudes in this area to those of the medical profession, and thus avoid interfering with the over-all program.

* The Bureau of Applied Social Research of Columbia University is currently undertaking a large-scale evaluation of medical school training. One of the problems being examined concerns the mechanisms through which the students learn to adopt an attitude of "detached concern" towards patients.

## chapter III

# RECRUITING
# VOLUNTEERS

## *Introduction*

THE ORGANIZATIONAL problems discussed in the two previous chapters
—maintaining membership interest and preserving organizational
goals—were said to stem from the process of delegating authority and
functions. It was also demonstrated that, in the case of the Foundation,
these problems are met primarily by the incorporation of a number of
control mechanisms into the organization's formal structure. In this
chapter, attention is given to the problem of recruiting new members—
a problem which is also endemic to all voluntary associations but which
stems not from the process of delegation but rather from the inherent
nature of organizations themselves. Since organizations are not *primary*
associations like nations, churches, and families, which obtain many if
not most of their numbers through natural reproduction, but rather
*secondary* associations, they are dependent for their survival upon the
continual incorporation of new individuals into their membership.

Practitioners in the fields of social work and community organization are of course generally aware of the fact that voluntary associations must actively recruit new members, as are the leaders and staff
members of most organizations.[1] But writers who have approached the
topic of voluntary associations with an interpretative or theoretical
orientation seem generally to have assumed that the members of voluntary associations join on their own initiative, since these associations
are usually defined as "interest groups" which exist to further the interests of their membership.

An examination of the wide range of voluntary associations in
America, however, reveals that the term "interest group" is much too
narrow a definition. Consider, for example, the classification of associations developed by Sherwood Fox on the basis of his analysis of some
5,000 voluntary associations. By noting the functions which each

association performed, Fox makes a distinction between *majoral, minoral,* and *medial* organizations. *Majoral associations* are those associations which serve the interests of the major institutions of society. Business, professional, scientific, educational, labor, and agricultural associations belong to this category. *Minoral associations,* on the other hand, are those which serve the interests of significant minorities in the population. Women's clubs, fraternal groups, hobby clubs, and various associations formed to protect the rights of different ethnic minorities in the population are all examples. Finally, *medial associations* mediate between major segments of the population. Social welfare organizations, which mediate between the community and the underprivileged population; veterans' groups, which mediate between war veterans and the Government; and voluntary health associations, which mediate both between research scientists and the public, and between individuals suffering from a disease or disorder and the medical profession, are examples of medial associations.[2]

These three broad types of associations differ markedly in the way their members are characteristically recruited. Membership in majoral associations is for the most part merely an adjunct to the peformance of an occupation. For this reason, active recruitment is either unnecessary or is limited to making the existence of certain facilities known to the occupational group. The recruitment of doctors into the American Medical Association, scientists into a professional society, farmers into a grange or marketing cooperative, and skilled workers into a trade union, for example, is generally of this character. Most eligible people join majoral associations either because they are compelled to or because it is a matter of self-interest, of establishing and maintaining good relationships with their occupational colleagues.

Membership in minoral associations, on the other hand, is more likely to be a matter of individual initiative. The purest case is perhaps that of the hobby group, whose members many only be in touch with each other through an organization publication, and who join and drop out as the intensity of their personal interest dictates. Most minoral associations conform closely to the image of a voluntary association as one in which membership is based upon "true" volunteering. Both majoral and minoral associations, accordingly, are examples of what are generally called "interest groups."[3]

Finally, membership in medial associations, particularly voluntary health associations, comes about for the most part as a result of active recruitment on the part of the organization. The fundamental reason for this situation, as far as voluntary health associations are concerned, is that our society has developed other institutionalized methods of dealing with health problems. The family and the schools, for example, are charged with teaching children the basic tenets of hygiene; national and local governments are responsible for the maintenance of public health standards and practices; and the medical and nursing professions are responsible for restoring to health individuals who become ill. From the point of view of the individual, this allocation of responsibility means that, although concerned in a general way with the health of his community, he has no compelling obligation to do more than take the common-sense steps necessary to protect the health of himself, his family, and his community. From the point of view of a voluntary health association, this allocation of responsibility means that there is no specific mechanism which it can utilize in order to obtain new recruits. Unlike a church, for example, a voluntary health association cannot depend on natural reproduction or religious conversion as a source of new members; unlike a military organization, it has no such coercive mechanism as conscription legislation; unlike a government bureaucracy, a business firm or a professional or trade association, it cannot depend upon the occupational structure for recruits; unlike fraternal or social organizations, it does not have recreational facilities to offer as an inducement; and unlike automobile clubs or veterans' groups—to cite only a few examples of other types of voluntary associations—it cannot obtain new members from any clearly-defined segment of the population. As a result, a voluntary health association has two possible courses of action. It can either make a general, impersonal appeal for volunteers, or it can make use of relationships *which were established for other purposes*. Most voluntary health associations adopt both courses of action; as will presently be demonstrated, the Foundation relies strongly upon the latter.

Information concerning the procedures utilized by the Foundation to recruit Volunteers could conceivably be obtained in three different ways. The recruiting procedures recommended in various manuals published by the Foundation for the guidance of Chapters might be examined; Volunteers could be asked to report how they normally went about the task of recruiting other Volunteers; and Volunteers could be asked to tell how they themselves were recruited.

The first of these techniques proved to be of little value in this research, since the manuals do not go into any detail concerning this topic, and in any case report only those procedures which are recommended, not those which are actually used. The second technique also proved to have limited utility, since most Volunteers who themselves had recruited others could not estimate which one procedure they had used most frequently. Accordingly, the data presented in this chapter were obtained by asking Volunteers how they themselves had become members of the Foundation. The section which follows immediately is devoted to an analysis of the process of joining the Foundation, viewed as an instance of individual decision-making. This is followed by a presentation of case histories which describe in Volunteers' own words how this decision was reached. The final section of the chapter examines the problem of recruiting Volunteers not from the point of view of the individuals concerned but as an example of how informal organization within an organization makes it possible for the formal mechanisms to operate.

## Joining the Foundation

### MOTIVES FOR JOINING HEALTH AND WELFARE ASSOCIATIONS

"Voluntary social work," according to Barber, "has its sources in certain of the fundamental values of American society; these values do not exist in all societies and so cannot be taken for granted."[4] Without question, the value which is cited most often as being responsible for the participation of Americans in health and welfare organizations is "humanitarianism." The Foundation, for example, tells its State Representatives that "the impelling reason why most people become National Foundation Chapter members is their realization of the need for medical assistance by those members of their community who have been or may be stricken with infantile paralysis."[5] Similarly, in publications distributed to the public, the American Cancer Society describes itself as "an expression of the spirit of democracy, and of the belief that each individual has a responsibility to himself, his neighbor, his community, and his country";[6] the American Heart Association states that it is a voluntary association "because its members are private citizens in many walks of life who have dedicated themselves to the fight against heart disease";[7] and the Red Cross calls itself "an expression of our concern for one another in time of need."[8]

The United Funds and Community Councils of America (formerly the Community Chests and Councils of America), which serves as a clearing-house for many voluntary associations, also believes humanitarianism is a major determinant of participation in health and welfare organizations. "In giving services, generously and without pay," we are told, "a volunteer fulfills one of the first obligations of good citizenship, which is to care what happens to people in his own community."[9] Humanitarianism is also described as the value which instigated the entire social welfare movement:

The pioneers in social welfare were volunteers. Before the caseworkers, before the group workers, before the health specialists, there were laymen who saw unmet human needs in their own communities and moved to meet them. They were the crusaders, the spurs to civic conscience; they were guided by a warm and sincere desire to right human wrongs.[10]

And voluntary participation today is described as an activity which is based upon a desire to help others: "It has been estimated that more than twenty-five million Americans *give* of their time, effort and skills, without pay, to help make their communities better places to live in."[11]

The assumption underlying all the statements cited above is that most volunteers participate "because" they share certain humanitarian values. They realize "needs"; feel "responsibility"; have "dedicated themselves"; express "concern"; care "what happens to people in the community"; are guided by "a warm and sincere desire to right human wrongs"; and give "their time, effort, and skills . . . to help make their communities better places to live in." What is the scientific status of assertions such as these? This is a difficult question to answer, since the evidence upon which the assertions are based is never specified. In general, however, it can be assumed that most of these assertions were made because of the compatibility of the fact of participation in this type of association with the dominant value of humanitarianism. In this sense, they correspond to what Selznick has termed "unanalyzed abstractions."[12] Explanations of this kind, however, are risky ventures at best, for two reasons. First, in the case of a complex society composed of people of diverse cultural, religious, and ethnic origins, there is generally very little agreement concerning which are the dominant values. Robin Williams, for example, prefaces his ambitious attempt to outline the major value-orientations in American society with the qualifying remark that "America does not have a completely consistent and integrated value-structure." Nevertheless, he was able to isolate, as "first approximations," fifteen value-orientations.[13] More recently, Cora Du Bois has attempted to describe "the dominant value profile of American culture," but found it necessary to restrict her analysis to the dominant values of middle-class Americans.[14]

A second problem inherent in any attempt to explain participation by reference to the dominant value of humanitarianism—and hence to the motives underlying participation—stems from the fact that motives can never be accepted as adequate explanations for the behavior of individuals; at the very least, it is necessary to consider external influences as well as motives. In the pages which follow, an attempt is made to describe the act of becoming a Foundation Volunteer by specifying the different types of influence which actually play an important role.

If motivations cannot be accepted as adequate explanations for joining the Foundation, what other information is needed? This general problem has been formulated by Arthur Kornhauser and Paul Lazarsfeld in these terms:

Any bit of action is determined on the one hand by the total make-up of the person at the moment, and on the other hand by the total situation in which he finds himself. . . . The action is a joint product of factors in the individual and factors in the situation. Explanations must always include both the objective and the subjective, and these are always in inseparable interrelationship.[15]

And again:

One proceeds in his analysis of any bit of action by analyzing those motives and mechanisms that appear significant, and also by studying the outside conditions which appear most clearly related to those inner dispositions. Explanations are found by working back and forth between individual dispositions and external influences. The behavior of the moment is always governed by both.[16]

If this formulation of the problem is accepted as a research directive, it is apparent that reasons other than motivations—referred to by Kornhauser and Lazarsfeld variously as "factors in the situation," "outside conditions," and "external influences"—must also be taken into consideration. The reasons to be considered in this analysis are discussed below; it is first necessary, however, to outline the broad purposes of the discussion which follows.

It is self-evident that the intrinsic nature of any phenomenon determines to a very large extent the research strategy employed in explaining it. But another set of conditions also determines research strategy: the purposes for which the explanation is to be used. Katz and Lazarsfeld, for example, in introducing their inquiry into the reasons why women make certain decisions—why they buy specific products, adopt new fashion styles, hold various opinions concerning public issues, and attend specific movies—describe these two determinants of research strategy in these terms:

The general question *why* doesn't really make sense. It has to be translated into a series of specific questions aimed at discovering whether a specific set of factors did or did not play an important role. What factors we will need to study will be determined partly by the purposes of the study and partly by the general nature of the area under investigation.[17]

Inquiries into the reasons for individual action are frequently undertaken because the investigator wants to know whether or not some specific factor "did or did not play an important role." An advertiser wants to know whether or not his advertising has caused people to buy his products; a criminologist wants to know whether or not crime dramas on television contribute to juvenile delinquency; a political sociologist wants to ascertain the role played by campaign "issues" in determining voting decisions, etc. The goals of the present inquiry, however, are somewhat different. First, the reasons why individuals join the Foundation are investigated in order to ascertain the procedures most frequently adopted by Foundation Volunteers in recruiting other Volunteers. Second, and of equal importance, it is necessary to learn the reasons why individuals join the Foundation in order to gain some insight into the impact which participation actually has upon individual Volunteers. That is, in keeping with the interest in organizational theory which guides this volume, it is necessary to establish a "base line" against which to measure changes in individual interests, attitudes, and motivations brought about by the experience of participation itself. Ideally, such a "base line" should be established by studying individuals *before* they became Volunteers. If a research design of this nature were feasible, the information obtained from Volunteers after they had participated for several years would provide an excellent measure of changes actually effected by participation. Since obtaining first-hand information about this period of the lives of Volunteers is impossible, the best alternative is to use for the purpose of establishing a "base line" the retrospective accounts given by Volunteers of the experiences which led to their joining the Foundation.

### THE NEED FOR A TYPOLOGY OF RECRUITS

It is obvious that no two Volunteers joined the Foundation under identical circumstances. Accordingly, one method of describing the phenomenon of joining would be to present 234 case histories. Such a presentation, however, would be more than tiresome reading; it would also make it impossible to compare the frequency and nature of different *types* of experiences. For this reason, the research strategy adopted in this chapter is the development of an empirically-derived *typology* of individuals recruited by the Foundation. With such a typology as a working tool, it will be possible to observe the differential impact of Foundation participation upon different types of recruits.

To anticipate, it will be demonstrated that four types of individuals are recruited into the Foundation. For purposes of both description and convenience these types are referred to as Polio Veterans, Humanitarians, Good Citizens, and Joiners. The specific experiences which characterize each type of recruit are noted in the discussion which follows. It is important to stress here, however, that this is a typology of recruits, *not* of Volunteers, since the information upon which the classification is based concerns only experiences and attitudes prior to joining the Foundation.*

### INITIAL TYPOLOGICAL DISTINCTION

In order to construct a typology of recruits it is first necessary to divide the Volunteers into sub-groups containing individuals whose actions are comparable. In the case of joining the Foundation, two possible bases for an initial division of individuals present themselves. First, since joining voluntary associations tends to become part of a person's pattern of life—either because he enjoys one organization and then seeks out others, or because he becomes known to other people through participation in one organization and thus comes to be invited to join other organizations—there is logically an important difference between people for whom the Foundation was the first voluntary association they had ever joined and those who were members of other organizations prior to joining the Foundation. Unfortunately for this purpose, practically all of the Volunteers studied were members of other organizations before they joined the Foundation, so this distinction could not be used.

A second distinction, however, proved to be very important: that

---

* This distinction is essential, since a major theme of the subsequent analysis is that the actual experience of membership in the Foundation often results in the acquisition by Volunteers of interests and attitudes which differ from those which they had at the time they joined. If this typology were not based solely upon pre-Foundation experiences, this subsequent analysis would obviously be tautological.

between Volunteers who had had direct contact in some way with polio before they joined the Foundation, and for whom this contact was judged to have influenced their decision to join the Foundation, and those who had not had this contact. The former group constitutes a minority of Volunteers. In spite of the fact that the local program of the Foundation is entirely concerned with some aspects of the organized fight against infantile paralysis, only 18 per cent of the Volunteers joined the organization as a result of personal experience with the disease. Of these a clear majority (88 per cent) had had polio themselves, or a member of their immediate family had had the disease. The remaining 12 per cent of this group had come into direct contact with polio through their experiences as public health officials, physical therapists, or in similar occupations.

For a majority (82 per cent) of Volunteers, therefore, it was not prior contact with polio which was the crucial experience they had before becoming Volunteers, but rather experience as a volunteer worker in other community organizations.

*Polio Veterans.* This differentiation between Volunteers who had had prior experience with polio and those who had not constitutes a fundamental "typological distinction." Volunteers who had had such experience are described here as Polio veterans, since their reasons for becoming Volunteers are directly related to their prior contact with polio. An analysis of the accounts of their experiences given by Polio Veterans reveals that having had polio, or having been intimately associated with its victims, gave them a unique perspective of the program of the Foundation. For some Polio Veterans, this personal experience produced a feeling of affinity with other victims; they knew "what it means," either physically or emotionally, to be struck by polio's frightening symptoms. The Campaign Director in Cattlefeed City, for example, related how his experience had led him into Foundation activity in these terms:

Ever since my little girl had it I was interested. And then the epidemic. In [a nearby community] they had three deaths in one week. I really seen the fear in them people. That's when I must have really got interested in it.

Another Volunteer, who organized a Polio Parents Committee after she joined the Desert City Chapter, explained that she had joined in the first place because of her personal experience. "The parents themselves needed help—psychological, not financial—it's like Alcoholics

Anonymous," she told the interviewer with considerable emotion. "If you have had it happen to yourself, you know what they're going through. . . . I know what we went through, and I thought if people could share their experiences it would help. We went through such hell that I thought what we learned should be generally useful."

For other Polio Veterans, the experience of having been afflicted by polio, and of having overcome its debilitating aftereffects, stimulated the urge to use themselves as living symbols of encouragement to recent victims. The Chapter Secretary in Upstate City, for example, felt impelled to join the Chapter because "I found people looked to me as one who'd had it, and was able to participate in a lot of activities. I found that people worse off would call me and compare their illness, and by talking to them I was able to give them encouragement. It's a long drawn-out deal, but it's not hopeless."

The assistance received from their local Chapter was the reason given by other Polio Veterans for joining the Foundation. They spoke of knowing "what the Foundation means to polio victims—a feeling of great relief that immediately frees you of worry," of "having seen many others who had been helped," of knowing about "the good work of the Foundation." A Soybean City Volunteer, who had contracted polio before the Foundation was established, and who had subsequently spent many months at Georgia Warm Springs undergoing treatment, learned from personal experience how much the Foundation has accomplished. "When I had polio," he reported, "the doctors didn't even know. They argued about my case. The National Foundation has done a lot to establish centers to train doctors." Personal experience was also decisive in the case of the Mothers' March Chairman in Power City, who recalled that "I never realized how wonderful it was or what they did until my boy got polio a summer ago. . . . I found out then about the Foundation and all the Volunteers."

There is evidence also that for some Volunteers the experience of having participated in the unique "polio culture" found in treatment centers exerted as much influence upon their joining the Foundation as did the traumatic impact of intimate contact with the disease itself. Georgia Warm Springs is of course the quintessence of this culture, and the comments of Volunteers which evoked memories of life at this treatment center are illustrative of the pervasive quality of its appeal. It is described as having a "special" atmosphere, almost a mystique, which is intangible and indescribable, and which can only be understood by initiates, who have learned that "there is something about the place" which makes one a convert.

The fact that fewer than one in every five Volunteers is a Polio Veteran highlights an important characteristic of the Foundation: unlike some special purpose associations, it is not composed primarily of people who have a direct, personal stake in the organization's program.

There is, of course, a clear historical reason for this characteristic of the Foundation's membership. It will be recalled that most Chapters were initially established as off-shoots of the local Committees for the Celebration of the President's Birthday.* Since the members of these Committees were in many cases people who were either Democratic Party leaders or job-holders, the proportion of Polio Veterans among them was not much greater than in the population as a whole. As the years passed, many of these original members dropped out; as the patient care program was broadened in scope, an increasing number of people received assistance from it, and thus incurred a sense of obligation to the Foundation. But these changes have not been of sufficient magnitude to alter the fundamental character of the Foundation's membership.†

*Prior experiences in community organizations.* Volunteers who are not Polio Veterans had had a wide variety of experiences in other community organizations prior to becoming Volunteers. Some merely "took this on," as they often phrased it, as part of a general life pattern of voluntary participation. "I just love all this," declared a Volunteer in Steamboat City, referring to his years of work not only for the Foundation but for every major voluntary association in his community. "I can't understand why people don't do more. I ran a one-man drug store for years, but found time to do this sort of thing." And a Gas City Volunteer provided this realistic appraisal: "I was ripe. If someone had asked me to do something definite for the Red Cross, I probably would have done that." The Treasurer of the Harbor City Chapter explained, "I'm always tied up in some outside activity. I had just wound up as Chairman of the fund-raising committee for the church. That made a nice bridge."

Sometimes this life pattern is regretted, as in the case of the Gas City Volunteer who remarked cynically, "Once you're out on the limb,

---

* See pp. 45–46.
† Although no comparative data are available, the phraseology employed in the publications of other voluntary health associations suggests that a much larger proportion of their volunteer membership is comprised of people who have had direct contact with the disease attacked by that association.[18]

they've got you." More generally, participation in community organizations is recognized as an inevitable aspect of community life. "You can't stop" is the gist of these comments. In more specific terms, "once you do a job for one you get called all the time. . . . At my community, a little residential town, you know everybody and everybody works on everything. There is a drive every month and the same people are doing the job." One Campaign Director, in referring to his activities in the Rotary Club, the Masons, the P.T.A., and his past participation in three other fund-raising campaigns, concluded that "it seems like there's always something."

Finally, for a small number of Volunteers (fourteen in all), the most crucial determinant of their participation in the Foundation was that of prior participation in local Democratic Party activities. These Volunteers are of course those who first joined in the mid-1930's as members of a local Committee for the Celebration of the President's Birthday. Postmasters are particularly likely to have been asked to serve on these Committees. "I was involved before we had an organization," reported a Volunteer in Lakeside County. "I was Chairman of the early drive when we raised the first money in the Ball—the first two years. . . . Weren't we appointed Chairmen by the President? We were automatically, as postmasters, I think."

### THE ROLE OF PERSONAL GOALS

The typological distinction between Volunteers who had and had not had personal experience with polio prior to joining the Foundation has made it possible to delineate one type of recruit, the Polio Veteran. Polio experiences, however, cannot be considered as adequate reasons for joining the Foundation, since a large majority of people who have had such experience do not become Volunteers. Furthermore, Volunteers who had not had personal experience with polio cannot be considered as constituting a distinctive type of recruit, since this is a residual category which includes all Volunteers other than Polio Veterans. It is thus necessary to extend the analysis by taking other categories of reasons into consideration.

The next category of reasons to be examined concerns the goals of Volunteers at the time they joined; that is, the future state of affairs which they envisioned at the time they joined. Table 2 presents—for Polio Veterans and Other Volunteers—the proportion who joined the Foundation primarily in order to achieve each of five major goals.

### Table 2—Personal Goals of Volunteers

| Goals | Polio Veterans | Other Volunteers | All Volunteers |
|---|---|---|---|
| **Self-oriented** | | | |
| Fulfill obligations to the community | 60% | 33% | 38% |
| Fulfill job obligations | 9 | 26 | 23 |
| Advance personal status | 5 | 26 | 22 |
| **Other-oriented** | | | |
| Help others | 12 | 8 | 9 |
| Eliminate polio | 14 | 7 | 8 |
| | 100% | 100% | 100% |
| N | (42) | (192) | (234) |

The distinction between "self-oriented" and "other-oriented" goals requires a word of explanation, since it is not immediately apparent that there is a meaningful distinction between the two types. On the surface, for example, a desire to "fulfill obligations to the community" seems as "other-oriented" as a desire to "help others" or "eliminate polio." The distinction between the two types of goals, however, stems from a consideration of the individuals Volunteers envisioned would be the immediate beneficiaries of their participation. In the case of those Volunteers who desired to fulfill community obligations, as will be demonstrated below, their primary concern was with fulfilling obligations which they themselves felt to be binding; in this sense, such goals are "self-oriented." Nevertheless, the distinction is in some ways arbitrary. Volunteers who desired to "help others," for example, may also have had as a primary motivation a desire to relieve themselves of an oppressive sense of obligation. After taking everything into consideration, however, it was decided that this dichotomy made a necessary distinction. The full meaning of these two types of goals will become clearer through the discussion which follows.

*Self-oriented goals.* The importance of the distinction between Polio Veterans and other Volunteers is apparent from the fact, reported in Table 2, that most Polio Veterans were motivated to become Volunteers because of a desire to fulfill a sense of obligation to the community —in contrast to only a third of other Volunteers. Since the community provides the funds which support both the Chapter's patient care program and the Foundation's research, education, and training programs, and since Polio Veterans were for the most part specific beneficiaries of these programs, they naturally felt a sense of obligation to the community in general, and to the Foundation in particular. In the words of one grateful parent in Market Town, "I can't pick up $5,000 and hand it back to the Foundation. The next best thing is to thank them by getting other contributions." Volunteering, for many Polio Veterans, thus represents a chance to discharge what can be an almost oppressive sense of obligation. "When you accept help you always feel that you'd like to repay," is a common expression of this feeling. "It won't help [my son] but it will help his children—my grandchildren," is the way one mother of a polio victim—the Defense Town Mothers' March Chairman—expressed this attitude. "You might say it's my little way of paying them back," she continued, "and I'd be a terrific ingrate if I didn't do it."

Volunteers who have not had personal contact with polio, on the other hand, often found the generic expression "civic duty" to be most expressive of their feelings of obligation to the community. "It was my civic duty to accept it and do my part," reported the Cattlefeed City Mothers' March Chairman, and the Corn City Chapter Secretary declared that "I felt that we should all do some civic work. I felt a certain civic responsibility that I hadn't been able to express before."

Sometimes a sense of community obligation is expressed in such prosaic gestures as that of the Volunteer in Pinetree County who reported that she was always her community's representative on every major committee, and that "during World War II, I kept the car filled with gas just for emergencies if anything needed to be done." And sometimes it is formulated as a necessary antidote to the atomizing, mechanistic tendencies of modern society. For example, a March of Dimes Chairman in Suburb County, who is the manager of a local supermarket, did not have to look far afield for an illustration of the major characteristic of American society which he hoped to alter by voluntary participation:

As fast and inconsiderate as the American public is now, 40 per cent of John Public is looking out just for John Public. We need more community spirit. The whole country is just like a big store, now, just like Safeway. That's a wonderful company, but it tends to be impersonal.

Volunteers who regarded joining the Foundation as the fulfillment of a job obligation are not necessarily less civic-minded than those who saw it as a civic duty, but the nature of their job happens to be such that a certain amount of voluntary participation is expected of them. The Chapter Chairman in Pulpwood City, for example, who is an insurance agent, reported that "a man in my business always is [involved]," and then reeled off the name of every fund-raising campaign in the community to which he felt duty-bound to contribute time and effort. School officials are particularly subject to these pressures. "When you are a high school principal," according to the Mountain County Chapter Chairman, "you just have to take on these things." A member of this Chapter's Executive Committee, also a high school principal, used similar language, perhaps because he had first joined at the invitation of the Chairman. "Every school man should do something of this sort," he reported. And in referring (significantly, in the present tense) to the days of the pre-Foundation President's Birthday Ball, a postmaster and the Chapter Treasurer in Mountain County noted that "there's no directive from the Post Office Department—it's just expected of you."

Prominent among Volunteers who saw in Foundation activity an opportunity for advancing their own status in the community are lawyers, especially young lawyers in small and medium-sized communities who find taking part in voluntary activity one socially-approved method of getting to be known by the public. Since lawyers cannot advertise, accepting a March of Dimes position is one way of laying the groundwork for future business. "Through this," one Defense Town lawyer declared, "people get to know me." And a successful attorney in Fabric Town provided a remarkably candid summary of this pattern of participation:

Professional and business men must look after their own interests, and it would be ridiculous not to recognize this. Insurance men, for example, are certainly interested in publicity, yet it would be unfair to say they are not also interested in the cause. It works both ways. . . . For example, I took it for advertisement purposes. Here in Fabric Town, they have used every new lawyer for drives. It's well known that we work every new lawyer to death in the town, because it is good business. . . . Whether the National Foundation admits it or not they will always need and find more young lawyers . . . who have not made their name.

Lawyers are of course not the only people who have found that voluntary participation may serve to increase their status. The Campaign Director in Suburb County, for example, confessed his political ambitions to the interviewer and noted that "there isn't a better enterprise that I could identify myself with." An aspiring member of the middle-class in Greenback City—the Secretary of the Chapter—confided that she had joined principally because "some of the nicest people in the community" were involved, although she hastened to add, "not that I wanted my picture in the paper or anything like that." And the Chapter Chairman in Gas City recalled that he had been asked to join by a member of the Executive Committee whose husband was a contractor. "I've sold him a lot of supplies," he reported, "and, you know, it's kinda hard to say 'no' to a customer."

The fact that many Volunteers were motivated to advance their own status in the community when they joined the Foundation lends support to the frequent assertion that voluntary associations serve the latent function in our society of providing an avenue through which people can achieve a higher status through their own efforts. The Kluckhohns, for example, assert that:

Associations help place individuals in society because most statuses in American society are achieved statuses, not dependent upon family line placement. Joining is thus an instrument of social mobility—hence entrance requirements and ceremonial initiations. But this is only part of the story.[19]

And Williams has pointed out that fraternal and civic associations in particular may constitute an avenue to success, "through the opportunities provided for personal acquaintance, knowledge of business opportunities and the like; and for the young professional or businessman membership may be a *sine qua non* for success in some local communities."[20]

*Other-oriented goals.* Among both Polio Veterans and Other Volunteers, individuals with "other-oriented" goals are nearly evenly divided between those with desires to "help others" and those with a desire to "do something" about the threat of polio. Polio Veterans, however, are more likely than Other Volunteers to have had either of these goals (Table 2).

Humanitarian impulses appear in a number of different guises. There is first of all the diffuse altruism of Volunteers such as the Campaign Director in Fabric Town, who said that he joined because "I like and wanted to help my fellow men," or the March of Dimes Volunteer in University City who joined "because I realized there was such a need for it." Second, there is the protective fervor of those Volunteers whose principal motivation was love of children. "I tell you, I'm crazy about children—I've never struck a child in my life," reported the Mothers' March Chairman in Glass City in explanation of her participation, and the Chapter Chairman in College Town declared that "if we can do anything to help the youngsters, that is where the effort should be—I felt like it was my duty." Third, there is the urge to put moral precepts into practice. "You have to do something *outside* your-self," according to a Pinetree County Volunteer, because "if you can't branch out and do for others . . . you don't deserve to prosper yourself." Finally, there is the vague idealism of such explanations as that given by a College Town March of Dimes Volunteer, which makes up in in-tensity what it lacks in focus:

Oh, there's so much misery in the world that you can help! That was my reason mainly. Help the community, help those that cannot help themselves. I think that the National Foundation stands for everything that Democracy means . . . gives everyone an equal opportunity in the community.

Polio Veterans are of course more likely than Other Volunteers to have had as a goal a desire to "do something" about polio, but this goal is by no means confined to them. A wide variety of explanations were provided by Volunteers with this goal. For some, the speed with which polio attacks its victims provided a sufficient reason for joining the Foundation. In explaining why a concern with polio had drawn her into the Foundation, one Wheat County Volunteer noted that when you get polio you're "whole one minute and crippled the next." Others focused their comments on the possibility that polio can be prevented. "I wanted this thing licked, and I wanted to do what I could do to help it," explained the Chairman of the Mothers' March in Lumber City. "This thing had to be whipped and it seems it was possible," was the comment of a Volunteer in Upstate City. For other Volunteers, polio is a personal threat which evokes an almost superstitious fear. The Up-land County Mothers' March Chairman, for example, confessed that she "wouldn't have felt right" refusing to work for the March of Dimes because she was obsessed with the presentiment that "one of the family would have come down with it the next day." And the Chapter Chair-man in Greenback City explained that he had joined because he had three daughters and hoped that "if I do my bit maybe the good Lord will spare my little girls from such a crippling disease."

*A methodological note.* Ascertaining the personal goals of Volun-teers presented more difficulties than was the case in learning about the most significant prior experience they had had, or learning whether or not they had been asked to join, and if so, who had asked them. One reason for this is that actual experience as a Volunteer often leads to such radical changes in attitudes toward the activity that Volunteers were often vague during the interviews about what goals they initially had had in mind, or were unable to draw a clear distinction between their initial goals in *becoming* a Volunteer and their present goals as Volunteers.

Another difficulty inherent in this analysis stems from the fact that some Volunteers were *unwilling* to recall their initial goals. Thus, many found it easier to give an "expected" answer than an answer which a more objective appraisal of the situation might evoke. For this reason, Volunteers often found it easier to impute certain motives to others than to accuse themselves of such behavior, as was the case with the Eastern City March of Dimes Volunteer who noted that "certain people have the need for society. They have a drive to do things. With others, it's good public relations. They learn names. They meet people. Personal public relations, I'd call it."

Confronted with these difficulties, it was often necessary to go beyond a literal interpretation of the interview transcript itself, a procedure which was easier in this research than would otherwise be the case since the analysts who made the assessments had actually conducted the interviews themselves. In most cases, a Volunteer's own estimate of his goals was assumed to be correct. In other cases, it was necessary to make use of statements prior to or following the formal interview, or to take into account what one Volunteer said about another, or to deduce that when a Volunteer was imputing goals to others he was actually talking about himself.

For these reasons, these data on personal goals are subject to a certain margin of error, caused by misjudgments. It is felt, however, that the number of Volunteers whose goals were incorrectly judged is sufficiently small so as not to distort the over-all picture of joining presented in this chapter.

*Humanitarians.* As the preceding review of the statements of Volunteers indicates, the contrast between recruits with "other-oriented" goals and those with "self-oriented" goals is sufficiently sharp to suggest that personal goals provide another basis for delineating a distinctive type of recruit. Accordingly, Volunteers with "other-oriented" goals—unless they are Polio Veterans—are here called Humanitarians, since their fundamental concern was with the welfare of others.

The program, the goals and the publicity of the Foundation all contain the necessary ingredients for attracting people who are deeply motivated by a concern for their fellow men. The pathos of the crippled child, exhibited annually on a million posters, the promise of help to victims of a tragically disabling disease, and the hope of wiping out what is widely regarded by the American public as a major threat to the nation's children—these are the aspects of the Foundation which attracted most Humanitarians.

## INITIAL IMAGES OF THE FOUNDATION

By taking into consideration two types of reasons—prior experiences and personal goals—it has thus been possible to delineate two types of recruits, Polio Veterans and Humanitarians. But these two reasons cannot be said to account satisfactorily for participation as a Volunteer, since neither having had personal experience with polio nor having other-directed goals necessarily lead to membership in the Foundation. A person who for some reason is motivated to support the fight against polio can do so by affiliating with the Sister Kenny Foundation, for example, or by becoming a Red Cross Gray Lady and requesting assignment to a polio ward, or by contributing generously to the March of Dimes. Similarly, people interested in "helping others" can find many outlets for their interest other than Foundation activity. Accordingly, it is necessary to extend the analysis beyond a consideration of these two reasons, and examine the image of the Foundation held by Volunteers at the time they joined.

When asked specifically, "What did you know about the Foundation before you joined?" some Volunteers reported that they had known only about "Roosevelt, Warm Springs, and all that," or that "it was a worthwhile cause." Others were able to provide fairly complete descriptions of their image of the Foundation at that time. And still others replied candidly that they had known absolutely nothing except that someone had asked them to join, or "help out" as it was more frequently described. It was possible, however, to differentiate between Volunteers whose major image of the Foundation was that of "people" belonging to or supporting an organization and those who regarded it as an organization with certain specific "purposes." Table 3 shows the proportion of Polio Veterans, Humanitarians, and Other Volunteers who had different variations of these images at the time they joined.

Table 3 shows quite clearly that different types of recruits characteristically regarded the Foundation in different ways. A large majority of both Polio Veterans and Humanitarians saw it as an organization having specific purposes or goals, but among Other Volunteers, a smaller majority was primarily attracted to the "people" aspects of the Foundation. These distributions suggest that the category "Other Volunteers" can be meaningfully divided into two groups: Good Citizens, who saw the Foundation as an organization having "purposes," and Joiners, who regarded it primarily in terms of the "people" involved in the activity. This distinction will become clearer after a presentation of a sampling of the statements made about each of these images of the Foundation.

### Table 3—Initial Image of the Foundation

| Image | Polio Veterans | Humanitarians | Other Volunteers | All Volunteers |
|---|---|---|---|---|
| **Purposes** | | | | |
| An organization with goals | 80% | 61% | 35% | 46% |
| An organization with a program | 14 | 14 | 6 | 8 |
| **People** | | | | |
| Individual members | 4 | 14 | 41 | 31 |
| Sponsoring organizations | — | — | 16 | 13 |
| Public reputation | 2 | 11 | 2 | 2 |
| | 100% | 100% | 100% | 100% |
| N | (42) | (28) | (164) | (234) |

*An organization having "purposes."* More than half of all Volunteers initially viewed the Foundation primarily as an organization with a particular mission. For most Volunteers in this group, the fact that it was an organization which benefited the children of the community or which simply "did good" was sufficient. Others specifically saw it as an organization to further research into the causes and prevention of polio. A Pinetree County Volunteer, for example, had first heard about the then-experimental Salk vaccine at a pharmacists' convention. "Having kiddies of my own," he said, "if we can stamp it out, I am for doing all I can." A women Volunteer in College Town felt that "it was a very worthwhile thing to be part of an organization that could put funds in research and stop the disease if possible," and a grateful mother in Harbor City whose son had been stricken and helped by the Chapter noted that "only by raising money for research can this thing be eliminated."

The Foundation's patient care program was mentioned by other Volunteers as being a part of their initial image. The Chapter Chairman in Soybean City, for example, recalled that the assistance given by the Chapter to the son of a friend was what had initially attracted him. "In fact," he said, "I was surprised by the liberal terms they had for the patients." The Campaign Director in Payday Town, located in the heart of the Deep South, was impressed by the fact that "the National Foundation guarantees to anyone regardless of color, income, etc., the best treatment that can be provided. . . . That to me is the great thing." And the egalitarian philosophy underlying the patient care program was cited by most of the Negro Volunteers interviewed as being of much importance to their decision. "This is one organization which doesn't draw lines" is the way a Negro March of Dimes Chairman in Greenback City summed up this philosophy. For all those who initially viewed the Foundation as an organization having specific purposes, the important consideration was not "who" was carrying on the program but "what" the organization actually did or stood for.

*An organization of "people."* Nearly half of all Volunteers, however, were initally more interested in (or impressed by) the personnel or reputation of the Foundation than they were by its actual program. Most Volunteers in this group were attracted simply by the personality of the individual who asked them to join. A March of Dimes Chairman in Upstate City, for example, when asked why he had joined, recalled that it was because a prominent member of the community whom he admired had asked him. "It was Harry————," he reminisced. "I've known him, yes. I used to be one of his caddies when I was a kid." And a Chapter Volunteer in Desert City referred to "the wonderful people working on it, like Mrs. ———— (State Advisor on Women's Activities), Bob ———— (State Representative). Bill ———— (Chapter Chairman) was a great man. The epidemic the year before nearly killed Bill. He would inspire others to work for it. Bill came to me when they were going to put on the first Mothers' March. He asked me to put it on."

Other Volunteers were attracted by the fact that an organization to which they belonged was sponsoring one phase of the March of Dimes. "I'm Secretary of the Eagles," reported the Chapter Chairman in Market Town,"who have always sponsored the drive," and a Gas City Volunteer said that "our group [the Lions Club] is very interested in anything of this sort. We particularly sponsor any type of program for the unfortunates. So from that we were naturally interested in this." Similar comments were made by women Volunteers. "I became a Marching Mother in 1951. The Jaycee Wives organization asked me to march. I was a member and that was our project for the year," recalled one woman who is now a member of the Executive

Committee in Central City. A sorority member in Dirtroad County stated that "we all felt that it was a wonderful campaign and we all felt that we'd like our names associated with sponsoring this drive. This sorority is a national one, and most chapters have sponsored the polio drive."

The prestige and reputation of the Foundation was the primary component of the image held by other Volunteers. As a Valley City Volunteer pointed out, "it was a wonderful opportunity to serve on a board as important as the March of Dimes is. All of us want to be identified with something as fine as this." And the Chapter Chairman in Market Town who stated that he initially joined because he was Secretary of the Eagles also said he was impressed by the Foundation because "people will give time to it without glory or pay," and that this had convinced him "that there must be something back of the movement."

*Good Citizens and Joiners.* Since Good Citizens and Joiners together comprise 70 per cent of all Volunteers, it is important to stress further the distinction between them. It will be recalled that these two types of recruits are distinguished from Polio Veterans by the fact that they had not had personal contact with polio prior to joining the Foundation, and from Humanitarians by the fact that they had "self-oriented" rather than "other-oriented" goals in mind when they joined. They are distinguished from one another by their initial images of the Foundation.

Despite the fact that both types had "self-oriented" goals, the statements made by Good Citizens and Joiners about these goals reveal an important difference between them: as their name suggests, Good Citizens are more likely to have desired to fulfill a sense of obligation to the community, while Joiners are more likely to have wanted to fulfill job obligations or advance their personal status (53 per cent and 72 per cent, respectively).

Good Citizens and Joiners, accordingly, differ from one another not only because of differing initial images of the Foundation, but also because they characteristically had different goals. The Volunteers cited above, for example, who spoke of "civic duty" or of the voluntary participation expected of people in their occupations, are for the most part Good Citizens, while those who—like young lawyers—spoke of the need to become widely known in the community are Joiners. Good Citizens often spoke of their sense of identification with their community. "I grew up with this place," was the way one Gas City Volunteer expressed this identification; his thoughts were echoed by a Pinetree Volunteer who noted simply that "I've been a part of our community." Joiners, on the other hand, are more likely to have regarded the opportunity to become a Volunteer as a chance to further their own interests. The statements made by Joiners cited above need not be repeated here; perhaps the best method of summarizing their motivations is to note that, like Willis Wayde, the hero of John Marquand's novel about a latter-day George Babbitt, Joiners have learned that voluntary participation has many rewards:

Willis learned, in the years he and Sylvia were starting out in Orange, the importance of being identified with the place where you lived and of being a useful individual in it. One was bound to derive real personal satisfaction from being on church committees or collecting for the Republican campaign or helping with festivities at the country club, and eventually such activities paid off in a very practical way. Local bankers and businessmen whom you had never met began recognizing you as a good sound citizen who was willing to give time and energy to a cause, and this recognition in turn helped the standing of the company you represented.[21]

Since the Joiner is so often made the target of satire, it is well to remember that he is a product of a society in which primary group relationships have come to have increasingly less meaning for the individual. The decline of the extended family has placed limits upon the number of primary group relationships which are possible with one's kin, the secularization of society has limited the role of the church as a source of intimate relationships, and urbanization has resulted in a decline in relationships between members of the same community. Although a number of recent studies suggest that the traditional sociological portrait of modern man as a creature deprived of intimate relationships has been somewhat over-drawn,[22] Clyde Kluckhohn's vivid description of his plight certainly contains a great deal of truth:

Mass economic upheaval following upon unprecedented economic growth; lack of attention to the human problems of an industrial civilization; the impersonality of the social organization of cities; the melting pot, transitory geographic residence, social mobility, weakening of religious faith—all of these trends have contributed to make Americans feel unanchored, adrift upon a meaningless voyage.

"Why," Kluckhohn goes on to ask, "are Americans a nation of joiners?" In part, he says, joining is:

A defense mechanism against the excessive fluidity of our social structure. Weary of the tension of continual struggle for social place, people have tried to gain a degree of routinized and recognized fixity by allying themselves with others in voluntary associations.[23]

Kluckhohn is not alone in stating that Americans join voluntary associations in order to find some sort of substitute for primary group relationships. Robert Angell notes that the fact that voluntary associations are necessary at all "reveals the depth of the clefts in our social structure. . . . What fails to develop from the natural forces of a true community life we attempt to foster by rational organizations;"[24] Herbert Goldhamer states that a social setting in which the community no longer operates as an all-inclusive social group is favorable to the development of associations;[25] Sherwood Fox observes that "alienated from sources of intimate, stable group support, individuals find substitutes in the numerous secondary groupings, including voluntary associations;"[26] and Robin Williams says that voluntary associations fill the void left by the dissolution of older patterns of group interaction—family, neighborhood, work group, and church.[27]

## TYPES OF RECRUITS: A SUMMARY

The preceding discussion has considered three categories of reasons for joining the Foundation. Since each category has been dichotomized, it is *logically* possible to derive eight types of recruits from this analysis, as demonstrated in the following diagram:

|  | REASON A | | REASON A' | |
|  | Reason B | Reason B' | Reason B | Reason B' |
| Reason C | Type 1 | Type 2 | Type 3 | Type 4 |
| Reason C' | Type 5 | Type 6 | Type 7 | Type 8 |

Only four types of recruits have been derived from the analysis, however, for two reasons. First, as shown below in Table 4, none of the Volunteers studied belong to two of the eight types. Second, one type contains only seven Volunteers. By eliminating the two logically-possible but empirically-nonexistent types, and by combining two other types into one, a total of four types was delineated.* Table 4 summarizes the entire procedure followed in deriving these four types of recruits.

* The procedure of combining "cells" in a table such as Table 4 is technically known as "the reduction of property-space through the simplification of dimensions."[28]

### Table 4—Types of Recruits: A Summary

| PRIOR EXPERIENCES | PERSONAL EXPERIENCE WITH POLIO | | PARTICIPATION IN COMMUNITY ORGANIZATIONS | |
|---|---|---|---|---|
| Personal goals | "Other-oriented" | "Self-oriented" | "Other-oriented" | "Self-oriented" |
| Image of the Foundation: | | | | |
| "People" | 0 | 0 | 7 | 66 |
| "Purposes" | 11 | 31 | 21 | 98 |
| TYPE OF RECRUIT | Polio Veterans | Humanitarians | Good Citizens Joiners | |
| Number of recruits | 42 | 28 | 66 98 | |
| Per cent of all Volunteers | 18 | 12 | 28 42 | |

## TRIGGER EVENTS

Although the delineation of four types of recruits has shed considerable light on the problem of why Volunteers joined the Foundation, one more category of reasons must be considered: the specific events which led to their becoming members. These events have been identified in a number of ways in other studies of reasons for individual behavior. Peter Rossi, for example, in his study of why people move from one house to another, devotes attention to "precipitants," e.g., being evicted from the old house or having an increased income.[29] Kornhauser and Lazarsfeld, in discussing purchasing decisions, speak of "precipitating influences."[30] Philip Ennis, in his analysis of why people switched from drinking coffee to drinking tea, uses the term "precipitating factor."[31] In discussing reasons for changes in voting intentions, Hazel Gaudet notes the importance of various "occurrences" or "events."[32] In analyzing the reasons for traffic accidents, Stannard Baker uses the term "key event."[33] Finally, Katz and Lazarsfeld, in discussing the influences leading to decisions in marketing, fashions, movie attendance, and opinions on public affairs, discuss the role of "trigger events."[34] For present purposes, the term "trigger event" is used as being most descriptive of what took place in most instances of joining the Foundation.

The most frequent trigger event was the occasion of being asked to join by a friend: 52 per cent of all Volunteers joined the Foundation in response to an invitation extended by someone whom they knew personally. Another 20 per cent were asked to join by some other member of the community; 18 per cent were asked to join by an organizational or occupational colleague; and 10 per cent volunteered on their own initiative. Polio Veterans are more likely than other Volunteers to have volunteered on their own initiative; Humanitarians and Joiners are more likely to have been asked by an organizational or occupational colleague; and Good Citizens are more likely to have been approached by a community member whom they may not have known personally. These inter-type variations reflect of course characteristic differences in the types of experiences which preceded membership in the Foundation. Of more significance than these differences, however, is the fact that in the case of 90 per cent of the Volunteers some trigger event was a necessary component of their joining the Foundation. The specific nature of these trigger events is discussed in the concluding section of this chapter.*

### VOLUNTEERING

Although "volunteering" has been classified above as a trigger event, it is more accurately described as a residual category which includes all Volunteers who said that no one had asked them to join the Foundation, but who joined on their own initiative. Accordingly, it was necessary to inquire of these Volunteers what circumstances had led them to take this initiative; that is, what trigger event had taken place.

A total of twenty four of the Volunteers interviewed joined without receiving a specific invitation. In the case of ten of these twenty four "true" Volunteers it was the circumstance of having had polio in their family which triggered their decision—nine of these ten Volunteers had received financial aid from the Foundation, and sought to repay their local Chapter by participating as a Volunteer.

Five other Volunteers belonged to organizations which assumed responsibility for some phase of the March of Dimes; they heard about the project, became interested, and volunteered. A polio epidemic was the trigger event which tripped off the decision of three Volunteers—in every case they initially volunteered to serve as a Polio Emergency Volunteer in their local hospital. Finally, a number of chance events served to activate the predisposition of others. One man was told by his wife that the March of Dimes needed some help, so he telephoned the Chairman and offered his services. Another Volunteer, a young lawyer who had been stricken with polio during World War II, was spurred into the decision by the March of Dimes campaign itself; the campaign publicity reminded him of his sense of obligation, and he volunteered.

* See pp. 109–115.

One Volunteer became a Polio Emergency Volunteer when she substituted one day for her sister who could not visit the hospital. One
woman resigned from her job as the secretary of the State Representative, and then became a Volunteer; another was lunching with friends
and heard them discussing the need for assistance; and a wife "naturally helped out" when her husband was asked to be Campaign Director. In every case, then, some crucial event took place which activated
the decision.

It cannot of course be concluded from this discussion of trigger
events that individuals became Volunteers "because" they are asked,
or "because" some event took place which led them to volunteer their
services, since many invitations and other opportunities to join are
bypassed. It is impossible to document this assertion with the data
available, since all of the Volunteers interviewed in this research had
(by definition) *not* refused this invitation. However, comments such
as the following statement by a March of Dimes Chairman in Glass
City indicate that invitations—although they may be necessary conditions for membership—cannot be viewed as sufficient conditions:

(*Are you active in other community organizations?*) No, I don't *aim* to
volunteer. I say "no" as often as I can. Yes, the Red Cross as Chairman,
and also our Military Fund. I am Co-Chairman—I believe it was for the
USO. I turned the Cancer down. I don't think I've ever been asked for
Heart. I've been getting three requests in a row—Red Cross, Polio, and
Cancer.

Why did this Volunteer, as well as other Volunteers, not decline to
join the Foundation when the opportunity presented itself? In large
part, this question has been answered by the previous description of
the four types of recruits. But part of the question remains unanswered,
and must remain so, since many Volunteers are unclear in their own
minds as to the exact nature of the relationship between what Kornhauser and Lazarsfeld call "factors in the individual and factors in the
situation."[35] As a result of their own uncertainty as to their "real"
reasons for joining, many Volunteers relieved themselves of responsibility, and reported that they were "talked into it." The Campaign
Director in Lumber City confided that he had been "sucked into it,"
and a March of Dimes Chairman in Pinetree County—using a colloquial expression more common in his part of the country—claimed
that "they 'hornswoggled' me into it." But as the discussion thus far
in this chapter has demonstrated, statements such as these cannot be

accepted as completely satisfactory reasons for joining the Foundation.*

## Case Histories

The analytic approach to the process of joining the Foundation used thus far in this chapter has made it possible to identify and comprehend the various components of the decision to join, but it has in the very nature of the case made it difficult to demonstrate the relationship between "factors in the individual and factors in the situation." In order to make this relationship more vivid, sixteen brief case histories are presented below, illustrating in the words of Volunteers themselves the experiences of the four types of recruits and the circumstances surrounding each of the four major trigger events. It is of interest to note in these excerpts from the interviews how Volunteers themselves are often quite unaware, until questioned further by the interviewer, that both "inside" and "outside" factors played a role in their being recruited into the Foundation.

### POLIO VETERANS

*Asked by a friend.* Mrs. ——, a member of the Executive Committee in Defense Town, is the wife of an engineer at a large aircraft factory. She was present at the very first meeting of the Chapter. When asked who had asked her to join, she replied, "Who do you suppose? Mrs. —— (the Chapter Chairman). You can't escape her!" And when asked what was the most important reason why she joined, she replied in these terms: "Our son got polio . . . so I knew a great about the Foundation. . . . Of course, I probably would have joined the Chapter anyway because of Mrs. ——".

*Asked by a member of the community.* Mrs. ——, a Chapter Volunteer in Harbor City, is the wife of an accountant. When asked to tell the interviewer a little about herself, she immediately replied, "Obviously I'm a member of this because one of our sons got polio eight

---

* Statements of this character do call attention to the fact, however, that joining the Foundation is in some ways a "passive" act. In this respect, trigger events as reasons for joining have somewhat the same character as reasons for auto accidents; witness, for example, the tendency of many Volunteers to preface their accounts of how they became Volunteers with the phrase, "Well, it happened this way," as if they were about to explain how they had happened to hit a telephone pole.[36]

years ago." But when asked specifically how she had first become involved, she admitted that she had been asked to join. "My first contact was three years ago when I was asked to be City Chairman for the Mothers' March."

*Asked by a colleague.* The Campaign Director in Desert City, the regional agent for an insurance company, explained how he had joined:

*(Who first approached you?)* Mr. _____. *(Had you known him before?)* I had known him through business connections. Real estate, loan and finance matters are often referred to him at the bank. . . . *(What did you know about this work before you joined?)* Well, of course I became interested when my son got polio, November 12th. . . . *(Did the Foundation assist you?)* They did call and offer help. We didn't need it, but the fact that they made the offer was great.
*(What would you say is the most important reason why you joined?)* If they had been indifferent to us or had not shown any interest in my son's case, I would not have taken the job. When you have seen polio at first hand, you can't help but be more interested.

*Volunteered.* Mr. ———— owns a chain of hamburger stands in Power City, and is a member of the Chapter Executive Committee. When asked how he first became involved in Foundation activities he told this story:

It was a family incident. A brother of mine became afflicted with polio and, well, the Foundation went to bat for him. He didn't have any money, he was newly married, and just finished college. I made the contact for him with the Foundation. They were so nice that I thought I would volunteer and repay at least some of their efforts.

### HUMANITARIANS

*Asked by a friend.* Mrs. ———— is a member of the Executive Committee in Pinetree County; her husband is the president of a local bank. When asked the most important reason why she joined, she replied:

I always figured you have to do something outside yourself. It's the same as in Sunday School where I teach. If you can't branch out and do for others, you don't deserve to prosper yourself.

But when asked specifically how she became a member, Mrs. ———— recalled that an old friend—"We were working girls together, I worked in the bank and she worked for the Automobile Association"—had asked her to join the Chapter six years ago.

*Asked by a member of the community.* Mr. ————, the Campaign Co-Director in Oil City, is an assistant to the president of a local bank.

When asked to report the most important reason why he joined the Foundation, he replied: "It is important for people to do work for things they believe in. . . . I think that those who, as everyone should, want to wipe this thing out should get in and help." But when asked how many years he had worked on the March of Dimes, he told this story:

I have been doing this for three years. I was asked to do it originally by [the Chapter Chairman]. I had been connected with him on some other campaigns, principally the Community Chest.

*Asked by a colleague.* The Campaign Director in Steel City is both the manager of an insurance office and a county commissioner for welfare problems. He cited as the most important reason why he joined the Foundation "an interest in children and their welfare," but when asked who had first approached him he replied: "Sam did. The welfare work had some bearing on it. I get called often as welfare director on these cases and often I make a call on the family.

*Volunteered.* Mrs. ———, an elementary school teacher, has served as a Polio Emergency Volunteer in Steel City for the past ten years. "When we had our bad epidemic," she reported, "I worked all night. We were quarantined and I got claustrophobia. I spent eight hours a day with little kids." (*Who asked you to join?*) "I just saw it in the paper and went over to the meeting."

### GOOD CITIZENS

*Asked by a friend.* A Mothers' March Captain in Market Town, whose husband is a partner in an insurance agency, provided this account of her joining the Foundation:

(*Who first approached you?*) Mrs. ———. We had gone to school together. . . . We revived our friendship when I came down here. She asked me to come down to a board meeting. . . . I was on the spot and I was flattered that she thought I could do it. . . . She was a good salesman.

*Asked by a member of the community.* Mrs. ——— was described by the interviewer as "the Mary Margaret McBride of Gas City." She was interviewed in the radio studio after her morning broadcast, and asked how many years she had been a Volunteer:

I started my program in 1949. They called and asked for some publicity and of course I was very interested in doing something for it. . . . I have two children myself, so I was interested in the whole polio problem. So I told them anything at all, I'll do it.

Her interest continued, and she is now Publicity Chairman for the Gas City March of Dimes.

*Asked by a colleague.* The Chapter Chairman in Steel City, who runs a drug store, is one of the relatively few Volunteers who joined in the 1930's, before the Foundation itself was established. He was asked by the interviewer to tell a little about himself:

I imagine you would be interested to know that my real background in this is probably through politics. I was on the Democratic Central Committee here, in 1926. When polio started, they brought in the postmaster here, and he headed it at first. But I worked with him on the Birthday Ball, of course.

*Volunteered.* Mr. ——— owns a suburban drug store near Cattlefeed City, and is the March of Dimes Chairman for his community. He volunteered for this position, but under conditions which many American males will find familiar:

(*Who first approached you?*) Well, I'd probably give that credit to my wife. When they were having those drives in Cattlefeed City and no one here seemed to take hold she said, "Why don't you send out for their stuff and find out?" I called up . . . and they sent me some of the material.

### JOINERS

*Asked by a friend.* Mr. ——— is a reporter for one of Eastern City's newspapers, and serves as Publicity Chairman for the March of Dimes. He has a similar position in several other community organizations, and when asked to give the most important reason why he joined the Foundation replied: "Only two. A sense of duty and a personal friendship with the person who asked me."

*Asked by a member of the community.* The Secretary of the Eastern City Chapter runs a small publicity and advertising agency, and is also active in Republican politics both locally and at the state capital. He was asked how he first became involved in the Chapter:

The Chapter had had a grand fight. Then the State Representative and one holdover started looking for new people. I was one of the persons they came to. (*What did you know about the Foundation before you joined?*) Not too much. I knew, of course, its general program. I was primarily interested in what I could give the Chapter in the way of publicity. . . . A question of publicity seems important to me because I'm a publicity man myself. Also, the State Representative called on me. He was and is a very fine fellow.

*Asked by a colleague.* Mr. ———, a March of Dimes Volunteer in Payday Town, owns a furniture store. He was asked by the interviewer to tell a little about himself:

I came in on this seven years ago. I belong to the Lions Club—they were asked to sponsor the March of Dimes and they asked me to head it as Payday Town county Chairman. (*What did you know about the Foundation before you joined?*) Not too much except for its reputation.

*Volunteered.* The Campaign Director in University City is a pharmacist, and is one of the three Joiners who volunteered on their own initiative:

(*Who first approached you?*) I don't know if any single person asked me. I just volunteered my services as a Jaycee. (*What did you know about the Foundation before you joined?*) I would say practically nothing except what I'd seen on TV and heard on the radio. (*What would you say is the most important reason why you joined?*) Just because I wanted to be an active member of the Junior Chamber of Commerce. I have a more active feeling about polio now.

## Recruiting Volunteers

### THE UTILIZATION OF ROLE RELATIONSHIPS

It was noted in the Introduction to this chapter that a characteristic of all medial associations, and particularly of voluntary health associations, is that their members are not, for the most part, people who joined on their own initiative—they are recruited by the organization. In the case of the Foundation, only 10 per cent of the Volunteers studied joined without a specific invitation. It is accordingly of some interest to examine the ways in which Foundation Volunteers actually go about the business of recruiting new Volunteers.

Since relatively few people feel obligated to join the Foundation as a matter of course—in the same way, for example, that a doctor feels obligated to join his county medical society—Foundation Volunteers must make use of obligations which have been incurred in other ways. These other obligations are best described as "role relationships."

The concept "role relationship" is derived from a consideration of society as a system comprised of myriads of interpersonal relationships. A fundamental requirement of any social system is that people must "behave in given situational conditions in certain relatively specific ways, or at least within relatively specific limits."[37] Individual participants in the system are thus guided in many of their actions by considerations which result from their membership in a particular interpersonal relationship; that is, they feel "a sense of obligation" to behave in a certain way.[38] Because obligations of this kind apply only to behavior in certain situations, they differ from such obligations as those "to oneself" or "to God," in that avoiding the disapproval of others is the underlying reason for taking steps to fulfill them.*

From this point of view, a large proportion of social behavior can be decribed as the fulfillment of obligations which derive from various role relationships. In fact, it is generally difficult to persuade people to take any specific course of action, including joining a voluntary association, unless they view this action as a necessary component of the proper fulfillment of some role obligation. For this reason, among others goverments ask their citizens to buy bonds in war-time because of their obligation to their country or to "the boys overseas," and advertisers tell women that their obligation to their husbands requires that they keep their skins young and smooth.

No attempt can be made here to specify all of the role relationships in which Americans are involved. Rather, attention will be given to those relationships which this research has revealed are most frequently utilized by Foundation Chapter and March of Dimes Volunteers in order to obtain new recruits: *friendship, community membership,* and *organizational membership.*

It will be recalled from the discussion presented earlier in this chapter that each Volunteer interviewed was asked to recount the circumstances under which he or she became a Foundation Volunteer, and that 90 per cent of the Volunteers reported that someone had asked them to join. These invitations were described as "trigger events," since they serve to activate the predispositions of Volunteers. These same responses, however, may be used as indicators of the role relationship which was utilized by the recruiter. Accordingly, if the person who extended the invitation was a friend, it was assumed that the obligations which result from interpersonal or friendship relations were utilized; if this person was a Volunteer whom he or she didn't know, or a State Representative, or any one else who approached the new Volunteer because of his reputation for civic-mindedness or some related reason, it was assumed that obligations stemming from community relation-

---

* If role obligations come to be fully incorporated into the personality system, however, avoiding the disapproval of others becomes a secondary consideration, since in such cases role obligations are in effect "obligations to oneself."

ships were utilized; and if this person was a co-member of some other community organization, or a co-worker at his place of work, or a business or professional associate, it was assumed that organizational relationships were called upon. That is, the *role relationship* between the recruiter and the recruited was used in this analysis as an "indicator" of the *role obligation* utilized.

### INTERPERSONAL RELATIONSHIPS

The role relationship most frequently employed in recruiting is that of friendship: 58 per cent of all Volunteers who were recruited into the Foundation were asked by a friend. This is perfectly in accord with the conclusions reached in various studies of how people are influenced: what to buy, what to think about public issues, what entertainment to seek, whom to vote for—all have been shown to be decisions in which personal influence plays a very large part.[39]

Volunteers do not of course extend invitations to their friends indiscriminately; rather, they select people who have already demonstrated their competence and interest in community activities. Typically, this means that Volunteers select people with whom they have worked in other community volunteer activities. During the interviews, Volunteers repeatedly stressed the fact that taking part in one community activity leads to friendships which in turn lead to participation in other activities. March of Dimes Volunteers in particular are often recruited on an "exchange for services rendered" basis. That is, Volunteers frequently turn to people whom they have helped on other campaigns, and explicitly or otherwise use an obligation incurred in the past as the basis for expecting an acceptance at this time. "After all," confided the Chapter Chairman in Oil City, "some guy helps you out and then you can't turn him down. R——— now, he had helped me many times, so when he asked me to take this on, I didn't mind at all." Many Volunteers profess to regret this situation, complaining that "one thing leads to another," but there is no doubt that the utilization of obligations which originate in personal friendships is of crucial importance for maintaining a constant influx of new members into the Foundation.

### COMMUNITY RELATIONSHIPS

Community and organizational relationships were used with nearly equal frequency—in 22 and 20 per cent of all invitations, respectively.

In the case of invitations which invoke the obligations attendant upon community relationships, an appeal is made not to an individual's sense of duty toward his friends, or toward an organization, but rather toward the community at large. This type of approach is particularly effective among people who are self-consciously aware of their reputation as community leaders affiliated with all "good causes." The Campaign Director in South City, for example, explained his acceptance in these terms: "I think this is one way of fulfilling one's responsibility to the community."

Often obligation to the community is invoked by a Volunteer—or even a prestigeful non-Volunteer who is willing to help the Chapter out —by telephoning or calling upon a prospective recruit and asking if he will perform a community service by taking part in Chapter or March of Dimes activities. The Chairman of Women's Activities in Harbor City, for example, reported that as a newcomer to the city she was pressed into service by one of the community's social leaders. She couldn't refuse the invitation, she said, because "you'd be a cad if you didn't work in this town. I don't see how any woman has the time for bridge or relaxation—they don't leave you a minute."

A common method of making use of community membership obligations is to telephone or write to someone in the community who has had polio in the family recently, and who has received help from the Chapter, and ask if he would like to take part in the activities. A March of Dimes Chairman in College Town, for example, explained that "She got my name from the hospital and thought anyone who had gotten help would be able to help, a very good assumption. I was always surprised why no one had asked me before." And the Chapter Chairman in Payday Town reported his experiences as follows: "I was released from Warm Springs in July 1949. In the Fall of 1949 Mr. ——— asked me to help. . . . I said, 'Yes, of course.' I was Chairman of the March of Dimes for three years . . . then I became Chapter Chairman."

But the most frequent invitation of all, accounting for two out of every three invitations which invoked the obligations of community membership, came from the State Representative, part of whose job it is to ensure that every Chapter in his jurisdiction is making full use of the volunteer resources of its community. Sometimes State Representatives approach people directly. The Chapter Chairman in Old-town, for example, reported that the State Representative "went to the priest . . . and said he needed some active people to be on the Chapter. The priest referred him to me and I said I would like to help." More often, however, a Chapter or March of Dimes officer will learn of a potential Volunteer, and will ask the State Representative to extend the invitation, in the hope that his prestige as an official representative of the national organization will carry more weight.

## ORGANIZATIONAL RELATIONSHIPS

Invitations extended in the name of an organization, and which accordingly invoke the sense of obligation which people feel toward an organization, come about in a number of ways. Often a community organization is asked by the Chairman to assume responsibility for one phase of the March of Dimes, and individual members of the organization are subsequently asked by one of their co-members to carry out specific assignments. The American Legion Auxiliary, the Lions Club, the Junior Chamber of Commerce, and the P.T.A. are among the groups which most often adopt the March of Dimes as an organizational "project." Nearly half of all Volunteers whose relationship to an organization was utilized were approached in this way, but this proportion still does not fully reflect the importance of organizational activities as a mechanism for recruiting, since (as already related) many people who were approached by friends would not have made these friendships had they not participated in other organizational activities.

A third of the invitations which made use of the obligations of organizational membership were extended to business and professional associates, which reflects the fact that many business firms consider participation in community volunteer activities as an employee responsibility. In fact, during periods of intensive volunteer activity, such as the March of Dimes, some firms will ask an employee to serve as a full-time Volunteer, remaining, of course, on the payroll of the firm during this period.

Finally, many of the Volunteers who joined during the early years of the Foundation were asked by fellow Democrats to help out with the President's Birthday Ball. One-quarter of all Volunteers who were invited to participate by an appeal to their organizational loyalty (ten Volunteers in all) were asked by members of a local Democratic organization.

RECRUITING AS A PATTERN OF INFORMAL ORGANIZATION

It is very difficult for a voluntary health association to make explicit provisions in its various manuals for the recruitment of new members, since its local units have no legitimate claim over any specific individuals. Voluntary associations are generally defined as "interest groups," and the tacit assumption is generally made in the literature on interest groups that people having certain interests will seek out those groups most likely to serve them. As previously noted, however, voluntary health associations are faced with a particularly unstructured situation with respect to recruitment, since our society has developed institutionalized methods for dealing with health problems that do not necessarily include voluntary health associations. For these reasons— lack of guidance from the organization and the absence of institutionalized patterns—voluntary associations tend to develop informal patterns of recruitment.

The major informal pattern developed by Foundation Chapters and March of Dimes organizations—the utilization of role relationships which were established for other purposes—has constituted the major focus of this section. It has been shown that each of the three major role relationships utilized represents a pattern of informal organization. Interpersonal relationships, for example, often entail the pattern of reciprocity, in which the basic claim that the recruiter has over the recruit is the fact that he has helped him out in some similar activity in the past. When the obligations of community membership have been utilized, very often the basis for expecting an acceptance is the fact that the recruit has been helped by the Chapter in the past, and therefore feels some sense of unfulfilled obligation. And the obligations attendant upon organizational relationships have been put to maximum use by defining cooperation with Foundation activities as a responsibility of another community organization, and thereby enlisting the support of individuals whose primary obligation is to that organization. All of these patterns are best described as *informal* patterns, since no official provisions are made for them in the various manuals published by the Foundation.

It should not, however, be concluded from the foregoing that the utilization of role relationships is necessarily an approach to the problem of recruitment which is rationally planned by Chapter and March of Dimes leaders. On the contrary, Volunteers generally approach the problem of recruitment in an extremely pragmatic manner, and take advantage of any opportunity which presents itself. Although they are more or less conscious of the fact that role relationships are utilized, they certainly do not describe their behavior in these terms. It is only when information pertaining to a large number of specific instances of recruiting is gathered together and examined systematically that actual patterns emerge.

## chapter IV

# ASSISTING
# POLIO
# VICTIMS

## Introduction

ALTHOUGH RECRUITING Volunteers must certainly be considered part of the program of local Chapter and March of Dimes organizations, it is an activity whose very nature requires that it be carried out through a pattern of informal organization. Patient care activities, in contrast, are formally designated as the pimary responsibility of local Chapters, and an elaborate set of organizational procedures has been established to channel funds raised during the March of Dimes to polio victims in need of financial assistance. This chapter is devoted to a description and an analysis of this program.

The patient care program is of course the major activity of the Foundation, and is undoubtedly the activity which has the most far-reaching implications for American society. In terms of dollars alone, the program is impressive. Over the years, 68 per cent of all the funds raised during the March of Dimes have been spent to assist polio victims—233 million dollars in the period 1938–1955.[1] Even in 1955, when large sums were spent for gamma globulin and the Salk vaccine, 56 per cent of all March of Dimes proceeds was spent to pay doctors' and hospital bills.[2] Over and above the financial importance of the program, however, is the fact that it must be regarded as the major program of the Foundation simply because Volunteers view it as such. In fact, as will presently be demonstrated, many Volunteers regard it as the *raison d'etre* of the entire organization.

In this chapter, the patient care program is discussed from three points of view. The first section describes in some detail the climate of public opinion concerning polio within which the program is carried out—a climate which has a direct bearing both upon Volunteer interest in the program and public support of it through the March of Dimes. The second section describes the nature and scope of the program itself, and demonstrates how the Foundation's corporate-type structure makes an assistance program of this magnitude technically feasible. A third and final section presents some of the reasons underlying the central role played by the patient care program in maintaining volunteer interest in the organization which sponsors it.


## Public Concern Over the Threat of Polio

An important characteristic of the Foundation's over-all program is its inherently noncontroversial nature. Practically no one in our society objects to the Foundation's objective of eliminating epidemic polio, although some may quarrel with the specific measures adopted to attain this objective. But the Foundation's program is more than simply noncontroversial; it is also one which commands widespread public interest, since concern over the threat of polio is common among all segments of the American population.

In order to obtain a measure of public concern over the threat of various diseases, those members of the general public interviewed in the course of this research were asked a number of questions designed to ascertain different dimensions of concern over various diseases. Table 5 summarizes the opinions of the American public concerning the four diseases which were mentioned most frequently as cause for concern.

**Table 5—Concern over the Seriousness of Four Diseases**

| Dimensions of concern[a] | Polio | PER CENT WHO MENTIONED EACH DISEASE Cancer | Heart diseases | Tuberculosis | N |
|---|---|---|---|---|---|
| Serious | 44 | 71 | 56 | 20 | (2000) |
| Most serious | 16 | 48 | 25 | 3 | (2000) |
| Most widespread | 9 | 28 | 46 | 17 | (1324) |
| Most fear-inspiring | 12 | 54 | 13 | 4 | (2000) |

Table 5 brings out several points quite clearly. First, cancer is regarded as a serious disease by a large majority of the population—hardly surprising in view both of its actual incidence and the widespread publicity which it has received in recent years.[4] Second, heart diseases are regarded as serious by a smaller majority of the population, and, quite accurately, often cited as the most widespread of these four diseases. Third, nearly half of the public also judges polio to be a serious disease. Relatively few people, however, judged it to be the *most* serious disease, and only small percentages believe that polio affects more people than any other disease, or fear it more than any other. Heart diseases and cancer, respectively, received most mentions in response to these questions. When polio is compared with tuberculosis, however, its saliency among the American public becomes apparent. Although tuberculosis is judged, correctly, to affect more people than polio, polio is more frequently judged to be a serious disease, the *most* serious disease, and the most feared disease.*

## THE ROLE OF INFORMATION

What accounts for the fact that polio, which has a much lower incidence than these other three diseases, evokes such a relatively high level of public concern? One obvious answer is that polio receives a great deal of publicity in the mass media, and is accordingly discussed a great deal by Americans. For example, in all four of the medium-sized cities studied in this research, a majority (64 per cent) of the public reported having heard more about polio in the past year than about any other disease.[5] Furthermore, judgments of seriousness are related to the extent to which a disease has come to people's attention, since, in the case of each disease, the percentage of people who cited it as most serious is greater among those people who have heard most about it. For example, 30 per cent of those people who had heard most about polio cited polio as the most serious disease, in contrast to 18 per cent of those who had heard most about heart diseases and 15 per cent of those who had heard most about cancer.

## THE IMPACT OF FOUNDATION PUBLICITY

Can the relatively high level of public identification of polio as a serious disease be attributed to the fact that this research was con-

---

* Although they cannot be discussed in detail here, a number of other comparisons among diseases are of interest. People under forty years of age, for example, are more likely to select polio than heart diseases as most serious, while people over forty are more likely to select heart diseases. Similarly, upper socio-economic groups are more likely to select heart diseases, and lower socio-economic groups polio. Negroes are much more likely than whites to think tuberculosis is most serious, and much less likely to select heart diseases.

To mention a few more comparisons: Negroes are much more likely than whites to think tuberculosis affects more people than any other disease, although the incidence of tuberculosis among Negroes in the southern city in which this question was asked is actually quite low. Men are more likely than women to fear heart diseases more than polio, and vice versa; and one out of every five Negroes fears tuberculosis more than any other disease.

ducted during the month of February, immediately after the March of Dimes, at a time of the year when, with the exception of the annual summer increase in polio incidence, the public might be expected to be most aware of polio? The evidence from this study indicates that it cannot, for two reasons. First, cancer is judged to be more serious than polio, even among people who reported hearing more about polio in the past year. Yet the most recent Cancer Crusade, sponsored by the American Cancer Society, was held a full ten months prior to the research in these four cities. Furthermore, the Christmas Seal Sale of the National Tuberculosis Association had been conducted in these cities in November and December, and the American Heart Association's annual Heart Fund Appeal was in full swing in each of the cities at the time the research was being carried out. Yet neither tuberculosis nor heart diseases were mentioned as most serious as often as polio or cancer. Since these campaigns utilize different techniques comparisons among them must be made with caution. Nevertheless, campaign publicity appears not to be a major determinant of judgments of seriousness.

A second body of evidence is also persuasive on this point. The residents of these four cities were asked not only to name the disease which they had heard most about in the past year but also a number of questions designed to ascertain their level of familiarity with the kinds of information about Foundation activities used as publicity materials during the March of Dimes. It is thus possible to compare the extent to which polio is judged to be the most serious disease not only among those who have and who have not heard most about it in the past year, but also among those whose level of information concerning Foundation activities is high and low. Table 6 presents the results of this comparison.

Table 6 brings out three points quite clearly. First, it is evident that, regardless of socio-economic status, people who have heard most about polio are more likely than those who have not to regard it as the most serious disease. Furthermore, among those who have, as well as among those who have not, heard most about polio, people having a low socio-economic status are more likely than those having a higher status to regard polio as the most serious disease.

Second, when the level of knowledge of Foundation activities among people who *have* heard most about polio is examined, a rather striking difference is revealed. People who know a great deal about Foundation activities (i.e., who were effectively exposed to March of Dimes publicity, as well as to year-round publicity) are less likely than

### Table 6—Hearing About Polio, Knowledge of Foundation Activities, and Judgments Concerning the Seriousness of Polio

|                                               | PER CENT WHO THINK POLIO IS THE MOST SERIOUS DISEASE, BY SES* | | | |
|-----------------------------------------------|:---:|:---:|:---:|:---:|
| Knowledge of Foundation Activities[6]         | Heard Most About Polio in the Past Year | | Heard Most About Another Disease | |
|                                               |     | N   |     | N   |
|                                               | *High SES* | | | |
| High                                          | 14  | (132) | 5   | (61) |
| Low                                           | 28  | (32)  | 5   | (38) |
|                                               | *High Middle SES* | | | |
| High                                          | 24  | (120) | 15  | (66) |
| Low                                           | 38  | (72)  | 18  | (72) |
|                                               | *Low Middle SES* | | | |
| High                                          | 26  | (158) | 15  | (59) |
| Low                                           | 33  | (138) | 16  | (91) |
|                                               | *Low SES* | | | |
| High                                          | 57  | (35)  | 21  | (14) |
| Low                                           | 39  | (143) | 22  | (93) |

* See Appendix B for a description of the procedures followed in constructing the Socio-Economic Status (SES) Index.

those who know less about them to judge polio to be the most serious disease. March of Dimes and other Foundation-inspired publicity has seemingly influenced the judgments of these people, but in precisely the opposite direction from that sometimes alleged by critics of the Foundation's information program.[7] Rather than convincing these people that polio is the most serious disease confronting the nation today, it has had the opposite effect.

Third, the phenomenon discussed above is observed only among the three upper socio-economic groups; among the lowest group, the reverse is true. Although comparatively few low status people have both heard most about polio in the past year and know a great deal about Foundation activities, a majority of those who are in this category named polio as the most serious disease. The impact of knowledge of Foundation activities upon this group, in other words, was the opposite of its impact upon people of higher status. In their case, it served to convince them that polio is the most serious disease.

An explanation for this seemingly anomalous situation is not hard to find. The March of Dimes campaign, and Chapter publicity throughout the year, has implicitly a dual character. It certainly brings to the attention of the American people the fact that polio is an ever-present danger. But it also contains a message of hope. "Medical care is available to you if you should get polio" is one message which this publicity contains; another message, particularly in the 1954 and subsequent campaigns, is that "Research is winning the fight against polio."

Consequently, people who know a great deal about Foundation activities are more likely than others to have been informed of major steps which have been taken to combat polio, and have accordingly more of a basis to counteract the otherwise frightening impact of having heard a great deal about polio. Polio information, in effect, serves to mitigate against the influence of scare headlines or back-fence gossip.*

Why then were people from the lowest socio-economic group more likely to judge polio as most serious if they knew a great deal about Foundation activities? Simply because they missed the point. All of this group are economically depressed manual workers who have not graduated from high school, and the twin message of danger and hope contained in Foundation publicity was apparently not understood. If polio is not the most serious disease which this nation faces, these people seem to reason, why is so much attention given to the March of Dimes?

In the face of this evidence, it seems reasonable to conclude that information concerning Foundation activities serves to convince only a relatively small percentage of the population that polio is the most serious of all diseases. And those who *are* convinced are the uneducated and economically-depressed groups who are most likely to misinterpret the message of any information campaign.[8]

To recapitulate briefly: It has been demonstrated thus far in this section that a substantial percentage of the American public regards polio as a serious disease and cites it as the disease about which it has heard most in the past year. Furthermore, people who have heard most about polio are more likely than others to regard it as the most serious disease. However, it has also been demonstrated that this high level of public concern is not the result of exposure to publicity about polio during the March of Dimes, since people who were most effectively exposed to this publicity are less likely to regard polio as a serious disease. Accordingly, in order to understand some of the reasons underlying the high level of concern over polio it is necessary to examine the extent to which the defining characteristics of polio itself are determining factors.

* Among people who have heard most about a disease *other than* polio, knowledge of Foundation activities has very little effect upon their judgments of polio's seriousness. Since they had not been sensitized to polio by hearing a great deal about it, information concerning the Foundation could not have served to mitigate the impact of scare publicity. Accordingly, the small percentage of this group which named polio as the most serious disease was apparently influenced by considerations other than either hearing about it or being exposed to information about the Foundation.

### THE EFFECT OF POLIO'S UNIQUE CHARACTERISTICS

No attempt is made here to discuss polio from a medical point of view, although every effort has been made to ensure that the characteristics of polio which are described are not at variance with the prevailing state of medical knowledge. Rather, discussion is focused upon those characteristics of polio which this research has revealed have brought the disease most dramatically to the attention of the American people. Attention is given to the following characteristics of polio:

*1.* It is an epidemic disease.
*2.* It is a children's disease.
*3.* It is a crippling disease.
*4.* It is most prevalent in prosperous communities.

In the case of each of these characteristics, a summary of the evidence demonstrating both the characteristic itself and public awareness of it is presented prior to a discussion of the relevance of the characteristic to the observed level of public concern.*

*Polio is an epidemic disease.* Although cases of polio have occurred since the earliest recorded history—the first known picture of a polio victim is that carved on an Egyptian tablet some 3,000 years ago— only recently has it become an epidemic disease. The first epidemic of which there is any record took place early in the 19th Century, on the island of St. Helena.[9] But this epidemic seems to have been directly related to the extreme isolation of St. Helena's population; it was not until a century later, in fact, that polio became a truly epidemic disease.[10]

Technically, polio in America is both an endemic and an epidemic disease.[11] For present purposes, however, the term "epidemic" is used in the common-sense meaning of "nonconstant." In this sense, polio may be described as an epidemic disease because it generally strikes different communities in force each year, because it occurs more frequently in some years than it does in others, and because it occurs more frequently in the warm summer months than in other seasons. All three of these tendencies contribute to the high level of public concern.

An accurate record of the annual incidence of polio in the United States is available only for the years since 1914. But in the forty-one-year period 1915–1955 the year-to-year variation has been very marked. During fifteen of these years there were fewer than 5 cases

* It should be noted that the characteristics of polio discussed in this section apply to the situation which existed prior to the widespread use of the Salk vaccine.

of polio per 100,000 population; during thirteen years there were between 5 and 9.9 cases; during seven years there were between ten and 19.9 cases; and during six years there were 20 or more cases per 100,000 population. In many consecutive years, furthermore, the rate has varied more than 100 per cent.[12]

The periodicity of its incidence must also be counted among polio's epidemic characteristics. In the five-year period 1951–1955, for example, there were in the entire United States an average of fewer than 300 new cases of polio per week from January until the end of May. In all five of these years, the number of new cases started to rise sharply in early June, reaching an average peak of slightly more than 2,500 new cases in late August or early September. Then the number of new cases again declined sharply, until mid-December, when again an average of fewer than 300 new cases per week were reported.[13] In short, a large proportion of each year's cases occurred in the four warm summer months of June, July, August, and September. The reasons for this incidence pattern are not fully understood.[14]

Finally, polio's epidemic nature is shown by the year-to-year variation in the counties throughout the United States which have a high incidence. This is true both nationally and in the counties served by the thirty-seven Chapters studied intensively. In fourteen of the thirty-seven counties, for example, the number of new cases in one or more years was more than twice the mean for the four-year period preceding the research. In the same fourteen counties, the number of cases during one or more years was only half the four-year mean. In another nine counties, there were one or more years in which the number of new cases was less than half the four-year mean, and in one county there was one year in which the number of new cases was more than twice the four-year mean. In short, in only thirteen of these thirty-seven counties was the number of new cases—as measured by these criteria —relatively constant throughout the four-year period.

The epidemic nature of polio contributes to a high level of public concern in a number of ways. First, the very fact that it does have epidemic characteristics means both that it is contagious and that its incidence, both nationally and locally, is unpredictable. The feelings of uneasiness generated by any contagious disease, the uncertainty generated by unpredictability, and the generally increasing rate of reported incidence all contribute to the fact that polio is an extremely newsworthy disease, since newspapers and other media by their very nature devote special attention to unpredicted and dramatic events.

Since public concern has been shown to be related to the extent to which people have heard about polio, it is apparent that coverage of polio news in the mass media has contributed to this concern.

The seasonal pattern of polio incidence also contributes to public awareness, and hence to concern. Since a majority of each year's cases occur within the space of a few months, the total annual incidence has a much greater impact upon the public than would be true if new cases were evenly distributed throughout the year. Furthermore, like auto accidents over holiday weekends, summer outbreaks of polio have come to be standard news items which newspapers cover because of widespread reader interest.

Finally, the year-to-year variation in the communities throughout the country which have high incidence rates also serves to maintain public concern. In order to demonstrate this, it is necessary to provide a word of explanation concerning the nature of polio incidence as a determinant of the attitudes of individuals.

Since the polio incidence rate of a community is a variable which characterizes the total community, not the individuals living in it, any attempt to examine the impact of this rate upon the attitudes and behavior of individuals involves establishing correlations between an ecological variable and a number of individual variables. If a positive correlation is anticipated, it is assumed that individuals must in some way be "aware" of the incidence rate. They may acquire this "awareness" directly, through personal experience which brings them into contact with the objective situation brought about by a high polio incidence rate (for example, they may know many people whose children have had polio, or read a great deal about local polio incidence in the newspapers), or they may become "aware" indirectly, through exposure to a highly-publicized March of Dimes campaign—which in turn may be partially a result of knowledge of the polio incidence rate on the part of the March of Dimes leaders. In either event, people become aware of the polio incidence rate through some personal experience.

This assumption—that people are in some way "aware" of an ecological variable—characterizes much research which attempts to correlate ecological and individual variables; the limits to which it can be accepted in the special case of polio incidence, however, must be noted.

Consider for a moment another ecological variable: mean annual precipitation. If a person lives in a city such as Mobile, Alabama, which has a high annual precipitation (62.4 inches of rain a year), the chances are that he is directly aware of this characteristic of his environment. He says to visitors, for example, "Yes, we have a lot of rain here," and he buys a new umbrella soon after losing his old one. Similarly, a person living in Phoenix, Arizona, which has only 7.75 inches of rainfall per year, is almost certain to know that it seldom rains. In fact, the arid climate may very well have contributed to his decision to move to Phoenix from some other city. So the assumption that individuals are aware of ecological variables is not a difficult one to accept in the case of annual precipitation. Geographical determinists of the Ellsworth Huntington persuasion, in fact, accept it unconditionally, and attempt to explain both character structure and behavior accordingly.[15]

Polio incidence, however, is an ecological variable of another kind. In the first place, since polio is an epidemic disease, the incidence rate changes from year to year. Although some communities in the United States have histories of either generally low or generally high incidence, when only a few years are considered these long-term tendencies may not be apparent. In the second place, since polio even in years of high incidence affects comparatively few people, it is quite possible to live in a high polio incidence community and be completely unaware of this characteristic of the environment. Similarly, it is possible to live in a low incidence community, but through some personal contact with polio, or through exposure to an unusual amount of information concerning polio, actually assume that the incidence rate is high. Unlike mean annual precipitation, accordingly, polio incidence does not affect some people who logically should be affected by it, and affects others who should not, logically, be affected at all.

Each of these two characteristics of polio incidence has important implications for the correlational analysis attempted in this study. The fact that the rate in any one community may change drastically from year to year means that some measure of recent polio incidence must be obtained. In this research, it was determined that the best measure available was a weighted average for the three preceding years. Three years were selected in order to give allowance to the impact of previous high or low incidence upon attitudes and behavior; a weighted average in which the most recent year contributed 50 per cent of the average was used in order to compensate for the fact that recent experiences have generally a more decisive impact than earlier ones.*

* See Appendix B for a description of the weighting procedures followed.

For present purposes, the major implication of the relatively low incidence of polio is that even people who are aware, in a general way, of the polio incidence rate of their community cannot necessarily be expected to hold opinions toward polio which are congruent with this knowledge, and many people may in fact hold opinions which are contrary to the objective facts of polio incidence in their community.

How, then, does the year-to-year variation in the communities throughout the country which have a high polio incidence serve to maintain a high level of public concern? Table 7 shows the relationship between polio incidence and concern over polio.

### Table 7—Polio Incidence and Concern Over Polio

| Polio Incidence Rate of County* | Serious | PER CENT OF EACH SES GROUP WHO JUDGE POLIO TO BE:[16] Most Serious | Most Fear-inspiring | N |
|---|---|---|---|---|
| | | High SES | | |
| High | 57 | 15 | 15 | (112) |
| Medium | 43 | 15 | 11 | (665) |
| Low | 37 | 10 | 8 | (186) |
| | | Low SES | | |
| High | 55 | 22 | 15 | (175) |
| Medium | 41 | 18 | 12 | (623) |
| Low | 43 | 15 | 12 | (164) |

* 1951–1953 weighted average.

Note, in Table 7, that in areas of recently-high polio incidence a higher percentage of the population expressed concern over polio on all three measures of concern used. This is particularly true of people from the high socio-economic status group, who are of course more likely to be aware of the objective facts of polio incidence. But the percentage differences between areas of high and low polio incidence are not large, for the reasons discussed earlier: people are often both unaware of the polio incidence rate of their community and are influenced by a polio incidence level which occurred prior to the years studied. For this reason, concern over polio never vanishes completely, and is reinforced from time to time by a reoccurrence of a high level of incidence.

*Polio is a children's disease.* The most highly-publicized victims of polio have always been children and adolescents—hence, of course, the term "infantile paralysis". And although the past decade has witnessed a significant shift in the age composition of new polio cases, e.g., an increasing tendency for people twenty years of age and older to be afflicted, over 75 per cent of the new polio cases in recent years were still among people less than twenty years old, and more than 50 per cent were among children less than ten years old.[17]

In the eyes of the public generally, polio is not only regarded largely as a children's disease; it is also regarded by a substantial majority (75 per cent) as the *most* serious children's disease which currently threatens American children.[18]

Since polio is largely identified as a children's disease, and since a majority of the households in America contain children under twenty-one years of age, this identification in itself contributes substantially to the general level of concern. Furthermore, the fact that most victims are children means that a majority of any one community's cases affect one clearly-defined segment of the population. This serves to dramatize the danger of polio more effectively than would be the case if polio incidence were randomly distributed among the population. And the impact of this age clustering is of course increased by the fact that the public at large is more concerned over the health of children than over the health of the adult population.

*Polio is a crippling disease.* Polio cripples its victims much more frequently than it kills them—particularly in recent years when improved diagnosis and emergency treatment have been developed. In the years 1915 through 1929, for example, the ratio of the death rate to the case rate ranged from a low of 20.5 per cent in 1927 to a high of 41.4 per cent in 1918, while in the years since 1950 the ratio has been less than 6 per cent each year.[19] Statistics concerning the crippling effects of polio are not available on a nationwide basis. In one study conducted of a 1941 epidemic in Maryland, however, it was found that 50 per cent of the patients had no aftereffects, 29 per cent had slight aftereffects, 18 per cent had marked aftereffects, and 3 per cent died.[20] Furthermore, polio is one of the leading causes of the deformities and crippling conditions which afflict children.[21]

For purposes of this discussion, the most important consequence of polio's crippling aftereffects is that it is comparatively easy to identify a victim of polio. For this reason, people are generally aware of the fact that someone whom they know has had polio, either recently or sometime in the past—although people may of course simply assume that an acquaintance has had polio, when in fact his deformity may have some other origin. In this respect, polio differs markedly from cancer, tuberculosis, or heart diseases, the presence of which may be known only to the individual's immediate family. Because of this high visibility of polio's crippling aftereffects, three-quarters as many people claim to know someone who has had polio as claim to know someone who has had cancer, in spite of the fact that the incidence of cancer is higher than that of polio, and approximately the same percentage of the population knows someone who has had polio as knows someone who has had either a heart disease or tuberculosis.

### Table 8—Acquaintance with Victims of Four Diseases

| | PER CENT WHO KNOW A VICTIM OF EACH DISEASE, BY SES[22] | | | | |
|---|---|---|---|---|---|
| | Cancer | Heart Diseases | Polio | Tuberculosis | N |
| High SES | 76 | 63 | 62 | 54 | (963) |
| Low SES | 72 | 60 | 54 | 55 | (962) |

As shown in Table 8, people of higher socio-economic status are more likely to know victims of specific diseases, which in part reflects the fact that they generally know more people in the community. Tuberculosis is an important exception; because it has a much higher incidence among poor people than among the rich, its victims are as widely known among the lower socio-economic status group as among the higher one.

The probability that a person will know a victim of polio is of course greater in areas which have recently had a high polio incidence. In areas of recently-high polio incidence, 78 per cent of people of high socio-economic status, and 67 per cent of people of low socio-economic status, know someone who has had polio. In areas of recently-low polio incidence, on the other hand, only 60 per cent of the high SES group, and 49 per cent of the low SES group, know a polio victim. But the fact that even in areas of low incidence more than half of the population knows someone who has had polio is dramatic evidence of polio's high visibility,* since less than 125 persons out of every 100,000 in the American population is actually crippled by polio.[23]

*Polio is most prevalent in prosperous communities.* Both the increase in the epidemicity of polio in recent decades and the increase in the annual incidence rate are a reflection of the fact that hygienic and living standards have improved greatly during this period, since infants living in areas of poor sanitation and much faecal pollution almost uniformly are infected by and thus become immune to infantile

---

* Since the incidence rates used in this comparison are for the years 1951–1953, many counties which had a low incidence during this period might well have had a high incidence in earlier years. This fact undoubtedly contributes to the relatively high level of acquaintanceship with a polio victim in areas of low polio incidence.

paralysis at an early age.[24] As a result of this phenomenon, polio is most prevalent in middle and upper income communities, i.e., communities with a high living standard and adequate sanitary facilities. In spite of the fact that American communities do not vary as greatly with respect to sanitary facilities as do those in many other countries, the county-to-county correlation between the income level of the counties served by Foundation Chapters and the incidence of infantile paralysis has been quite high. For example, 35 per cent of the counties served by Chapters which have a high median family income also had a high level of polio incidence, and only 12 per cent had a low incidence. In counties with a low median family income, on the other hand, only 7 per cent have had a high incidence, and 41 per cent have had a low incidence. Table 9 presents the data upon which these statements are based.*

### Table 9—Incidence of Infantile Paralysis in Counties Served by Foundation Chapters, by Median Family Income

| Polio Incidence Rate† | MEDIAN FAMILY INCOME OF COUNTY* | | |
|---|---|---|---|
| | High | Medium | Low |
| High | 35% | 31% | 7% |
| Medium | 53 | 50 | 52 |
| Low | 12 | 19 | 41 |
| | 100% | 100% | 100% |
| N | (720) | (1575) | (778) |

* Data for the year 1949 (1950 Census). See Appendix B for a description of the criteria used to establish cutting points.

† 1950–1952 weighted average.

The correlation between income level and reported polio incidence relates to public concern in two ways. First, since public concern is related to polio incidence, it is apparent that concern is at its highest level in communities with a high income level. Since individuals who have high incomes contribute more frequently to the March of Dimes than do those having low incomes, and since per capita receipts during the March of Dimes are greater in areas having a high income level, that portion of the American public which is most threatened by polio

* Median family income varies greatly from region to region in the United States. Similarly, it varies according to the level of urbanization of an area. Since polio incidence was, in the years studied, also related to both region and level of urbanization, it is necessary to consider these variables when examining the relationship between income level and polio incidence. When these variables are controlled, however, the positive relationship remains. In highly-urbanized as well as rural counties, and in all regions of the United States, counties with a high median family income are more likely than other counties to have a high polio incidence rate.

is also the portion which has the greatest financial ability to contribute
to the March of Dimes.* Second, since participation in voluntary associations in America is highly correlated with socio-economic status,
the very groups in the population most threatened by polio are also
those most likely to include individuals interested in becoming Volunteers. For this reason, polio's incidence rate serves to identify the threat
of polio in the minds of both potential and actual Volunteers as one
which concerns *people like themselves,* not just the underprivileged.
Their interest in the Foundation's program is consequently intensified.


## *The Scope and Nature of the Patient Care Program*

The previous section has shown that the Foundation is faced with
a climate of opinion concerning polio which is extremely favorable
toward any remedial measures which it might adopt, both in terms of
obtaining a sufficient number of Volunteers to carry out its program
and with respect to securing public support during the March of Dimes.
Concern over the threat of polio is relatively high in America, in part
because people hear a great deal about the disease, in part because of
polio's unique characteristics.

As described previously, the Foundation's program for combating
polio is many-faceted.† In recent years, the development of the Salk
vaccine has caused public attention to focus upon the scientific research
program, which has always absorbed a large share of March of Dime
funds—more than 25 million dollars was spent for virus research and
the vaccine field trial in the years prior to the public announcement on
April 12, 1955 that the Salk vaccine provided effective protection
against paralytic polio.[25] But the research program is sponsored and
coordinated by National Headquarters—as is the Foundation's extensive program of professional education—and it is the patient care
program which, except during the March of Dimes, absorbs the major
share of Volunteer time and energy.

### EXTENT OF THE PROGRAM

Polio is a costly disease. Expensive equipment and medical specialists are often necessary during a patient's recovery period, and care

* See pp. 180–181.
† See pp. 72–73.

must often continue for years—sometimes decades—after the disease
is contracted. In fact, because of the continuing need of many patients
for medical care, the number of patients who receive financial assistance
from the Foundation in any given year exceeds the number of people
who first contracted polio during the year. Table 10 summarizes the
expenditures of the Foundation's patient care program during the years
immediately preceding and following this research.

**Table 10—Foundation Expenditures for Patient Care, 1951–1955** [26]

| Year | New Polio Cases | Patients Receiving Foundation Assistance (approximate) | Patient Care Expenditures (millions) | Proportion of all Foundation Expenditures (per cent) |
|---|---|---|---|---|
| 1951 | 28,386 | 63,000 | $20.9 | 69.7 |
| 1952 | 57,879 | 80,000 | 24.9 | 69.0 |
| 1953 | 35,592 | 77,000 | 29.7 | 62.1 |
| 1954 | 38,476 | 74,000 | 28.5 | 48.6 |
| 1955 | 29,270 | 69,000 | 27.6 | 56.4 |

The information presented in Table 10 highlights two important
aspects of the Foundation's patient care program. First, it indicates
that, regardless of the number of new polio cases in any given year,
patient care expenses account for a majority of the Foundation's total
expenses. The only exception during this five-year period was in 1954,
when the mass field trials of the Salk vaccine absorbed 28 per cent of
the Foundation's income. Second, it shows that the number of patients
who received assistance in any given year is far in excess of the number
of people who contracted polio during that year. This reflects, of
course, the fact that many patients are assisted for a number of years
after they were first stricken by polio. The magnitude of this type of
continued assistance can be illustrated by noting the specific experiences
of the thirty-seven Chapters studied intensively. In the three years preceding this research—1951 through 1953—5,801 people contracted
polio in the thirty-seven counties served by these Chapters. Of these,
3,997 (69 per cent) received financial assistance from the local Chapter in the year they contracted polio—evidence that the patient care
program assists not merely an underprivileged minority, but a majority
of the people who become polio patients. Another 5,237 people who
had contracted polio during a previous year also received assistance,
bringing the total number of patients assisted during this three-year
period to 9,234—nearly twice the number of new polio cases.[27] The
patient care program, accordingly, is much larger in scope than the
polio incidence rate in any given year would suggest.

A program of this scope obviously cannot be carried out by local Chapters alone. National Headquarters participates in a number of ways. First, it grants funds directly to institutions caring for polio patients. In 1954 and 1955 alone, for example, more than four million dollars was granted by the national office to twenty-nine hospitals and universities throughout the country for the support of respirator centers and other institutions caring for polio patients.[28] Second, nurses, doctors, and other professionals are hired by the national office during epidemics; emergency equipment, such as iron lungs, is sent to Chapters; professional training courses are held during epidemics; and literature on methods of patient care is distributed both to the public and the medical profession. Third, and of perhaps most importance from the Chapter point of view, headquarters funds are advanced to those Chapters which have used all of their own funds for patient care.

### CHAPTER RESPONSIBILITIES

In spite of these services furnished by the national office, however, major responsibility for administering the patient care program rests with local Chapters. Specific Chapter responsibilities under the program are described to Volunteers in the patient care manual as follows:

1. To get in touch with the patient's family immediately upon learning of case.
2. To pay for care of polio patients who need financial assistance.
3. To provide expenses for the training of doctors, and nurses, at polio refresher courses and institutes.
4. To survey patient care facilities and resources and promote improvement where needed.
5. To plan with health authorities for full utilization of community resources in anticipation of high polio incidence.
6. To cooperate with hospitals and other community agencies concerned in planning an over-all program of polio patient care.
7. To guide the purchase of polio equipment by fraternal and civic groups so that it will be of maximum benefit to existing hospital and clinical facilities for the treatment and rehabilitation of polio patients.
8. To make provisions for transportation of patients to and from hospitals and clinics.
9. To develop and train, in cooperation with local medical, nursing, hospital and public health groups, volunteers (PEVs) to assist with the care of polio patients in hospitals, clinics and homes.[29]

These responsibilities encompass a wide range of activities. Some apply only to Chapters located in communities which have a hospital accepting infantile paralysis patients; other involve actions for which the need may arise only infrequently; and still others involve chiefly the maintenance of some form of liaison with public and hospital officials. But the first two responsibilities listed—getting in touch with the families of polio patients and paying for medical and hospital care—require action on the part of practically all Chapters at least several times a year, and constitute, as far as most Volunteers are concerned, the core of the patient care program. During polio epidemics, of course, these responsibilities are increased, and Polio Emergency Volunteers assist with the actual care of polio patients in hospitals and private homes.

How do local Chapters decide which polio patients need financial assistance? Since polio is a reportable disease, local health officers learn of each new case through doctors and hospitals, and in most communities they automatically transmit the name of the patient to the Chapter. The Chairman then sends a letter to members of the patient's family informing them of the services provided by the Chapter, and inviting them to arrange a meeting with a Chapter representative to discuss what assistance can be provided. In most instances the initial initiative is thus taken by the Chapter, rather than by the patient or his family. But the actual decisions concerning which patients should be supported and how much assistance should be granted are made by the Chapter Executive Committee. The Medical Advisory Committee, comprised of doctors and other professionals, is generally only called upon when special problems arise and to make a periodic review of the need for continued care of patients being financially assisted by the Chapter. To guide them in making these decisions, Volunteers are told that "our philosophy of assistance is broader and more flexible than that of state agencies which have legally established criteria for determining eligibility for assistance. Our chief concern is that the polio patient receives the best care available, and we stand ready to assist in payment for this service where it is needed."[30]

If "eligibility criteria" are not used, how can Volunteers determine whether or not financial assistance should be given? Although elaborate forms for use in interviewing the families of polio patients are provided by National Headquarters, the evidence from this research is that these forms are not used in many cases, and cannot in any event provide more than general guidelines for making a decision. In short, Volunteers must use their own judgment in each individual case; the various manuals prepared by the national office do no more than stipulate the kinds of payments which cannot be made and provide such general suggestions as "it has been the experience of Chapters that four out of five families require some financial assistance."[31]

In this connection, it is important to note that although the Foundation's program of assistance to polio patients is officially and colloquially called a patient "care" program, the term is something of a misnomer. As the following excerpts from the *Chapter Reference Book* indicate, Volunteers are continually reminded that *assistance,* not *care,* is the major function of the program:

We must remember that polio patients are neither "Chapter" nor "National Foundation" patients. The treatment of every patient rests solely in the hands of his physician. It is the job of your Chapter to *aid* the physician in charge—by making available to him all of your Chapter resources which will assist him in the treatment and care of the polio patient. . . . The National Foundation does not practice medicine nor give care to patients. The function of your Chapter is to cooperate with, not supplant, service already existing in your community.[32]

The patient care program, in short, serves primarily a *mediating* function. In this respect it is similar to the activities of such organizations as the Parent-Teachers Association, which exists not to supplant the school system, but to bring about closer cooperation between teachers and parents. Since the medical profession has the basic responsibility in our society for the care of the sick, it is apparent that any organization comprised of laymen which *did* presume to assume this responsibility for itself would meet with widespread opposition from the medical profession.

### PATIENT CARE AS A COMMUNITY SERVICE

The most important aspect of the patient care program, as far as Volunteers are concerned, however, is the fact that Chapters are encouraged to view the patient care program as a community service, not as a form of charitable assistance to the needy. This philosophy is explained as follows:

We are not dispensing charity in any sense of the word. *While we expect a family to do what it reasonably can financially,* we do not insist that it prove itself totally indigent to obtain needed care. If it is evident that the high cost of polio care would result in undue hardship, force the family to sell a car that it needs, mortgage its home or otherwise drastically lower its standard of living, the Chapter should offer to pay for all or that portion of the cost that cannot be reasonably met by the family.[33]

The "community service" philosophy underlying the patient care program is expressed in two ways. First, as noted above, assistance is not confined to the totally indigent, but is given to any family which would have to lower its standard of living by paying the total costs of medical and hospital care. Second, assistance is not confined to paying purely medical bills. In addition to paying these, Chapters are permitted to pay for nursing care, physical therapy, appliances, surgery, transportation to and from hospitals and clinics, foster home care, and psychiatric or psychological services. Furthermore, payments are not limited to those which benefit specific individuals. Chapters may purchase special equipment for use in local hospitals and contribute funds for recruitment of professional hospital personnel during epidemics. [34] In short, Chapters are urged to do everything possible to extend "a neighborly hand to those in need of its services."[35]

## CORPORATE STRUCTURE AND THE PATIENT CARE PROGRAM

A major structural characteristic of the Foundation is that, unlike many voluntary associations, it is not a federation of state or local affiliates, but a unified organization with a corporate-type structure. Local Chapters are component units, or "branch offices," of the national organization. Our concern here is not with the origins of this structural characteristic or with its consequences for the organization as a whole; rather, the discussion which follows is confined to the implications of this structure for the functioning of the patient care program.

Since polio is an epidemic disease, the need for patient care funds does not remain constant within any one Chapter from year to year. In some years, a Chapter will have sufficient resources in its bank account to meet the needs of the patients on its roster, or may even have surplus funds. In other years, the funds available may fall far short of those required. In order to distribute funds to communities which need them, a system has been established by the Foundation which permits emergency aid funds to be advanced to those Chapters which have depleted their own funds. By the same token, when additional funds are not needed by a Chapter it is expected to return to the national office a portion of the funds which it has received in previous years, in order for other Chapters to have sufficient resources for their immediate needs.* In the years 1951 through 1955, approximately two-thirds of

* This regulation was enforced only infrequently, however, until 1955, when the Board of Trustees called upon Chapters to turn in 50 per cent of their surplus funds to National Headquarters. Almost $4,600,000 was transferred from these Chapters to Chapters in need of funds to meet unpaid bills.[36]

all funds expended for patient care were obtained from Chapter funds
—the 50 per cent of the March of Dimes proceeds which each Chapter
retains for its own use—and approximately one-third was obtained
from emergency aid funds transmitted to Chapters directly from National Headquarters.†[37] The importance of this system of emergency
aid—this "transfer of funds within one organization, to meet financial
necessities as they arise," as it is officially described[38]—is obvious.
Without it, the patient care program in its present form could not exist.
Suppose, for example, that instead of this system, each Chapter retained for its own use three-quarters of its March of Dimes proceeds
rather than the 50 per cent it returns under the present division of
funds. The result would be that some Chapters would accumulate large
surpluses, and others would be unable to care for more than a small
percentage of the polio patients in their territory. Since the existence of
either large surpluses or unassisted patients would serve to discredit the
Foundation in the eyes of the public, a system of this kind would be
patently inoperable.

Does this system of emergency aid require a corporate-type formal
structure for its efficacy? It is here contended that it does, since only
a national headquarters with authority over its local units could possibly coordinate such a vast system. If the major focus of authority was
in a state organization, as is the case with several voluntary health
associations, an equitable distribution of funds within the state could
easily be made. But the incidence of polio varies greatly from state to
state as well as from county to county.[39] For this reason, only an organization which is established along county lines, and in which ultimate authority resides in the national office, could possibly coordinate
the machinery necessary to enable the Foundation to fulfill its pledge
"to assist every infantile paralysis patient in the land to obtain the best
available medical treatment and care, regardless of age, race, creed, or
color."[40]

A subsidiary advantage of the Foundation's corporate structure as
far as the patient care program is concerned is that it makes an active
volunteer membership absolutely essential. Decisions must be made
each year concerning the types of payments to be authorized for some
70,000 to 80,000 patients. Since the professional personnel in the
national office could not possibly make all these decisions without em-

† During these years, from three to five per cent of all patient care expenditures was
in the form of direct expenditures by National Headquarters for equipment, transportation of nurses, physicians, etc.

ploying an expensive, and perhaps inefficient, administrative staff, the burden of decision-making is delegated to local Chapters. If state organizations existed, on the other hand, it might be administratively feasible for them to require that all Chapters submit applications for patient aid to their offices for approval. This in turn would undoubtedly lead to a decline in Volunteer interest, since a major aspect of the patient care program from the Chapter point of view is that decisions concerning the expenditure of funds are made by Volunteers *in the community where the funds are raised.* Volunteer control, in turn, is only possible because polio is a disease having a relatively low incidence and yet requiring relatively expensive medical treatment. If Chapters had, say, five or six times as many patients on their rosters as they have at present, it might well be that only in small communities could Volunteers attend to all the administrative details which would be involved. And if the expenditure per patient was considerably less than it currently is, it is highly probable that Volunteers would not consider it worth their while to devote evenings and weekends to the decisions involved.*

## Volunteer Involvement in Patient Care Activities

Although fulfilling the responsibilities entailed in patient care is the major year-round activity of local Chapters, not all Volunteers take an active part in the program. March of Dimes Volunteers, of course, generally have no direct relationship to the program. Furthermore, in some Chapters, most of the details are handled by the Chairman and a few members of the Executive Committee. Although other Volunteers in these Chapters are informed in a general way concerning the number and types of patients currently being assisted by the Chapter, their knowledge is more likely to come from conversations with other Volunteers and through attending the annual meeting, where the events of the past year are generally reviewed. In other Chapters, on the other hand, nearly all Chapter Volunteers participate, at least to the extent

* As indicated in Table 10, p. 131, the average expenditure per patient is $250–350. These figures fail, however, to reflect the fact that many Chapters expend many thousand dollars for a single patient. During the interviews Volunteers always stressed the two or three patients whose expenses had been several thousand dollars, rather than the large number of patients whose illness had cost the Chapter only a few hundred dollars.

of interviewing the families of patients or transporting patients to clinics. And when an epidemic strikes, the number of tasks to be done increases enormously. More bills must be paid, professional groups must be assisted in training Polio Emergency Volunteers to work in hospitals, the cooperation of the press and radio stations must be obtained in appealing for needed equipment, educational material furnished by National Headquarters must be distributed, and the public must be kept informed of everything that is being done to meet the emergency situation.[41]

Active participation in the program is not, however, a necessary condition of emotional or intellectual involvement in it. In order to tap other aspects of involvement, Volunteers were queried at some length about their own views of the program. In the course of the interviews, 22 per cent of all Volunteers stated that the patient care program was the activity which interested them most; 51 per cent stated that they regarded the patient care program as a major "strong point" of the Foundation's over-all program; and 58 per cent selected patient care as the "key" to the Foundation's success in obtaining public support.

As might be expected, these responses are highly intercorrelated. That is, Volunteers who hold one of these three views are more likely than others to hold the other two. Accordingly, in order to obtain a broader measure of involvement in the patient care program than that provided by any one response, an Index of Patient Care Involvement was constructed. Volunteers with index scores of 2 or 3 are considered to be "highly involved" in the patient care program; all others are considered to be "not highly involved." According to this criterion, 44 per cent of all Volunteers are "highly involved" in the program.* Since patient care is a Chapter activity, Chapter Volunteers generally scored higher than March of Dimes Volunteers: 54 per cent of the Chapter Volunteers are "highly involved," in contrast to 30 per cent of the March of Dimes Volunteers.

### INVOLVEMENT IN PATIENT CARE AMONG DIFFERENT TYPES OF RECRUITS

Most Volunteers joined the Foundation through first participating in the March of Dimes, and almost all of the Volunteers who did join the Chapter directly remained as Chapter Volunteers. A substantial

* See Appendix B for a description of this Index and the method of scoring employed.

proportion of those who first joined the March of Dimes, on the other hand, eventually transferred to Chapter activity. Table 11 examines the extent to which these four patterns of joining are related to involvement in the patient care program.

**Table 11—Mode of Entry and Involvement in the Patient Care Program**

| | PER CENT "HIGHLY INVOLVED" IN THE PATIENT CARE PROGRAM | | | |
|---|---|---|---|---|
| Mode of Entry | Chapter Volunteers | | March of Dimes Volunteers | |
| | | N | | N |
| Chapter | 62 | (69) | 67 | (3) |
| March of Dimes | 43 | (60) | 29 | (102) |

Table 11 demonstrates that a clear majority of those Volunteers who initially joined the Chapter are "highly involved" in the patient care program regardless of whether or not they "transferred" to the March of Dimes. Among Volunteers who initially joined the March of Dimes, however, it is chiefly those who later joined the Chapter who have a high level of involvement in patient care. Similarly, among present Chapter Volunteers, those who initially joined the Chapter are more likely to be "highly involved" than those who initially joined the March of Dimes.

Experience as a Chapter Volunteer, as well as an initial interest in Chapter activities, obviously contributes strongly to involvement in the patient care program. This point is brought out even more forcefully in Table 12, which examines the level of involvement in the patient care program among different types of recruits.

**Table 12—Type of Recruit and Involvement in the Patient Care Program**

| | PER CENT "HIGHLY INVOLVED" IN THE PATIENT CARE PROGRAM | | | |
|---|---|---|---|---|
| Type of Recruit | Chapter Volunteers | | March of Dimes Volunteers | |
| | | N | | N |
| Joiners | 50 | (50) | 19 | (48) |
| Good Citizens | 51 | (38) | 39 | (28) |
| Humanitarians | 54 | (13) | 40 | (15) |
| Polio Veterans | 68 | (28) | 43 | (14) |

It is quite clear that Chapter Volunteers, regardless of how they joined the Foundation, are more highly involved in the patient care program than are March of Dimes Volunteers, and that among both groups of Volunteers, Polio Veterans are most likely, and Joiners least likely, to have a high level of involvement in the patient care program. This is fully in accord with our expectations, since the personal experiences of Polio Veterans have predisposed them toward an interest in this program. But note the percentage differences among the Joiners, who it will be recalled from the previous chapter were attracted by the "people" of the Foundation rather than by its "purposes." Among the minority of Joiners who initially joined the Chapter, as well as among those who transferred to the Chapter, fully half are highly involved in the patient care program. The experiences which they have undergone within the Foundation, it appears, have brought about a radical transformation of their image of the organization. For them, it is no longer simply a group of people with whom they enjoy associating, or an organization whose sponsorship they respect, but rather an organization which provides an essential service function within the community. Those Joiners, on the other hand, who remained March of Dimes Volunteers did not undergo any such transformation; only one in every five has acquired a high level of involvement in patient care.

## LENGTH OF SERVICE AND INVOLVEMENT IN PATIENT CARE

The relatively high level of involvement among March of Dimes Volunteers suggests that some factor other than direct participation in the program may be involved, and the possibility arises that length of service may be related to involvement in patient care. Table 13 presents data reporting upon this relationship.

*Table 13—Length of Service and Involvement in the Patient Care Program*

|  | PER CENT "HIGHLY INVOLVED" IN THE PATIENT CARE PROGRAM | | | |
|  | Chapter Volunteers | | March of Dimes Volunteers | |
| Years Active | | N | | N |
| One | 52 | (7) | 10 | (30) |
| Two to five | 50 | (60) | 37 | (59) |
| More than five | 57 | (39) | 45 | (11) |
| "Since the beginning"* | 61 | (23) | 40 | (5) |

* Many Volunteers could not recall in which of the "early years" (1934 through 1938) they first participated. Hence, the general term "since the beginning" refers to any of these years.

As Table 13 demonstrates, the longer Volunteers have belonged to the organization, the more likely they are to be involved in the pa-

tient care program. This is true of Chapter Volunteers, all of whom
are of course relatively highly involved, and it is dramatically true of
March of Dimes Volunteers. Only 10 per cent of the new recruits
among March of Dimes Volunteers are highly involved, in contrast to
over 40 per cent of those who have been active for more than five years.
It is thus apparent that length of tenure, combined with the consequently increased opportunities to observe the operation of the program, contributes substantially to involvement in patient care activities.
As discussed above, there are also important historical reasons for the
greater involvement of Foundation "old-timers."*

Volunteers who have been members for a number of years have had
increased opportunities to become involved in the patient care program
for two reasons. First, tenure in itself provides greater opportunities
for familiarity. Personal relationships with other Volunteers become
intensified, opportunities to perform some assignment related to the
summer onslaught of polio are increased, and so forth. Second, the
longer a Volunteer has been a member, the greater is the likelihood
that he will have been a member during a year of high polio incidence,
when the Chapter's patient care program performed a much more ob-
servable community service. Accordingly, it is necessary to turn to an
examination of the relationship of polio incidence itself to involvement in the patient care program.

POLIO INCIDENCE AND INVOLVEMENT IN PATIENT CARE

Since the counties served by Foundation Chapters vary in size from
small rural ones to large metropolitan centers, and since polio is an
epidemic disease, the actual number of new polio cases varies greatly
from county to county. In the four years preceding this research, for
example, one of the thirty-seven counties studied intensively had had
only one new case of polio, and another three counties had had fewer
than ten cases. At the other extreme, three counties had had a total of
more than 500 cases each during this four-year period.

In order to compensate for differences in population size, polio
incidence is usually measured by the number of new cases per year
per 100,000 population. For present purposes, however, the actual
number of new cases provides the best measure of polio incidence,
since there is generally only one Chapter serving each county, regardless of its size. It is well to bear in mind, however, that the number of

* See p. 47.

polio cases is not necessarily an accurate measure of actual patient care activities, for two major reasons. First, not all new polio patients require assistance from the Chapter. Second, the patients assisted by Chapters include those who have contracted polio at some time in the past, but who need therapy, remedial surgery, or orthopedic appliances of some kind, as well as those who have contracted it recently. Our present interest is in the impact of the *perceived* prevalence of polio, and for this purpose the actual number of new polio cases seems the best measure available. Since memories of past high incidence may persist for several years, the total number of new cases in the four preceding years is used in this chapter as an index of the prevalence of polio.

It is accordingly possible to examine separately the involvement in the patient care program of Volunteers serving in counties having a low, medium, or high incidence of polio. Table 14 shows the relationship, among both Chapter and March of Dimes Volunteers, of polio incidence to involvement in the patient care program.

**Table 14—Polio Incidence and Involvement in the Patient Care Program**

| | PER CENT "HIGHLY INVOLVED" IN THE PATIENT CARE PROGRAM | | | |
| --- | --- | --- | --- | --- |
| Level of Polio Incidence* | Chapter Volunteers | | March of Dimes Volunteers | |
| | | N | | N |
| Low | 45 | (20) | 24 | (21) |
| Medium | 57 | (54) | 30 | (44) |
| High | 55 | (55) | 35 | (40) |

\* The cutting points between "low" and "medium" and between "medium" and "high" are of course arbitrary. The eight counties classified as having had a low incidence had between 1 and 25 new cases during this four-year period; the fourteen counties classified as having had a medium incidence had between 42 and 110 cases; and the fifteen counties classified as having had a high incidence had between 162 and 1,062 cases.

As expected, both Chapter and March of Dimes Volunteers serving in counties which have had many polio cases in recent years are more likely than others to be "highly involved" in the patient care program. In fact, it is almost inconceivable that the reverse situation should prevail. But the percentage differences are not very large, and a substantial percentage of Volunteers even in counties of low incidence are involved in the patient care program.

The relatively low correlation between polio incidence and involvement in the patient care program represents a striking departure from the correlation patterns previously discussed. The high correlations observed when organizational affiliation, type of recruit, and length of service as a Volunteer are examined all confirm our common-sense expectations, which in turn are based upon our knowledge of what kinds of activities the patient care program actually involves. By the same token, common sense would lead us to suspect that involvement in the patient care program would be *much* greater in Chapters which have had to cope with a large number of new polio cases. This, however, is not the case.

One possible explanation of this seemingly anomalous situation is that the actual number of new polio cases is of less importance than the incidence *rate*. That is, a few cases may have as much impact upon Volunteer attitudes in small counties as do a few hundred cases in large cities. Although this is undoubtedly a contributing factor, it does not alone account for the comparative absence of an observed difference in involvement in the three categories of Chapters, since within each category no differences occur between the large and small counties. Accordingly, the possibility arises that the patient care program may be viewed somewhat differently in the three categories of Chapters, and that each of these views is related in a different way to patient care involvement.

In order to explore this possibility, it is necessary to go beyond the available statistical data and ascertain what Volunteers serving in communities having had different levels of polio incidence actually said about their involvement in the patient care program. The discussion which follows is based upon an analysis of these statements. Since Chapter Chairmen are the Volunteers who are most directly and consistently concerned with carrying out the Chapter's responsibilities under the patient care program, their views are given more attention than are the views of other Volunteers.

*Low incidence Chapters.* The correlation between polio incidence and involvement in the patient care program is strongest in the case of Chapter Chairmen. Only three of the eight Chairmen serving in counties with low polio incidence are "highly involved" in patient care, in contrast to ten of the fourteen Chairmen in medium incidence Chapters and ten of the fifteen Chairmen in high incidence Chapters. This reflects, of course, the fact that Chairmen in low incidence counties actually have very few responsibilities under the program, and devote most of their energies either to the annual March of Dimes or to "telling the polio story" to the community. Yet a majority reported that their greatest source of satisfaction from participating as a Volunteer came from *being in a position to help people* in the community, if and when polio struck. Their statements vary in intensity, ranging from generic expressions such as that uttered by the Chairman of the Hometown Chapter—"The greatest satisfaction would be taking care of patients, if we have any. . . ."—to the description of his activities provided by the Chapter Chairman in Dirtroad County. In spite of the fact that his county had only one polio case in the four preceding years, this Chairman thinks of himself as an intermediary between doctors and hospitalized patients, and as the family counselor of distraught relatives. For him, the roles of psychologist and benefactor have their own rewards: "To see the gratitude of the kids when you call on them. And even the family, . . . when they see that the financial burden is taken care of and taken away from them."

For the Chairman of the University City Chapter, contact with the families of polio victims is also satisfying, but for a slightly different reason: his gratification stems from being the representative of a volunteer movement which places its resources at his disposal so that he can offer assistance to the distressed in time of crisis:

Since . . . I've been in the homes of people who have had it, it has broadened me. I have a mixed emotion. Naturally, when you come into a home where there has been polio, it's pretty hard to say those things [i.e., to offer consolation]. The patient is not there, yet you can come back and say, "*We* have got some help for you." It is pretty gratifying to be the instigator of that. All this good is done 100 per cent by Volunteers.

Three other Volunteers in this Chapter also placed emphasis upon *being in a position* to offer financial relief to families faced with the prospect of staggering medical bills. Since University City had fewer than a dozen polio cases in the four preceding years, the importance of these statements lies in the emphasis placed upon the potentialities of the program rather than upon the realities of cumulative experience. The patient care program, in short, is highly valued by Volunteers who have not had a great deal of experience with it because it is a legitimate and indispensable community service. One University City Volunteer summed up one reason for this attitude in these terms: "There is a real need. . . . Responsible members of the community should feel a duty to step in and do the job. Otherwise we would find probably governmental assumption of this type of welfare function."

*Medium incidence Chapters.* Although a majority of the Chairmen in these Chapters are "highly involved" in the patient care program, in none of these counties is there a sense of polio being a major threat to the health of the population. Patient care in most of these Chapters is a steady routine handled, for the most part, by the Chairman alone or (in the larger cities) in conjunction with the Executive Secretary employed by the Chapter.

A characteristic of the views expressed by the ten Chairmen in these Chapters who are "highly involved" is the stress placed upon the satisfactions derived primarily from association with a program devoted to community service, from being the recognized *community agents* of the program. Furthermore, it is the broader aspects of the patient care program, rather than the specific gratifications which come from tendering assistance to individual victims and their families, which interest most of these Chairmen. In speaking of the activities which have given them the greatest feeling of accomplishment, for example, these Chairmen referred less to individual cases they have dealt with than to anonymous groups of people. They perceive the patient care program, in short, first in terms of its social functions, and only secondarily as a source of personal satisfactions. The statements of two of these Chairmen—in South City and Pulpwood City, respectively—reflect this almost professional detachment:

I spend more time talking to families than on anything else, trying to see them more than once, for what the National Foundation calls "emotional handholding."

We try to put their minds at rest. This is in line with my own profession—life insurance. There is no greater satisfaction than to relieve people in times of stress. That's why I'm in life insurance.

For other Chairmen who devote most of their time to the patient care program, the gratitude of patients and parents is the most rewarding aspect of their work. Summing up his experiences, the Mountain County Chairman expressed himself with increasing emotion, actually repressing tears, with these words:

(*What has given you the greatest sense of satisfaction?*) To have mothers or victims come to the annual meeting and to listen to the way they get up to thank the members of the Executive Committee for what the Chapter has done. Victims, children, come in with crutches, wheelchairs. To have some mother get up to say what the Chapter has done. Fathers come into my living room at night to thank me. . . . You can tell by their clothes that they don't have much money, but you can tell that they're sincere. Doing something for humanity, that's all.

Most of the other Volunteers in Chapters having had a medium level of polio incidence spoke as observers rather than as administrators or actual participants in patient care activities; for them, the program provides a laudable but somewhat diffuse justification for their disparate activities. It is the ultimate rationale for their individual efforts, but not necessarily a source of immediate, personal satisfactions. "Helping crippled children," assisting "victims," being involved in a community activity which "relieves people from worry"—these are the recurrent themes mentioned by these Volunteers. But it is evident that their involvement in their local Chapter or March of Dimes organization depends also upon a diversified range of more tangible rewards derived from their actual contacts with fellow Volunteers, or from specific accomplishments in organizing or in raising money, or simply from being able to participate in an enjoyable group activity.

*High incidence Chapters.* A strikingly different pattern of involvement in patient care activities exists in high incidence Chapters, where the role of patient care as a source of satisfactions is more clearly defined. The responsibility for administering assistance to polio victims constitutes a major year-round task which has provided opportunities for widespread Volunteer participation in six of these fifteen Chapters; in the remaining nine Chapters, located in large cities, in which the patient care program is largely in the hands of the Executive Secretary or is routinized in local hospitals, Volunteer participation centers for the most part on March of Dimes activities. It is important to remember, however, that whatever the activities which absorb the time of most Volunteers, the presence of a large number of patients in the community constitutes a vivid reminder of the immediate purpose for the existence of the Chapter and March of Dimes organization.

We will first examine the views of the patient care program expressed by the Chapter Chairmen who are most directly involved in administering the program—either alone, in conjunction with Executive Secretaries, or together with other Chapter Volunteers. Three of these Chairmen are in communities where polio had struck with epidemic or near-epidemic force in the previous two years. Their references to these crisis situations are charged with emotion, for they regard themselves as having been part of a dramatic battle against disease in their own communities. The Chairman in Corn City regarded his battle as chiefly against the apathy of the community's doctors:

We had an epidemic here in 1952, . . . but the doctors, you know how they are, they refused to declare an epidemic, an emergency situation. I appealed before them. . . . Well, they didn't do anything. So I went and organized things in the hospital, hired nurses and orderlies, worked day and night. The load was terrible. At one time four nurses walked off—they couldn't stand it any more. I worked day and night. I lost twenty pounds in four months, but still the doctors wouldn't do anything. Finally, on Labor Day they declared an emergency. They held a meeting and the head nurse who had been overworked told them . . . that if I hadn't been there it couldn't have been done, that they hadn't helped a bit. Well, finally they thanked me for what I had done. The epidemic cost me five thousand dollars because I couldn't attend to my business during that period. . . . I imagine patient care is my biggest effort. . . . There is hardly a day goes by around here that I don't have anything to do with patient care even in a poor year like this. What I mean is we have very few cases.

The Chairman in Suburb County found that dealing with parents was the most difficult task:

(*What has given you the greatest sense of satisfaction?*) The feeling I get in calling on these patients, which I try to do. . . . To hear them tell me in their own words how grateful they are for the work we are doing. . . . Naturally . . . they're in hysterics sometimes. I try to sell them on the idea that it's going to be all right. I've seen so many of these cases that after I check with the doctors and take a look I can tell right away if the patient will get full recovery or partial recovery. . . . Sometimes I have to sit there and deliberately lie. I have checked and sometimes I know it will be a long time. After the first shock, that first few days, you can go around to the parents and sit down and explain it to them.

And the Chairman of the Friendly City Chapter found that his greatest satisfaction came from comforting stricken children:

I have to [talk to victims' families], practically to all of them. Of course, this past year, there were very few cases, but the year before, I spent two hours a day at the hospital. . . . Maybe I'm a sentimental old coot, . . . [but] probably being around these kids and helping them over the hump has been the most satisfying.

In contrast to the intensity of commitment revealed in statements such as these are the more dispassionate, objective appraisals of satisfactions made by other Chapter Chairmen whose primary activity is the patient care program. There are many reasons for this difference in emphasis, largely stemming from differences in the ways Chapters are organized to handle the patient care program. But one obvious explanation which presents itself is the fact that polio incidence in relation to population size has been much lower in all but one of these Chapters than it has been in the Chapters previously discussed. Although this one Chapter, Harbor City, is among the top five Chapters in terms of actual polio incidence of all the thirty-seven Chapters studied, it is located in a large metropolitan area and employs an office staff. Accordingly, the patient care program is handled more with a big-city emphasis on businesslike efficiency than with the informality which generally prevails in smaller communities. Nevertheless, the Chairman of this Chapter pointed out that what sets the Foundation apart from other activities in his mind is his knowledge of what the patient care program does to put polio victims back on their feet. Citing an individual case of remarkable recovery as an example, he concluded by saying: "Well, we stayed with the case four or five months. His business picked up. We got a letter from him, saying that he would take at least one-half the cost. . . . Now he's taking care of himself completely. That's what you can see in this work.

To recapitulate: The intensity of satisfactions derived by Volunteers is directly related to frequency of contact with patients and grateful relatives and to the opportunities for action in "crisis" situations. That is, intensity is related to polio incidence. But involvement in the patient care program has dimensions other than intensity, and regardless of the actual incidence of polio many Volunteers regard the patient care program as an essential component of their Chapter program. Patient care, accordingly, is regarded as a necessary community service in Chapters which have had a low incidence, as a steady routine in Chapters with a medium incidence, and as the *raison d'etre* of the Chapter when incidence has been high. And when the crisis of a polio epidemic has occurred, patient care has become the major source of gratification for Volunteers on all levels of the organization, as was the case, for example, in Greenback City, where, as one member of the Executive Committee put it, "Everybody pitched in—it was a crusade." Perhaps the purest example of the maximum rewards offered by *direct* participation in the patient care program is contained in the moving story told by another Committee member in Greenback City, who discussed his involvement in these terms.

Let me put it this way: you can't talk of enjoying this. There's something immoral about saying you do. . . . But if I didn't enjoy patient care I wouldn't have performed the duties of a nurse during the epidemic, carrying bed pans at the temporary unit. There were three of us who called ourselves the "Bed Pan Boys." I'll never forget the night we had an emergency tracheotomy! I was holding this child's head while the doctor was performing the operation, and she relaxed and died in my arms.

## chapter V

# RAISING
# FUNDS

## Introduction

AS FAR as Volunteers are concerned, the heart of the Foundation's local program is providing financial and other assistance to polio victims, but an assistance program of this magnitude would obviously not be possible without the financial contributions of the public at large. These contributions are obtained through the efforts of Volunteers; accordingly, fund-raising is itself a vital component of the Foundation's program. As a matter of fact, most Volunteers are initially recruited into the Foundation as March of Dimes Volunteers, and for those Volunteers who do not participate in patient care activities fundraising is the major rationale for their membership in the Foundation. For these reasons, a discussion of the Foundation's local program must include an analysis of the March of Dimes as a Volunteer activity.

As with so many aspects of American life, the Foundation and its broad program are products of organized philanthropy. According to Donald Young, the president of the Russel Sage Foundation, "it is difficult to imagine what life in the United States would be like without philanthropic giving."[1] In terms of dollars alone, the contribution of philanthropy to American society is impressive. According to a recent estimate Americans contribute each year nearly four billion dollars to private philanthropies. Religious organizations receive half of this total, and health and welfare associations nearly half of the remainder.[2]

Philanthropic giving takes a number of forms, and organizations supported by gifts—in contrast to those supported by membership dues —may be grouped into general categories based upon the types of gifts which support them. Colleges and other educational institutions often receive substantial support from alumni and wealthy individuals;

churches generally derive the bulk of their income from the annual pledges of their members; and many small health and welfare agencies depend upon the contributions of a few wealthy individuals. Many community service organizations, such as youth organizations, derive their income largely from the Community Chest or some other joint campaign, which is in turn supported by wealthy individuals, business corporations, and the smaller contributions of individual citizens. The United Jewish Appeal and the American Red Cross, which annually raise more money than any other welfare associations, are supported by large contributions from both wealthy individuals and business concerns, as well as by small contributions from many individuals. The four major national voluntary health associations,* however, obtain the major portion of their income from small gifts, ranging in size from a few pennies to ten dollars or so, contributed by millions of individuals.

There are two exceptions to this dependence upon small gifts. All four associations seek contributions from wealthy individuals and from corporations, but only a small proportion of their total income is derived from these sources. Second, with the exception of the Foundation, individual units of these associations sometimes receive funds from their local Community Chest, although such units normally conduct their own campaign as well.† In spite of these two exceptions, however, the income of all four of these voluntary health associations is derived largely from small gifts contributed by many millions of people.

It goes without saying that a campaign geared to the small gift given by millions of people requires an army of fund-raisers if it is to be successful. This chapter is concerned with those characteristics of the March of Dimes campaign which make it possible for the Foundation to recruit and retain such an army. The first section describes the organization of the campaign; the second section points out the major satisfactions which Volunteers derive from participating in March of Dimes activities; the third section deals with the crucial problem of participation in the March of Dimes by Chapter Volunteers; and the fourth and final section analyzes the assessments made by Volunteers of the reasons why the American public gives such generous support to the March of Dimes. The extent and nature of actual public participation in the March of Dimes is described in the chapter which follows.

---

* The National Foundation for Infantile Paralysis, the National Tuberculosis Association, the American Cancer Society, and the American Heart Association.

† See p. 55 for a discussion of the participation of other voluntary health associations in Community Chests and similar united campaigns.

## The Organization of the March of Dimes

The major structural differences between local Chapters and March of Dimes organizations have been described earlier, and need not be spelled out in detail here. It is necessary only to reiterate that local Chapters are relatively small, year-round organizations whose members for the most part also play an active but generally not a top leadership role in the March of Dimes campaign. March of Dimes organizations, on the other hand, are quite large, even in small counties, and are ephemeral. The leaders start holding informal meetings in the Fall, but the vast majority of March of Dimes Volunteers is not recruited until December or in some cases early January. At the end of January, or early in February, the organization is disbanded.

As a result of these structural differences, participation as a Volunteer involves a quite different type of commitment in each organization. Consider first the amount of time which Volunteers spend in Foundation activities. Some Chapter Volunteers, as already indicated, spend many hours a week handling the affairs of their Chapter; others devote only a few hours each month to one or another committee meeting. But meetings and correspondence and conferences with the families of patients—to say nothing of the enormous work load which accompanies a polio epidemic—add up over the course of a year to a considerable time commitment on the part of many Chapter Volunteers. Most March of Dimes Volunteers, on the other hand, devote relatively little time to the organization. Table 15 reports the number of hours spent on the March of Dimes by Volunteers in the four cities in which intensive studies were conducted.

### Table 15—Hours Devoted to the March of Dimes*

| Hours | Chairmen | | Deputy Chairmen | | Other Volunteers | |
|---|---|---|---|---|---|---|
| | Dec. | Jan. | Dec. | Jan. | Dec. | Jan. |
| More than 40 | 12% | 25% | 2% | 6% | — | 2% |
| 21 to 40 | 8 | 15 | 4 | 4 | — | 2 |
| 11 to 20 | 14 | 29 | 4 | 27 | — | 5 |
| 10 or less | 66 | 31 | 90 | 63 | 100% | 91 |
| | 100% | 100% | 100% | 100% | 100% | 100% |
| N | (80) | (80) | (167) | (167) | (212) | (212) |

* Includes all March of Dimes Volunteers who responded to the mail questionnaire used in the four cities in which special studies were undertaken. See Appendix A for a description of this phase of the field work.

Note first the amount of time spent by the various March of Dimes Chairmen—a group which corresponds approximately to the March of Dimes Volunteers interviewed personally in the thirty-seven Chapters. A majority of even this group of Chairmen spent less than ten hours in December making preparations for the campaign, and a majority spent less than twenty hours during the month of the campaign itself. A quarter of the Chairmen, however, spent more than forty hours during the month of January—certainly a large block of time to devote to one voluntary association in the course of one month. However, although comparable data are not available, it seems highly probable that the vast majority of Chapter Volunteers spend more than forty hours on Foundation activities in the course of an average year.

Among March of Dimes Volunteers other than Chairmen, moreover, even smaller blocks of time are devoted to the fund-raising campaign. In fact, a majority of this group—and a majority of all March of Dimes Volunteers—devoted fewer than ten hours to the campaign, even during the peak month of January. There are of course many exceptions, particularly among the top leadership, but the over-all conclusion which can be drawn from these data is that March of Dimes activity is not particularly time-consuming for most participants.

An equally important difference between the involvement of Chapter and March of Dimes Volunteers in Foundation activities is the degree of specificity of their tasks. Although Chapters are assigned specific functions, and in turn delegate even more specific functions to committees, the year-round activities of Chapter Volunteers are relatively diffuse in contrast to those involved in fund-raising. This is best illustrated by noting the differences in the organizational charts which National Headquarters provides local organizations as blueprints for them to follow. Although more complex charts are suggested for large-city Chapters, the basic Chapter organizational chart consists only of the Chapter membership, the Executive Committee and the Medical Advisory Committee.[3] Contrast this simplicity with the relatively complex organizational chart recommended for March of Dimes organizations (Chart 1, below).

Needless to say, all March of Dimes organizations are not as highly specialized as the model organization portrayed in Chart 1. But most counties have more than one population center, each of which has several activities Chairmen serving as deputies to the City Chairman, and each activity Chairman recruits a staff of his own. The net result, accordingly, is not only a large organization, but a highly specialized one as well.

## Chart 1—March of Dimes Organization[4]

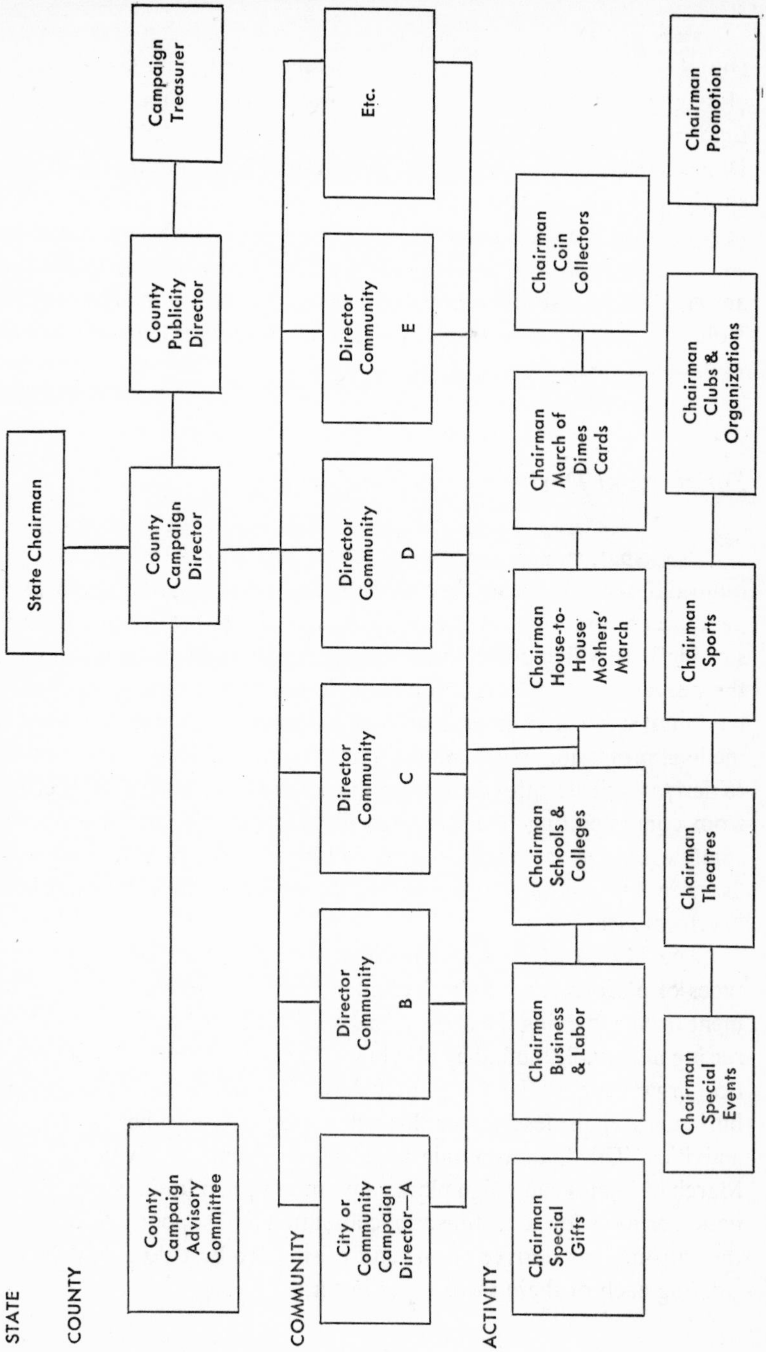

STATE

COUNTY

COMMUNITY

ACTIVITY

State Chairman

Campaign Treasurer

County Publicity Director

County Campaign Director

County Campaign Advisory Committee

City or Community Campaign Director—A

Director Community B

Director Community C

Director Community D

Director Community E

Etc.

Chairman Special Gifts

Chairman Business & Labor

Chairman Schools & Colleges

Chairman House-to-House Mothers' March

Chairman March of Dimes Cards

Chairman Coin Collectors

Chairman Special Events

Chairman Theatres

Chairman Sports

Chairman Clubs & Organizations

Chairman Promotion

The discussion in this section has pointed out that the March of Dimes campaign is designed to obtain small gifts from large numbers of people, and that this objective requires a large number of Volunteer fund-raisers if it is to be achieved. It has also been noted that March of Dimes activities are for the most part both of brief duration and highly specialized. These conditions lead naturally to the question of why so many people are willing to take part in an activity which on the surface seems to offer so few rewards. The section which follows attempts to answer this question by describing some of the satisfactions which Volunteers derive from participating in the March of Dimes.

## Satisfaction Derived from Fund-Raising

Participation as a Volunteer fund-raiser offers satisfactions of a quite different character than those derived from participation in the patient care program. While Chapter Volunteers are rewarded by the satisfactions which come from considering themselves benefactors, or the purveyors of information of vital importance to the welfare of the community, or the intermediaries between polio patients and the medical profession, participants in the March of Dimes are more likely to derive intrinsic enjoyment from the activities themselves, rather than from contemplating their broader significance. The key word which summarizes the satisfactions provided by the patient care program is "service"; the parallel term to describe the rewards of fund-raising is "performance."

The March of Dimes campaign provides opportunities for three types of performance. First, Volunteers obtain a sense of accomplishment from achieving the short-term, pragmatic goal of the campaign—raising money. Second, they obtain satisfactions from putting into practice organizing skills which they have learned either through their businesses or professions or through taking part in other fund-raising activities. Third, they obtain satisfactions from creativity, since the March of Dimes campaign places a premium upon initiative and imagination as tools for attracting public attention and support. Accordingly, the satisfactions derived from fund-raising are best described by considering each of these three types in turn.

### THE SATISFACTIONS OF ACCOMPLISHMENT

The point has already been made that a major distinguishing feature of the March of Dimes campaign is that it has a finite goal—raising as much money as possible during the month of January. It is important to note, however, that National Headquarters does not actually set quotas which local organizations are expected to meet, although it does announce to Volunteers how much money is needed to meet anticipated expenses. Since in recent years the costs of both research and patient care have been increasing, there is a tendency for March of Dimes Volunteers to compute on their own initiative how much more than last year's total must be raised in the county if the sum is to contribute its proportionate share to the increased national budget. As a result, Volunteers talk about a "quota" as if one had actually been given them. The Campaign Director in Eastern City, for example, declared that his "greatest satisfaction was exceeding the quota last year." Referring to the current campaign, he remarked that it was impossible to tell about its outcome at that point, but that "if we were assigned last year's quota we could have made that. Still hope to meet [this year's quota]."

The fact that March of Dimes Volunteers assign quotas to themselves is symptomatic not only of their need to define the task ahead but also of their need to interject a note of challenge into an activity which might well become routine. The March of Dimes has such widespread public acceptance that most local organizations can raise a good share of their proceeds with minimum effort: it is the final 10 or 20 per cent which presents a challenge to the enterprising Campaign Director. There is evidence also that for some March of Dimes leaders the element of competition which they themselves inject into the campaign gives added spice to their activities. Witness, for example, the statement of a March of Dimes Chairman in Glass City, who declared that what was important to him was "to see each year's drive larger than the past."

Volunteers who serve as Chairmen for several consecutive years have themselves as competitors. "I've been Chairman three years," recalled the Campaign Director in Power City, "and each and every year we've had higher contributions." And new Chairmen are in competition with their predecessors. A Chairman in Suburb County, for example, reported his greatest satisfaction came from "sweating to outdo the people who did it before," and a Chairman in College Town boasted he had netted in his first year as a Volunteer "three thousand dollars more than the person who preceded me. The next year, I got three thousand more."

## THE SATISFACTIONS OF ORGANIZING

Although National Headquarters distributes a *March of Dimes Guide* to each local organization, and even distributes training films which describe how to organize a campaign, the actual organization of the campaign is in the hands of the local Chairmen. Because the campaign has so many facets, it is often possible to recruit Chairmen for special activities who know from their professional or business experience a great many of the details involved in organization. Newspaper and radio editors become Publicity Chairmen; high school principals become Chairmen of Schools and Colleges; managers of beverage distribution companies become Chairmen of Coin Collectors; proprietors of movie houses become Theater Chairmen; local sports figures become Chairmen of the Sports Committee, etc. This detailed organization not only provides many individuals with the satisfaction of being "in charge"; it also makes the task less formidable, since it is "all part of a day's work."

It is not however the utilization of their professionally-learned skills which gives Volunteers the greatest sense of satisfaction, but rather the fact that the campaign affords opportunities for the display of *amateur* organizing skills. The joys of generalship are most apparent in statements which make reference to the "fun" of organizing. "I think the part I enjoyed most in the drive," recalled a Chairman in Corn City, "was organizing fund-raising activities, contacting the people, getting them to help me and helping them get rolling." Witness also the prideful account provided by the Fabric Town Campaign Director:

I have thirty-two people under me, all of them local Chairmen. When I call up Mr. X, he sets up an even larger organization than I have for the whole county. It's like a pyramid, with other small pyramids. Eventually you get everybody in on it. You've got to know how to organize.

For other Volunteers the task of organizing the campaign offers a different type of reward: a sense of participation in a "team," of finding a ready response from people who are approached to donate time and effort. "Just the way this campaign alone is run is terrific," the

Market Town Campaign Director commented enthusiastically. "When a new idea comes up you just throw it to someone else and they run with it." For the Campaign Director in Pulpwood City, a signal satisfaction was "the fun of getting people together who are willing to work. You get a sense of accomplishment." And the College Town Campaign Director noted that the most rewarding aspect of his activities had been "finding the warmth and response in the people you're working with. They're truly inspired. It brings out the best in them. That's outside of the satisfaction you get from raising the money you hoped for."

### THE SATISFACTIONS OF CREATIVITY

The March of Dimes is accepted by Volunteers as a challenge not only to their energy and their organizing skills, but to their imagination as well. The interview transcripts are replete with accounts of feats of local improvisation which give the campaign almost a Mardi Gras character. To cite one example, here is a story told with gleeful pride by a March of Dimes Chairman in Suburb County:

I'll never forget one thing we did. We pulled into the Market Basket [supermarket] Friday night. We said [over a loudspeaker]—the parking lot was full of cars you see—"There's a *killer* loose in this vicinity!" People jumped out of cars—that got a lot of attention you see. Then we informed them that it was infantile paralysis that was loose. Next day downtown everybody was talking about it, and they gave "like mad." I think the drive would be a real success if kept hot and strong the whole month.

There are other similar examples of Volunteer efforts to keep the March of Dimes "hot and strong" all month. Typical of these activities are the wheelbarrow collections in another town in Suburb County, in which passersby were "cornered" by determined Volunteers until they contributed; the Robin Hood campaign in Oldtown, where the Sheriff "held up" passing motorists for donations; the public auction in Market Town, at which the clothes of the fattest man in town, a well-known bank official, were sold to the highest bidder; and the emergency Mother's March held in a small town near Lumber City, in which the volunteer firemen donned their wives' dresses and canvassed the entire town in the fire truck. By and large these ebullient schemes were thought up by Volunteers themselves, although sometimes the idea first came to their attention in the campaign guide, which publishes each year stories of particularly successful special events. Through the medium of this guide, one man's "bright idea" becomes a standard feature of the next year's nationwide campaign.

The immediate significance of this type of behavior, and of the obvious satisfactions which it brings to participants, is that the campaign is, to quote one Volunteer, "full of pep and vinegar"—an energetic, original project of amateurs, not a packaged program promoted by professional fund-raisers. Of more fundamental importance, however, is the fact that fund-raising can assume, in some of its phases, some of the characteristics of legitimized play. In the eyes of Volunteers there is apparently no loss of dignity involved in the "high jinks" which serve as a release for the type of spontaneous creativity usually associated with the conventions of fraternal associations, or with college class reunions. In this case, however, decorum can be set aside by the participants with impunity, since the ultimate purpose which is served by the "stunts" they create and the "gimmicks" they invent is fundamentally serious and respected by the community at large.

### THE MOTHERS' MARCH ON POLIO

The campaign activity which has the broadest appeal for March of Dimes Volunteers as a participant activity and which is widely regarded as the single most effective technique for obtaining mass support is the Mothers' March on Polio. This activity differs from the standard house-to-house canvass in the fact that solicitors are invited into each house— the lighted porch light serves as the invitation. Characteristically, the Mothers' March was first "invented" by Volunteers—in Wausau, Wisconsin in 1951—and has since spread throughout the country. It is a "wind-up" event held at the end of January.

The Mothers' March is both a highly-organized activity and one which provides many opportunities for local improvisation. Organization-wise, it borrows much from military strategy. The woman in charge of each ward is a Colonel, and her assistants are Block Captains and Lieutenants; the event itself is a *march* against a common enemy. The headquarters office features a large map of the city, divided into areas of responsibility; in cities the size of Philadelphia, for example, 65,000 Marching Mothers are needed for complete coverage. And the quasi-military character of the event is highlighted by the fact that timing is an important feature: the goal is to visit every house in the county during one hour—usually between seven and eight o'clock in the evening. "Turn on Your Porch Light! Fight Polio Tonight!" is the theme of the advance publicity.

These features are standardized, recommended by National Headquarters and utilized almost everywhere. But the methods of heralding the event, and of obtaining public cooperation, are infinitely diversified. The use of bells, sirens, whistles, and searchlights to announce the start of the Mothers' March is suggested by National Headquarters, but there is a wide variety of local imaginative refinements. In Oil City, for example, a metronome was set ticking before a microphone in the local radio station a half hour before the March. The night march in a rural suburb in Pulpwood City was turned into a noonday "Dinner Pail March" by an energetic housewife who recognized the difficulties of covering a sparsely-settled community in the dark. Volunteers in Pinetree County, balked by deep snow the last day of January, sent out Marching Mothers early in February. And in the Spanish-speaking sections of Oldtown, votive candles were set on window sills in neighborhoods where many houses had no electric lights and no porches.

The account of one researcher who participated as an observer in the Mothers' March in South City serves to shed light on the role which the event plays in the lives of Volunteers having different responsibilities and from different social backgrounds.

The leadership of the March of Dimes in South City, as in many other communities throughout the South, is concentrated in the hands of an upper-class group which is active in a variety of civic and social projects. Accordingly, when the researcher assigned to South City expressed a desire to watch Volunteers actually conducting the March, the Chairman immediately suggested visiting a ward in the best residential section of the city, but agreed finally to arrange a visit to a ward in a grid-type neighborhood. Roughly one-third of this ward is shabby and run-down, another third consists of well-kept, turn-of-the-century frame houses intermingled with stucco bungalows of more recent vintage, and the final third, located on the periphery, consists of newly-built housing projects. These areas are largely occupied, respectively, by workers in a brick and tile factory; by white collar employees and tradesmen; and by skilled workers, newcomers to the city who work for the most part at a nearby defense plant.

The Mothers' March Colonel in charge of this ward, the wife of a chemical engineer, was participating in the March for the second year. She was assisted by her husband, who had borrowed a neighbor's

car and stood ready to share the job of picking up the jars of money
collected by Block Captains and their assistants. While waiting for the
seven o'clock starting signal, the Colonel volunteered the following
comment:

The reason why the March is so popular is that it costs only one hour of
time. Of course that's not actually so when you are on the organizing end of
things—I worked for three weeks before tonight. I like this better than any
other drive. In other drives—the Red Cross, Cancer—people will turn you
down. This is the only drive I like to work on. Lots of people give who don't
have children.

The researcher accompanied one Marching Mother on her route
around the block. She reported that perhaps three-quarters of the
houses had the porch light on, and that the occupants were ready with
a quarter, fifty cents or a dollar bill when the Marching Mother rang the
bell. One house on the block was completely dark, but the porch light
was on. Remembering her instructions, the Marching Mother rang
the bell. The door opened, and an elderly woman stepped from the
dark house on to the porch and offered a dollar bill. "I think this is
what you want," she said. For a moment the void which separates the
world of the blind from that of the seeing was temporarily bridged, and
the researcher learned what all blind people know as a matter of course:
the blind only use lights to help others.

Subsequently the researcher accompanied the Colonel as she drove
through the ward, stopping every few blocks to collect the jars filled
with money from the Block Captains. The following are some of the
remarks made as the car stopped and as the Block Captains placed the
jars on the rear seat:

First stop—(*Block Captain:*)
　　It was lots of fun. You know, I don't get to see my neighbors 'cause I
　　work—except on *this!*
Second stop—(*Block Captain:*)
　　I like to give time on this, for my part, although my husband—he's a
　　great one for these things—he gives [money] at work. I didn't know
　　about the vaccine—all I know is what I read in the *Readers' Digest*.
　　But I think it would sure be wonderful if you could beat this like all
　　the others. You know, like smallpox.
Third stop—(*Colonel to researcher, after collecting a jar:*)
　　They thank you for asking them. This little girl [i.e., a young woman]
　　asked me to *let* her work for us. She's new in the neighborhood. Her
　　husband's a fireman.
Fourth stop—(*Block Captain:*)

Now you be sure to let me know if anything like this comes up again. I love to help.
Fifth stop—(*Block Captain:*)
You're welcome. I was glad to do it. I enjoyed doing it!
Sixth stop—(*Block Captain:*)
There's five dollars of our own in that [jar]. That's a dollar apiece for all of us.
Seventh stop—(*Block Captain:*)
We've done right well. I got eight dollars—now isn't that nice. I didn't think I'd get two.
Eighth stop—(*Block Captain whose husband is the warden of the South City jail:*)
Some of the prisoners in the jail gave too. They asked my husband to let them.
Ninth stop—(*Colonel to researcher, after collecting a jar:*)
She works at the post office and she took this [jar] to work with her.

The researcher ended the evening at the largest bank in South City, where all the Colonels brought their carloads of jars. The Chapter Chairman, the Chapter Secretary, and several members of the Chapter Executive Board were all there, since all had taken an active part in the campaign. It is interesting to note that for these Volunteers the Mothers' March was a gala social event, and they were all dressed accordingly. What was most striking, however, was the air of intense preoccupation with which all of these Volunteers watched the giant tally sheets hung on the wall on which the collections from the various wards of the city—and from communities throughout the county—were recorded. The dominant concerns were "Will we make it [the goal]?" and "How was it going at this time last year?" It was obvious that the Mothers' March Chairman, to whom everyone deferred as the General in command, was under a severe strain as she sat receiving calls from all over the county. All eyes were on her, for this was the public test of her organizing skills and qualities of leadership.

This report on two groups of South City Volunteers—workers and leaders—thus offers a study in contrasts, yet it is quite apparent that for both groups the Mothers' March was an intimate challenge and a very real source of satisfactions. For each, participation offered opportunities for displaying leadership and initiative, for concerted action, for recreation, and for doing something "beyond themselves." For each, furthermore, the March was not only a fund-raising activity, but an institution, a community ritual which takes place every year. In a sense, then, the Mothers' March on Polio is a synthesis of the month-long campaign which precedes it, offering Volunteers on all levels of responsibility the same satisfactions of achieving a goal, of organizing, and of participating in a dramatic, enjoyable experience.

## Interest in Fund-Raising Among Chapter Volunteers

Since March of Dimes Volunteers were queried at length during the interviews concerning their fund-raising activities, and since they play no part in the year-round program of the Chapter, the previous section has been chiefly concerned with the satisfactions these Volunteers derive from fund-raising. But Chapter Volunteers are by no means inactive during the March of Dimes campaign; in fact, 70 per cent of the Chapter Volunteers interviewed played an active role in the campaign that year. Since in many counties there are relatively few opportunities for a large number of Volunteers to participate actively in the patient care program, the March of Dimes campaign provides one concrete activity in which those Chapter Volunteers who are so motivated can take part. This section describes the nature of the participation of Chapter Volunteers in the March of Dimes, and discusses the importance of this participation for the success of the Foundation's local program.

In the course of the interviews with Foundation Volunteers all phases of the Foundation's local program were discussed; accordingly, it was possible for the interviewer to ascertain in the case of most Volunteers which activity actually interested them most. Virtually all March of Dimes Volunteers were found to be primarily interested in fund-raising—hardly surprising since this is the only activity with which they have first-hand familiarity. But it is of some interest to note that more than one quarter of all Chapter Volunteers (28 per cent) are also primarily interested in fund-raising.

Since participation in fund-raising is an official obligation of Chapter Volunteers, and since the March of Dimes can only serve as an effective recruiting organization for the Chapter if Chapter Volunteers become acquainted with the interests and skills of March of Dimes Volunteers, it is important to examine the conditions under which Chapter Volunteers are most interested in fund-raising. This problem is most meaningfully approached by examining in turn the differences among Chapter Volunteers which emanate from 1) their participation in other fund-raising activities, 2) their mode of entry into the Foundation, and 3) the actual polio problem with which their Chapter is confronted.

### PARTICIPATION IN OTHER FUND-RAISING ACTIVITIES

Although most Foundation Volunteers are active members of other community organizations, March of Dimes Volunteers are more likely than Chapter Volunteers to take part in other fund-raising activities.* But among those Chapter Volunteers who do take part in the fund-raising activities of other organizations, 32 per cent cited fund-raising as their major interest in the Foundation's program, in contrast to 18 per cent of those who do not participate in other fund-raising campaigns.

### MODE OF ENTRY INTO THE FOUNDATION

The importance of the March of Dimes as a recruiting organization for local Chapters has previously been noted: nearly half of all Chapter Volunteers originally participated as March of Dimes Volunteers.† One consequence of this recruitment pattern is that it increases the likelihood that local Chapters will include in their membership Volunteers who are primarily interested in carrying out the Chapter responsibility of assisting during the March of Dimes campaign. Thirty-seven per cent of those Chapter Volunteers who initially joined the March of Dimes are primarily interested in fund-raising, in contrast to 20 per cent of those who initially joined the Chapter directly.

By the same token, the patterns of recruitment which result in the incorporation into local Chapters of four types of recruits also ensure that Chapters will have some members who are primarily interested in fund-raising. Here the contrast is even more marked: among Polio Veterans and Humanitarians, relatively few Volunteers are primarily interested in fund-raising (11 and 15 per cent, respectively); among Good Citizens and particularly among Joiners, on the other hand, fund-raising as much more of an appeal (29 and 40 per cent, respectively).

### THE LOCAL SITUATION

Since half of the proceeds of the March of Dimes remain in the treasury of local Chapters for the support of the local patient care program, Chapter Volunteers naturally have a vested interest in the success

* See p. 61.
† See p. 39.

of the March of Dimes. The scope of their major program, in fact, is
directly related to the amount of money which is raised each year. For
this reason, the provision in the *Manual for Chapters* that "the annual
fund-raising appeal must be supported fully by every Chapter and
branch chapter and the greatest possible cooperation and assistance
must be given to the local director appointed within its territory"[5]
is for the most part complied with not because it is a directive from
National Headquarters, but rather because it is in the best interest of
Chapter Volunteers to raise as much money as possible. Does the participation of Chapter Volunteers in the March of Dimes actually increase
the amount of money raised? Presumably it does, since the success of
the March of Dimes is directly related to the number of dedicated Volunteers who take part in it. But of greater interest for present purposes
is the fact, reported in Table 16, that Chapter Volunteers are more
likely to be primarily interested in fund-raising in counties in which
the March of Dimes is relatively *unsuccessful*.

**Table 16—Success of the Local March of Dimes and Interest in Fund-
Raising**

| PER CAPITA RECEIPTS FROM PREVIOUS MARCH OF DIMES[6] | PER CENT OF CHAPTER VOLUNTEERS WHOSE MAJOR INTEREST IS FUND-RAISING | N |
|---|---|---|
| Under $.25 | 37 | (38) |
| $.26–.34 | 28 | (32) |
| $.35–.46 | 24 | (29) |
| Over $.46 | 20 | (30) |

Table 16 indicates that the interest of Chapter Volunteers in fund-
raising is *inversely* correlated with March of Dimes success. The direction of causality is clear; the interest of Chapter Volunteers obviously
does not hinder March of Dimes success. Rather, it is in counties which
have had difficulty raising enough funds for the needs of the patient
care program that Chapter Volunteers are most likely to be interested.

A majority of Chapter Volunteers thus comply with the National
Headquarters request that they take part in the annual March of Dimes,
but only a minority regards fund-raising as its major area of interest.
Specifically, Chapter Volunteers who take part in the fund-raising campaigns of other organizations, who initially joined the March of Dimes,
and who entered the Foundation as Joiners are more likely than other
Chapter Volunteers to be primarily interested in fund-raising.

The active interest of this minority is important for the conduct of
the Foundation's local program for a number of reasons. First, since

the March of Dimes serves as the primary recruiting mechanism for
new Chapter Volunteers, it is important that present Chapter Volunteers take an active part in it, so they can become familiar with people
who are potential recruits for the Chapter. Second, the March of Dimes
serves a very useful function as a Chapter activity which can maintain
the interest of Chapter Volunteers who—either because of their own
predispositions or because of low polio incidence—are not active
participants in the patient care program. Third, the fact that Chapter
Volunteers who serve in counties which have relatively unsuccessful
March of Dimes campaigns are more likely than other Chapter Volunteers to be primarily interested in fund-raising contributes to the total
amount of money raised during the campaign. Without the active interest of these Volunteers, it may be concluded, even less money would
be raised in these counties.

## Volunteer Assessments of Reasons for Public Support

### THE ROLE OF THE MARCH OF DIMES

In many voluntary associations the annual fund-raising campaign
is a source of membership frustration and disappointment, since the
goal is seldom reached and so many requests for contributions are
denied. The March of Dimes differs sharply from campaigns such as
these, since practically all of the Volunteers interviewed reported both
a willingness on the part of the public to contribute and yearly increases
in the amount of money raised. This phenomenon is significant not
only as an indication of the widespread public acceptance of the legitimacy* of the March of Dimes but also as evidence of the existence
of an added dimension of the appeal which fund-raising has as a Volunteer activity. Implicit in their comments is the idea that fund-raising is
fully enjoyable only when giving approaches a spontaneous gesture of
generosity, devoid of coercive overtones. Public support, in other
words, is what makes the crucial distinction between fund-raising and
soliciting; Volunteers work most willingly if they are recognized as
community servants, not as unwelcome intruders. Witness, for example, a statement made by the Campaign Director in Pinetree County:

* The term "legitimacy" is used here not in the sense of "legality," but rather in
the Weberian sense. "Sanctity" is a near-equivalent.[7]

You get a big kick out of some of the sources of money. Like these kids up here, the individuals that will give surprisingly large contributions. I've had working people—for example, a common laborer—come in and give twenty dollars. I saw his billfold and he had one dollar left in it. He told me that he had his rent paid for a week, and he had a meal ticket for two weeks, but he wanted to be sure the money left over got into the March of Dimes.

As is the case with their evaluations of the Chapter as a community organization, most Volunteers chose to explain public willingness to support the March of Dimes in terms of comparisons with other community campaigns, particularly those of the Red Cross and the Community Chest.* The Chapter Chairman in Eastern City, for example, interviewed in his office in the used-car department of the Chevrolet agency, explained his own experience with public support in these terms: "I can go down to our shop, to our mechanics, with a March of Dimes container and those fellows are happy, happy to give. If I go down with a Red Cross or Community Chest or Heart box, they'll give, but they won't be so happy about it." Much the same sentiment was voiced by the Campaign Director in Payday Town, who said he had personally approached every businessman in his community—"every grocery store, filling station, bank, all the merchants"—and that he had never heard a word of criticism against the campaign. "Only two people actually said 'No'," he told the interviewer. "I like it because of the response," he continued. "This doesn't happen with the Red Cross."

*Method of approach.* The two reasons which Volunteers most frequently offer to explain both public support for the March of Dimes and its appeal to them personally are its method of approach and the modesty of its demands. The recurrent theme in comments referring to the first of these reasons is disapproval of the pressure tactics which Volunteers allege often characterize the campaigns conducted by other community organizations. Although avowed admirers of advertising skills—as evidenced by their wholesale approval of National Headquarters publicity materials—most Volunteers claim to resent the use of baldly "hucksterish" techniques in fund-raising if they seem to violate the right of independent choice of their fellow citizens. Witness this comment of the Corn City Chapter Secretary:

I solicited one year for the Red Cross, but I never will again. (*Why is that?*) Well, they gave me a list of cards with suggested amounts that people should give, and I don't plan to ask for definite amounts. Some of the people are in no position to give the help they expected. It was just too commercial.

* See pp. 206–207 for a discussion of the "scapegoating" function served by the Red Cross.

Similarly, the South City Campaign Director noted that the March of
Dimes, in contrast to the Community Chest, uses a "good approach."
He pointed out that "no one says to the corner grocer, 'Jim, we've got
you down for $100'." Thus, neither the petitioner nor the prospective
donor is embarrassed—a fact which Volunteers stress as a major distinguishing feature of the March of Dimes. "There isn't anything else
like this," reported the University City Chapter Chairman. "The Community Chest is not really voluntary. They go down and say, 'What are
you going to give?' It's not forced, but! Whereas this activity is strictly
voluntary."

*Modesty of demands.* Although Volunteers staunchly defend the
right of the individual to determine how much he should give, there is
a widespread feeling that everyone should give *something,* and there is
little hesitancy at obtaining "forced" token contributions. The establishment of highway "tolls" and similar activities provide ample evidence of the near-universality of this belief. Coercion of this type is
justified, in their opinion, because of the modesty of the demand. One
Market Town Volunteer explained this philosophy in these terms:

It's only a dime you have to give. If you go around and ask for big money—
take the Red Cross—they want a dollar or five dollars. It's much harder.
But the dime part—it was copied after Woolworth's I believe—every child
can take part in that.

Interpreting the reaction of the prospective donor, another Market
Town Volunteer explained that "if you do not have prestige in terms
of family, money, possessions or business, you get the feeling that if
you don't contribute to a campaign you're looked down upon. On
Polio, if you contribute a dime, you're a member of the organization."

### THE ROLE OF THE PATIENT CARE PROGRAM

Although Volunteers view the March of Dimes campaign itself as
conducive to public support, they also believe that the public supports
it because of the Foundation's activities in combating polio. And of
all of the Foundation's activities, the patient care program is most
frequently regarded as being most popular with the American public.

Since no Volunteer believes that the patient care program is other
than a necessary and important community service, and since all
Volunteers think that in some way the existence of the program en-
hances the fund-raising capacities of the Foundation, the question at
hand is not the intrinsic merits of the program, but rather the *relative*

merits of the patient care and research programs as "selling points" during the March of Dimes. Volunteers were asked during the interview to state their own views of the relative merits of the two programs, but not all were able to give a definite answer. Some were reluctant to make comparative evaluations on the basis of their limited knowledge and others chose to select other attributes of the Foundation as primarily responsible for public support. Some Volunteers, for example, believe that the prestige of President Roosevelt is in itself a reason for widespread public support; others feel that the public responds merely to the portrait of the crippled child on the March of Dimes poster; and still others believe that campaign techniques alone are the decisive factor. Several Volunteers, for example, observed that "you can sell iceboxes to Eskimos if you go about it correctly." A majority, however, stated a preference for either the patient care or the research program, and more than four out of every five of those who did express a preference stated that patient care is more important than research in terms of securing public support. Accordingly, the opinions of these patient care advocates deserve prior attention.

An analysis of the opinions of this group revealed that advocacy of patient care is not systematically related to the actual level of polio incidence; similar percentages of Volunteers advocate patient care as a selling point in high incidence, medium incidence, and low incidence Chapters. Three explanations may be advanced to account for this. First, patient care advocacy is closely related to involvement in the patient care program, which was shown above to be only slightly related to polio incidence. Second, advocacy of patient care is not necessarily based upon actual participation in the program. In counties which have had very little polio in recent years, all Volunteers—as a matter of course—have had limited contact with patient care; and in Chapters which have had a great deal of polio, it is primarily the Chapter Chairman and other Chapter Volunteers who actually participate, through handling administrative details and through actual contact with polio victims and their families. Third, advocacy of patient care as the major reason for public support is by no means based upon direct evidence. Through contact with other Volunteers, through exposure to Foundation publicity materials, and through exposure to the ethos of the Foundation, these Volunteers come to believe that patient care is the mainstay of the total program (or, in the case of research advocates, that its importance is exaggerated).

For these reasons, the "psychological" proximity of polio is as important to Volunteers as its actual proximity, and arm-chair judgments of the importance of patient care are as important as ones based upon first-hand experience. For if Volunteers believe—in areas of both high and low polio incidence, on the basis of either actual experience or *ad hoc* reasoning—that the patient care program is the major source of public support, then for them it *is* the mainstay, and attention should be given to their views. In the oft-cited theorem of W. I. Thomas, "if men define situations as real, they are real in their consequences."[8]

In defining the patient care program as the major reason for public support, Volunteers based their assumptions upon one or another of three major premises. First, patient care—in contrast to research—is the more understandable, tangible and emotionally appealing argument; in short, it provides the best publicity material. Research, on the other hand, lacks this appeal. Second, patient care has also a marked practical appeal, based on self-interest. The public believes, this argument runs, that March of Dimes contributions are a form of insurance premium. Third, patient care is a unique and indispensable community service. Since it is a cooperative movement for local aid, the public supports it as it supports other community services.

*Emotional appeal.* In advancing the thesis that patient care activities are superior to the research program as emotionally appealing arguments for obtaining public support, Volunteers made a clear-cut distinction between their own private understanding and appreciation of the research objective of the Foundation and their estimation of its lack of popular appeal. This is symptomatic of their own self-image as "insiders," informed "experts" who, as members of the organization, know the true facts. The public, however, is either naïvely uninformed or still in the process of learning about the fight against polio. This dual perspective is evident in statements such as that of the Chapter Vice-Chairman in Eastern City, who reported "I don't think they think of research. *We* think of research, of course, but the givers are thinking of the victims." Similarly, the South City Campaign Director noted that "I would tend to give more [for research], but the general public has not caught on. . . . Having pored over this stuff for months, my thinking is therefore not the same as the average person in the street." "Being closer to the literature," according to the March of Dimes Chairman for the Negro community in South City, is what makes the difference. "I would have a better perspective—the leaders are informed on research, but the public thinks of the child."

One reason why patient care is by far the better theme to stress in appealing for public support, some Volunteers argue, is that it is more easily comprehended. Explanations of the objectives of the research program, in contrast, are more difficult for the public to grasp. "The gamma globulin and vaccine stories, and research in general, are difficult to get across," according to a Pulpwood City Volunteer, since "they are rather sophisticated concepts for the layman." Moreover, patient care can be symbolized more readily and with greater impact, patient care advocates maintain, referring in particular to their greater success with the 1953 coin collector representing an iron lung than with the 1954 model representing a test tube.

Finally, some patient care advocates stressed the dramatic, emotional appeal of the program. "We're after dollars," one Soybean City Volunteer remarked, "and you get dollars by awakening sympathy, by talking about patient care, not by talking about 23 million dollars for a vaccine." Patient care appeals to the heart, a Harbor City Volunteer maintained, and "heart-strings and purse-strings are closely tied together." Other Volunteers referred to the fact that "all the drives that try to get rid of the human interest element become flops," and that the patient care theme is the epitome of this human interest appeal. "Polio cases," intoned the Secretary of the Eastern City Chapter, "are the be-all and the end-all." This last theme was mentioned repeatedly by Volunteers, who strengthened their point by citing examples of how other organizations have fared which do not have the advantage of the patient care argument for use in fund-raising campaigns. A March of Dimes Chairman in Wheat County summarized this point in concise terms:

The March of Dimes has been the most successful of any . . . you can see how you actually help the child through financial assistance. Cancer and Heart have forgotten that angle; they play up research. How much more could they get if they offered assistance to the cancer patient? In the National Foundation you can actually see what's going on. When you see an iron lung, you know that the Foundation is connected with helping the situation there, helping the child that's crippled.

*The appeal of self-interest.* One-fourth of all patient care advocates stressed not the emotional advantages of the patient care program, but its appeal to self-interest. A Fabric Town Volunteer summed up the situation succinctly: "The March of Dimes offers the chance to buy the cheapest paid-up insurance policy you can get—only a dime." For these Volunteers, this aspect of patient care activities represents the strongest argument with which to appeal for support from the public.

The Mothers' March Chairman in Pulpwood City, for example, attributed the success of the Foundation in its fund-raising campaigns to the fact that people know they would be helped if it happened to them. "In talking to women," she explained to the interviewer, "I've gotten the answer, 'I can't refuse because I know that if I need help I'll get it.' " Similarly realistic appraisals of the underlying reason for March of Dimes support are evident in the comment of a Mountain County Volunteer that "it all has to do with the fact that you don't have to worry—we'll take care of that," or in the assertion made by a Volunteer in College Town that "more than anything else" the patient care program gives the assurance that "if some member of your family becomes afflicted with polio you wouldn't have the burden of the expense."

Even more typical of this posture are those statements made by Volunteers which—while singling out the value of this appeal to legitimate self-interest—assign an equal value to the fact that patient care is tendered without the stigma of charity. It is the non-charity approach these Volunteers maintain, that invests the program with the character of group insurance, rather than philanthropy. "We stress what we believe," the Chapter Chairman in Central City told the interviewer. "It could happen to you, and the Foundation stands ready at all times to advance money. It's not charity, it is a trust fund, established by you and you and you to take care of you when you need it." In Suburb County, the Campaign Director reported that he had stressed the fact that "There's no charity involved. It's direct monetary aid, without numerous forms to fill out and taking the pauper's oath and that sort of thing. And here too they don't have to ask for it. The first contact is made by the Chapter." And for a Volunteer in Pulpwood City, to cite one more statement of this theme, the most important feature "in the long run" of the Foundation's over-all program is "the factor of getting together and assisting without the stigma of charity. . . . It's a new kind of community spirit."

*A community service.* The feature of the patient care program which won the most widespread approval as a "selling point" by Volunteers, however, is neither its emotional appeal nor its appeal to self-interest. Rather, it is the fact that the funds raised during the March of Dimes are spent *locally* for the care of polio victims in their own communities. In fact, 59 out of 100 patient care advocates expressed the opinion that the local spending aspect of the program is the most compelling argument for obtaining public support, and the one which has contributed most to establishing the Foundation's activities as a legitimate community enterprise in the eyes of the public. This is so, these Volunteers maintain, for two reasons. First, local spending for patient care is a feature unique to the Foundation. "Most organizations take the money out," commented a Wheat County Volunteer. "It goes to the headquarters. In the March of Dimes you can always say 'the money will stay here in the local area.'" Second, these local expenditures serve as tangible reminders of the mutual assistance function of the Foundation, which these Volunteers claim is a more telling argument with practical-minded Americans than is either altruism or humanitarianism. "Keeping it on the local level you are getting results," reported the Campaign Director in Steel City. "We've been getting money for expenses and research work, but people think of the money spent here." And an Oil City Volunteer maintained: "People like the local emphasis. They like to know that the money is used here." This explanation was offered in more dramatic terms by an Upstate City Volunteer:

The money which is passed on to the Foundation and the Chapter comes back to the people very specifically, and the people who do benefit act as missionaries, so that people are aware there is financial security they can call on from the National Foundation.

Finally, an even more realistic and somewhat shamefaced appraisal of this natural concern was given by a Harbor City Volunteer. "Aren't we selfish? We feel bad when you people on the East Coast are hit, but we're really not affected by it. The local cases make us more willing to help."

Even if only a small part of the March of Dimes income is actually spent locally, some Volunteers contend, the fact that half of the total sum is ear-marked and retained for use in the community as a hedge against emergencies is of key importance, since it transforms the Chapter into a trust organization acting in the interest of local citizens. The appeal of this policy to the general public, this argument runs, is that it coincides with the legitimate desire to "look after one's own." It is this sum—"the fifty per cent kept *here*"—that counts, according to a March of Dimes Volunteer in Upland County, simply because "people like the feeling of security it gives." In the opinion of the Chapter Secretary in University City, this local emergency fund is the main reason—"90 per cent of the reason" as he measured it—for the Foundation's success to date. "People are queer," he informed the interviewer, and "if they don't feel they are getting something back for it, the greatest per cent won't dig in. The fact that half of it is kept in this county is one reason for the large amount that can be taken in." Finally, here is a first-hand account, provided by a Chapter Volunteer in Central City, of this argument at work:

I've used this argument with people not interested and who had children: "Now listen, what would you do if your children got polio and we didn't have enough money to take care of them?" And the argument works.

## THE ROLE OF THE RESEARCH PROGRAM

The fact that a large majority of Volunteers believe that the patient care program is more effective than the research program in terms of securing public support reflects of course the situation in the early part of 1954, when the Foundation's research program had not yet involved a large number of Volunteers. Shortly after the interviews took place, however, Volunteer participation increased enormously. Throughout the country parents of small children were anxious to learn how the vaccine field trials of 1954 affected them, and, one year later, how they could get their own child vaccinated with the Salk vaccine. Accordingly, Volunteers addressed groups, distributed pamphlets, and explained the program to their acquaintances. In the 217 communities in which the Salk vaccine was actually tested during the 1954 field trials, Volunteer support was particularly essential. Volunteers came from the medical profession: in the course of a few months some 20,000 doctors and 40,000 nurses assisted on a volunteer basis. School systems contributed others: 50,000 school teachers and principals helped in the administration of the vaccine to school children. And over 200,000 lay Volunteers helped with the many tasks which the vaccine field trials entailed.[9]

In the light of these subsequent developments it is of interest to examine the comments made by the small group of Volunteers— twenty-four in all—who maintained *prior* to the development of the Salk vaccine that the Foundation's research program is a better "selling point" than patient care activities. These Volunteers advanced as a rationale for their contention the fact that patient care is only an *interim* goal, whereas efforts to discover a preventive which would eliminate epidemic polio represent progress toward the Foundation's *ultimate* goal. And, they added, public support can only be obtained for this final objective.

This attitude is revealed most specifically in such comments as that of the Campaign Director in Pulpwood City, who noted that "after all, we want to stop it, to eliminate it, not just care for people," or in the warning of the Chapter Treasurer in Wheat County: "You can't say that you are raising money to take care of people. The main thing is we are raising money to wipe this out." "Buying a crutch is not the answer to this thing," according to the Harbor City Campaign Director. "The research, the vaccine, that polio can be prevented—*that* should be the story."*

It is worth noting that these Volunteers, in affirming the superiority of research over patient care as a "selling point," seem to be projecting their own predispositions into their evaluations. In contrast to the patient care advocates, they make less of a distinction between their own private opinions and what they deem to be the best argument for use in convincing the public. Moreover, this contention also reflects a more fundamental attitude toward the Foundation itself. For these Volunteers, the Foundation has clearly a self-liquidating purpose; its main function is to eliminate polio, and the patient care program is a subsidiary activity. Not only do research advocates believe that this final objective should be kept in sight, but they also are convinced that the research argument has the greatest impact upon the public, since Americans in general are research-minded, and already "sold" on the infallibility of science and on the actual accomplishments of research for the prevention of polio. "They all feel that this time it's going to be it," is the opinion of the Campaign Director in Fabric Town, referring to the forthcoming 1954 vaccine field trials, "and that they [polio researchers] have found the cause of the disease. . . . The public knows the money goes for this sort of thing. You need dollars for research."

If the public is not already "sold," other research advocates contend, there is ample evidence that it is aware of the potentialities of polio research, since the precedent-setting victories over smallpox and diphtheria have set the stage for public recognition of gamma globulin and the Salk vaccine as tangible advances which presaged a final victory over the disease. "They look forward to the time when it will be like smallpox," a Lakeside County Volunteer declared, and giving to the March of Dimes represents, above all, the chance "to

---

* It is illustrative of the diversity of opinion often found within one Chapter that the Deputy Campaign Director in Harbor City is the patient care advocate, cited above, who maintained that "heart-strings and purse-strings are closely tied together."

conquer polio" to discover "how little Johnny and Mary will be protected against polio."*

* In sharp contrast to the views of the Volunteers reported above, which are four to
one in favor of patient care as the best "selling point" during the March of Dimes, are
the opinions of the rank-and-file March of Dimes Volunteers who were queried by
means of a mail questionnaire. When asked, "If you were in charge of publicity for the
March of Dimes, what would you place most emphasis upon?," more of these Volunteers
elected research than elected patient care. (42 per cent favored research, 35 per cent
favored patient care, and 23 per cent did not express a preference.) In short, there is a
definite relationship between position in the organization and judgments concerning the
Foundation activity which has most public appeal. Four out of five of the Volunteer
leaders who were personally interviewed, and who expressed a preference, are patient
care advocates, while more than half of the rank-and-file Volunteers who expressed a
preference feel that research is the best "selling point."

## chapter VI

# GIVING TO
# THE MARCH
# OF DIMES

## Introduction

THE STRUCTURAL and operational features of the Foundation which enable it to attract and hold a large and interested corps of Volunteers have been recurrent themes in this volume, but little has been said concerning the reasons underlying the financial support which the American public gives to the Foundation during the annual March of Dimes. Since the funds contributed during this campaign are an indispensable part of the Foundation's program, it is necessary to present some reasons for the success of the March of Dimes. In contrast to the previous chapter, which discussed the role played by *Volunteers* in making the campaign a success, this chapter is concerned with the reasons underlying *public* contributions to the March of Dimes.

One method of documenting the assertion that the March of Dimes is a highly-successful fund-raising campaign is to compare it with the campaigns of other organizations. There are six national organizations whose campaigns have sufficient similarity to make comparisons meaningful: Community Chest organizations, the American Red Cross, the Foundation, the National Tuberculosis Association, the American Cancer Society, and the American Heart Association.* Community Chest organizations exist in some 1,900 cities and towns throughout the United States, and the other five organizations hold campaigns in virtually every county in the country. In order to provide an indication

---

* Professional workers in these organizations often refer to the Red Cross, the four voluntary health associations considered here, and the National Society for Crippled Children and Adults as the "Big Six."[1] The Easter Seal Campaign of the National Society for Crippled Children and Adults is not included in the discussion which follows, since its total proceeds are less than those of any of the six campaigns discussed.

*176*

of their relative success, Table 17 presents the 1954 income of the
fund-raising campaigns of these six organizations.

**Table 17—1954 Income of Six Health and Welfare Associations***

| Association | 1954 Income⁸ |
|---|---|
| 1,900 United Community Campaigns (Community Chests, etc.) | $302,500,000 |
| American Red Cross | 85,502,867 |
| National Foundation for Infantile Paralysis | 67,907,000 |
| National Tuberculosis Association | 23,200,000 |
| American Cancer Society | 21,670,153 |
| American Heart Association | 11,350,195 |
| | $512,130,215 |

* Includes income from the annual fund-raising campaigns only.

As Table 17 indicates, the 1954 income from the fund-raising campaigns of these six organizations was over a half billion dollars, which
represents a third of the entire amount which Americans contribute to
philanthropies other than religious and educational institutions during
an average year.[3] Nearly three-fifths of this total was contributed to
Community Chest Campaigns for the support of some 21,000 local
health and welfare agencies.

Although Community Chest Campaigns and the Red Cross Drive
had more *income* in 1954 than any of the four voluntary health association campaigns, more *people* contributed to the March of Dimes and
the Christmas Seal Sale than to either the Community Chest or the
Red Cross. Based upon data collected during the present study of the
Foundation, Table 18 shows, for each socio-economic group in the
population, the proportion of contributors to each of the six major
campaigns.*

* A brief note on the validity of these data is needed. Obtaining accurate information concerning the extent to which people have contributed to fund-raising campaigns
is extremely difficult, both because people's memories are often very short with respect
to minor expenditures and because it is easy for people to indulge in "white lies" when
asked whether or not they have contributed money to a worthwhile campaign. Although
the first of these factors undoubtedly resulted in some under-reporting of contributions,
their net effect is undoubtedly over-reporting.

Given the fact of over-reporting, there are two corrective procedures possible. The
first is to devote less attention to the percentages of people who claim to have contributed than to the relative standing of the different organizations, or to comparisons
among sub-groups within the population.

A second corrective procedure is to eliminate from the "contributor" group those
individuals for whom there is other evidence which suggests that they did not in fact
contribute, or who contributed only through a payroll deduction—which cannot be
considered a voluntary contribution. See Appendix B for a description of the corrective procedures followed during this analysis. Table 18 and all subsequent tables
reporting upon contributions to these campaigns are based upon data corrected by
the procedures described in Appendix B.

### Table 18—Contributors to Six Fund-Raising Campaigns

PER CENT WHO CONTRIBUTED, BY SES

| Campaign* | High | High Middle | Low Middle | Low | Total† |
|---|---|---|---|---|---|
| March of Dimes | 81 | 76 | 66 | 55 | 69 |
| Christmas Seal Sale | 74 | 65 | 57 | 42 | 59 |
| Red Cross Drive | 58 | 54 | 50 | 43 | 52 |
| Community Chest‡ | 46 | 43 | 32 | 24 | 36 |
| Cancer Crusade | 44 | 33 | 33 | 17 | 32 |
| Heart Appeal | 38 | 33 | 29 | 15 | 29 |
| N | (411) | (552) | (548) | (414) | (2000) |

\* Since the interviewing took place in February, 1954, these data apply to the following campaigns:

| March of Dimes | January, 1954 |
|---|---|
| Christmas Seal Sale | December, 1953 |
| Red Cross Drive | March, 1953 |
| Community Chest | September-November, 1953 |
| Heart Appeal | February, 1953 and/or February, 1954 |
| Cancer Crusade | April, 1953 |

† Columns add to less than the total, since the socio-economic status of seventy-five respondents was not ascertained.

‡ These data are from a national sample. Accordingly, many people living outside of the 1,900 cities and towns which have Community Chest campaigns did not have an opportunity to contribute to the Community Chest. In the four cities, all of which have Community Chest campaigns, 57 per cent of the population contributed to the Community Chest.

The most striking aspect of the data presented in Table 18 is that the Community Chest and the Red Cross Drive—in spite of their greater income—had fewer contributors than either the March of Dimes or the Christmas Seal Sale. Their larger income, in other words, is obtained through a smaller number of large contributions. In 1954, for example, seventy-four Community Chests throughout the United States received nearly 40 per cent of their total income from business and industrial firms.[4] But all four voluntary health campaigns receive mostly small gifts, so it is of utmost importance that the campaign reach as many people as possible, from all social strata. As Table 18 indicates, one reason for the success of the March of Dimes is that a majority of people from even the lowest socio-economic group contributes to it.

How is it that the March of Dimes has been so successful in obtaining contributions from such a large segment of the American population? A number of answers to this complex question have already been given in previous chapters; a brief recapitulation is in order here. First, the Foundation has a large group of interested and active Volunteers—more Volunteers, in fact, than many organizations have contributors. Since most Volunteers make contributions, and are able, at the very least, to obtain contributions from their close friends and colleagues, the size of the Foundation's membership alone contributes a great deal to its success in fund-raising. Second, polio is a disease which is widely-known in America, and about which a substantial segment of the American population feels concern. Its epidemic nature, its crippling aftereffects, its selection of children as the major victims, and its tendency to strike more frequently in prosperous communities than it does in others all serve to maintain a high level of public interest and concern. Third, the Foundation's patient care program, according to the testimony of Volunteers, is a major asset with respect to obtaining public support, since people respond favorably to the fact that the funds they contribute are used locally to assist polio victims.

In this chapter, a different mode of explanation is attempted. Instead of answering the question of why the public supports the March of Dimes so generously by inference from the state of public opinion concerning polio, or by reporting the views of Volunteers themselves, the attitudes and behavior of the public itself are examined. In the course of the chapter, accordingly, it will be possible to reach some conclusions concerning public response to the Foundation's local program.

## Public Participation in the March of Dimes

The views of Volunteers concerning the reasons why the public supports the March of Dimes were not of course expressed on the basis of any systematically collected evidence of public sentiments. The comments cited in the previous chapter were based in part upon conversations held with a few contributors and in part upon the predispositions of the Volunteers themselves. Since Volunteers think so highly of the patient care program, they naturally tend to project their own feelings on to the public at large.*

If we disregard for a moment the testimony of Foundation Volunteers, however, and consider only the components of the campaign itself, it is possible to derive logically a number of characteristics which the March of Dimes, or any other fund-raising campaign based upon small contributions, must have if it is to achieve maximum success. Since most contributions are small, the March of Dimes must obtain some contribution from a substantial proportion of the national popu-

* See pp. 137–148.

lation. By the same token, it must obtain more than one contribution from many people. Since many people are unaware of the Foundation's financial needs, and the specific uses to which funds are put, a successful campaign must obtain contributions not only from people who are informed on these matters but also from those who are not informed. Furthermore, since polio has a relatively low incidence rate, a successful campaign must reach people who have not had first-hand familiarity with the disease as well as those who have direct experience with it. Finally, contributions must be obtained from people who are relatively unconcerned about the threat posed by polio as well as from those who are very concerned. This chapter is devoted to a discussion of the extent to which the March of Dimes campaign fulfills these five logically-derived requirements.

WIDESPREAD PUBLIC PARTICIPATION

It was noted in the Introduction to this chapter that people of higher socio-economic status are more likely than others to contribute to the March of Dimes—as well as to other fund-raising campaigns.* This phenomena is reflected on a nationwide scale by the per capita receipts during the March of Dimes of counties having different income levels. As Table 19 demonstrates, richer counties are more likely than poorer ones to contribute substantial sums to the March of Dimes.

**Table 19—1953 March of Dimes Proceeds in Counties Served by Foundation Chapters**

| 1953 per capita proceeds[6] | MEDIAN FAMILY INCOME OF COUNTY[5] | | |
|---|---|---|---|
| | High | Medium | Low |
| $.47 and over | 33% | 20% | 2% |
| .35–.46 | 30 | 22 | 4 |
| .26–.34 | 24 | 23 | 12 |
| .25 and less | 13 | 35 | 82 |
| | 100% | 100% | 100% |
| N | (720) | (1575) | (778) |

* See Table 18, p. 178.

The very marked correlation between the income level of counties and their total per capita contributions to the March of Dimes reflects of course a higher level of all kinds of expenditures in richer counties. Richer counties also have more automobiles, more bathtubs, and a higher movie attendance per capita. But per capita proceeds from the March of Dimes are of course a quite different matter than *individual* contributions; as Table 20 demonstrates, people who live in poor counties, regardless of their own personal income, are *more* likely to contribute to the March of Dimes than are people living in rich ones.

### Table 20—Contributors to the March of Dimes

| Median Family Income of County | PER CENT WHO CONTRIBUTED | | | | | |
|---|---|---|---|---|---|---|
| | $5,000 and over annual income | | $3,000–4,999 annual income | | Less than $3,000 annual income | |
| High | 76 | (258) | 73 | (501) | 52 | (328) |
| Medium | 86 | (59) | 82 | (130) | 63 | (183) |
| Low | 85 | (40) | 84 | (84) | 67 | (357) |

The distributions reported in Table 20 are of course quite the opposite of those reported in Table 19. More money is raised in richer counties, but more people contribute in poorer ones. How may this anomaly be explained?

Consider for a moment the relationship between the median family income of a county and the personal family income of the people living in it. In rich counties, people who have an income of $5,000 or more are not regarded as being particularly rich; by the same token, upper income people in poor counties—who constitute only a small proportion of the population in such counties—are very rich, comparatively speaking. Similarly, people living in rich counties who have a family income of less than $3,000 are regarded by others as poor, while people having the same income in poor counties are not necessarily viewed as being badly off—many people in such counties may have an even smaller income than they have. For these reasons, personal income is not very meaningful as an absolute figure; it acquires its greatest meaning when it is placed in proper perspective by the median family income of the county.

The implications of these relationships for the success of the March of Dimes are quite apparent. Contributing is not related to *actual* income, but to *relative* income. Because of this relationship, the March of Dimes reaches a substantial proportion of the population in all types of counties—rich and poor alike. In rich counties, people contribute more *generously,* which accounts for the strong correlation between median family income and per capita receipts, but even in the poorest counties most people give *something.*

#### MULTIPLE CONTRIBUTIONS

*Comparisons among campaigns.* Each of the six major fund-raising campaigns attempts to use as many techniques as possible; at the same time, most concentrate upon one or two techniques which in the past have proved successful. The most specialized campaign is the Christmas Seal Sale, which is largely confined to mailing seals to everyone in the community, with a request that a contribution be returned.* The Red Cross and most Community Chest organizations rely largely upon a house-to-house convass. The March of Dimes, the Cancer Crusade, and the Heart Appeal, on the other hand, have developed more diversified techniques.

In the four cities studied intensively, all six organizations held active campaigns in the year preceding the research. Table 21 shows both the percentage of the adult population of each city which contributed to each campaign and the mean number of gifts made by each contributor.†

### Table 21—Mean Gifts per Contributor in Six Fund-Raising Campaigns, Four Cities

| Campaign | Per Cent Who Contributed | Mean Gifts Per Contributor |
|---|---|---|
| Christmas Seal Sale | 77 | 1.02 |
| March of Dimes | 70 | 1.34 |
| Community Chest | 57 | 1.13 |
| Red Cross Drive | 50 | 1.07 |
| Heart Appeal | 45 | 1.03 |
| Cancer Crusade | 43 | 1.05 |
| N | (1324) | |

In these four cities the March of Dimes and the Christmas Seal Sale reached more people than any of the other four campaigns, but except in the case of the March of Dimes, most contributors gave only once. The overwhelming majority of people who purchased Christmas Seals, for example, said that they had contributed only through the mail. March of Dimes contributors, on the other hand, contributed an average of 1.34 gifts to the campaign. Just as Community Chest Campaigns and the Red Cross Drive have greater success than health cam-

---

* In recent years, however, local Tuberculosis Associations have attempted to increase their income by selling seals in public places such as post-offices.

† Data concerning the number of gifts contributed were obtained by asking each contributer how he had made his contribution—through the mail, in a coinbox, to a personal solicitor at the door, attending a benefit, or in some other way. The data presented in Table 21 under-estimate the actual number of gifts per contributor for two reasons. First, even if a person had dropped coins in a number of boxes, attended several benefits, etc., he would have been credited with only one contribution. Second, as mentioned previously people's memories are short in such matters, and it is very probable that many respondents told the interviewer how they had made one contribution, but neglected to mention others they had made. Under-reporting, however, does not affect the *relative* standing of the campaigns listed in Table 21.

paigns because they receive *larger* gifts, the March of Dimes has greater success than the other three health campaigns in large part because many people make contributions *several* times.

*Sources of income.* The multi-faceted character of the March of Dimes campaign is illustrated in Table 22, which shows for each of the four cities the proportion of all receipts during the 1954 campaign received from each major fund-raising activity.

**Table 22—Sources of Income During the 1954 March of Dimes, Four Cities**[7]

| Source of Income | Eastern City | Central City | South City | Desert City |
|---|---|---|---|---|
| Mothers' March on Polio | 23% | 42% | 26% | 21% |
| Special events* | 49 | 10 | 12 | 28 |
| Employer-employee gifts | 10 | 11 | 1 | – |
| Collections in schools and colleges | – | 12 | 11 | 14 |
| March of Dimes Cards (mailed contributions) | 9 | 12 | 3 | 9 |
| Coin boxes | 5 | 8 | 1 | 4 |
| Armed Forces contributions | – | 4 | 44 | 14 |
| Special gifts | 4 | 1 | 2 | 10 |
| | 100% | 100% | 100% | 100% |

\* Includes collections in motion picture theaters, radio and television receipts, contributions from clubs and organizations, benefit performances, sports events, etc.

Several aspects of Table 22 deserve special comment. First, note the great diversity in sources of income among the four cities. This diversity is in part a reflection of the fact that the actual conduct of the campaign is in the hands of Volunteers, who place special emphasis upon the activities which interest them most and which they feel have the greatest chance for success, and in part it is an outgrowth of the local situation. Eastern City, for example, has no armed forces installations nearby, but takes advantage of the fact that its population is very civic-minded and "events" conscious. A fraternity from a near-by college, for instance, ran a car-wash in front of the City Hall for two weeks: hundreds of local citizens paid two dollars to have their car washed, and each two dollars went to the March of Dimes. Events such as this brought in nearly half of the total sum collected. Central City, on the other hand, received the largest share of its income from the Mothers' March on Polio. A large Army post on the outskirts of South City contributed nearly half of its total receipts, while Desert City had a much more "balanced" campaign than the other three communities.

Second, it is noteworthy that only in Desert City, the most prosperous of the four cities, did special gifts play a significant role in the total campaign, yet only 10 per cent of its receipts came from this source.

Finally, it is quite apparent that regardless of local conditions all four campaigns obtained an important share of their income from the Mothers' March on Polio, which in recent years has accounted for about one-fourth of the nationwide income from the March of Dimes. This phase of the campaign was described in some detail in an earlier chapter, in which its importance as a Volunteer activity was indicated;* our purpose here is to demonstrate the role played by the Mothers' March in these four communities.

*The role of the Mothers' March.* The goal of the Mothers' March on Polio is to have a Marching Mother stop in at every house in the community which has its porch light on during the designated hour. This goal, however, was not fully realized in any of these four cities. The Eastern City campaign achieved the best coverage—72 per cent of all households—and the Desert City campaign the poorest. Only 46 per cent of the households in Desert City were approached during the Mothers' March. In all four cities, people from higher socio-economic groups were more likely to be reached than were others.

There are a number of reasons for this imperfect coverage. The Mothers' March on Polio is not a door-to-door solicitation, but a campaign in which the solicitor is invited to enter: the lighted porch light serves as her signal. Although Volunteers reported that Marching Mothers often stopped in at houses at which the porch light was not lit—"just in case they forgot to light it"—many houses were undoubtedly passed by because no signal appeared. Some people might not have heard about the Mothers' March, and so didn't turn on their lights, although unawareness was minimized in these four cities by extensive advance publicity. Others might have heard about the Mothers' March, but forgot to turn on their light; others might not want to have been bothered; still others might have gone shopping or visiting or to the movies that evening. Or, in spite of the best of planning, their neighborhood might not have been covered.

In all four of these cities the Mothers' March was run by middle- and upper-class women. In Central City, the Jaycee (Junior Chamber of Commerce) wives conducted the campaign; in the other three cities, it was a project of the Parent-Teachers' Association. It is quite conceivable, accordingly, that these women covered their own neighbor-

* See pp. 158–162.

hoods, and neighborhoods similar to their own, more thoroughly than they did working-class neighborhoods. Furthermore, the crucial element of the Mothers' March—the lighted porch light—is itself a determinant of differential success. Many working-class people live in multiple-family dwellings, or in houses without porch lights, or in houses which are not visible from the street. All of these factors serve to explain the failure of the Mother's March to obtain complete coverage in these communities.

If the Mothers' March were the only campaign technique utilized, accordingly, March of Dimes receipts would be much lower than they are. But in these four cities, a majority (57 per cent) of even those people who were *not* reached by the Mothers' March nevertheless contributed to the March of Dimes in some other way. Among people who *were* solicited during the Mothers' March, 81 per cent contributed. These percentages demonstrate of course the importance of the Mothers' March to the March of Dimes campaign, since people who are solicited directly are more likely than others to contribute.* But they also show the importance of a multi-faceted campaign, since most people who were missed by the Mothers' March contributed nevertheless. In fact, the proportion of contributors among this group is higher than the proportion of contributors to either the Heart Appeal, the Cancer Crusade, or the Red Cross Drive among *all* respondents, and equal to the proportion of contributors to the Community Chest.† The importance of multiple contributions to a campaign based upon the strategy of the small gift is thus apparent.

## CONTRIBUTIONS FROM INFORMED AND UNINFORMED PEOPLE

The two requirements of the fund-raising program discussed thus far—widespread public participation and multiple contributions—are best described as *characteristics of the entire campaign*. The requirements that contributions be obtained from informed and uninformed people, from experienced and inexperienced people, and from concerned and unconcerned people, on the other hand, pertain to *characteristics of contributors*. For this reason, a somewhat different method of presenting the material is required. This discussion, accordingly, as well as the two which follow, is divided into two parts. In the first part

* They also document the assertions of Volunteers that they often stopped in at houses which did not have the porch light on. If this were not the case, 100 per cent of those who were visited would have contributed.

† See Table 21, p. 182.

of each discussion, the extent to which the American public is informed about Foundation activities, has had experience with polio, and is concerned over polio is described; in the second part, the relationship of these characteristics to contributing to the March of Dimes is examined.

*Information concerning Foundation activities.* The judgments of Volunteers concerning the relative importance of the patient care and research programs in securing public support during the March of Dimes, reported earlier,* are predicated upon two assumptions. First, since the March of Dimes by its very nature requires contributions from a large proportion of the public if it is to succeed, Volunteers assume that people are generally aware of the uses to which the funds are put. Second, they assume that knowledge of the program which the money supports is a factor which increases the probability that individuals will contribute. It is accordingly necessary to examine the extent to which these assumptions are valid.

Almost everyone in America knows in a general way about the March of Dimes—as evidenced by the fact that 83 per cent of the American public, when asked which health campaigns they had heard about, mentioned the March of Dimes. Knowledge of the fact that the funds collected during the March of Dimes are used for patient care is less widespread, however, since there are a number of other ways in which the funds raised to combat polio could be, and are, utilized: research, public education, professional training, etc. Furthermore, knowledge of the fact that funds are used for patient care is a quite different matter than knowledge of the fact that an organization exists in the community to which people can turn for financial assistance. In fact, 70 per cent of the public knows in a general way that funds are used for patient care, but only 42 per cent knows that they could turn to the Foundation Chapter in their community if polio should strike their family.[8] Patient care as a *general concept,* therefore, is much more widely known than the *organizational mechanism* which has been established to administer it. Volunteers, it is quite apparent, often tend to overestimate the extent to which the public knows about their Chapter and its activities.†

* See pp. 167–175.
† Some Volunteers, however, have a more realistic view. Witness, for example, the Campaign Director in Harbor City, who, when asked if he thought most people in the county knew about the Chapter and its patient care program, replied "It has had pretty good publicity, but there's a high per cent of boobs in any community."

How do people come to learn about the local patient care program? Exposure to campaign publicity is certainly one way, although an examination of the publicity materials used both nationally and in the thirty-seven Chapters studied intensively has revealed that very little attention is devoted to the community service aspects of the Foundation's program. But campaigns are by no means the only source of information. People talk with others about both community activities and the experiences of their friends, and through these countless conversations knowledge of this service function is disseminated throughout the community. And, since people of higher socio-economic status generally have many opportunities to talk informally with a large number of people, they are quite likely (59 per cent) to know about their local Chapter's patient care program. Among people of low socio-economic status, on the other hand, only 23 per cent know of the program.

The fact that people from the lowest income group—who are of course most in need of the type of assistance furnished by the patient care program—are least aware of the fact that they could receive assistance from the Foundation if polio should strike in their family provides additional confirmation for a finding which has emerged from research in various areas. People who could benefit most by knowing certain items of information, or by holding certain attitudes, are also least likely to have this information or these attitudes. Herbert Hyman, for example, in a paper which summarizes many of the correlates of socio-economic status, has demonstrated that poor people are less likely than rich people to place a high valuation upon the importance of sending their children to college, or the importance of having a job which is widely regarded as prestigeful.[9] The two most important routes to a higher status—education and job advancement—are thus least appreciated by the people who could benefit most by them. Paul Lazarsfeld, on the basis of data first presented in *The American Soldier,* has pointed out that less educated soldiers, who were, by and large, most discriminated against by the Army's promotion system, were also less critical of the system.[10] And in summarizing his findings of a study of youth in Austria, Lazarsfeld notes:

The underprivileged youth has seen less, read less, has heard about less, has in his whole environment experienced fewer changes than the socially privileged, and he simply knows of fewer possibilities.[11]

Although high status people are two and a half times as likely as
low status people to know about the patient care program, it is clear
that socio-economic status is not the only important factor. Rather, as
mentioned earlier, high status people have more opportunities to find
out about community activities in general, since they meet and talk to
more people. Furthermore, they are more likely to participate in community organizations, which in itself leads to opportunities to find out
about what's going on in the community. Table 23 shows the importance of community organizations as communications centers.

**Table 23—Membership in Community Organizations and Awareness
of the Local Patient Care Program**

| | PER CENT WHO ARE AWARE OF THE PROGRAM | | | | | |
|---|---|---|---|---|---|---|
| SES | Membership in two or more organizations | | Membership in only one | | Membership in none | |
| | | N | | N | | N |
| High | 70 | (162) | 46 | (125) | 56 | (124) |
| High middle | 54 | (172) | 44 | (161) | 43 | (219) |
| Low middle | 53 | (104) | 46 | (161) | 34 | (283) |
| Low | 30 | (56) | 22 | (132) | 22 | (226) |

Socio-economic status is clearly a primary determinant of awareness of the patient care program, but on each status level people who
belong to two or more community organizations are more likely than
others to know about the program. This is less true of low status people
than of others, since the community organizations to which they belong
are likely to be separated from the main stream of community life. But
people in the two middle status groups who belong to community organizations are nearly as likely as people in the upper status group who
don't belong to any organizations to be aware of the patient care program. Participation in community organizations, in other words, serves
as a funtional equivalent for high status among these people. Although
their social status makes it unlikely that they will obtain much information about community activities in the course of conversations with the
banker or the banker's wife, they are nearly as likely to find out what is
going on by attending meetings at the Elks Club, or by sewing with
the members of the Order of the Eastern Star.

Although the patient care program is the major local activity of
the Foundation, it is not of course the only aspect known to the public.
In order to provide an indication of the relative awareness on the part
of the public of different aspects, Table 24 presents the percentage of
people who scored high on each of seven knowledge items.

## Table 24—Knowledge of Foundation Activities

|  | PER CENT WHO SCORED HIGH ON EACH KNOWLEDGE ITEM, BY SES | | | |
| Knowledge item | High SES | N | Low SES | N |
| --- | --- | --- | --- | --- |
| Patient care program | 80 | (963) | 61 | (962) |
| President Roosevelt | 71 | (963) | 47 | (962) |
| Chapter in the county | 66 | (593) | 48 | (731) |
| Chapter patient care program | 52 | (963) | 33 | (962) |
| Research theme | 49 | (593) | 36 | (731) |
| Sponsorship of March of Dimes | 47 | (963) | 23 | (962) |
| Nonparticipation in Community Chest | 45 | (593) | 22 | (731) |

People having a high socio-economic status are considerably more informed about all Foundation activities than are people having a low status. But of much greater importance in terms of the present discussion is the rank order of the knowledge items presented in Table 24. A clear majority of the population knows that March of Dimes funds are used for patient care of some kind. And a bare majority knows that President Roosevelt founded the Foundation* and that a local Chapter exists in the county. But less than half of the public knows either of the other four knowledge items presented in Table 24. Even among people of high socio-economic status only 52 per cent know about the local patient care program; only 49 per cent were aware that research had been the major theme of the recent March of Dimes campaign; only 47 per cent were able to identify the Foundation as the organization which sponsors the March of Dimes; and only 45 per cent knows that the March of Dimes does not participate in the Community Chest.

The average citizen, accordingly, knows that a campaign called the March of Dimes is held each year to raise funds to assist polio patients; and there is a fair probability that he knows both that President Roosevelt founded the Foundation and that there is a local unit of the Foundation in his county. But it is unlikely that his knowledge of Foundation activities extends beyond these basic facts. Clearly, if the March of Dimes depended greatly upon public awareness of the Foundation's activities it would not be as successful as it is in obtaining contributions from a majority of the population.

* Interestingly enough, people under forty years of age are as likely to know of President Roosevelt's role in the Foundation as are people over forty, in spite of the fact that they were at most only twenty-three years of age at the time the Foundation was established. The fact that 59 per cent of the population knows that President Roosevelt founded the Foundation is itself an indication of a relatively high level of public awareness. During the peak of presidential election campaigns, for example, public opinion polls frequently show that less than half of the public can name both vice-presidential candidates.

*Information and contributions.* It is quite clear from the data presented in Table 24 that many people contribute to the March of Dimes without much specific knowledge of the Foundation's activities. Although a majority in all socio-economic groups contributes, a majority of high status individuals are uninformed concerning three of the seven knowledge items, and a majority of low status people are uninformed concerning six of the seven. A more direct measure of this phenomenon could of course be presented by showing the percentage of contributors among people who scored high and low on each of these items. This procedure, however, would burden the text with tables; accordingly the mean percentage of contributors among people with high and low scores on the seven items has been computed in Table 25.

### Table 25—Contributors to the March of Dimes, by Knowledge Score

| | PER CENT WHO CONTRIBUTED TO THE MARCH OF DIMES, BY SES | |
|---|---|---|
| Knowledge score* | High SES | Low SES |
| High | 82 | 75 |
| Low | 70 | 55 |

\* The percentages reported in Table 25 are the mean percentages of contributors among people who scored high and low on the seven knowledge items presented in Table 24.

Among both high and low status people, a majority contributed to the March of Dimes—regardless of their knowledge scores—but there is nevertheless a substantial difference between the percentage of contributors among people with high and low scores. This is particularly true among low status people, who, if they are highly-informed, are more likely than uninformed high status people to contribute to the March of Dimes.

Do these data indicate that people contribute to the March of Dimes *because* they know these facts about Foundation activities? That they do so at least in part is suggested by the frequent statements of Volunteers, based upon first-hand contact with contributors. But in the light of what we know about how the March of Dimes campaign is organized, and about the specific fund-faising techniques which are utilized, a much more plausible explanation accounting for these percentage differences presents itself. People who are most knowledgeable about Foundation activities are precisely the people who participate most widely in community activities: they work at more prestigeful occupations, have a wider circle of acquaintances, and belong to more community organizations. As a result, they are more likely to come into contact with some phase of the March of Dimes campaign, and thus more likely to contribute. In short, the basic strategy of the March of Dimes campaign—to ensure that the mechanisms for making small contributions are widely available in the community—is most effective in reaching people who "get around" in the community. The fact that these are also the people who are best informed about Foundation activities appears to be a secondary determinant of March of Dimes contributions.

It will be recalled that Volunteer leaders believe that the patient care program is the major "selling point" during the March of Dimes, while rank-and-file Volunteers place more emphasis upon the research program.* Does the finding reported in Table 25 that there is a relatively minor relationship between knowledge of Foundation activities and contributions to the March of Dimes prove both groups of Volunteers to be wrong? In one sense it does, since when knowledge of the patient care and research programs are individually correlated with contributions, neither program turns out to have a higher correlation than the other. But in another sense both groups of Volunteers are right, since people who know of either program are somewhat more likely to contribute. Much more important than these correlations, however, is the fact that the mere existence of these two programs places the stamp of community approval upon the March of Dimes campaign; it ensures, for example, the cooperation of newspaper and radio editors, public officials, employers, and union leaders. Without such community approval, it may be concluded, the March of Dimes could not carry out an extensive campaign which reaches a majority of Americans—informed and uninformed people alike.†

CONTRIBUTIONS FROM EXPERIENCED AND INEXPERIENCED PEOPLE

*The proximity of polio.* Since polio is a relatively infrequent disease, in contrast, for example, to cancer and heart diseases, most people have not had first-hand contact with it. That is, neither they nor a member of their family has ever had polio. On the other hand, many people have had some form of second-hand contact with polio; they have read something about it in newspapers and magazines, they have heard people talking about it, etc. Furthermore, since the crippling aftereffects of

---

* See pp. 167–175.

† Ignorance of the uses to which funds are put is of course not confined to March of Dimes contributors, although it was not possible to obtain comparative data concerning other organizations during the interviews. Norman Miller has made a similar observation concerning Jewish philanthrophy.[13]

polio are highly visible, there is a high probability that the acquaintances of a person who has had a severe attack will be aware of his experience. Needless to say, this is not necessarily the case with many
other diseases.

People are apt to come into contact with polio in a variety of ways.
They may be living in an area of high polio incidence; they may know
someone who has had polio, or have heard a good deal of talk about
the disease; they may be parents of young children, agonizingly aware
of its threat; or they may know someone who has been helped by the
local Chapter. Since these five experiences all refer to the actual psychological "proximity" of polio to individuals, this generic term has
been adopted to describe them.* Table 26 summarizes the extent to
which the American public has had each of these five experiences.

### Table 26—The Proximity of Polio

| Proximity item[14] | PER CENT WHO SCORED HIGH ON EACH PROXIMITY ITEM | N |
|---|---|---|
| News about polio | 64 | (1324) |
| Acquaintance with a victim | 59 | (2000) |
| Young children in family | 37 | (1983) |
| Acquaintance with a Chapter-assisted victim | 18 | (1324) |
| High polio incidence | 15 | (2000) |

The most frequent experience of all is simply having heard a great
deal about polio in recent years. More than half of the public knows
someone who has had polio, and more than a third are parents of young
children, and hence particularly concerned over the threat of polio.
But fewer than one out of every five persons knows someone personally
who has been helped by the local Chapter, and only 15 per cent live in
areas which have had a recently-high level of polio incidence. Contact
with polio and its victims, although by no means rare, is manifestly not
a part of the everyday experience of most Americans.

*Proximity and contributions.* Do experiences of the type reported
in Table 26 increase the probability that a person will contribute to the
March of Dimes? Table 27 answers this question by reporting the percentage of March of Dimes contributors among people who have and
have not had each of these five experiences.

---

* The *most* "proximate" experience is of course having had polio oneself. Since the
incidence of polio is comparatively low, very few of the respondents in either the
nationwide or the four city survey had had polio themselves. Those who had were
classified as having known someone who had had polio, or as having known someone helped by the local Chapter.

**Table 27—Contributors to the March of Dimes, by Polio Proximity Scores**

| Proximity item[15] | PER CENT WHO CONTRIBUTED | | | |
|---|---|---|---|---|
| | High score | N | Low score | N |
| News about polio | 73 | (830) | 66 | (494) |
| Acquaintance with a victim | 72 | (117) | 65 | (827) |
| Young children in family | 76 | (741) | 65 | (1242) |
| Acquaintance with a Chapter-assisted victim | 80 | (243) | 68 | (1081) |
| High polio incidence | 72 | (299) | 68 | (361) |

As might be expected, people who have had each experience are more likely than those who have not to be contributors to the March of Dimes. But except for two experiences—having young children, and knowing someone who has been helped by the local Chapter—the percentage differences are quite small. And, significantly, both of these experiences are relatively infrequent. Young parents contribute to the March of Dimes more frequently than other adults, but only 37 per cent of the population are young adults;* people who know someone who has been helped by the Chapter contribute more frequently, but only 18 per cent know such a person. It can thus be concluded that if the March of Dimes depended for the bulk of its contributions upon people who had had even second-hand experience with polio it would not reach such a large proportion of the American public as it currently does.

The relatively low correlation between the polio incidence of a county and the percentage of March of Dimes contributors in its population deserves special mention, since it has already been noted that both polio incidence and March of Dimes proceeds are higher in rich counties than they are in poor ones.† The net conclusion which can be drawn from these two correlations is that March of Dimes proceeds must be higher in areas of high polio incidence than they are in others. As Table 28 demonstrates, this is in fact the case: among counties having a high, medium, or low median family income, those which have had a recently-high level of polio incidence are most likely to have had outstandingly successful March of Dimes campaigns.

* Young parents contribute more frequently than other people not only because of concern over polio. They are also *socially* more vulnerable to solicitation. Their children are asked to contribute at school, and they themselves are more likely than childless people (or parents of older children) to be home when a solicitor calls.

† See p. 180.

### Table 28—1953 Per Capita March of Dimes Proceeds in Counties Served by Foundation Chapters

|  | MEDIAN FAMILY INCOME OF COUNTY[16] | | | | | | | | |
|  | High | | | Medium | | | Low | | |
|  | POLIO INCIDENCE RATE OF COUNTY* | | | | | | | | |
| 1953 per capita proceeds[17] | High | Medium | Low | High | Medium | Low | High | Medium | Low |
| $.47 and over | 48% | 27% | 18% | 39% | 13% | 8% | 13% | 1% | 1% |
| .35 – .46 | 27 | 30 | 36 | 25 | 22 | 17 | 16 | 3 | 2 |
| .26 – .34 | 16 | 30 | 22 | 18 | 28 | 19 | 18 | 12 | 10 |
| .25 and less | 9 | 13 | 24 | 18 | 37 | 56 | 53 | 84 | 87 |
|  | 100% | 100% | 100% | 100% | 100% | 100% | 100% | 100% | 100% |
| N | (253) | (384) | (83) | (484) | (793) | (298) | (54) | (406) | (318) |

\* 1950–1952 weighted average.

Since there is such a strong positive correlation between polio incidence and *total* March of Dimes proceeds, why is there only a slight positive correlation between polio incidence and *individual* March of Dimes contributions? One answer to this question can be derived from a consideration of the data reported in Table 29, showing the relationship of polio incidence to the impact of the March of Dimes upon the public.

### Table 29—The Impact of the March of Dimes

|  | PER CENT WHO SCORED HIGH ON EACH IMPACT ITEM BY POLIO INCIDENCE RATE OF COUNTY* | | |
| Impact item[18] | High | Medium | Low |
| Popularity | 49 | 47 | 40 |
| Saliency | 90 | 83 | 77 |
| Contribution | 72 | 69 | 68 |
| N | (299) | (1340) | (361) |

\* 1951–1953 weighted average.

The March of Dimes clearly has a greater impact upon people who live in areas of high polio incidence than it has upon others: it is a more popular compaign, it is more salient, and it is contributed to more frequently. But while the percentage-point different between high and low polio incidence areas is nine in the case of popularity and 13 in the case of saliency, there is only a four-percentage point difference in the case of actual contributors to the March of Dimes.

It will be recalled that the polio incidence rate of a county is a variable which characterizes the population as a whole, and not necessarily all the individuals living in the county.* Only rarely, in fact, are people actually aware of the relative standing of their county vis à vis the national polio incidence rate. If a community has had a severe polio

\* See pp. 124–125.

epidemic most people are of course quite aware of it, but a high—in contrast to an epidemic—incidence can easily escape the notice of most people. Volunteers, however, are fully aware of the incidence of polio, since a majority of all polio victims receive some assistance from the Chapter.

Confronted with a high polio incidence, Volunteers are naturally motivated to conduct a particularly active campaign, since funds are needed to assist victims. As a result of active campaigns in counties which have had high polio incidence, the public is more aware of the March of Dimes (Table 29), and more money is raised (Table 28). But the proportion of the public which contributes to the campaign is not appreciably altered (Table 29), since the campaign itself is planned in such a way as to obtain *some* contribution from almost everyone. What is altered is the *intensity* of the campaign. More Volunteers participate, the campaign receives greater publicity, and more fund-raising techniques are utilized. As a result, more people know about the campaign, more large contributions are obtained, and—most important of all—more people make more than one contribution. As a result of an intensive campaign, the total amount of money raised is increased considerably, but the proportion of the public which contributes is not appreciably increased.

The crucial distinction between Volunteer and public awareness of polio incidence rates thus explains why more money is raised in areas of high polio incidence than it is in areas of low incidence, without any appreciable difference in the proportion of the public which contributes. It also highlights a major reason for the success of the March of Dimes in obtaining its objective of reaching a large majority of the population: contributions are received from people who have not—as well as those who have—had some form of personal experience with the disease which their dimes and dollars are used to combat.

### CONTRIBUTIONS FROM CONCERNED AND UNCONCERNED PEOPLE

*Concern over the threat of polio.* The extent to which the American public is concerned over the threat posed by polio was discussed in some detail earlier.* It was demonstrated that although polio is generally regarded as a more serious disease than tuberculosis, it is not regarded as being as serious as either cancer or heart diseases. Among children's diseases, however, polio is overwhelmingly viewed as most serious.

* See pp. 117–130.

Concern over polio, moreover, is not evenly distributed through-out the population. In terms of *individual* characteristics, people who have heard more about polio than about any other diseases in the past year or so are more likely to express concern, and concern is more widespread among parents of young children than it is among other adults. In terms of *community* characteristics, people living in areas of recently-high polio incidence are more likely than others to be concerned.

Since the funds collected during the March of Dimes are used to provide financial assistance to polio victims, to develop improved methods of treatment, and to support research activities directed toward eliminating polio as an epidemic disease, it is reasonable to assume that people who are concerned over the threat of polio would be more likely than others to contribute to the March of Dimes. The extent to which this assumption is correct must accordingly be examined. Before the data relating to this assumption are presented, however, it is necessary to comment briefly on the relationship of individual predispositions and motivations to contributions to fund-raising campaigns.

Consider first the distinction between major and trivial decisions. In housing studies, for example, it is possible to distinguish between the motivations of people who decide to rent an apartment and those who decide to buy a house, since where you will live for the next few years or for the rest of your life is a major decision.[19] Of somewhat less concern to most people, but nevertheless of considerable importance, are decisions concerning which presidential candidate to support in an election.[20] But whether or not to drop a coin in a box on the drug-store counter, or give a child a few dimes for his March of Dimes Card, or turn on the porch light on the evening of the Mothers' March are trivial decisions for most people, and involve a quite different set of motivations than is the case with major decisions. As a matter of fact, in the case of most March of Dimes contributions, as well as, of course, contributions to other health and welfare campaigns, the real decision to give is actually made *before* the campaign gets underway. People either like or do not like to drop coins in boxes for "good causes"; they either accede to or refuse the requests of their children for small coins to bring to school; and they either feel or do not feel that an important part of being a "good neighbor" is to turn the porch light on for the Marching Mother who lives down the street. One obvious reason for the success of the March of Dimes in obtaining contributions from so many people is the fact that most people do have these particular attitudes.

March of Dimes Cards, sent through the mail, present a somewhat different situation, since an on-the-spot decision must obviously be made: the card must either be thrown in a waste basket or returned with a check, a dollar bill, or at least a few coins. This decision, although hardly a major one, is certainly a motivated one, and an examination of the reasons why people either returned or destroyed the card would be very enlightening. Unfortunately for this purpose, however, March of Dimes Cards play a relatively unimportant part in the total campaign.* Accordingly, it is reasonable to assume that most people contribute to the March of Dimes under conditions which involve a very low level of motivation and very little actual decision-making. This does *not* mean that contributors do not have a reason for giving; rather, that these reasons are in many cases not directly related to the "decision" made at the time the contribution was made, and may be quite unrelated to concern over the threat of polio.

In addition to the distinction between major and trivial decisions, it is also necessary to consider the distinction between actions which do and do not require individual initiative. Both moving to a new house and voting in a presidential election, to use the same illustrations cited above, require the exercise of some initiative; contributing to voluntary health campaigns, on the other hand, requires very little. A fundamental strategy of these campaigns is to make the necessary *mechanisms* for contributing widely available. Hence, coin collectors are placed in retail shops; personal solicitors are recruited in businesses and organizations, and for door-to-door and street soliciting; businessmen's luncheon benefits are arranged; "telethons" and "radiothons" are held; etc. Everywhere a reasonably active person turns during one of these

* The Christmas Seal Sale provides an interesting contrast to the March of Dimes in this respect. In most communities, both campaigns send mailed appeals to virtually every household—telephone books, city directories, and automobile registration lists providing the major source of addresses. Yet based upon the data presented in Tables 21 and 22, it is quite apparent that the rate of return is much higher in the case of the Christmas Seal Sale than in the case of the March of Dimes. It is very doubtful, however, that this differential rate of return indicates that motivations play a more important role in the case of contributions to the Christmas Seal Sale, for two reasons. First, the correlation between motivations and contributions is just as low in the case of the Christmas Seal Sale as it is—as will presently be demonstrated—in the case of the March of Dimes. Second, contributors to the Christmas Seal Sale receive a tangible reward for having contributed—useful Christmas seals for use in sending out Christmas cards. It is quite reasonable to assume, therefore, that many contributors to the Christmas Seal Sale are as motivated by considerations of "custom" or "practicality" as they are by a desire to contribute to an organization which is combating tuberculosis.

campaigns, especially in middle-sized cities, he is greeted by an "out-stretched palm" or its equivalent. This not only makes contributing an action which requires little motivation, it also increases the number of multiple contributions which are obtained. To cite a concrete example, it is difficult for a woman who is solicited in a super-market to refuse by saying, "Sorry, but my husband gave fifty cents at the factory."*

*Concern and contributions.* The preceding discussion of the relationship between motivations and contributions to fund-raising campaigns casts serious doubts upon the assumption that people who are deeply concerned about the threat of polio are more likely to contribute to the March of Dimes. In order to show the extent to which these doubts render the assumption invalid, Table 30 presents the proportion of March of Dimes contributors among people with high and low scores on each of four attitude items.

### Table 30—Contributors to the March of Dimes, by Polio Attitude Score

| Attitude item[21] | PER CENT WHO CONTRIBUTED | | | |
| | High score | N | Low score | N |
|---|---|---|---|---|
| Seriousness | 73 | (873) | 64 | (1127) |
| Crippling aftereffects | 72 | (911) | 67 | (1089) |
| Fear | 73 | (103) | 70 | (792) |
| Emotional involvement | 74 | (486) | 66 | (499) |

People with high scores on each of these four items are somewhat more likely than others to contribute to the March of Dimes. It would of course be quite remarkable if this were not the case—i.e., if people who think polio is serious, who think its crippling aftereffects make it serious, who fear polio, and who are emotionally involved in polio did not contribute to the March of Dimes more frequently. But note also how small the difference is, ranging from a low of three percentage points in the case of "fear" to a high of nine percentage points in the case of "seriousness." It is particularly significant that contributors are found almost as frequently among people who scored low on the Fear of Polio Index as among those who scored high, since critics of the Foundation have sometimes alleged that the success of the March of Dimes is based upon the fact that the American public has been in-

---

* It is interesting to note in this connection that the Red Cross and the Community Chest, which depend more upon larger contributions from fewer people, frequently give contributors lapel pins to wear, which serve, it would seem, the latent function of providing a guarantee against further solicitation.

doctrinated to the point where it is unduly fearful over the threat of polio. Jerome Ellison, for example, reports that "a considerable body of philanthropic opinion feels that the Foundation has oversold the disease with too much 'scare copy.' "[22] The data presented in this chapter, however, do not support assertions such as these.*

It is possible to conclude, therefore, that one reason for the success of the March of Dimes is the fact that the campaign is successful in reaching not only people who are concerned over the threat of polio but also those who are less concerned. Furthermore, nearly identical differences between the proportions of contributors among concerned and unconcerned people were obtained when the relationship between concern over cancer, tuberculosis, and heart diseases and contributions to these campaigns was examined, indicating that the relatively greater success of the March of Dimes is a reflection of different aspects of campaign organization, rather than of a higher level of motivation (motivation, that is, which is related to concern over the threat of polio) among the public at large.

* See also pp. 118–121.

# CONCLUSIONS

*chapter VII*

# VOLUNTEERS
# AND THE
# FOUNDATION

## Introduction

PREVIOUS CHAPTERS have described the Foundation from several points of view. Its Volunteer membership has been described; its local activities have been reviewed; the organizational framework within which these activities are carried out has been analyzed; and the reasons underlying public support of the March of Dimes have been discussed. These four topics have been given rather detailed attention, since a central thesis of this study is that the ultimate character of an organization is determined by its membership, its formal structure, its activities, and the environment within which its activities are carried out.

These descriptions of the Foundation and its environment have included a number of explanations for the success which the Foundation has had in attracting and retaining an active and interested Volunteer membership. In particular, the Foundation's formal structure, its methods of recruiting Volunteers, its patient care program and its fund-raising activities have all been cited as bearing directly upon the topic of Volunteer participation. This chapter extends the analysis of the reasons underlying Volunteer participation one step further by describing how Volunteers themselves actually regard the organization. To anticipate, it is demonstrated in this chapter that the images which Volunteers have of the Foundation as a voluntary association go far toward explaining their continued participation and interest in its program.

A brief review of the Foundation's structure is necessary at this point. It will be recalled that the Foundation has a corporate-type structure, and that National Headquarters delegates certain functions to the local Chapters: providing financial assistance to polio patients and their families; informing the public of current developments concerning infantile paralysis and the steps currently being taken to combat it; and, through participation in the annual March of Dimes campaign, raising the funds necessary to support both the local and national programs. In order to carry out these responsibilities, two parallel organizations have been established in local communities, generally along county lines: a permanent Chapter which is an integral part of the national organization and a March of Dimes organization which is in effect reconstituted each year. The tasks assigned to Chapters are the responsibility of the Officers, the Executive Committee and various other committees appointed by the Executive Committee; the March of Dimes, on the other hand, is the responsibility of a Campaign Director who is officially appointed by the State Chairman and who recruits a staff comprised both of Chapter members and other individuals in the county.

Two procedural aspects of the local program, described earlier, might also be reviewed here. First, in sharp contrast to the situation which prevails in many voluntary health associations, the local program is carried out almost entirely by *lay* Volunteers. Chapters appoint a Medical Advisory Committee to help with details of the patient care program, but doctors are not permitted to hold office in a local Chapter. Furthermore, paid Executive Secretaries are found only in large cities. Second, the local program is geared entirely to the accomplishment of specific tasks, rather than toward the maintenance of wide membership participation. This means that—with the important exception of the March of Dimes—relatively few Volunteers are needed to carry out the day-to-day activities of the Chapter. Moreover, comparatively few bureaucratic procedures involving purely internal matters have been established. Chapters do not have regular meeting places, for example, and except in medium-sized and large cities they do not even have office space. Chapter meetings are held only once or twice a year, no initiation or investiture ceremonies are held, and most Chapter business is conducted over the telephone or at committee meetings. In most of these respects, Foundation Chapters differ sharply from such voluntary associations as veterans' groups, fraternal orders, social clubs and the like.

What do Volunteers think of their local organization as an *organization,* rather than as the embodiment of worthwhile purposes? In any organization there is necessarily a gap between the formal goals and the down-to-earth procedures designed to achieve them; i.e., regardless of the degree of consensus concerning the organization's goals, there is always some degree of disagreement concerning how the goals may best be attained. It can be anticipated, therefore, that some Volunteers will regard the local organization which has been established to achieve the Foundation's purposes in somewhat negative terms.

On the other hand, there are sound reasons for expecting that most Volunteers are favorably disposed toward their local organization. Membership is purely voluntary, and Volunteers who become disaffected can simply withdraw from the organization. It can thus be anticipated that the judgments of the local organization provided by most Volunteers are strongly biased in favor of the Foundation.* For this reason, the first section of this chapter describes the predominant images which Volunteers have of their organization not in the abstract, but in comparison with other organizations. The second section of the chapter describes the images which Volunteers have of the Foundation from a quite different point of view; it is concerned with the ways in which Volunteers actually perceive the Foundation's formal structure, i.e., its characteristic mode of delegating authority and functions. A final section describes the process through which these perceptions take place.

## Comparisons with Other Organizations

Since the preliminary phase of this research revealed that Foundation Volunteers are at the same time generally active members of other community organizations, it was decided to ascertain their specific opinions of the Foundation by asking them to compare their Chapter or March of Dimes organizations with others with which they were familiar. The rationale for this decision is the following: It was felt that in making comparisons Volunteers would not only be better able to articulate their feelings, but would also be less likely to respond by parroting in unqualified terms the publicity formulas which themselves had grown accustomed to using as recruiting or fund-raising arguments.

In comparing their own organization with others in the community, Volunteers consistently revealed a preference for the Foundation. And

---

* The favorable bias of its members is a phenomenon which is of course not confined to the Foundation. Arnold Rose, for example, reports that in a union local in which nearly half of the membership confessed that they had joined initially because they were forced to do so—since they worked in a union shop—more than 90 per cent of the membership thought the union was run either "very well" or "fairly well." Since Rose describes a number of features of this union which indicate that it is by no means a model trade union, the bias of its membership is apparent.[1]

in so doing, they spoke not only with the authority of experience but also as strong advocates, defending, as it were, their own involvement in Foundation activities. This bias does not of course necessarily detract from the accuracy of their observations, but it did result in obviously one-sided judgments of other community organizations. This is particularly true of the Red Cross, since nearly half of the Volunteers elected to express their approval of the Foundation's local program in terms of their own experiences with the Red Cross.* Furthermore, statements about the Red Cross are more emphatic and emotionally charged than are statements about other voluntary health associations or about the Community Chest, which in general are either more tempered or neutral. For these reasons, comparisons with the Red Cross predominate in the review of Volunteer attitudes which follows.

Comparisons with the Red Cross are in one sense inevitable. More Volunteers have had experience with it than with any other single organization; it is the only other major national organization with a specific program of local assistance; and in most communities it is the only health and welfare organization which annually raises more funds than the Foundation by means of public contributions. Furthermore, at the time of this research a major activity of local Red Cross units was obtaining voluntary donations of blood for use in extracting gamma globulin, and many Volunteers felt that the American public was giving credit to the Red Cross for instigating this polio prevention program— credit which should be given to the Foundation. It should also be noted that many Volunteers, in choosing to compare the Red Cross with the Foundation, were merely making use of a convenient symbol; the Red Cross, in other words, serves as a verbal crutch for the less articulate. In fact, the almost totally negative terms in which it is characterized suggest that the reference is in many instances to a stereotype—rather than reference to the Red Cross as a community organization.† This stereotype is to some extent a war-born phenomenon. It will be remembered that many servicemen during World War II gave vent to the traditional animosity of the soldier toward the civilian noncombatant by criticizing the Red Cross. The ubiquitous Red Cross worker became the personification of civilian "brass" and the activities of Red Cross

* At no point in the interviews, however, were Volunteers asked to compare the Foundation with the Red Cross. The selection of an organization with which to compare the Foundation was left entirely to the Volunteers.

† A recent article on the Red Cross in the *New York Times,* for example, was headed "Red Cross Target for Varied Abuse. False Rumors Keep Cropping Up About it, but Cannot Mar Its Record of Good Deeds."[2]

field units were subject to acrid and sometimes petty criticism which often obscured their real worth. The official historian of the Red Cross has summarized this phenomenon as follows:

The returning soldiers who had resented the charges made at Red Cross service clubs, disliked the attitude of some of the Red Cross girls, and otherwise found fault with the Red Cross overseas program, affected no small part of the public with their critical reaction. Gallup polls revealed this sharp decline in popular favor. One reported that whereas sixty per cent of the people had in 1944 placed the American Red Cross first among the charitable organizations to which they were willing to contribute, only twenty-one per cent felt this way in 1947. While the end of the war largely accounted for this shift in opinion, it also reflected a more skeptical attitude toward the value of some Red Cross activities.[3]

That returning soldiers brought home somewhat hostile attitudes is quite clear from the comments of many Volunteers. As a March of Dimes Chairman in Pinetree County put it bluntly, "Anyone who's been in the service hates the Red Cross' guts."

Although it was not within the province of this research to investigate this phenomenon, this explanation has been included in order to point out that in criticizing the Red Cross, Volunteers were not necessarily evaluating its local program. Rather, they were more likely to be referring to the "negative" of their positive image of the Foundation. Like the narrators in Robert Browning's dramatic monologues, Volunteers described themselves in the process of describing others.

Two themes predominate in the comments made by Volunteers in comparing their own organization with others in the community. The Foundation is praised because of its truly "volunteer" character and because of the simplicity and economy of its operations. Volunteers who stressed each theme serve in all types of Chapters and occupy different Chapter and March of Dimes positions. Regardless of their vantage point, however, their comments reflect a double perspective: the private opinion of the Volunteer and his evaluation of how the public reacts to his organization's activities.

### VOLUNTEER CHARACTER

Volunteers who referred to the personnel of the Foundation in making comparisons with other organizations reveal a deep-rooted antagonism toward hierarchical and bureaucratic organizations in general. Specifically, Volunteers resent those professionals whom David Riesman has characterized as "the full-time planners of other people's short-time bursts of energy and masochism,"[4] i.e., those people whose

jobs are generally described as "organizer" or local "representative."
The Chapter Chairman in Pinetree County, for example, in referring
to the Red Cross, for which he had worked as a volunteer fund-raiser,
voiced his resentment of the paid representative who had been sent into
the community to supervise the drive. "My feeling is that if they have to
send someone here to oversee it, they could run it," he declared.
"People resent someone coming in here with a Packard station wagon
on a salary to supervise fund-raising," he continued, and the Red Cross
is "top-heavy with salaries." In contrast, Volunteers for the March of
Dimes "think up their own stunts . . . people like the fact that it's all
volunteer." In the same vein, the South City Campaign Director recalled that "last year when I was working on the Red Cross, I was
asked always, 'How much does so-and-so make?' It's really delightful
to be able to say, when working on the March of Dimes, "Mr. O'Connor
doesn't get a dime.' " Another Volunteer in this Chapter expressed his
approval of the absence of professionals in the local program of the
Foundation by calling it "one of the very best selling points of the whole
organization. It's what sold me from the very beginning. I wouldn't do
this for the National Foundation if they offered me four thousand
dollars a year." The Secretary of this Chapter pointed out that "Volunteers are a great appeal, especially with those charity racket scandals."
And the Mothers' March Chairman, in comparing her experiences in
the Red Cross and the March of Dimes, declared: "You find a resistance to the Red Cross . . . because people feel there are too many paid
executives." Fund-raisers for the March of Dimes did not encounter
this resistance, she reported, since people are "generally aware that [it]
. . . is run on a small expense account."

For some Volunteers, criticism of the "top-heavy" administrative
structure of the Red Cross appears to be a way of expressing a cultur-
ally-conditioned defiance of authoritarian behavior in general, of attempts to "push people around." A characteristic expression of this
posture of independence is this statement by a March of Dimes Volunteer in Pinetree County:

I remember how the Red Cross works. Red Cross moves in and just starts
with the idea, "I'm the boss and I'm running the joint." If Polio moves in
with a "rep" they start training people to take over. The Foundation
furnishes the equipment and the know-how, but they get local people to do
it themselves. The others come in in big rigs. We had a flood here and the
Red Cross came in, but I'm telling you, the Red Cross couldn't raise fifty
cents here now.

The Red Cross is of course not the only organization which Volunteers accuse of treating volunteer workers as if they were subordinates, although, as mentioned earlier, most comparisons made by Volunteers were with the Red Cross. For example, a member of the Executive Committee (and former Chapter Chairman) in Greenback City, who has been active most of his adult life in a wide variety of community organizations, made this comment:

The volunteer organization [of the Foundation] is of primary importance. Let me give you an example. Here we have a Civil Defense organization just like in other places. But it's a failure—just as it is all over the country. And I can tell you why, too. A General is at the head of it. And Generals think they can make plans and tell people what to do. It doesn't work with Americans. You can't push them around. They won't take orders. They'll do things if they want to, and if they have to.

In the minds of many Volunteers who relate their views to a broader social ethic, the characteristic of the Foundation which sets it apart from other organizations is its essentially "democratic" composition. Its membership is not confined to the social élite, to "the Big Names in the community." On the contrary, according to a Steamboat City Volunteer, "it's always the little people." And the Corn City Chapter Chairman noted that the Community Chest and the Red Cross are striking contrasts in this respect:

Let me put it this way. There are a lot of organizations that are national in scope . . . but when you get into your Community Chest and Red Cross, you find yourself on the "four hundred" level—people who are doing things because it is the thing to do. . . . It is like, let me say, "going slumming." I've noticed that because I'm on both.

There is abundant evidence, furthermore, that the Foundation represents to many Volunteers a revival of the tradition of community self-help which was once a standard feature of American community life, but which has been largely replaced by more institutionalized forms of assistance administered by professionals. "You have the feeling of belonging," reported the Chapter Secretary in Market Town, "that it's *our* organization, not just a Board of Directors off somewhere in a national headquarters." This feeling, combined with the absence of status consciousness among Volunteers and the atmosphere of easy informality which pervades relationships among them, fosters a sense of intimacy which, Volunteers maintain, is not found in other organizations. The Foundation has more appeal than the Red Cross, according to a Defense Town Volunteer, because the Red Cross seems impersonal: "For me, Polio seems different, closer, even though the meetings we have of the Chapter membership are so large. But you always get the feeling you can talk to people. You can go up to anyone at these meetings and get to know them immediately. You start talking polio. . . . Floods, disasters, blood donations are all good things, but there isn't the personal touch."

There were frequent references, furthermore, to the special ethos which Volunteers assert characterizes the Foundation. A Gas City Volunteer, for example, who had done publicity work for the Cancer Society, the Y.M.C.A., and the Easter Seals campaign, reported that "on my list the March of Dimes or the National Foundation is first. It just is that way. You feel [pause] a spirit of cooperation, of a whole family getting together. You feel that with the National Foundation. It is something you don't feel with these other organizations."

## SIMPLICITY AND ECONOMY

Although a major characteristic of the patient care program is its underlying philosophy of generosity—reflected both in the types of patients who are assisted and in the amount of money spent per patient —economy of operation is in the minds of many Volunteers a unique and praiseworthy feature of the local program. The Foundation is superior to other organizations, according to many Volunteers, because it both spends less money for administrative purposes and accomplishes its purposes with a minimum of administrative procedures. Witness the opinion of one South City Volunteer—an advocate of economy:

It's a real nice thing to say that the National Foundation has the lowest percentage of total cost than any other organization. . . . This applies both to my own feelings and to the general public. Yes, for the person who gives one dollar this is an important thing, and that person is the most important person in any drive.

The Mountain County Chapter Chairman, who is also a Director of his local Red Cross, observed that "people get more for their money. . . . We meet less sales resistance. The March of Dimes is much easier than the Red Cross to sell." The Campaign Director in Payday Town, who explained that he had worked for five years in the Red Cross and was now the local Treasurer, declared that he was "not too sold on it, however. It costs too much to administer it. They waste too much. It doesn't compare with this program." He then related his own experience in his own plant, where the response to the Red Cross Drive was only 20 per cent of the response to the March of Dimes. "It's the same for the county," he concluded, "businessmen especially like to know that there are low costs."

Many Volunteers praised what they consider to be the almost spartan simplicity of the Foundation's mode of operation. "The fact that you can do so much directly without red tape" impressed the South City Chapter Chairman. "It's a matter of pride," he continued, "that our office is free, our typewriters donated." The Red Cross is "the worst I ever saw," reported the South City Secretary. "The dollars they pour into those damn forms!" And the Secretary of the Eastern City Chapter, in summarizing the way his Chapter handles its relationships with polio patients, provided a succinct analysis of the difference many Volunteers observe between the approach of the Foundation and that of other welfare organizations: "We don't use the social worker approach, don't sit down with a long questionnaire."

### DISSENTING OPINIONS

Although the overwhelming majority of Volunteers praised the Foundation during the interviews, or made no critical comments, it is instructive to examine the reasons underlying the disaffection of the ten Volunteers who were judged by the interviewers to be either "hostile" toward or "disenchanted" with the Foundation.

All six "hostile" Volunteers are in fundamental disagreement with the Foundation's policy of not participating in Community Chest or other united fund-raising campaigns. Their friends and business associates are in every case active supporters of the local Community Chest, and they see no reason why the March of Dimes should not become a member. Their "hostility" is thus directed against only one of the policies of the Foundation.

Of the four Volunteers rated as "disenchanted," one is a polio parent who feels his business associates are taking unfair advantage of him by using his child for publicity purposes; one had had a fight with the State Representative immediately prior to the interview and was "about to resign"; one is a young lawyer who feels that he was "roped in" to the job of March of Dimes Chairman; and one is a socially-prominent businessman who feels compelled to participate as a Volunteer, but who takes a jaundiced view of the activity. It is of some interest that only in the case of the first of these four "disenchanted" Volunteers does there seem to be any awareness on the part of other Volunteers of their disaffection.

## Perceptions of the Foundation's Structure

The origins, nature, and consequences of the Foundation's formal structure have been recurrent themes throughout this volume. It has been demonstrated that the circumstances surrounding the Foundation's origins in the Georgia Warm Springs Foundation—and in its fund-raising organization, the Committee for the Celebration of the President's Birthday—are largely responsible for the initial emergence of the Foundation's corporate-type structure. It has also been demonstrated that the Foundation's capacity to solve or circumvent the two most pervasive problems of voluntary associations—maintaining membership interest and preserving organizational goals—is directly related to its corporate-type structure. Moreover, the major operational programs of the Foundation have been shown to be dependent upon a corporate-type structure for their proper functioning. The epidemic nature of polio makes it mandatory that National Headquarters be empowered to distribute funds to the Chapters that need them most, and the need for a coordinated research program makes it essential that the expenditure of research funds be centrally-controlled.

All of these previous discussions, however, have been oriented toward the functions which the Foundation's corporate-type structure serves for the organization and its capacity to carry out its program, and very little attention has been given to the relationship between the Foundation's structure and the participation of individual Volunteers in the Foundation's program. The present section is devoted to this topic.

How do Volunteers actually percieve the Foundation's formal structure? The relevance of this question stems from the need to clarify a more fundamental question which has until this point in the analysis not been given a satisfactory answer. How has the Foundation—which like other voluntary associations in America must carry out its program in accordance with a set of cultural prescriptions characterized by David Truman as "the democratic mould"—been able to retain an active and interested membership? Truman defines these prescriptions in these terms:

The attitudes themselves are vague, but they usually involve approval of such devices as periodic elections of key officials, broad participation by the membership in the group's policy making, either directly or through a system of elected representatives, written constitutions, and the like. These, in fact, become elements without which an organization cannot achieve "respectability" and "legitimacy" in the community.[5]

The Foundation has an ambivalent character with respect to these elements of democratic government. Local Chapters are open-membership organizations, and their officers are elected, at least nominally, by the membership. In most Chapters, furthermore, leadership turnover is fairly high. The policy-making body of the national organization, however, is the legal membership of the corporation, i.e., the Board of Trustees. Chapters do not have policy-making functions, since their legal status is that of administrative units of the national organization. Similarly, the March of Dimes is officially directed by National Headquarters, and the County Campaign Director is officially appointed by the State March of Dimes Chairman, who is in turn appointed by National Headquarters.

It is comparatively easy to demonstrate that a corporate-type structure is a fundamental requirement of the Foundation's national and local programs; it is more difficult to explain how the Foundation has been able to achieve both "respectability" and "legitimacy" in the community, and among its Volunteers, in view of the cultural prescription—"the democratic mould"—that national organizations should be based upon the principle of membership representation.

It must first be noted that not all voluntary associations are "expected" to have the same degree of membership representation. Automobile associations and hospitalization insurance plans, for example, which exist solely to provide services for their members, are not necessarily expected to have a democratic structure, and even when they do, few members take advantage of their opportunity to vote or express their opinions on the policies the organization should follow. Similarly, membership representation in the internal affairs of the organization is generally not considered to be a crucial requirement of organizations which exist primarily to cope with emergency situations, e.g., the Red Cross, since it is widely recognized that the democratic process can be slow and unwieldy.* At the other extreme, trade unions are "expected" to be very democratic, since they exist to represent the interests of their members. For this reason, they are often subjected to strong criticism when they adopt a policy or engage in a course of action which is allegedly contrary to the desires of the membership, or when their leadership remains unchanged over a period of years.[6]

Since the Foundation exists primarily to eliminate the threat of

* The Red Cross, however, has not been immune to criticism that its membership has no role in policy-making. In the years since World War II these criticisms have led to a number of important structural changes.[7]

infantile paralysis, rather than to represent the personal interests of its membership, it is less subject to the pressures of the "democratic mould" than are other voluntary associations. The nature of its program thus goes far toward explaining how its corporate-type structure —and the acceptance by local units of the authority of the national organization which this structure requires—have not detracted from either its "respectability" or "legitimacy" in the eyes of its Volunteers. Its corporate-type structure nevertheless poses a potential problem for the Foundation, since as Peter Blau has observed, "the hierarchy of authority in a bureaucracy, essential for coordination, often produces among its lower echelons profound feelings of inequality and apathy that impede identification with the organization's objectives."[8]

The hypothesis that some members would not accept the authority of the Foundation's corporate-type structure is of course based upon the assumption that all members actually perceive the structure in these terms. This assumption, however, turns out to be unwarranted. In order to demonstrate this, it is necessary to describe the two quite different perceptions of the Foundation's formal structure identified in the course of this research.

### TWO PERCEPTIONS OF STRUCTURE

In contrast to the situation which prevails in many national organizations, the Foundation's local program is quite standardized throughout the county. The patient care program differs from county to county more in magnitude than it does in content, and the broad outlines of the March of Dimes are established by National Headquarters and followed, with local variations, in most communities. All local organizations are subject to the same rules and regulations, and are in direct contact with National Headquarters through one of its employees—the State Representative. For these reasons, the expectation is that Volunteers share a similar image of the kind of organization to which they belong. More specifically, since the Foundation's formal structure is clearly of the corporate-type, it is logical to assume that most Volunteers would perceive it as such. However, this is not the case: as many Volunteers perceive the Foundation as a federation of local Chapters, serviced by a national office (46 per cent), as perceive it as a national organization with a corporate-type structure (46 per cent).*

March of Dimes Volunteers are more likely than Chapter Volunteers to perceive the Foundation as a national organization, which re-

---

* The perceptions of 8 per cent of the Volunteers were not ascertained.

flects the fact that the March of Dimes is officially directed by National Headquarters, not by the local Chapter. Nevertheless, more than a third of all March of Dimes Volunteers, and more than half of all Chapter Volunteers, perceive the Foundation's formal structure, i.e., the relationship which obtains between National Headquarters and their local organization, as being quite different from its formal reality.*

*A national organization.* Volunteers whose perception of the Foundation's formal structure is closely in accord with official reality adopt a number of different postures toward the organization. Some Volunteers accept the role of the local Chapter as a branch office of National Headquarters as a matter of course. The Chapter Vice-Chairman in Gas City, for example, described the role of his Chapter in these terms: "Our job is to act as agents for the National Foundation for the disbursement of funds. . . . Our job is to decide how to use the money most effectively." The Chapter Secretary in Market Town, when asked what sort of problems the State Representative helped her with, provided a definition of the State Representative's role which conforms perfectly to his official one. She said that he helped her with "medical problems, financial problems, patient care problems, transfer of cases, responsibility for equipment, office administration—and as a morale booster." Finally, another mirror image of the official structure is revealed in the comment of the Eastern City Chapter Chairman, who summed up his role in the Foundation in these terms:

I could put it in a phrase I use a lot. I picked it up years ago. I think it was first stated by Basil O'Connor. "When polio walks in your door, the Eastern City Chapter of the National Foundation for Infantile Paralysis walks through with it." It makes me happy to say, "We're with you."

Other nationally-minded Volunteers actually discount the importance of their local Chapter. A Chapter Volunteer in South City, for example, after reporting how often people shift back and forth between

* Direct questioning was not used during the interviews to ascertain perceptions of structure, since this would have alerted Volunteers to the fact that they belonged to an organization having a certain formal structure. The mode of their response to such questions, accordingly, would have been that of informing the interviewer of the *facts* concerning this structure. Since one of the purposes of the interview was to ascertain some of the *assumptions* which actually guide the day-to-day behavior of Volunteers, it was necessary to approach this topic indirectly. This was done by asking a number of questions concerning their actual experiences with National Headquarters personnel, and with carrying out policies established by National Headquarters. In responding to these questions, as well as to others which led them to speak in organizational terms, Volunteers supplied sufficient information for the interviewer-analysts to ascertain their underlying image of the organization's structure. (As already noted, this was not possible in the case of 8 per cent of all Volunteers.)

Chapter and March of Dimes activities, concluded: "In this particular Chapter, I think interest in the program is more important than actually belonging. Actually, belonging to the Chapter is a nebulous thing. . . . Your loyalty is to the program of the National Foundation, and then you work on all phases."

Several Volunteers even reported instances in which they had actually by-passed the Chapter organization in carrying out Chapter activities. "If I went through the Chapter it would take too long," complained a Volunteer in Wheat County, "so I just call up the State Representative and work with him and with the doctors here."

One indication of national-mindedness is the frequency with which references were made during the interviews to the personal qualities of National Headquarters personnel. There seem to be two explanations for this phenomenon. First, few national voluntary associations are as closely associated with specific personalities. Volunteers have every reason to feel a sense of identification with President Roosevelt, who founded the organization, and with Basil O'Connor, who has been President from the beginning. Second, because there are no state organizations, National Headquarters personnel must of necessity actually visit local Chapters more frequently than would otherwise be the case. In fact, in seven of the thirty-seven Chapters studied intensively, Volunteers reported that in recent years they had had *frequent* contact with personnel from National Headquarters, and in another eleven Chapters, Volunteers reported that they had *occasional* contact. Since only ten or fifteen staff members of National Headquarters are available for these trips into the field, this represents a remarkably high proportion of Chapters actually visited.

For some Volunteers, personal contact with National Headquarters personnel, either in their own community or at regional meetings, has fostered the feeling that their link with these staff members is a personal as well as an official one. Typically, they referred to these representatives by their first names. "I've known them all," declared one Volunteer, and reeled off the names of six staff members in addition to Basil O'Connor himself. "I met Mr. O'Connor . . . for the first time last year," the Gas City Chapter Chairman remarked, and then proceeded to describe him as a "very high type fellow, sincere and dynamic and smart as hell. I don't know what more you can say for a man."

Identification with National Headquarters personnel sometimes verges on adulation. "I think the heads of the organization are so uplifting," reported the Chairman of Women's Activities in Steel City.

"They are wonderful speakers. . . . I enjoy every meeting when they are there. You know, when we come home, that we're going to give everything we've got." A graphic example of this feeling of intimacy and admiration is the enthusiastic statement of the Steamboat City Chapter Chairman, which illustrates the sense of familiarity coupled with admiration which is characteristic of Volunteers who view the Foundation as a national organization:

I think those people at National are wonderful. I think we get quite a bit of help during the year. . . . The marvelous thing is that I can go up to New York and see these people. . . . It makes it a lot simpler if they know you, and you have a personal request. Most Chapter members know this. I don't think anyone stands in awe of [them]. Only Basil O'Connor. We stand in awe of him because of his unselfishness.

Later, while driving the interviewer to the airport, this Chairman expressed her identification with the national leadership in these terms: "Now you be sure to give my love to those people up in New York. And tell them we have everything under control." This identification with the national leadership seems in part to be an attempt to establish the legitimacy of their participation on the grounds that they have made what might be called a personal pact with National Headquarters personnel. Many Volunteers spoke of personal letters they had written to or received from the national office. Even the impersonality of the interview situation did not always seem to constitute a barrier to personal communication. "I don't care if you quote me by name or not," the Suburb County Chapter Chairman told the interviewer. "They all know what I think, back there in New York. They could pick out my quote a mile away. They'd say, 'That's old Bob!' "

*A federation of local Chapters.* In striking contrast to this recognition of and dependence upon the authority of National Headquarters are the views of those Volunteers who perceive the Foundation as a federation of loosely-affiliated Chapters. Since these views are patently not based upon the acceptance of official doctrine, they encompass a wide range of interpretations. For all Volunteers who expressed them, however, it is apparent that their involvement in the Foundation's program is predicated upon the assumption that it is primarily a *local* activity. Only seldom did they express serious criticism of National Headquarters; rather, their declarations take the form of denials of the official nature of the local-national relationship. National Headquarters is relegated to the background by these Volunteers, and its directives are for the most part either to be ignored or regarded as encroachments upon the jurisdiction of the local organization.

Sometimes these expressions of independence are truculent, as in the case of the Oil City Chapter Chairman who complained that National Headquarters personnel "must keep bankers' hours or something," since he was unable to see the staff members he wanted to during a trip to New York City. Sometimes they are expressions of complete unconcern. "They don't bother us and we don't bother them," noted the Chapter Secretary in Greenback City when she was asked about her contacts with National Headquarters. And sometimes they take the form of monumental indifference. "We have almost no contact with National," reported the Eastern City Chapter Secretary. "National sends through bulletins, but frankly we don't pay much attention to them. National is necessary, but not of any great interest."*

Another independent stance makes a clear-cut distinction between the activities which are the concern of National Headquarters and those which have been delegated to local units. The Foundation's campaign publicity, for example, is viewed with great respect by even the most federation-minded Volunteers. But in recognizing the legitimacy of National Headquarters activities, federation-minded Volunteers often go one step further and imply that the relationship between their organization and the national office is not hierarchical in nature. "We here don't feel obliged to do what the National Chapter [sic] would dictate," asserted the Gas City Chapter Chairman, "because we know the local situation. But in general, we have conferred with them on things like GG and the vaccine, and we do go along there, of course." Since the gamma globulin and vaccine programs are completely under the direction of National Headquarters, which asks Volunteers from time to time to assume various responsibilities relating to the local administration of the programs, the assertion by a Chapter Chairman that "we have conferred with them . . . [and] we do go along there, of course" is a striking illustration of the perception of the Foundation as a federation of loosely-affiliated Chapters.

## Conclusions

Since its corporate-type structure is essential for the efficient conduct of the Foundation's program, and since a structure of this type is

---

* It is of interest to note that Volunteers in the same Chapter often hold quite different images of the Foundation's formal structure. For example, this Chapter Secretary works very closely with his Chapter Chairman, who was quoted above as having derived his favorite expression from Basil O'Connor himself.

manifestly at variance with the image of voluntary associations as democratic organizations held by many Americans, the fact that nearly half of all Volunteers actually perceive the Foundation as having a federation-type structure is an important reason underlying continued Volunteer interest and participation. As far as these Volunteers are concerned, the Foundation *has* a democratic structure. What factors account for this differential perception of the Foundation's structure? The following is an attempt to find an answer to this difficult question.

Social psychologists, faced with the recurrent problem of explaining how different individuals may perceive an identical situation in quite different ways, have devoted a great deal of attention to the phenomenon of selective perception.[9] Briefly, two complementary approaches to the problem have been developed. First, a distinction has been made between two major factors which influence perception. On the one hand, perception has been shown to be influenced by *functional* factors, i.e., "those which derive primarily from the needs, moods, past experience, and memory of the individual."[10] On the other hand, perception is influenced by *structural* factors, i.e., "those factors deriving solely from the nature of the physical stimuli and the neural effects they evoke in the nervous system of the individual."[11]

A second approach to the problem of selective perception is to describe the various psychological processes at work. First, perception involves a great deal of *omitting.* Since it is impossible for an observer to note every detail of a situation, some details are simply not perceived. Second, perception involves *supplementing:* details which are in fact not present in a situation are nevertheless "perceived" in order to make the situation meaningful. Third, perception involves *structuring,* or giving form or organization to that which is perceived.[12]

By undertaking carefully controlled experiments social psychologists are able to vary the nature of different situations, and thus observe the conditions under which these three processes take place. The student of voluntary associations, on the other hand, cannot control the large number of factors which enter into perceptions of the structure of an organization by its members, and hence cannot approach the precision of measurement attained by social psychologists working under laboratory conditions. Nevertheless, these social psychological concepts serve the very useful purpose of providing a broad theoretical point of view with which to approach the problem of explaining contrasting perceptions of the Foundation's structure. Accordingly, the discussion now turns to an examination of the functional and structural factors which influence the perceptions of Volunteers.

## FUNCTIONAL FACTORS

*Regional differences.* The search for an explanation of differential perception of the Foundation's structure naturally began with an examination of the characteristics of the communities in which Volunteers holding either image live, since—although the Foundation's program is in theory identical throughout the country—the field research revealed that some local variation in working procedures does exist. Some of this variation is of course related to the size of the population served —small rural counties naturally face quite different problems than do large cities. Some Chapter and March of Dimes organizations are in effect unofficially sponsored by another community organization, while others are not. Some local organizations undergo a nearly complete turnover in leadership every year or so, while others utilize the same leadership year after year, etc. It was felt, accordingly, that local differences such as these might result in different perceptions of the Foundation's structure.

This expectation was fulfilled in part, but only in part. For example, in two of the thirty-seven communities all of the Volunteers interviewed were found to perceive the Foundation as a federation, while in four other communities all Volunteers were found to perceive it as a national organization. But these clusterings of people with similar perceptions do not contribute materially to an explanation, for two reasons. First, communities in which all Volunteers share the same image were not found to differ systematically in any respect from other communities. That is, no *community* correlates of the two images were detected. Volunteers having both images were found in both large cities and rural counties; in areas of both high and low polio incidence; in both old-established and newly-reorganized Chapters; and in counties which conduct successful fund-raising campaigns as well as in those which have less success. Second, in the overwhelming majority of communities (thirty-one out of thirty-seven), Volunteers who hold both images work side by side in carrying out the local program of the Foundation. The local situation, in and of itself, it must be concluded, does not determine perception of the Foundation's structure.

One interesting relationship between the local situation and perception was observed, however. It was found that the further a county is from the Foundation's National Headquarters in New York, the greater is the proportion of Volunteers who perceive the Foundation as a federation. In fact, in the Eastern counties studied, only 38 per cent of the Volunteers perceive the Foundation as a federation, while in the West this is true of more than half of the Volunteers, and in the Southwest, it is true of more than two-thirds of the Volunteers—as shown in Table 31.

**Table 31—Distance from National Headquarters and Perceptions of the Foundation's Structure**

| Region | PER CENT WHO PERCEIVE THE FOUNDATION AS A FEDERATION | N |
|---|---|---|
| East | 38 | (33) |
| South | 36 | (61) |
| Midwest | 45 | (64) |
| Southwest | 68 | (25) |
| West | 57 | (51) |

There appear to be three major reasons for these regional differences. First, it is probably true of organizations generally that local autonomy, either actual or perceived, increases with distance from the organization's headquarters. Surveillance is more difficult at a distance, and the fact of distance alone is likely to increase feelings of autonomy. Members of a far-off headquarters, it is widely believed, cannot possibly understand local problems.

Second, according to Volunteers in several of the Southwestern and southern West Coast counties studied, polio is less of a seasonal problem in these regions than it is in the rest of the country. For this reason, they feel that their situation is a special one, and one which a national organization cannot fully understand.

Third, there seem to be sound historical reasons for assuming that Americans in Southwestern and Western states actually have more firmly-held opinions concerning the inviolability of their local autonomy than do people living in other regions of the country. After all, Volunteers in two of the Southwestern counties studied are Texans, whose sentiments toward independence and local autonomy are probably not unduly overstated by the prevailing folk-lore.

*Orientations toward national organizations.* Regional differences explain only part of this phenomenon, however, since some Volunteers in every Eastern county except one perceive the Foundation as a federation, and some Volunteers in every Southwestern county except one perceive it as a national organization. But these regional differences do serve to call attention to the fact that the personal values held by

Volunteers do play a role in determining their perception of the Foundation's structure, since people who *want* to believe that something is true are often able to fulfill their desires. "As a rule," according to Lawrence Lowell, "men see what they look for, and observe the things they expect to see."[13] In the present context, it can be assumed that people who "expect" or "want" a national organization to have either a corporate or a federation-type formal structure will tend to perceive an organization to which they belong in accordance with their expectation or their desire.

Unfortunately for the purpose of testing this assumption empirically, the available data concerning the values of Volunteers were for the most part obtained in connection with discussions of Foundation activities, and would thus be redundant or self-confirming if used for this purpose. A number of rough indicators of non-Foundation personal values are of course available: social class, religious preferences, political affiliation, and occupation. None of these indicators are in any sense related to opinions concerning the ideal nature of the relationship between the national headquarters of an organization and its local units, however, and none were found to be related to perceptions of the Foundation's structure. Volunteers having both perceptions were found with approximately equal frequency among middle- and upper-class Volunteers, among Protestants and others, among Republicans and Democrats, among businessmen and professional people.*

The finding, however, that Southwestern and Western Volunteers are more likely than others to perceive the Foundation as a federation suggests so strongly that orientations toward local activities influence orientations toward the Foundation that it is unnecessary to reject the possibility that functional factors play a role in perception simply because adequate indicators are not available. The fact that one by no means atypical American community contains individuals with sharply

---

* Since Volunteers become members of the Foundation in various ways, it was thought that the particular experiences undergone by individual Volunteers might influence their perception of the Foundation's structure. It was hypothesized, for example, that Humanitarians might have a different image of the Foundation than Joiners, since they joined under such different circumstances. This turned out not to be the case, however, since both perceptions are found with equal frequency among all four types of recruits and among Volunteers recruited through the utilization of various role relationships. Furthermore, length of service as a Volunteer is not a determinant. Volunteers serving for the first year tend to regard the Foundation as a national organization somewhat more frequently than others, but no important differences were observed among Volunteers who had served for various numbers of years. By the same token, position in the organization is not related to perceptions of structure: holders of both images were found with equal frequency among Chairmen and among other Volunteers.

contrasting attitudes toward the community has been demonstrated by Robert Merton in his study of patterns of interpersonal influence in an Eastern Seaboard community he calls Rovere. Accordingly, it is instructive to note the differences he observed between the two types of influential people he calls "locals" and "cosmopolitans." Merton makes the distinction between these types of people in these terms:

The chief criterion for distinguishing the two is found in their *orientation* toward Rovere. The localite largely confines his interests to this community. Rovere is essentially his world. Devoting little thought or energy to the Great Society, he is preoccupied with local problems, to the virtual exclusion of the national and international scene. He is, strictly speaking, parochial.

Contrariwise with the cosmopolitan type. He has some interest in Rovere and must of course maintain a minimum of relations within the community since he, too, exerts influence there. But he is also oriented significantly to the world outside Rovere, and regards himself as an integral part of that world. He resides in Rovere but lives in the Great Society. If the local type is parochial, the cosmopolitan is ecumenical.[14]

The parallel between the orientation toward the *community* of the local and cosmopolitan individuals described by Merton and the orientation toward the *Foundation* of the federation-minded and nationally-minded Volunteers identified in this research becomes even clearer when the participation of local and cosmopolitan influentials in voluntary associations is examined. Merton found that these people differ not only with respect to their orientation toward Rovere, but also in terms of their participation in voluntary associations. Both types of influential individuals, he found, are inveterate joiners: cosmopolitans belong to an average of eight organizations per individual, and locals to an average of six. But they belong to different types of organizations:

The local influentials evidently crowd into those organizations which are largely designed for "making contacts," for establishing personal ties. Thus, they are found largely in the secret societies (Masons), fraternal organizations (Elks), and local service clubs. . . . Their participation appears to be less a matter of furthering the nominal objectives of these organizations than of using them as *contact centers.* . . . The cosmopolitans, on the other hand, tend to belong to those organizations in which they can exercise their special skills and knowledge. They are found in professional societies and in hobby groups. At the time of the inquiry, in 1943, they were more often involved in Civilian Defense organizations where again they were presumably more concerned with furthering the objectives of the organization than with establishing personal ties.[15]

The fact that local and cosmopolitan influentials characteristically join different types of voluntary associations led Merton to formulate an hypothesis concerning the different functions which participation serves for the two types:

Cosmopolitans are concerned with associations primarily because of the activities of these associations. They are means for extending or exhibiting their skills and knowledge. Locals are interested in associations not for their activities, but because these provide a means for extending personal relationships. The basic orientations of locals and cosmopolitan influentials are thus diversely expressed in organizational behavior as in other respects.[16]

Since Rovere is in no way an unusual American community, it can be assumed that most communities contain individuals with similar orientations toward organizational participation. And every community has a sufficient range of organizations to provide both types with ample opportunities to obtain satisfactions from participation. But if this situation is viewed not from the point of view of the individuals concerned, but rather from the point of view of the organizations in a community, and their capacity to carry out an active program, it becomes immediately apparent that it would be a distinct advantage for an organization if it were able to recruit *both* types of individuals. Both have skills to contribute, and both have an audience in the community which looks to them for leadership.

Is the Foundation able to recruit both local and cosmopolitan influentials? In view of the close parallel between the orientation toward the *community* of the local and cosmopolitan influentials described by Merton and the orientation toward the *Foundation* of federation-minded and nationally-minded Volunteers, it is not unreasonable to assume that the answer to this question is "yes."* Perceptions of the Foundation's structure, accordingly, are much more than merely examples of the widespread phenomenon of selective perception; they are in addition unplanned and distinctly advantageous components of the image of the Foundation held by its Volunteers.

## STRUCTURAL FACTORS

Although the Foundation's formal *structure* is clearly of the corporate type, it is important to note that the federation image represents

* Additional confirmation may also be derived from the fact that the Foundation recruits both Joiners and Good Citizens, who differ from one another in their original orientation toward the Foundation in a manner which closely resembles the different orientations of locals and cosmopolitans toward the organizations they join. See pp. 99–101.

a confirmation, albeit exaggerated and distorted, of one important aspect of the Foundation's *mode of operation*. For the principle of local autonomy is inherent in the activities which engage most of the attention of Volunteers—patient care and fund-raising. The patient care program first originated as a local activity, and both activities are by their very nature local programs. It is in a sense inevitable then that, among Volunteers who derive a sense of achievement from the opportunities for individual initiative offered by these programs, there should be some who structure the organization within their own minds so that it will conform with their own experiences. In fact, the problem of why some Volunteers perceive the Foundation as a federation is no more interesting, and perhaps less so, than the parallel problem of why some perceive it as a national organization.

A fundamental tenet of perceptual theory is that objects which are ambiguous lend themselves to restructuring more readily than do simpler or more familiar objects. In such situations, functional factors play a particularly important role in perception. Since the object itself is ambiguous, the person who perceives it must draw upon his own values and past experience if the object is to have any meaning for him.

Several aspects of the Foundation's program and mode of operation are fundamentally ambiguous in nature. This dual character of the Foundation, accordingly, greatly facilitates the process of selective perception. Four specific aspects of the Foundation's program and mode of operation which lend themselves to dual interpretation are discussed below.

*Manuals and publications.* It was pointed out earlier that the various manuals prepared by National Headquarters for the guidance of Volunteers describe the corporate-type structure of the organization in very specific terms. "A Chapter . . . is subject at all times to all rules, regulations and policies of the National Foundation,"[17] Volunteers are told. And again, "The National Foundation and its Chapters are one organization. . . . In a sense, a Chapter is like the branch office of a large corporation; National Headquarters is its home office."[18]

Many Volunteers, however, seldom have occasion to read these manuals. And even if they do, they are apt to be misled. Not deliberately, of course, for the manuals are as explicit as they could possibly be, but simply because official publications are most often used for guidance on specific issues. When they are read in this manner, it is quite easy for one sentence to be lifted from its context. Consider, for example, these excerpts from the *Reference Book for Chapters*. In the "Foreword," the following sentences appear:

The development of practical measures for serving each community must rest in the hands of local citizens. You in the Chapters can judge best what is needed. Your work is strengthened, however, by *its association with a national organization* with resources above and beyond those accessible locally.[19]

And in the section of this same manual entitled, "Chapter Relations with National Headquarters," Volunteers can read this phrase: "Within certain *limitations of broad principles and policies* set by National Headquarters, each Chapter is autonomous."[20]

The phrases "association with a national organization" and "limitations of broad principles and policies" are obviously so ambiguous in nature that a Volunteer seeking justification for his own contemplated action can easily interpret them as he wishes.

A Gas City Volunteer, for example, who is a strong advocate of local autonomy, asserted that she had never observed any instances of National Headquarters "dictating" policy to the Chapter. "We have a red-bound book [*Reference Book for Chapters*]," she said, "and we operate within this framework. It sets up a general framework for us, that's all." The fact that many passages in this reference book, and many others in the more legalistic *Manual for Chapters,* set very specific limits upon what practical measures may actually be taken by Chapters, and in what areas Chapters actually enjoy autonomy, has no bearing upon the perception of a Volunteer who never reads them. In brief, depending upon the nature of their own experiences in reading Foundation manuals and publications, Volunteers can acquire either a national or a federal image of the Foundation's formal structure.

*Chapter organization.* Since most Chapters are small, and since most activities are goal-related, there are few occasions for large meetings of Volunteers. Typically, the decisions made by Foundation Volunteers are made over the telephone, or over the luncheon table, or in one Volunteer's living room. The cumulative effect of being a participant in these decisions can, however, take two forms. Some Volunteers can perceive these activities as those of "agents for the National Foundation," and thus come to view the Foundation as a national organization. Others, more impressed by the fact that autonomous decisions, involving in many cases large sums of money, are made informally by Volunteers without the need to seek ratification from a higher headquarters, can as easily perceive this as evidence that their Chapter is an autonomous member of a nationwide federation. The organizational aspects of Chapter activities are so unstructured that either perception of the Foundation's formal structure can result. As in the case of manuals and publications, the actual image acquired is to a very great extent determined by the specific experiences of individual Volunteers.

*The patient care program.* The extent to which the patient care program provides Volunteers with opportunities to make autonomous decisions has previously been discussed in some detail. It is intended as a community service program and it is perceived as such by Volunteers. Since decisions are made locally, and since the funds necessary to finance the program are raised locally, participation in the patient care program often leads Volunteers to regard their Chapter as an autonomous local welfare agency. The South City Chapter Chairman, for example, affirmed the self-sufficiency of his local organization in these terms: "Last year we got a lot of equipment in gifts and that doesn't show up on the records. . . . We got two bubble-type respirators and iron lungs in the last drive. Frankly, I like it better when we get equipment."

Even the system under which local Chapters can apply to National Headquarters for supplementary funds—described above as being dependent upon a corporate-type structure for its proper functioning—can be invoked as evidence of the federated nature of the Foundation. Witness this statement by a Glass City Volunteer:

(*Which means more to you personally, the fact that the Chapter fights polio, or the fact that this is an effort for the benefit of people here in this community?*) I think maybe more that it is a local outfit. Of course I realize that if our county funds are depleted there's a chance for a loan from the National Foundation or some type of help.

Finally, an extreme version of the posture of independence which local interpretation of patient care policies often fosters is the emphatic declaration of another Chapter Chairman, who claimed he had told a headquarters representative that "just because it's a polio fund it doesn't have to go just to polio people." He went on to explain to the interviewer that "we help *all* crippled children. Anything at all, clubfoot, harelip—they just run 'em over here to me, and if it's reasonable we pay for it."

But sometimes a Chapter's funds become exhausted. Perhaps a polio patient needs an iron lung, and there is none in the local hospital. Suppose a patient's doctor recommends that therapy at Georgia Warm Springs is needed? In situations such as these, the importance of National Headquarters becomes apparent. Through the State Representative, or even directly, the machinery of National Headquarters can be set into motion, and the problem can be solved. Volunteers who have observed this machinery in action, it goes without saying, are provided with a forceful reminder of the fact that they are members of a national organization. An Upstate City Volunteer described one such experience:

In 1944 Mr. _____ called Mr. O'Connor one afternoon about four o'clock and told him we were out of funds. The next morning we had $25,000 here. And that's not all. We had to go back for $5,000 that summer. Before, I thought these people at National were just a bunch of "stiffies"—that we didn't need them. We were way out here in the sticks . . . and we got along very well. Well, last summer taught me a lesson. The people at National came down here and they were just wonderful.

The patient care program accordingly, in spite of the fact that its mechanics are quite uniform throughout the country, readily lends itself to dual interpretation, since Volunteers acquire either image of the Foundation's formal structure through participating in it.

*The fund-raising program.* The very nature of the March of Dimes campaign is a source of different perceptions of the organization. It is, first of all, a nationwide campaign timed to occur simultaneously all over the country during one month. It is, moreover, the one activity of the Foundation which is most consistently and widely publicized on a national scale. But at the same time it is also an activity which permits, indeed, places a premium upon local improvisation. Consequently, those Volunteers who have been involved in organizing the broad aspects of the fund-raising campaign, or who have been concerned with supplying the local mass media with publicity releases, have been particularly conscious of being part of a centrally-directed, coordinated effort, and of being dependent upon materials furnished by "headquarters." However, equally common phenomena are the references made by March of Dimes Volunteers—in particular those who have assumed responsibility for specific phases of the campaign of a "special events" nature—to local creative efforts. It is just this type of activity, which offers a wide latitude for personal creativity and interpretation, which strengthens or actually gives rise to these Volunteers' sense of autonomy. The prideful account of a Wheat County March of Dimes Volunteer who described with obvious relish to the interviewer his handling of a recent campaign is a case in point:

And the radio—sometimes I feel bad because the air is blue with polio news, but I don't hesitate a minute to shovel more onto them. . . . One guy —he's a station manager down there—can do more tear jerkers than they can think up in New York. I have a hobby, firecrackers. . . . This gave me an idea for the Mothers' March. The fire trucks are no good, they don't get enough attention, so to get the headlines, I put one aerial bomb in each district instead of that folderol of sirens. We had the bomb go off in each district. You don't have anything like that usually to disturb people.

The Foundation's policy on participation in joint fund-raising campaigns also lends itself to a dual interpretation. As described earlier, the nationwide policy of the Foundation is that fund-raising must be conducted as an independent activity. The participation of local units in Community Chest or other joint appeals is thus specifically forbidden.* In order to assist Volunteers tactfully to decline to participate in such campaigns, National Headquarters furnishes them with statements of the Foundation's policies, suggested letters to the directors of the joint campaigns, etc. But Community Chest drives and similar campaigns are themselves local organizations, and are thus free to attempt to persuade the March of Dimes to join in with them by any means at their disposal. In communities in which the Community Chest leaders tacitly accept the privilege of the March of Dimes not to participate, Volunteers need only decline to join by stating that the policy of their organization forbids it. But in communities in which these leaders do not accept the legitimacy of the Foundation's policy, the conflict between the Community Chest and the March of Dimes often develops into an open struggle between two rival organizations.

Volunteers faced with the first of these situations, accordingly, are openly reminded of the fact that they are members of a national organization. In reporting his experience, one Wheat County Volunteer told this story:

I almost got sucked in. They [the Community Chest leaders] said that they would conduct an audit and assign to each charity the amount that people gave to it, but that was just propaganda. I was straightened out on that when I saw the Director of Fund-raising for the Foundation.

But for Volunteers in communities where resistance to participate in the Community Chest involves more than a simple refusal, the conflict demands retaliatory measures to combat unfavorable publicity directed at the March of Dimes. It is necessary, in other words, that Volunteers

* See pp. 53–56.

take autonomous action in order to win community recognition and support, which in turn strengthens their image of the Foundation as a federation of local organizations. "I pulled a gimmick here that proved pretty good," an embattled Volunteer in Harbor City reported, since "we had to show that the community still supported the March of Dimes." He then related how he had persuaded the mayor, local religious leaders, and prominent businessmen to appear on radio and television programs to make special pleas on behalf of the March of Dimes, summing up his strategy in these terms:

So during the whole campaign you have your ecclesiastical leaders, your business leaders, your first citizens, who told how much support was needed. So while we were getting buffeted and kicked in the teeth by the Community Chest, we had a united community on the other side.

Volunteers who have had experiences such as these naturally tend to think of themselves as leaders of an autonomous organization, while Volunteers whose experiences in fund-raising have made them more conscious of being participants in a coordinated, national campaign tend to perceive the Foundation as a national organization.

*Intermittent participation.* Formal organizations differ markedly with respect to the amount of time their members devote to organizational activities. Monasteries and military organizations, to cite two extreme examples, demand almost full-time participation from their members. Government bureaucracies and industrial or business organizations generally require participation for at least forty hours a week. An important characteristic of all voluntary associations, however, is that most members are only part-time and intermittent participants. Although some associations are able to attract leaders who have the leisure to devote a great deal of time to organizational activity, this is generally not true of the Foundation.

The typical Volunteer is an extremely busy person. He is in his most active years of life—more than three-fourths of all Volunteers are under fifty years old—and he must work hard to establish and maintain financial security for himself and his family. He has a growing family, and, like most middle-class Americans, has no household servants. And he belongs to two or three voluntary associations other than the Foundation. Consequently, there are definite limits upon the amount of time and energy he can devote to Foundation activity.

Even the complicated details of running the March of Dimes campaign are handled pretty much with the "left hand." As demonstrated earlier, only 40 per cent of the various March of Dimes Chairmen in the four counties studied intensively devoted more than twenty hours to March of Dimes activities, and 31 per cent devoted less than ten hours.* During the other months of the years, moreover, even fewer hours are expended, although the annual total is impressive. But the patient care program often requires that only a few Volunteers spend a great deal of time attending to its details, and in large cities, where there are often many patients in need of financial assistance, an Executive Secretary may be employed to handle at least the bookkeeping aspects of the program.

Because participation is intermittent, and tangential to the lives of Volunteers, most Volunteers observe only a small sampling of the entire range of Foundation activities in their communities, and are only partially informed concerning the national program. If the activities they have observed seem to suggest that the Foundation's structure is that of a federation, the twin processes of *supplementing* and *structuring* take place. From their partial knowledge Volunteers construct an image of the organization which conforms to the small sample of the organization which they have observed. By the same token, if they observe specific instances of the Foundation's functioning as a national organization, they tend to perceive its structure as having that form.

*Goal-related activities.* The extent to which the local activities of the Foundation are largely goal-related—in contradistinction to organization-related activities—has been discussed earlier, in connection with the ways in which the Foundation's structure mitigates against its goals being displaced,† and need not be repeated here. For present purposes, the important consequence of this emphasis upon goal-related activities is that the individual Volunteer only infrequently comes into contact with the actual organizational mechanisms of the Foundation. For example, the typical Volunteer generally has no need to consult the Chapter *By-Laws;* he does not have to make arrangements for ceremonial occasions; and he attends only one or two membership meetings a year. Instead, he is chiefly engaged in carrying out pragmatic tasks: interviewing the families of patients, driving patients to a clinic, raising funds, talking to community groups, etc. It is quite possible, accordingly, to be an active Volunteer for many years without having much

* See Table 15, p. 151.
† See pp. 72–75.

contact with the Foundation *as an organization.* Yet it is precisely in official literature, and in purely organizational procedures, that the corporate nature of the Foundation's structure becomes most apparent. Goal-related activities, in short, serve as a structural source of selective perception of the Foundation's actual formal structure.

*chapter VIII*

# THE
# REWARDS OF
# VOLUNTEERING

## Introduction

IT IS quite apparent from the material presented in the previous chapter that Volunteers respond favorably to the organizational aspects of the Foundation. They like the fact that many important decisions are made by Volunteers, not by a professional staff; they approve of the simplicity and economy of the patient care program and the March of Dimes; and, regardless of their own preferences concerning the proper structure of a national organization, they find the Foundation's pattern of national-local relationships congenial. The prevalence of these attitudes of course goes far toward explaining the continued participation of Volunteers in the Foundation's program.

Other chapters in this volume have also contributed to an explanation of this phenomenon. Chapter I, for example, discussed the structural features of the Foundation which enable it to maintain the interest of its members at a high level. Chapters IV and V described how patient care and fund-raising are activities which, in addition to being utilitarian in purpose, provide Volunteers with many opportunities for obtaining personal satisfactions.

This chapter approaches the topic of Volunteer participation from a somewhat different point of view: it discusses the nature of the rewards Volunteers derive from their participation. In one sense, the chapter is more specific than previous ones, in that many different instances of satisfying experiences are cited; in another sense, it is much more general, since an attempt is made to relate the experiences of Volunteers in Foundation activities to the patterns of life characteristic of American society.

*233*

## Major Rewards

Emphasis has been placed in this volume upon the activities and opinions of Volunteers which both relate to and further the achievement of the Foundation's expressed purposes—providing assistance to polio victims, raising funds to finance the program, and eventually eliminating infantile paralysis as an epidemic disease. These purposes are of course both highly specific and extremely "rational" in nature, and an equally specific and rational program has been developed in order to achieve them. National Headquarters is responsible for providing general coordination and direction to the organization, and for supporting research into the cause, treatment, and prevention of polio, while local Chapters are responsible for patient care, for informing the community concerning the nature of the disease and the steps which are being taken to combat it, and, through taking part in the March of Dimes, for raising the funds necessary to support both the local and national programs.

Because of the specificity and rationality of its program, the Foundation would appear to be characterized by what Rudolf Heberle has called a "purposive-rational, society-like type of texture."* Social reality, however, seldom conforms perfectly with official reality, and during the course of this research it was learned that many Volunteers view the Foundation in quite different terms. More specifically, they view it as an organization whose activities make it possible for them on the one hand to achieve a larger measure of self-fulfillment and on the other hand to avail themselves of an opportunity to subordinate their personalities in a transcendent cause—to participate, as it were, in a social movement. Before this significance of this phenomenon can be discussed, it is necessary to describe the specific nature of these rewards.

### OPPORTUNITIES FOR SELF-FULFILLMENT

A recurrent theme in discussions of contemporary American society concerns the difficulties which many individuals have in finding an adequate way in which to express their own personalities. The theme is of course not new—more than a century ago Henry Thoreau noted that "the mass of men lead lives of quiet desperation"[2]—but the increased pace of America's industrialization has caused numerous ob-

---

* The term "texture" is used by Heberle to describe the "socio-psychological" relations between members of a group, in contrast, for example, to the "structural" relations discussed in the previous chapter.[1]

servers to conclude that the failure of many Americans to achieve a measure of self-fulfillment constitutes a distinguishing characteristic of our times. Clyde Kluckhohn notes that many Americans are "adrift on a meaningless voyage,"[3] and David Riesman has recently characterized American society as "the lonely crowd."[4] Evidence to support these assertions can be found at every turn; consider for example the constant stream of self-help books flowing from the nation's publishing houses. Practically all of these books offer two bits of advice: get involved in some activity which assists other people, and acquire some skill in a field not related to your livelihood. In the face of this advice, it is of some significance that when Volunteers were asked what had been the most rewarding aspects of their participation in Foundation activities, a majority mentioned either the opportunities provided to help others or the skills which they had achieved in the course of carrying out their Foundation assignments.

*Helping others.* The individual Volunteer has many opportunities to feel that he is "doing good," since the activities of the organization are oriented toward others—polio victims—rather than toward the members themselves. Significantly, however, only a small percentage of all Volunteers originally entered the Foundation primarily for humanitarian reasons.* But once he is a member, the fact that a Volunteer is involved in a humanitarian enterprise becomes very apparent. He helps others by raising money to fight a crippling disease, by disbursing funds to relieve the burden placed upon the family of a polio victim, or simply by enlisting the cooperation and support of others for these activities. Activities of this kind, understandably enough, are often viewed as personally rewarding. Witness, for example, the statement of a Chapter Volunteer in Gas City:

(*What has given you the greatest feeling of satisfaction and accomplishment?*) Over the years, I'd say the mere fact that I've been in a position to help some of these poor devils. The poor bastards, they have nothing, so we can give them four hundred dollars, a thousand dollars. . . .

Or the almost identical comment of a March of Dimes Chairman in Hometown, who found that "help and service to mankind . . . just in general giving help to some poor devil who can't help himself" is what gave him the greatest sense of self-fulfillment.

Being a "good citizen" by contributing voluntarily to the benefit of others has provided many Volunteers with a sense of self-fulfillment.

* See pp. 89–96.

Working on the Executive Committee, declared a Chapter Volunteer in Gas City, "makes me feel like the richest man in the world. Here in my business, I can work and make a success of it, but there is more to life than that. You have to have something else." And the Lakeside County Chapter Chairman noted that "if you haven't improved the conditions around you under which you live, you haven't done much for your community and your country."

These statements, and the many others in the interviews which express the same sentiments in somewhat different words, are notable for their emphasis on the opportunities offered by Foundation activities for fulfilling idealistic yearnings. Volunteers who regard their activities in these terms generally said, either explicitly or by intimation, that working on their local Chapter or March of Dimes campaign had allowed the fulfillment of a deeply-rooted desire to "do right" by others. Significantly, this altruistic compulsion is generally related to direct participation in Foundation activities, rather than to nominal affiliation. Life in the average middle class American community, of which the thirty-seven communities studied are a fair representation, is essentially placid, remarkably free of any great economic struggle or political strife, pleasantly routinized and predictable. In these communities, opportunities for intercession on behalf of others and for participation in dramatic crises are infrequent. For this reason, Foundation activities fill a vacuum in the lives of many Volunteers. Here, for example, is the testimony of a Chapter Volunteer in Market Town, who is the proprietor of a roadside bar-and-grill:

I'm interested in good causes. I try to get others to do as much good as they can. I'm in a line of business here that I'm not happy with. . . . You look around and try to do something good and this is one thing where you *know* you can do good. I don't see how anybody can be happy without doing something for their fellow man.

Humanitarian fervor in connection with Foundation activity assumes particular significance when one realizes that there are, in reality, many institutional and informal means in most communities for helping others: church charities, youth organizations, other health and welfare projects, etc. Many Volunteers, however, regard Foundation activity as a *unique* opportunity to "do good." The opportunity *is* of course unique in the sense that many voluntary health and welfare associations provide only vicarious satisfactions. Direct experiences, however, provide direct rewards, as evidenced by this comment of the Chapter Secretary in Lakeside County:

When I come in [to the hospital] and say, "I'm Mrs. _____," they look to you and lean on you. If [people] could see their faces you wouldn't have to ask people to be Volunteers—they'd ask *you*.

*Being an expert*. Although Foundation Volunteers have had for the most part no specialized preparation for their work, and the activities themselves are of such a nature that any intelligent person who "knows his way around" in the community can perform them, the average Volunteer thinks of himself as a quasi-professional, as a man who knows more about the tasks of combating polio, and raising money than his neighbors. Objectively speaking, Volunteers are of course correct in this self-evaluation, since most people are only vaguely informed about the problems of polio, and relatively few people in any community have actually organized and supervised a fund-raising campaign. For present purposes, however, our interest in not much in the technical skills acquired by Volunteers as it is in the many satisfactions they obtain from practicing them.

Close contact with the medical profession is one source of satisfaction, since in our society, the doctor, the "man in white," has been idolized in film and fiction as the prestige figure above all others, the embodiment of "science." Before becoming a Volunteer, a Chapter member in Power City recalled, "My only relationship with doctors . . . was sickness in the family, but now it's different. Lots of times, when we visit hospitals, we give opinions on things." Speaking of his relationship with local doctors, a Chapter Volunteer in Wheat County noted, "We understand their problems and they understand ours." And a Chapter Volunteer in Harbor City reported with pride his familiarity with the hidden world of medicine:

Patient care . . . has been an education for me. Now I have no trouble to go into a doctor's office, to get in and get the information. Then the interesting bits of information I get in this way lets me go to the family to help them, reassure them. I can spread the word, tell people in lay language what can be done. I have also had the opportunity to set [*sic*] in on Medical Advisory meetings. . . .

Because Volunteers have an opportunity for close contact with doctors, they also feel that they are the *equals* of doctors. "They're my committee," affirmed the Glass City Chapter Chairman. "I appointed them with a view to working with them and solving problems we knew would arise." And because doctors are often regarded as equals, they are not immune to criticism. Parallel of course to the American tendency to idolize doctors is the tendency to criticize them for their exclusiveness, their sense of superiority, their charges. Foundation Volunteers, armed with first-hand experience and some knowledge of their own, often take satisfaction in deflating the medical ego. "He's nice and cooperative," said the South City Chapter Chairman of the chief of the Orthopedics Department at a local medical school, "although I don't agree with his treatment." And a Wheat County Volunteer reported with pride that "they don't pull the medical ethics story on *me*. They tell me all the facts. Of course, we're giving them some tools to clean up the abuses in their own profession. . . . They're willing to work with us on that."

Since Volunteers often do have close contact with polio patients, and since doctors are generally regarded as prestigeful persons, there is also a tendency for Volunteers to identify with doctors, to adopt the role of doctor, and to obtain a sense of self-fulfillment in this way. National Headquarters is of course aware of this tendency, and warns Volunteers not to think of patients as being Chapter patients.* But the temptation is too great for many Volunteers to resist, and the interviews are replete with references to "my patients," or "our patients." Speaking of one particularly serious case, the Chapter Chairman in Suburb County noted that "his vital capacity was about 300 cc's. Now it's up to around 600. But a fellow like him . . . ought to have about 3500 vital capacity. . . . We decided to try the rocking bed." Volunteers speak of being able to tell "right away" whether or not a patient will have full recovery, and of having to lie deliberately to the family at times; of their awareness of what it means psychologically to contract polio; and of their skill at relieving the tension in the minds of the parents of a child with polio. And many have a favorite story concerning their success with a particular patient. A Polio Emergency Volunteer in Steel City, for example, told of:

> . . . a little girl who was a dancer and had to have braces. She was very restless, and the mother told me, "She has never liked to stay still." She calmed down and agreed to be quiet after I told her if she wanted to dance again she would have to be able to walk first.

Although Volunteers who perform the role of a doctor naturally begin to feel they are doctors, this is not the only source of such satisfactions. The Chapter Chairman in Cattlefeed City, for example, a successful businessman who never went beyond high school, confessed that his activity in health organizations stemmed directly from his

* See p. 134.

thwarted desire to become a doctor. "I guess that's why I'm so active in health organizations," he said. "I always wish I had been a doctor. I was all set to go to pre-med when the banks crashed in 1932. . . ."

Direct contact with patients and doctors is not required for a Volunteer to obtain satisfactions from being an expert, since patient care is only one part of the local program. As a local spokesman for the Foundation, a Volunteer may speak for the Chapter in advising the public and in answering requests for information. Volunteers welcome this role, and are eager to disseminate information, upon invitation or otherwise. "Everybody knows of the Chapter, from the calls I get," reported the Chapter Chairman in Corn City. "Women call and say their children have such and such symptoms," he continued, "and they ask me do their children have polio. You tell them to call the doctor and they say, 'Oh, no! I want you to tell me! . . . They call me Mr. Polio in this city." And a Defense Town Volunteer noted, "I ask people to read their [polio] insurance policies carefully and not to buy a policy that doesn't have complete coverage—they ask my advice on that a lot."

During the March of Dimes campaign Volunteers often have an opportunity to give radio talks, or to hear their words repeated over the radio. "The radio usually calls on me," reported the Vice-Chairman in Gas City, "I'm generally spokesman for the Chapter." And the Campaign Director in Market Town, whose days are spent making loans in a small household finance company, found during the campaign that "I used to wake up in the morning and the first thing I'd hear on the radio was, 'Chairman ———— says such and such.' And then they would give some March of Dimes news."

Fund-raising itself requires special skills in which Volunteers take pride. A Mothers' March Captain in Harbor City, for example, prides herself on her ability to recruit Marching Mothers. Learning that a women's organization might be persuaded to supply volunteer workers, she called its president:

I called her when I heard that Mayor ————— had appointed her. I told her that I thought Mayor ————— was a good mayor—things like that. That's the way you work on them. So she came down and brought her group down.

Persuading people to contribute money is an art by itself, according to the Chapter Chairman in Defense Town, who noted, "You have to have the personality that will get you in to see your giver. . . . When they see me coming, they pull out their money, or they reach for the broom." And for those Volunteers who lack such skills, there are always other jobs to be done. "I've never been in a position to get people to do things," reported a former Postmaster in Lakeside County, who has been active in fund-raising since the first President's Birthday Ball. "I just keep records," she continued. "I know where to find information. I used to be in the courthouse and I still know the people. I'm not good at soliciting money, but some people can't count."

## PARTICIPATION IN A SOCIAL MOVEMENT

One indication of the fact that Volunteers receive rewards not only from participating in a voluntary association, but also from being a part of a social movement, is the frequency with which words derived from military or crusading terminology were used with reference to participation in the Foundation. The leitmotiv of these statements is a sense of pride and satisfaction in being part of a nationwide movement—a "citizens' army"—which has banded together thousands of people who are powerless to combat polio alone, but whose cumulative efforts have made a coordinated attack possible. "We're a small group here, but there are thousands tied in all over the country," was the way a Chapter Volunteer in Wheat County expressed this thought. In recruiting other Volunteers, a March of Dimes Volunteer in Pulpwood City told the interviewer, "I stress banding together to fight a common enemy." For a March of Dimes Chairman in Pinetree County, the greatest sense of satisfaction was derived from being "one small part of a large group of people who are conquering a world-wide— what would you say—plague. I had one small part in the attempt to stamp it out. If this was in medieval times, we would say a 'demon.'" Another enthusiastic Volunteer, the Chapter Chairman in South City, chose a different metaphor. Emphasizing "what a tremendous thing the Foundation is doing by banding together people to fight disease," he likened the organization to a "ground swell."

The Foundation differs from many special purpose associations in that it is neither a "social protest" organization nor one which seeks to inculcate moral principles. On the contrary, it is an organization which has set for itself very pragmatic goals which are fully in accord with the dominant values of American society, and which it seeks to achieve through the medium of culturally sanctioned activities. For this reason, Volunteers who assert that the Foundation has "ideological" overtones, or is the embodiment of a "way of life," may be said to derive satisfactions from participation in a social movement.

Some of these Volunteers focused their comments upon the impact of Foundation activity upon their own lives. "Working for the Foundation has made me broader, more tolerant," the Steamboat City Chapter Chairman reported. And she thinks other women would have a similar experience, since "the Foundation has an immense potential among women, maybe all over America." Other Volunteers, less articulate, are nevertheless impressed by the fact that participation in the Foundation has a pervasive influence upon people's lives. "I think you'll find the people who work for polio don't know why," is the way these ideological overtones were expressed by a Wheat County Volunteer. "People working for polio have a special spirit," he continued, and "I don't know where they get it." Even minor details can evoke an idealistic fervor. "People don't charge for gasoline," reported a College Town Volunteer. "I never charge for gasoline on my trips. That again is on an emotional basis. It's humanity serving humanity."

One version of the notion that the Foundation is an expression of a "way of life" concerns its function as a moral force in society. Some Volunteers find that participation evokes what is perhaps best described as a missionary zeal. "It's a pretty wonderful feeling to be part of the whole thing," the College Town Chapter Chairman declared. "I'm a great believer in helping other people," he continued, "regardless if they live in College Town or New York. They are still humans—even abroad. The effort should be to spread [the Foundation] all over the world. If you could take the effort that the Foundation exerts and put it all over, just think how wonderful it could be!" Perhaps the most eloquent expression of the Foundation as both a personal ideology and one which represents a moral force in society is the one voiced by the Chapter Secretary in Market Town:

This is established not as a charity, but as a way of life. . . . For the people, by the people, of the people. . . . It reminds me of the translation of the Bible and the statement of King James in the Preface of why people should be able to read it. . . . If I could express it in its essence, it is a feeling for others. . . . It's something that people feel. It's intangible. It's having a semblance of understanding of people who went before you, a feeling that you want to be a part of it. It's like what makes you want to live. The thing that makes you a human being. You see man as he would like to be, but on a level which he has not as yet achieved.

A measure of the ideological convictions of this Volunteer is provided by the remainder of her statement as well, in which she explicitly minimized the pragmatic program of the Foundation:

It's not just crippling. If I never saw a patient and just explained to you the part of the *Chapter Manual* as it deals with the human relations aspect of the program, you would still want to do it. You say you want to get out of it and you don't. You think the problem can't be resolved, but you don't leave it.

Finally, some Volunteers interpret the "way of life" which they believe the Foundation symbolizes as being consonant with their own conceptions of the meaning of democracy. For those who are unable to articulate their political beliefs in general terms, the Foundation becomes identified in their own mind with the label of the political party which they support. The Chapter Chairman in Steel City, for example, an active Democrat, provided this criticism of the medical profession: "You take these doctors locally. They feel we spend too much money. It's the Republican idea, in contrast to the Democratic idea of help thy brother." For some Republican Volunteers, on the other hand, the Foundation represents a reversal of a dangerous trend. "We went astray here in this country a few years ago," the Lumber City Campaign Chairman reported. "We had leanings toward socialism," he continued. "I think a large part of the March of Dimes is our own people's answer to socialized medicine." More frequently, however, Volunteers see the Foundation's political meaning in broader terms, and see the organization as not only a demonstration but also a vindication of the American way. "It's the American way of life against a common enemy," explained a March of Dimes Volunteer in Harbor City.

A characteristic common to all of the statements cited above is that they are holistic evaluations of participation in the Foundation's activities. In this respect, they differ from the more circumscribed statements reported earlier, which have been concerned with such topics as comparisons between the Foundation and other organizations, evaluations of the patient care program, and perceptions of the Foundation's formal structure. Furthermore, the degree of affect or emotional envolvement which these statements contain suggests that they constitute more than mere favorable comments about an organization. Although these Volunteers did not use the term "social movement" in their discussions of the Foundation—typically they spoke of the "polio movement" or the "polio cause"—the tone and nature of their comments indicate that their satisfactions from participation in Foundation activities are of a different order than those realizable from mere affiliation with a voluntary association; that they are, in effect, the satisfactions attainable only through participation in a social movement.

## Conclusions

The opportunities provided by the Foundation's program for "helping others" and for "being an expert" require no special explanation, since they clearly derive from the nature of the activities in which Volunteers take part. But can Foundation Volunteers, on a purely objective basis, be considered to be participants in a social movement? This question cannot be answered without considering the various ways in which social movements can be defined. At one extreme, it is possible to speak of *general* social movements, in which the participants have an interest in common which they pursue in many different, and often noncoordinated ways. The labor movement, the youth movement, the women's movement, the peace movement, the soil conservation movement, and the anti-slavery movement are often cited as illustrations of general social movements.[5] If this broad definition is used, Foundation Volunteers are of course participants in a social movement—what Louis Dublin has called the "voluntary health movement."[6] A classification of this kind, however, although accurate for descriptive purposes, certainly does not provide a very useful basis for interpreting the statements of Foundation Volunteers, since the term "movement" has entered our language as a colloquial way of referring to any attempt to instigate social or even technological change, e.g., the "automation movement."

At the other extreme, social movements have been defined as being almost pathological in nature. Some writers, for example, assume that the leaders and followers of social movements are characterized by psychological frustration of some kind. Arnold Green states that participants in social movements are generally at odds with themselves and the world about them, and cites the Moral Rearmament and the Townsend Movement as examples of typical social movements.[7] Hadley Cantril, in a volume devoted to a psychological analysis of participation in social movements, illustrates his thesis with case studies of lynching mobs, the Kingdom of Father Divine, the Oxford Group, the Townsend Plan, and the Nazi Party.[8] And Talcott Parsons states that the first condition for the emergence of a social movement is "the presence in the population of sufficiently intense, widely spread and properly distributed alienative motivational elements."[9] By these criteria, Foundation Volunteers are clearly not participants in a social movement, since they are drawn largely from the most integrated, rather than the most alienated, segment of the American population.

Between these two extremes are those definitions of social movements which are more specific than the definition of a general social movement, but which do not suggest that only alienated individuals participate in them. Rather, they stress the fact that social movements involve activities on the part of organized groups to effect some change in society. Herbert Blumer, for example, states that social movements may be generically defined as "collective enterprises to establish a new order of life";[10] Rudolf Heberle describes a social movement as "a collective ready for action by which some kind of change is to be achieved, some innovation to be made, or some previous condition to be restored";[11] and Wendell King says that social movements involve "a systematic effort to inaugurate changes in thought, behavior, and social relationships."[12] According to criteria such as these, the Foundation obviously has many of the characteristics of a social movement, since it attempts to change not only the statistical incidence of infantile paralysis but also our society's mode of treating and preventing it.

No attempt need be made here to resolve this confusion concerning the range of behavior which may properly be included in the term "social movement," since the very fact that so many Volunteers obtain satisfactions from regarding their participation as extending beyond anti-polio activities is sufficient evidence that the Foundation represents to its members something more than a special purpose association. Our concern, rather, is to attempt to explain this phenomenon, and in so doing to contribute to an explanation of the reasons underlying widespread Volunteer dedication to the organization, and hence the Foundation's capacity to carry out its purposes so effectively. Since the phenomenon itself is complex, and assumes such a variety of forms, no single explanation can possibly be sufficient. The explanation which follows, accordingly, considers the role played by four different factors: the historical circumstances surrounding the Foundation's origins, the reading of Foundation publications, the prior dispositions of Volunteers, and Volunteer participation in the Foundation's program.

*The role of the Foundation's history.* Since the original impetus behind the creation of a new organization generally comes from a number of directions, it is difficult to select one event as the most crucial moment in an organization's history. In the case of the Foundation, however, a strong case can be made for selecting the visit of Franklin D. Roosevelt to Warm Springs, Georgia in the fall of 1924. Roosevelt had heard of the beneficial effects of the mineral pools at Warm Springs upon another victim of infantile paralysis, and had decided to try the pools himself. He found that the mineral water gave some strength to his legs, and decided to return regularly to Warm Springs. Other polio victims soon began to come to Warm Springs, and in 1927 the Georgia Warm Springs Foundation was established as a private philanthropy, financed for the most part by Roosevelt and a few other wealthy individuals.[13] Eleven years later, through circumstances recounted earlier,* a full-fledged national organization, the National Foundation for Infantile Paralysis, was established.

At some time between the years 1924 and 1938, however, an equally important transformation took place: a private philanthropy acquired many of the characteristics of a social movement. Some historians might select January 30, 1934 as the crucial date in this transformation, since that was the night of the first President's Birthday Ball, a fund-raising venture which was supported by the public far beyond the expectations of its sponsors. Others would regard this event as evidence of skillful organization, but not necessarily of widespread public interest and support, and would select instead a week in January, 1938, during the Foundation's first month of existence, when Eddie Cantor and the Lone Ranger suggested over a nationwide radio network that anyone who wanted to help fight polio could send a dime to President Roosevelt at the White House. As a result of these announcements, the American people contributed a total of 2,680,000 dimes which completely disrupted operations in the White House mail room for months.[14] And still others would say that the Foundation became a social movement as early as 1933, when the people of the state of Georgia contributed thousands of dimes and dollars toward the construction of Georgia Hall.† In any event, there is little doubt that the transformation of the Georgia Warm Springs Foundation into a social movement was closely related to the popularity of President Roosevelt, who was endowed, in the minds of millions of Americans in the 1930's, with many of the characteristics of a "charismatic" leader. Max Weber first introduced the term "charisma" into sociological discourse, and defined it as follows:

The term "charisma" will be applied to a certain quality of an individual personality by virtue of which he is set apart from ordinary men and treated as endowed with supernatural, superhuman, or at least specifically exceptional powers or qualities. These are such as are not accessible to the ordinary person, but are regarded as of divine origin or as exemplary, and on the basis of them the individual concerned is treated as a leader.[15]

* See pp. 44–46.
† See pp. 42–43.

Weber's purpose in introducing the concept of "charisma" was to identify a type of authority which differs from either "rational" or "traditional" authority. "Both rational and traditional authority," he wrote, "are specifically forms of everyday routine control of action; while the charismatic type is the direct antithesis of this. . . . The only basis of legitimacy for it is personal charisma, so long as it is proved; that is, as long as it receives recognition and is able to satisfy the followers or disciples. But this lasts only so long as the belief in its charismatic inspiration remains."[16]

A major interest of Weber was the process through which charismatic authority becomes transformed into rational or traditional authority, since such a transformation is necessary if charismatic authority is not to be a purely transitory phenomenon. "In its pure form," he wrote, "charismatic authority may be said to exist only in the process of originating. It cannot remain stable but becomes either traditionalized or rationalized, or a combination of both."[17] This process, termed by Weber the "routinization of charisma," is of course a central concern of students of social movements, since most, but not all, social movements originate as the following of a charismatic leader, and develop in time into large-scale organizations.[18]

The Foundation, like many voluntary associations, has thus passed through three distinct stages: a modest beginning as the private interest of a charismatic leader, a period of mass enthusiasm, and finally the establishment of a formal organization. It has even undergone a process which Weber regarded as crucial to the survival of a charismatically-led organization: "the designation on the part of the original charismatic leader of his own successor. . . ."[19] Basil O'Connor, who worked closely with Roosevelt in the Georgia Warm Springs Foundation, recalls this moment in the Foundation's history very clearly:

When Mr. Roosevelt decided to run for the New York governorship in 1928, he said to me: "Doc, you'll have to run Warm Springs now!" Fulfilling that assignment, and the one which followed as president of the National Foundation for Infantile Paralysis, have been the most enriching experiences of my life.[20]

Can the historical origins of the Foundation as a charismatically-led mass movement be said to account for the fact that many Volunteers today regard their participation in Foundation activities as participation in a social movement? Is the Foundation an example of an organization which has undergone the "routinization of charisma," but which nevertheless retains many of the characteristics of charismatically-led movement? In one sense the answer to these questions must be affirmative. Basil O'Connor, Roosevelt's friend and colleague, is still president of the Foundation. A majority of the American population knows that President Roosevelt established the Foundation.* Every Volunteer who sees Foundation correspondence or publications is confronted with the phrase, "Franklin D. Roosevelt, Founder," and those who have occasion to visit National Headquarters in New York cannot help but notice the pictures of President Roosevelt hanging on the walls of the various offices. Furthermore, many Volunteers explicitly mentioned in the course of the interviews that both they and the public think of the Foundation in terms of President Roosevelt. "Most people think of Roosevelt," reported a March of Dimes Chairman in South City. "As far as they are concerned, he is a permanent President. . . . The name 'Roosevelt' is closely allied with the drive. . . . Polio and FDR are one and the same thing." And a Chapter Volunteer in Wheat County, when asked what he knew about the Foundation before he joined, said, "All I knew was 'just give dimes.' I was one to have great confidence in the fellow who started it . . . Roosevelt."

Nevertheless, the presence in the Foundation today of so many Volunteers who regard the Foundation as a social movement as well as a voluntary association cannot be attributed solely to the fact that the charismatic authority of Roosevelt has persisted in the minds of some Volunteers. In the first place, this view is found as frequently among newcomers to the Foundation as it is among "old-timers." Moreover, it is found as frequently among Republican Volunteers as it is among Democrats. And most important of all, many Volunteers who regard their participation in this light cannot be considered to be followers of the charismatic leadership of President Roosevelt. "I believe firmly in the Republican Party," the Campaign Director in Oil City told the interviewer. "I am very much against Mr. Roosevelt and all his works," he continued. "This whole thing started very politically, as you probably know. . . . I feel that in recent years the Foundation has successfully divorced itself from this political connotation and emphasis." And a Mountain County Volunteer reported that one of her strategies to raise money from her Republican neighbors was to include on her staff "a woman who cast the electoral vote for Eiesenhower— I guess that will show them that we are not Democrats." Accordingly, in order to understand this phenomenon, it is necessary to turn to a

* See p. 189.

consideration of factors other than the Foundation's origins as a mass movement.

*The role of Foundation publications.* In order to obtain the enthusiastic support both of their members and the public at large most voluntary associations make frequent use of what is perhaps best described as "inspirational" terminology in their various publications, and the Foundation is no exception. Although no systematic analysis of publications has been undertaken, an informal review of the various Foundation publications which might well have come to the attention of the Volunteers studied in this research has revealed numerous instances of the use of expressions which generally characterize "movements" rather than formal organizations. This is particularly true of references to the research program, which is referred to as "the fight against polio,"[21] or "the war on polio."[22] Volunteers are told that "the tide of battle"[23] has turned, but that "the enemy is still with us."[24] And all this has been possible because "the ranks of informed and enthusiastic volunteers grew steadily."[25]

Since its first years of existence, furthermore, the Foundation has officially been aware of the fact that its program has greater meaning than an attack upon a specific disease. An early booklet, for example, informed both the public and Volunteers that "your support of this cause is the expression of a free people in the conviction that the works of peace are lasting, and that the conquest of disease is among the most worthy of these."[26] Participation as a Volunteer is characterized as entailing more than mere membership in an organization; it is a calling, a profession—in the original meaning of the word:

For the volunteer, statistics have names and faces. He sees not the *case*, but the child. And, in his devotion to his high calling, he may forget the days, the months, and even the events that fuse into a total effort, describable as a nationwide program, and recorded in an Annual Report.[27]

Volunteers are also reminded of the fact that the Foundation's program has been without precedent; they are told, for example, that they are "pioneers in a field where none had walked before."[28] And an excerpt from a speech delivered by Basil O'Connor is included in one *Annual Report* as a reminder that the Foundation serves broader functions for society than that of combating polio:

Our native instinct for democracy and freedom finds one of its most powerful expressions in the right of free association. The existence in society of strong, robust, active voluntary groups is one of the best guarantees against the affirmative state indulging itself in illusions of omnipotence.[29]

Can exposure, over a period of months or years, to statements of this kind be said to have planted in the minds of Volunteers the idea that they are members of a social movement as well as a voluntary association? Are the statements of Volunteers cited above merely reflections of official doctrine? The answer to these questions is in part affirmative, since these publications are both read and respected. But it can also be argued that Volunteers, like other Americans, have become relatively immune to exhortatory language of this kind. It is of interest to note in this connection that other voluntary health associations make use of terminology which has a similar tone. The American Cancer Society, for example, calls its annual fund-raising campaign "the Cancer Crusade";[30] the American Heart Association refers to its fund-raising campaign as "giving from the heart";[31] and the National Tuberculosis Association speaks of "the success of the crusade which began 50 years ago."[32] Of much greater significance—since 43 per cent of all Foundation Volunteers have served as volunteers in the Red Cross—is the use of similar terminology by the Red Cross. Its volunteers, for example, are told that the organization is "not only a potent means for helping the distressed but also a great moral force in human society."[33] Yet as already indicated, many Foundation Volunteers who also belong to the Red Cross use the Red Cross as a convenient illustration of the kind of organization they think the Foundation is not.*

The actual role played by various official Foundation statements in the development of these attitudes among its Volunteers cannot, in the very nature of the case, be stated with precision on the basis of the data on hand. It would be unreasonable to conclude that these exhortations have no impact upon their readers; it would be equally unreasonable to conclude that ideologies can be so easily transmitted by the written word. In any event, it seems fair to assume that almost all Volunteers have to some extent been exposed to statements of this kind. These exhortations are, as it were, "constants" which at one time or another come to the attention of everyone. Accordingly, the discussion turns to variations in attitudes among different sub-groups of Volunteers. If systematic variations are found it will be possible to conclude that these attitudes represent something more than mere reflections of official ideology.

*The role of Volunteer predispositions.* A fundamental tenet of organizational theory, stressed by Selznick and others, is that individual participants in an organization always tend to resist being treated as

* See pp. 206–207.

means toward the accomplishment of goals, and interact as whole personalities, bringing to the organization their own problems and purposes.[34] The variety of ways in which Volunteers characterize the Foundation as a social movement lends support to this tenet, since there is evidence that Volunteers bring many of their own values to their participation in the Foundation, and select from the many facets of the Foundation's program those which agree most closely with their own convictions. The Democrats who see the Foundation as an expression of the traditional concern of the Democratic Party for the "common man," and the Republicans who see it as America's answer to the "socialistic" programs initiated by President Roosevelt, are examples of this phenomenon.

How can this tenet of organizational theory be empirically tested? Ideally, data on the values and predispositions of Volunteers at a time prior to their joining the Foundation should be obtained and correlated with their present attitudes. However, the methodological difficulties involved in interviewing people prior to becoming Volunteers effectively preclude this method. Another method is to compare the attitudes of Volunteers who were recruited into the Foundation with those who volunteered on their own initiative, on the assumption that "true" Volunteers are in some way more "ideologically" oriented. Unfortunately for this purpose, only 10 per cent of the Volunteers entered the Foundation on their own initiative. But if we examine the correlation between the role relationship used in recruiting Volunteers* and the percentage of Volunteers who regard the Foundation as a social movement an interesting finding emerges (Table 32).

**Table 32—Role Relationships Used When Recruited and Viewing the Foundation as a Social Movement**

| Role Relationship Used when Recruited | PER CENT WHO VIEW THE FOUNDATION AS A SOCIAL MOVEMENT | N |
|---|---|---|
| Community | 36 | (47) |
| Interpersonal | 57 | (121) |
| Organizational | 57 | (42) |
| None; volunteered | 71 | (24) |

A large majority of those Volunteers who entered the Foundation on their own initiative regard it as a social movement, while only 36 per cent of those who were asked to join the Foundation in order to fulfill their obligations to the community view it in these terms. This

* See pp. 109–115.

correlation suggests that there is in fact a relationship between a general "willingness" to become a Volunteer, or a predisposition to participate in a social movement, and attitudes toward such participation. The most "willing" volunteers—those who joined on their own initiative— are most likely to view their participation in these terms, and the least "willing"—those who joined in order to fulfill a sense of obligation to the community—are least likely to do so.* This evidence, coupled with the testimony of Volunteers themselves concerning the values which they believe the Foundation furthers in the course of its campaign against polio, suggests that the predispositions of Volunteers play an important role in determining their views toward their own participation.

*The role of Volunteer participation.* In an earlier chapter it was noted that each of the four types of recruits identified in this research entered the Foundation for different "reasons." For Polio Veterans, prior experience with polio was the most crucial experience which led them into the Foundation; for Humanitarians, "other-oriented" goals were most decisive. Good Citizens, on the other hand, were attracted by the program and purposes of the Foundation, and Joiners by the "people" of the Foundation. It will be recalled that this typology of recruits is based entirely upon the experiences and dispositions of Volunteers *prior* to participation in Foundation activities.† Accordingly, it is of interest to examine the extent to which each type of recruit, on the basis of experience in the organization, regards the Foundation as a social movement (Table 33).

**Table 33—Type of Recruit and Viewing the Foundation as a Social Movement**

| Type of Recruit | PER CENT WHO VIEW THE FOUNDATION AS A SOCIAL MOVEMENT | N |
|---|---|---|
| Polio Veterans | 45 | (42) |
| Joiners | 52 | (98) |
| Good Citizens | 58 | (66) |
| Humanitarians | 68 | (28) |

As Table 33 indicates, Humanitarians are more likely than other recruits, and Polio Veterans are less likely, to view the Foundation as

* These relationships are necessarily suggestive, rather than conclusive, since the role relationships utilized during recruitment are an imperfect measure of "willingness" to become a Volunteer, or of predispositions in general. It would of course be preferable to have more direct measures of these items.
† See pp. 84–85.

a social movement. These findings are fully in accord with the assumption that attitudes held prior to becoming a member of an organization are important determinants of subsequent judgments. Humanitarians, in fact, were for the most part initially attracted to the Foundation precisely because they regarded it as an organization which "did good" in general, rather than one which attacked a circumscribed problem. Polio Veterans, on the other hand, joined the Foundation for the specific purpose of assisting in the organized attack upon polio, and, accordingly, are most likely to continue to regard their participation in these terms. But note the largest single group of recruits, the Joiners. In spite of the fact that they had only a vague knowledge of the Foundation's objective and programs at the time they joined, they are nearly as likely as Good Citizens—who were fully aware at the time they joined of the Foundation's objective and program—to think of their participation as participation in a social movement. The crucial case of the Joiners, in other words, provides compelling evidence that the satisfactions which Volunteers obtain from participating in what they regard as a social movement stem to a very great extent from the nature of the Foundation's activities themselves. Historical factors most certainly play an important role in this respect, as does the reading of Foundation publications. Some Volunteers are more likely than others to have entered the Foundation with the *intent* of participating in a social movement, and thus find what they seek. But over and above these influences, the observations of Volunteers within their own Chapter and March of Dimes organizations, and the actual experiences which they undergo, provide many Volunteers with the emotionally satisfying experience of participating in a social movement.

## chapter IX

# THE FUTURE
# OF THE
# FOUNDATION

## *Introduction*

THE ANALYSIS of the local program of the Foundation presented in previous chapters has been largely static in nature: it has been concerned with those characteristics of the organization and its membership which have relevance for the continuation of the present program. These characteristics, the analysis has shown, serve to explain the success which the Foundation has had in recruiting Volunteers, in maintaining their active interest in the program, in providing financial assistance to every victim of infantile paralysis who needs it, in raising funds, and in making progress toward the Foundation's ultimate goal of eliminating the threat of epidemic polio. Any analysis of a goal-directed organization, however, cannot be confined to things as they are, since the future state of affairs toward which the organization's activities are oriented is very much a component of the contemporary organization. It must, in the very nature of the case, inquire into the relationship of present activities to future developments.

The relevance of this statement to the present analysis is rooted in the fact that the Foundation's major goal is by definition a finite one. A fundamental assumption underlying the original establishment of the Foundation was that infantile paralysis was a disease which medical science would eventually be able to bring under control and a major reason for the capacity of the Foundation to maintain through the years its high ratio of goal-related activities has been the very real possibility that the organization's goal would be realized—perhaps within the lifetime of the participants. The recent development of the Salk vaccine, and its use on a nationwide scale, serve as dramatic evidence that the full achievement of the Foundation's major goal will be realized in the not too distant future. In fact, Dr. Jonas E. Salk, who developed the vaccine, and Dr. Leonard E. Scheele, former Surgeon General of the United States Public Health Service, recently reported to the American Medical Association that by the middle of 1959 paralytic polio should be completely eliminated as a threat to both children and adults.[1]

The imminence of this full achievement of its major goal naturally raises the question of what will happen to the Foundation at that time. Will it simply go out of existence, will it continue on a more limited scale, providing assistance to persons already afflicted by polio, or will it—taking advantage of experience gained in conquering polio—turn its attention to another health or welfare problem? The seriousness of these questions, as they apply to organizations generally, has been noted by a number of students of voluntary associations and social movements. Wendell King, for example, states that "an apparently unanticipated and rarely desired outcome of achieving goals can be the abrupt demolition of the whole organization. Unless additional objectives are devised, the movement lies robbed of its reason for existence."[2] Their relevance to a concrete organization, however, has been only infrequently examined. This chapter is devoted to a consideration of these fundamental questions, not with the intent to provide definitive answers, but rather to stipulate some of the conditions which will determine the Foundation's future.

## The Succession of Goals

In order to achieve a perspective through which to approach the topic of the future of the Foundation it is helpful to recall the major conclusions reached by Philip Selznick in his analysis of the relationship between doctrine and action in the Tennessee Valley Authority. Organizations, Selznick notes, develop obligations over a period of time to act in a certain way, obligations which Selznick terms "commitments." He summarizes the importance of these commitments as follows:

The systematized commitments of an organization define its character. Day-to-day decision, relevant to the actual problems met in the translation of policy into action, create precedents, alliances, effective symbols, and personal loyalties which transform the organization from a profane, manipulable instrument into something having a sacred status and thus resistant to treatment simply as a means to some external goal. That is why organizations are often cast aside when new goals are sought. . . .

So long as goals are given, and the impulse to act persists, there will be a series of enforced lines of action demanded by the nature of the tools at hand. These commitments may lead to unanticipated consequences resulting in a deflection of original goals.[3]

Although Selznick's research was restricted to one organization, he clearly intended his conclusions to apply to other organizations as well. For this reason, it is appropriate to examine the extent to which this formulation of the consequences of organizational commitments may be said to characterize the situation which may soon confront the Foundation.

The passage cited is composed of two parts. First, it states that "day-to-day decisions" (i.e., those made in order to solve immediate and pressing problems) lead to "commitments," which in turn define the "character" of an organization. Second, it states that this process may have two consequences: an organization may be "deflected from its original goals" and it may be "cast aside when new goals are sought."

Although the major focus of this study has been the current membership and activities of the Foundation, rather than the details of its history, sufficient attention has been given to the circumstances surrounding the original emergence of various features of the organization to document the first of these two statements—that decisions made for the purpose of solving immediate problems often determine the ultimate character of an organization. It has been noted, for example, that the Foundation's almost total dependence upon a fund-raising strategy based upon obtaining small gifts from large numbers of people emerged from two decisions made in the Depression year 1933: to solicit gifts from the people of Georgia in order to finance the construction of a new building at Georgia Warm Springs, and to raise funds nationally by sponsoring President's Birthday Balls; that the characteristically middle-class composition of the Foundation's Volunteer membership may be traced in large part to the decision to ask postmasters, Democrats, and persons of civic prominence generally to organize these Birthday Balls; and that the patient care program is a direct outgrowth of the decision to permit local Committees for the Celebration of the President's Birthday to retain for use in their own communities a portion of the funds raised in 1935.* This brief listing of examples suggests

* See pp. 42–44, for a more complete description of these crucial decisions.

the general applicability to the Foundation of this aspect of Selznick's thesis: the Foundation's "character" today is clearly in many respects the result of decisions made with other ends in view.

The second part of Selznick's statement concerns the consequences which may result from the emergence of organizational commitments —goal displacement and the destruction of the organization itself. Sufficient evidence from other studies has been cited throughout this volume to suggest the near-universality of the phenomenon of goal displacement within organizations, and a number of reasons underlying the Foundation's capacity to maintain itself as a goal-oriented organization have been cited.† But what of the Foundation's capacity to maintain itself as an organization after its initial goals have been realized, and "new goals are sought"? Will its organizational structure be "cast aside"? It is to a consideration of these questions that the discussion now turns.

### EVIDENCE FROM OTHER ORGANIZATIONS

It should be noted first of all that Selznick is not alone in asserting the close relationship between organizational goals and organizational survival. Arnold Rose, for example, has stated that the purposes of voluntary associations are limited, and "almost never will an association act for a purpose different from the original one which brought the members together."[4] And the Kluckhohns have observed that "American associations are also a way that an antifeudalistic society chooses to 'get things done.' We form thousands of organizations to accomplish a specific purpose and then dissolve them."[5]

It is not difficult to find illustrations in American history which document the truth of these assertions. For example, two important voluntary associations in our early history, the Sons of Liberty and the Committees of Correspondence, were dissolved when the anti-British purposes for which they were established culminated in the American Revolution and the establishment of the Continental Congress. Sometimes organizations decline long before their goals are achieved, as, for example, the American Anti-Slavery Society, which split through internal dissension and controversy over policy matters some twenty years before the Emancipation Proclamation. And sometimes they are dissolved when their functions are taken over by governmental bodies, as happened to the Public School Society of New York City when the public school system was established.

† See pp. 69–77.

*The succession of goals.* Dissolution, however, is not the only course of action open to an organization when its purposes are either achieved or become irrelevant because of changes in the social environment; in fact, it is equally easy to find examples of organizations which have remained intact for the purpose of working toward new or sharply modified objectives. Peter Blau has called this process the "succession of goals," which he states is "the reverse of the displacement of goals."[6] He describes the process in these terms:

The attainment of organizational objectives generates a strain toward finding new objectives. To provide incentives for its members and to justify its existence, an organization has to adopt new goals as its old ones are realized. Unions illustrate this transformation of ends into means. After a union establishes the right of collective bargaining, this original objective becomes a means for the accomplishment of new objectives, such as pensions and seniority rights for workers.[7]

Unions are of course not the only illustration of the tendency of organizations to seek new objectives, nor do organizations necessarily wait until the achievement of their original objectives before they establish new ones. The American Legion, to cite one example, was originally established in order to preserve the spirit which characterized the American Expeditionary Force in World War I, but it very soon included in its objectives the protection of the rights of veterans and, particularly among local Posts, the instigation of community service projects. Dartmouth College, to cite another example, was originally founded primarily in order to educate and Christianize the Indians of New England, but it experienced no great difficulty in transforming itself into a general liberal arts college.

Voluntary health and welfare agencies exhibit similar tendencies. The Birth Control Federation, for example, in 1942 adopted the more comprehensive name of the Planned Parenthood Federation of America, and has since that time expanded its objectives to include treatment for infertility, education for marriage, and marriage counseling.[8] The American Social Hygiene Association, which has traditionally concerned itself with combating both prostitution and venereal diseases, has in recent years adjusted to the decline in organized prostitution and the drastic lowering of the incidence of venereal diseases, and has established such new objectives as supporting family life education and preparing high school boys for the social and psychological strains which they will undergo during military service.[9] In fact, thousands of organizations of all kinds have adapted in one way or another to external conditions affecting the relevance of their objectives, but there have been very few systematic analyses of such organizations from this point of view. It is therefore instructive to examine briefly the process of organizational adaptation as it has taken place in four organizations for which relatively complete information is available. Two of these organizations, the Woman's Christian Temperance Union and the Townsend Organization, have failed to adjust themselves to a changed environment, and exist today as fossil remains of their previous life. The other two, the Young Men's Christian Association and the American National Red Cross, have made highly successful adaptations.

*The Young Men's Christian Association.* Although there have been a number of organizational histories of the Y.M.C.A., Owen Pence's volume, *The Y.M.C.A. and Social Need,* is most useful for an examination of the Y.M.C.A. as an illustration of the process of organizational adaptation.[10] The book is sub-titled, "A Study of Institutional Adaptation"; more specifically, it is an examination of how the goals of the Y.M.C.A. have changed in response to various changes in the social environment, particularly the secularization of American society which has taken place in the past century.

Today the Y.M.C.A. places a great deal of emphasis upon the opportunities for recreation and physical exercise which it offers, but the first Association in London stated that its objective was "to improve the spiritual condition of young men engaged in the drapery and other trades"; the first Association in America, in Boston, expanded its objective to include "the improvement of the spiritual and mental condition of young men"; and the first New York Association included in its objectives the following:

The object of this Association shall be the improvement of the spiritual, mental, and social condition of young men . . . to bring them under moral and religious influences, by aiding them in the selection of suitable boarding places and employment. . . .[11]

With the passing years, as Pence shows, the Y.M.C.A. has devoted increasing attention to its physical and social goals, and less attention to its original religious and spiritual aims. This transition is summarized in these terms:

In contrast with the conception of earlier years, when the principal concern of the Association was with the securing of individual commitments to the Christian life, the realization has steadily grown in recent years that religious living and interest are so gravely conditioned by the total social experience that the two cannot be dealt with separately.[12]

And again, in more direct language:

In time, the Associations began to take their objectives for granted. In their place activity (that is, whatever met and satisfied expressed interests of members), became the real objective.[13]

The Y.M.C.A., therefore, is an example of an organization whose goals have changed not because they were achieved, but rather because of fundamental changes in the social environment in which its activities were carried out. The "spiritual improvement" of young men has come to be regarded as less relevant than it was in the 19th Century, and other activities have achieved greater relevance. As a result, the organization's membership has been broadened to include boys, women and non-Protestants; professionally-trained group leaders have often replaced the original laymen who served as volunteer workers; and an increased emphasis has been placed upon the construction of adequate buildings in which to carry out its broadened program.

Today the Y.M.C.A. is a highly successful organization, and it would be presumptuous to suggest that its success bears no relationship to the Christian ideals held by so many of its leaders. In fact, if its original objective had been to provide recreational facilities to "young men engaged in the drapery and other trades," it is highly probable that it would exist today only as some sort of athletic club in London. But the evidence is also quite clear that its success is in large part attributable to the fact that it has had the flexibility, in keeping with its Christian ideals, to redefine its objectives in accordance with the needs of the society which it serves.

*The Woman's Christian Temperance Union.* The central problem which led Joseph Gusfield to study the W.C.T.U. is the fact that changes in American drinking habits and the increased acceptance of drinking as a part of general social life "have presented the W.C.T.U. with an environment more hostile to the doctrine of total abstinence than was true in the years of the organization's formation and development."[14] In the face of this situation, Gusfield sought both to determine "whether the change in environment has led to changes in the goals and doctrine of the movement" and to explain "changes, or lack of change, in the organization."[15]

In many respects, the Y.M.C.A. and the W.C.T.U. have had similar histories. Both organizations were established at a time when a powerful middle class believed that its mission was to improve the social conditions under which the lower class lived. The Y.M.C.A. sought to improve these conditions by Christianizing and educating young men; the W.C.T.U. believed that working class people could enjoy the benefits of middle class life if they stopped drinking—"drink is the curse of the working classes" was a popular slogan of the 19th Century temperance movement.[16] And both organizations have survived in spite of a sharp decline in the popularity of these theories of humanitarian reform. But they differ greatly in the manner in which they have survived.

As previously indicated, the Y.M.C.A.'s history has been characterized by successive adjustments to its social environment. The W.C.T.U., on the other hand, has not adjusted:

Today the W.C.T.U. is an organization in retreat. Contrary to the expectations of theories of institutionalization, the movement has not acted to preserve organizational values at the expense of past doctrine.[17]

How has this been possible? As Gusfield shows, the W.C.T.U. has not abandoned its goal of establishing temperance norms, but has instead shifted its attention to a new audience. Originally the organization was composed largely of middle- and upper middle-class women who sought both to dissuade working class people from drinking and to improve their general welfare in other ways; today it is less upper middle-class and more lower middle- and working-class in composition, and its chief target is the drinking habits of middle-class groups. In short, the W.C.T.U. has elected *not* to change its goals to meet changed conditions, although Gusfield suggests two courses of action it might have taken:

One possible position would be a reversal of past doctrine and the embracing of a doctrine of moderate drinking. This would be the acceptance of the new standard of the middle classes. Another possibility might be a deemphasis of temperance aims and a substitution of other aims, such as those of a social welfare nature or an attack on "popular" enemies, such as drug addiction or juvenile delinquency.[18]

Instead, the organization has changed the composition of its membership, limited its goals to the discouragement of middle-class drinking, and shifted its strategy from active campaigning against intemperance to indulging in what Gusfield terms "moral indignation."[19]

*The Townsend Organization.* The Y.M.C.A. is an example of an organization which has succeeded through successive adaptations to its social environment; the W.C.T.U. is an organization which is in a

THE FUTURE OF THE FOUNDATION

state of decline because of its failure to adjust to changes in its environment; and the Townsend Organization, as Sheldon Messinger has demonstrated, is one which has nearly vanished because its major goal, alleviating or preventing economic dislocation, has at least temporarily been achieved—not, however, through the efforts of the organization.[20]

Dr. Francis E. Townsend first proposed his plan to end the Depression by retiring all United States citizens at the age of sixty on a monthly pension of $200 in September, 1933; by 1936 the Townsend Organization had 2,250,000 members. In 1935, however, the Social Security Act was passed, and by 1951 the organization had only 56,656 members, a loss of more than 97 per cent.[21] In the intervening years, the expansion of social security legislation, of pension plans by private employers, and of the national economy itself largely eliminated public interest in a program designed to end the Depression of the 1930's. In the face of these changes in the relevance of its original goals, how has the Townsend Organization survived at all?

Messinger outlines three organizational transformations which have taken place. First, there has been a tendency to support other measures affecting the aged, a tendency which the leaders themselves have checked since they realized it could lead only to a break-up of the organization. Second, there has been a tendency to obtain financial support by selling consumer goods of one kind or another, e.g., vitamin pills. Finally, there has been a tendency to convert membership meetings into social gatherings, and to hold other social events as well. On the basis of these tendencies, as well as of other aspects of the transformation of the Townsend Organization, Messinger draws this conclusion:

The organized arms of declining social movements will tend to adapt to these changed conditions in characteristic ways. We can broadly describe this adaptation by asserting that the dominating orientation of leaders and members shifts *from the implementation of the values the organization is taken to represent* (by leaders, members, and public alike), *to maintaining the organizational structure as such,* even at the loss of the organization's central mission.[22]

The Townsend Organization, in short, has adjusted to changes in its environment in ways quite different from those followed by the W.C.T.U. Instead of modifying its membership and its goals, it has virtually abandoned its original goals and has concentrated its attention, not very successfully, upon maintaining its organizational structure.

*The American National Red Cross.*[23] Like the Y.M.C.A., the Red Cross is a highly successful organization, and for much the same reasons: it has made successive adjustments to changes in its social environment. Its initial objective, as set forth in its first constitution, was "to hold itself in readiness in the event of war or any calamity great enough to be considered national, to inaugurate such practical measures in mitigation of the suffering and for the protection and relief of sick and wounded as may be consistent with the objects of the Association. . . ."[24] The organization was small in its early years, and floods and other disasters, the Spanish-American War, and most importantly, World War I, provided sufficient challenges to its resources to make any expansion of its objectives unnecessary. The end of World War I, however, found a greatly expanded Red Cross without an objective of sufficient scope to maintain the organization. There was a decline in membership interest, and the leaders feared the organization would suffer. Foster Dulles has summarized this crisis in the Red Cross's history in these terms:

The officers of the Red Cross, discouraged but not dismayed, were determined to find a way out in spite of chapter apathy. There was a natural desire on their part to see the American Red Cross maintain its position and still further broaden its field of usefulness, not only for the sake of whatever contributions could be made toward improving the conditions of American life, *but for the sake of the organization itself.*[25]

This crisis was surmounted by adopting a new program—"the preservation and improvement of the public health"—[26] and the Red Cross had no need to question the adequacy of its objectives until the Depression of the 1930's, when there was disagreement among the leaders concerning the role the organization should play in dispensing unemployment relief.[27] But the most severe test to date of the adequacy of the Red Cross's objectives came at the end of World War II, when again a greatly expanded organization found that its capacity to act outpaced its goals. Furthermore, there now existed a new threat to the organization—the increased intervention of the Government in welfare and relief activities as a result of the responsibilities it had assumed during the Depression and War years. "Clouds are appearing on the disaster relief horizon," wrote one Red Cross disaster worker in 1946. "Government today is rendering a number of services to disaster sufferers that were rendered by Red Cross disaster relief 10, 15, or 20 years ago."[28] This new crisis was summarized by Basil O'Connor, who was then National Chairman of the American Red Cross, at the 1949 annual convention, in a speech entitled "Can the Red Cross Survive?" Dulles summarizes this speech as follows:

The convention delegates were told that it was not only necessary to re-evaluate the mission of the American Red Cross, but to ask themselves the fundamental question of whether an organization founded in the remote past of the nineteenth century still had any place at all in the vastly altered world of the mid-twentieth century. O'Connor's own answer was strongly affirmative.[29]

It was of course not sufficient to give an affirmative answer to this question; it was necessary as well to establish new objectives and new activities. These were found in "the adoption of a national blood donor program as the core of its peacetime activities apart from disaster relief."[30] In this way the most recent crisis has been met, and the Red Cross has both maintained an active program and obtained adequate volunteer and public support in the postwar years. The decision to embark upon this program was made with full realization of its implications for the organization's survival:

Apart from meeting a very real need, the national blood program also appeared the best possible thing for the Red Cross to undertake on its own account. Just as health activities had been promoted after the First World War to give the chapters something to do as well as to advance public health, so the new project was expected to provide an outlet for volunteer activity in the new period of peace which would bring together, in one unified undertaking, the varied interests of the volunteer services.[31]

This brief review of the history of four organizations has of necessity mentioned only a few of the major conclusions reached by the authors cited. Nevertheless, it has called attention to the fact that organizations are by no means necessarily "cast aside when new goals are sought" and indicated some of the ways in which organizations have adjusted to changes in their environment and the relevancy of their goals. Furthermore, the histories of these four organizations suggest that the fate of an organization after its goals have been either achieved or rendered irrelevant cannot be determined on *a priori* grounds, but is rather a resultant of a given set of forces. "What," Blau asks, "determines whether displacement of goals or succession of goals predominates in an organization?"[32] Although he admits that this crucial question can be answered only in part, Blau does suggest two determining factors: "structural constraints in the organization" and acceptance on the part of the community. "When the community permits an organization . . . to become established and attain at least some of its first objectives in a relatively short period, it will probably find new fields to conquer in the course of its development."[33] It goes without saying that American society has permitted the Foundation to be established and to attain its first objectives; in fact, it has given it more encouragement and support than it has given any comparable organization. Accordingly, in order to pursue the inquiry implied in Blau's formulation of the problem of goal succession, it is necessary to examine what structural constraints might impede the Foundation from seeking new goals.

### THE FOUNDATION'S STRUCTURE AND THE FUTURE

The relevance of the Foundation's corporate-type structure to its capacity to carry out its program has been stated in some detail throughout this volume, and need only be summarized here. Local Chapters, for example, being *ad hoc* instrumentalities of the Board of Trustees, are subject to all rules, regulations and policies of the National Headquarters—a situation which enables National Headquarters, if the need should ever arise, to exert considerable authority over the activities of a local Chapter. The March of Dimes is officially directed by National Headquarters, and local Campaign Directors are appointed by the State Chairman, who is in turn appointed by National Headquarters. Here again, the structural machinery exists through which National Headquarters can exercise control over the activities of local organizations. The patient care program, although financed largely by the 50 per cent of all campaign receipts which is retained in the local community, is dependent, for its effective operation, upon the redistribution of funds by National Headquarters. The research program is entirely under the direction of National Headquarters, and Chapters are specifically prohibited from making grants to support research projects.* In short, if National Headquarters (i.e., the Board of Trustees) should decide to embark upon a new program, there is no organizational machinery to stand in the way. The new program would not need to be ratified by local Chapters, and there are no effective sub-groups within the organization which could offer effective resistance to it. The Foundation, in other words, has an organizational structure which would make "the succession of goals" quite feasible.

* See pp. 36–42 for descriptions of these aspects of the Foundation's formal structure.

## Volunteers and the Future

The statement that the Foundation's structure would permit "the succession of goals," although true in a legal sense, does not of course acknowledge the fundamental fact that the Foundation is a voluntary association. Its members are free to leave at any time, and no one is obliged to join. For this reason, no program sponsored by National Headquarters could possibly be successful if it did not command the enthusiastic support of Volunteers throughout the county. Witness for example, the ill-fated attempt of National Headquarters in the first year of the Foundation's existence to have full authority over the expenditure of all the funds raised during the March of Dimes.* In order to examine the Foundation's future prospects it is therefore necessary to examine the potential support for a new program which exists among the Foundation's Volunteer membership.

The interviews with Volunteers reported in this volume were held after the Salk vaccine had been developed, but immediately prior to the nationwide field trials of the vaccine, and hence before the public announcement on April 12, 1955 that a safe and effective anti-polio vaccine had at last been perfected. Nevertheless, many Volunteers believed at the time of the research that the vaccine would be effective, and some gave evidence that they had given thought to the impact of this development upon the Foundation. A sampling of these future-oriented remarks is given below, but the major conclusions concerning potential Volunteer participation in a future program of the Foundation must be drawn not from Volunteer reactions to the development of the Salk vaccine, but rather from Volunteer perceptions of the Foundation as an *innovating* organization.

The fact that voluntary associations, such as the Foundation, which carry on programs extending beyond the immediate interests of their membership serve the function of instituting change in society has been noted by many observers. Arnold Rose, for example, states that "voluntary associations provide a *social mechanism for continually instituting social changes,* so that the United States is a society in flux, constantly seeking (not always successfully, but seeking nevertheless) to solve long-standing problems and to satisfy new needs of groups of citizens as these needs arise."[34] Lipset and his colleagues have recently observed that voluntary associations are "a source of new opinions independent of the state and a means of communicating these new suggestions to a

* See pp. 44–45.

large section of the citizenry."[35] Speaking from a British perspective,
V. L. Allen has commented that "it is perhaps as pace-makers that
voluntary organizations have the most important and permanent function to perform in society. . . .[36] And in reference to the Foundation
specifically, Victor Cohn calls it "not just an attack on polio," but "a
pattern by which we Americans may be able to help solve many problems."[37] Observations such as these, however, are generally made by
outsiders, who are in a position to assess the role played by a voluntary
association in broad perspective. It is less frequent that a participant
in a voluntary association, involved as he is in day-to-day problems,
is able to detect the far-reaching implications of his organization.

Objectively speaking, the Foundation has obviously served as an
instigator of change. Not only has it pioneered in developing a coordinated mode of attack upon a specific disease, but it has also introduced
new concepts of fund-raising, of patient care, and of community
responsibility. The mass field trials of the Salk vaccine, which the Foundation sponsored, to cite another example of innovation, were a
completely new development as far as the history of immunological
verification is concerned—never before has the efficacy of a newly-
developed vaccine been tested on such a mass scale. It is of some interest, accordingly, to note that a considerable number of Volunteers
are alert to the fact that the Foundation, in keeping with its character
both as a social movement and a voluntary association, has served as
a "pacesetter" in American society.

This broad theme has a number of variations. For some Volunteers, the most important precedent-setting aspect of the Foundation is the fact that it has mobilized laymen in a coordinated attack
upon a disease. A March of Dimes Chairman in Defense Town, for
example, adopted what he termed "the sociological viewpoint," saying "we can fight polio if we can organize people. If we can organize
people like this, we can fight anything." This opinion was echoed by
that of the Harbor City Campaign Director, who asked rhetorically,
"Wouldn't it be a wonderful story to get polio licked, and then go on
to something else and get that licked and then go on to something
else?" Pausing a moment, he added the comment, "It would be a challenge, a career."

Other Volunteers focused their remarks more sharply upon specifically organizational accomplishments and potentialities. For example,
after verbally exploring the possibilities of other diseases which might

be conquered by techniques similar to those employed against polio, the Steamboat City Campaign Director concluded with this affirmation:

I really believe in this type of organization when people get together and get things done. I would like to see other organizations set up or something done in other fields . . . like mental health. But no one has had the organization that the Foundation has had. . . . I don't think this unique organization should pass out of existence. It should be utilized.

Another Steamboat City Volunteer, whose remarks achieve greater significance when it is noted that she is a Negro, commented upon the greater degree of "fraternization" which characterizes the Foundation in contrast to other organizations, and noted that "the organizational philosophy is excellent. If a group is organized to fight another disease with this type of organization, it will be equally successful." The March of Dimes, as a new approach to fund-raising, prompted the Oil City Chapter Chairman to declare that "it would be a shame for an organization of the calibre of the March of Dimes to fall apart." Finally, for some Volunteers the policy of the Foundation which permits funds to remain in the community for assisting polio victims is a precedent of such importance in terms of achieving public support that they believe it could and should be applied to the battle against other diseases. As a Wheat County March of Dimes Volunteer pointed out, "They could take over heart and cancer and do the same thing. The money could stay in the community and that should be the basis of the talk that would be given on it. You can say, 'it stays here for your protection.'"

Not all of the Volunteers interviewed, needless to say, were as articulate as these in expressing either their judgments of the Foundation's role as an innovating organization or their own hope that the organization would continue to exist after its objective of eliminating epidemic polio is achieved. Since Volunteers were not questioned concerning their views of the Foundation's future, only those who had given some thought to the matter prior to the interview took occasion to express their views. In fact, some Volunteers explicitly stated that in their opinion the Foundation should *not* undertake a new program. After polio has been conquered, according to the Chapter Vice-Chairman in Gas City, the Foundation "should get a big loving cup from the general population of the country and call it quits." Opinions of this kind were expressed only rarely, however, while thirty-five Volunteers —15 per cent of those interviewed—spontaneously recommended that the Foundation should continue to exist even after its major objective had been achieved. In the light of this evidence it seems reasonable to conclude that a considerable portion of the Volunteer membership of the Foundation has found its organizational characteristics sufficiently appealing, and its activities sufficiently rewarding, to be willing and anxious to take part in the organization should it seek to realize new goals.

## Conclusions

At the time of this writing there has been no official statement by the Foundation concerning its future plans, although the organization has indicated in a number of informal ways that it is seriously considering the possibility of undertaking a new program when epidemic polio has finally been brought under control.[38] For the present, the polio program continues to meet existing needs. Infantile paralysis still constitutes a threat to the American public; thousands of polio victims still need medical and financial assistance; sudden rises in incidence of an epidemic or near-epidemic character—in Boston in the summer of 1955, in Chicago in the summer of 1956—will probably continue to occur until a substantial proportion of the public has been given the three necessary injections of the Salk vaccine; and research is still needed in order to develop improved methods of both prevention and therapy.

Nevertheless, it is reasonable to assume on the basis of available evidence that the Foundation's major objectives will be reached within the next few years and that the organization will at that time seek to realize new goals. In the face of this situation, it is worth while to consider, on the basis of the materials presented throughout this volume, what kind of an organization it will become. What kinds of goals will it seek to obtain, what support will it have from the public and from its Volunteers, and what are its chances for success in some new venture?

Since the Foundation may fairly be said to represent majority rather than minority opinion in the United States, it is highly improbable that it will take the same course as has the Townsend Organization—dwindle in size and drift into half-hearted efforts to achieve irrelevant objectives. By the same token, given the character and accomplishments of the polio program, it is manifestly impossible for the Foundation to follow the path taken by the W.C.T.U.—limit its goals and change its strategy by aiming at a new target audience. In sharp contrast to both of these organizations, the Foundation has received social and financial support from a major segment of the American public and has had a goal which has relevance for all strata of American society.

In these respects the Foundation closely resembles the Y.M.C.A. and the Red Cross. Another point of similarity is the type of membership common to all three organizations—a membership drawn for the most part from the middle class, and from the upper middle class in the case of key positions in the national organization. In fact, the Foundation's membership is actually more representative of American society than the membership of either the Y.M.C.A. or the Red Cross, since the former is largely Protestant and the latter typically upper middle- and upper-class in composition.

In terms of any criteria, accordingly, the Foundation belongs in the "big leagues" of voluntary associations; like the Y.M.C.A. and the Red Cross, it is an institutionalized aspect of American life. It is therefore highly probable that it will follow a pattern similar to that established by these organizations: it will expand its operations by adopting a goal which has even *more* relevance for American society than that of eliminating infantile paralysis as an epidemic disease.

Although comparisons with the Y.M.C.A. and the Red Cross serve the useful purpose of setting the topic of the future of the Foundation in a broader organizational context, they cannot by themselves be adduced as convincing evidence that the Foundation will in the years ahead make a *successful* adaptation to the achievement of its major goals. This is true in part because the Foundation's future will be determined by decisions made by specific individuals as much as it will be by those organizational forces which can now be detected. It is also true in part because both the Y.M.C.A. and the Red Cross differ from the Foundation in the specificity of their original goals. Who is to say that it is not possible "to improve the spiritual condition of young men" by giving them an opportunity to play basketball, and can the national blood program of the Red Cross be called incompatible with the initial objective of inaugurating "such practical measures in mitigation of the suffering and for the protection of the sick and wounded as may be consistent with the objects of the Association?" The current goals of the Foundation, in contrast, are specifically concerned with problems of one disease, infantile paralysis.

It is of far-reaching importance, however, that in the course of working toward its goals the Foundation has made significant contributions in other areas. It has supported fundamental research in virology—to such an extent that William L. Laurence, Science Editor of the *New York Times,* has recently suggested that "its next goal should be to develop, with March of Dimes funds, an all-embracing multiple vaccine against all viruses attacking the nervous system."[39] It has assisted medical schools in developing new programs of professional education; pioneered in developing improved methods of assisting in the physical, social, and vocational adjustment of disabled persons; and in a number of other ways attacked problems which are not directly linked to the problems of infantile paralysis.[40] The very fact that the Foundation has always realized that an effective anti-polio campaign could not be carried out in isolation from other aspects of medicine and social welfare constitutes further evidence, accordingly, that the Foundation will make a successful adaptation to its post-polio program.

In the final analysis, however, the most compelling reason for predicting that the Foundation will in the future make a successful adjustment to the achievement of its major goal is that the organization has in fact *already* been transformed, in large part by its Volunteers, into something other than a special purpose association. For those Volunteers who, in spite of the fact that they may initially have been recruited as Polio Veterans or Good Citizens or Joiners, have come to regard the organization as a "social movement" or a "pacesetter" have altered not only the character of their own participation but the character of the Foundation as well. Implicit in these perceptions is the notion that the Foundation has an institutionalized status which transcends its current goals. Since the Foundation includes among its Volunteers so many who are able to conceptualize their involvement in terms of its ultimate implications (for themselves, or for society as a whole), rather than only in terms of a limited, pragmatic goal, it has already become an organization as deeply committed to its mode of operation as to its current purposes. In a word, it is an organization which is as committed to a means as it is to an end.

The reasons underlying commitment to means as well as to ends have constituted the major subject matter of this book. The organizational structure of the Foundation provides Volunteers with an opportunity to acquire, through making decisions and assuming responsibilities, a vested interest in the organization; a vested interest, however, which does not interfere with progress toward organizational goals. The

major activities of Chapter Volunteers—informing the public concerning the facts about infantile paralysis and providing financial and
other assistance to polio victims—are both rewarding in themselves
and suggest to Volunteers the possibilities inherent in the community
action approach to health and welfare problems. The March of Dimes,
through its basic strategy of obtaining small gifts from millions of contributors, has become not only a fund-raising campaign, but an institutionalized aspect of American life.

These characteristics of the Foundation have led many Volunteers
to perceive the organization as a "social movement," and have thus
provided Volunteers with an ideological rationale for their own participation. Through perceiving the Foundation as a "pacesetter," other
Volunteers—more alert to specific pragmatic implications, and better
able to extrapolate from present experience to future possibilities—
have been able to become involved in an endeavor which has both continuity and the logic of consistency. The very existence of these perceptions is thus a strong indication that the activities of Volunteers have
been more than a campaign against polio, more than a means to an end,
and more than the pursuit of a realizable goal: they have in themselves
been instrumental in bringing other ends in view.

APPENDICES

*appendix A*


# THE
# SAMPLES
# STUDIED


## *I. General Public Surveys*

### 1. THE NATIONWIDE SURVEY

A NATIONWIDE SURVEY of public attitudes toward various diseases and public contributions to fund-raising campaigns was conducted by the American Institute of Public Opinion, Princeton, New Jersey, in February, 1954. The questions used in the analysis are indicated in the references of this volume; the questionnaire instrument itself is on file at the Bureau of Applied Social Research. The description of the survey which follows is adapted from an unpublished report of the Institute.

The regular national sample of the American Institute of Public Opinion was used for this survey. This sample is what is generally termed a modified probability sample. The design provided for stratification by region and, within each region, stratification by geographical distribution, three rural-urban strata, and the Census economic areas. After ordering localities in accordance with these criteria, a systematic sample of localities was drawn from each region, with the probability of selection of a locality proportionate to its size. Within large urban communities, small clusters of blocks were drawn at random with probability proportionate to size. In smaller communities and rural regions sampling areas were drawn with equal probability.

Interviewers were assigned to selected areas and required to work within the boundaries of such areas. Within the area they chose respondents on the basis of age and sex quotas. Interviewing was carried out by the regular field staff of the American Institute of Public Opinion. The total sample consisted of 2,000 adults drawn from 300 sampling points.

### 2. THE FOUR-CITY SURVEY

A survey of public attitudes toward various diseases and public contributions to fund-raising campaigns was conducted in four cities by the Bureau of Applied Social Research of Columbia University in February

*275*

1954. The question used in the analysis are indicated in the references of this volume; the questionnaire instrument itself is on file at the Bureau of Applied Social Research.

The four cities in which interviews were conducted were selected on the basis of the following criteria:

1. Each city is broadly representative of the urban population of one major region of the United States—East, Midwest, South, and West.

2. Each city contains a majority of the population of the county in which it is located.

3. Each city is in the 50,000 to 100,000 population category.

Needless to say, these four cities are not a representative sample of any universe of cities. This phase of the research, however, was carried out primarily not in order to study the attitudes of urban dwellers, but rather to obtain measures of the relationship between Foundation activities and public response to the Foundation's program. In each of the four cities interviews were held with Chapter and March of Dimes Volunteers, and first-hand observations were made of the March of Dimes campaign in progress at the time of the research.

The four-city samples are probability samples of the population of the city and those suburbs which are encompassed in the most recent City Directory. The addresses listed in the City Directory, in other words, constitute the universe from which each sample was drawn. The procedure used to select respondents was as follows:

1. A goal of 400 interviews in Desert City, and 300 in each of the other three cities, was set.

2. An estimate of the number of addresses listed in each City Directory was made, and divided by the number of interviews desired. This procedure provided the sampling interval $(n)$. Starting with a randomly-selected number between 1 and 10, every $n$th address in the City Directory was selected.

3. If a selected address was a place of business, the first dwelling preceding or following this place of business was alternatively selected.

4. Dwellings under construction were included in the sample on the assumption that they would have been both completed and occupied in the interval between the compilation of the City Directory and the time of the field work. By the same token, dwellings listed as "unoccupied" were included.

5. In Desert City, where 5 per cent of the residential buildings were constructed since the compilation of the City Directory, twenty new addresses were randomly selected from lists of building permits and added to the sample.

Interviewing in the four cities was supervised by a staff member of the Bureau of Applied Social Research, who recruited and trained a local interviewing staff. In Desert City, Spanish-speaking residents were interviewed by Spanish-speaking interviewers, using a Spanish-language version of the

questionnaire. In South City, Negroes were interviewed by Negro interviewers.

Interviewers were assigned addresses selected by the procedure outlined
above, and instructed to interview either the "man of the house" or the
"woman of the house." Quotas were set to ensure that neither men nor
women would be disproportionately represented in the sample. If no one
was at home after two call-backs, or if an interview was refused, interviewers were instructed to obtain an interview at the adjacent address. The
total sample consisted of 1,324 adults, distributed as follows:

| | | |
|---|---|---:|
| Eastern City | | 293 |
| Central City | | 316 |
| South City | | 296 |
| (Whites) | (195) | |
| (Negroes) | (101) | |
| Desert City | | 419 |
| Total | | 1,324 |

## II.   Surveys of Volunteers

### 1. THE EIGHTY-FIVE-COUNTY SURVEY*

A survey of Foundation Volunteers was conducted by the American
Institute of Public Opinion in January and February, 1954. The questionnaire instrument used is on file at the Bureau of Applied Social Research.
The description of the survey which follows is adapted from unpublished
reports of the Institute.

In selecting the sample, all counties served by Foundation Chapters
were first stratified according to region. Within each region counties were
then stratified according to the Foundation's State Representative's rating
given each Chapter, and within each rating stratum, according to the 1950–
1952 weighted polio incidence rate of the county. The number of counties
drawn from each stratum was directly proportional to the stratum's 1950
population. In this manner, eighty-five counties were selected.

Interviewers were instructed to obtain six interviews in each county, if
possible with the following individuals:

1. Chapter Chairman
2. Chapter Secretary (or Executive Secretary)
3. Chairman of Women's Activities
4. Other Chapter Volunteer
5. March of Dimes Campaign Director
6. Other March of Dimes Volunteer

* The eighty-five-county survey of Volunteers is referred to in only three or four
places in the text. Accordingly, unless otherwise indicated references in the text are to
the thirty-seven-county survey. The eighty-five-county survey was undertaken primarily
to obtain quantitative data for comparison with the more intensive research undertaken
in the thirty-seven counties.

### Table 34—Selected Characteristics of the 85-County Sample

| Characteristic | | Chapter Volunteers | March of Dimes Volunteers |
|---|---|---|---|
| Years active | 1 | 7% | 27% |
| | 2–5 | 47 | 49 |
| | 6–9 | 18 | 12 |
| | 10 or more | 28 | 12 |
| Age | 20–30 | 7% | 16% |
| | 31–40 | 31 | 38 |
| | 41–50 | 33 | 26 |
| | 51–60 | 18 | 15 |
| | Over 60 | 11 | 5 |
| Sex | Men | 53% | 54% |
| | Women | 47 | 46 |
| Parental status | Have children under 21 | 56% | 74% |
| | Do not | 44 | 26 |
| Political preference | Democratic | 42% | 44% |
| | Republican | 40 | 44 |
| | Independent | 15 | 9 |
| | Not ascertained | 3 | 3 |
| Religious affiliation | Protestant | 76% | 73% |
| | Roman Catholic | 20 | 24 |
| | Jewish | 2 | 2 |
| | None | 2 | 1 |
| Number of memberships in community organizations | 4 or more | 67% | 72% |
| | 2 or 3 | 27 | 25 |
| | Only the Foundation | 6 | 3 |
| Occupation; husband's occupation | Professionals; semi-professionals; business executives | 37% | 29% |
| | Business proprietors; junior executives | 39 | 46 |
| | Clerical-sales employees | 10 | 7 |
| | Skilled, semi-skilled workers | 5 | 12 |
| | Other; not ascertained | 9 | 6 |
| | N | 100% (256) | 100% (190) |

Specially selected and trained members of the Institute's regular field staff conducted the interviews. Each interviewer was instructed to make arrangements for obtaining interviews through the Chapter Chairman and the March of Dimes Campaign Director. Because of variations among Chapter and March of Dimes organizations, however, the interviewing plan was not followed in detail in all eighty-five counties. Interviews were held with 520 individuals, distributed as follows: 256 Chapter Volunteers,

190 March of Dimes Volunteers, 48 Executive Secretaries, and 26 nurses and physical therapists.

Table 34 describes selected characteristics of the Foundation Volunteers who comprised the eighty-five-county sample.

## 2. THE THIRTY-SEVEN-COUNTY SURVEY

A survey of Foundation Volunteers was conducted by the Bureau of Applied Social Research in January, February, and March, 1954. The questionnaire instrument used is on file at the Bureau of Applied Social Research.

In selecting the sample, all counties served by Foundation Chapters were first stratified according to region. Within each region counties were then stratified according to their population size. Within each of these strata counties were then stratified according to their 1950–1953 weighted polio incidence rate (high and low) and their per capita contributions to the 1953 March of Dimes (high and low). From these strata fifty-one Chapters were purposively selected. Three criteria were used in making these selections. First, no Chapters were selected which had also been selected for study during the eighty-five-county study. (This eliminated the largest metropolitan areas in the country, since the eighty-five-county sample was selected with probability of selection proportionate to population size). Second, Chapters were selected in such a way that the resultant sample would contain counties having different economic characteristics, e.g., industrial, trade, and agricultural counties. Third, an attempt was made to select small counties which are only a few hours' journey from the large counties selected. (This procedure was followed because of the limited time and funds available for the field work.)

By this method of purposive selection, fifty-one counties were selected, and administrative arrangements were made to visit them. During the course of the field work, however, it became evident that there was insufficient time to visit this many counties, and fourteen counties which did not fulfill indispensable positions on the check-list of selection criteria were eliminated from the sample. In all, thirty-seven counties were studied: eighteen during the month of January, at the peak of Volunteer activity, and nineteen during the months of February and March.

The Chairman of the Foundation Chapter in each county selected was sent a letter, asking him to arrange appointments for interviews with the following Volunteers:

1. Chapter Chairman
2. Chapter Secretary
3. A Volunteer having had experience with the patient care program
4. An active Volunteer not a Chapter Officer
5. March of Dimes Campaign Director
6. A March of Dimes Chairman

Four staff members of the Bureau of Applied Social Research conducted all interviews with Foundation Volunteers. Upon arriving in a com-

## Table 35—Selected Characteristics of the 37-County Sample

| Characteristic | | Chapter Volunteers | March of Dimes Volunteers |
|---|---|---|---|
| Years active | 1 | 5% | 29% |
| | 2–5 | 47 | 56 |
| | More than 10 | 30 | 10 |
| | "Since the begining"* | 18 | 5 |
| Age | 20–30 | 5% | 10% |
| | 31–40 | 34 | 49 |
| | 41–50 | 33 | 24 |
| | 51–60 | 21 | 16 |
| | Over 60 | 7 | 1 |
| Sex | Men | 55% | 57% |
| | Women | 45 | 43 |
| Parental status | Have children under 21 | 63% | 71% |
| | Do not | 37 | 29 |
| Social class† | Upper | 10% | 13% |
| | Upper middle | 36 | 28 |
| | Middle | 49 | 45 |
| | Lower middle | 5 | 14 |
| Religious affiliation | Protestant | 80% | 83% |
| | Roman Catholic | 15 | 16 |
| | Jewish | 5 | – |
| | None | – | 1 |
| Political preference | Democratic | 46% | 48% |
| | Republican | 45 | 43 |
| | Independent | 8 | 8 |
| | Not ascertained | 1 | 1 |
| Occupation; husband's occupation | Professionals; semi-professionals | 38% | 33% |
| | Business proprietors | 23 | 23 |
| | Business executives | 25 | 21 |
| | Public office holders | 6 | 8 |
| | Clerical-sales employees | 3 | 6 |
| | Skilled, semi-skilled workers | 2 | 6 |
| | Other; not ascertained | 3 | 3 |
| Number of memberships in community organizations | 4 or more | 69% | 73% |
| | 2 or 3 | 28 | 25 |
| | Only the Foundation | 3 | 2 |
| | | 100% | 100% |
| N | | (129) | (105) |

* See note appended to Table 13, p. 140.

† See p. 289 for the definition of social class used.

munity, he (or she) immediately telephoned the Chapter Chairman, who had previously received notice of his arrival. Arrangements were made to carry out all interviews within a three- or four-day period. Interviewers made verbatim notes, which they recorded on discs after the interview was completed. The discs were then mailed to the Bureau's headquarters in New York, where transcriptions were typed upon McBee Key Sort Cards. Interviewers also submitted reports upon the communities they visited and the Chapter and March of Dimes activities which they observed.

Because of variations among Chapter and March of Dimes organizations, the interviewing plan was not followed in detail in all thirty-seven

## Table 36—Selected Characteristics of Rank-and-File Volunteers

| Characteristic | | Chairmen; Deputy Chairmen | Other Volunteers |
|---|---|---|---|
| Years active | 1 | 29% | 30% |
| | 2–5 | 55 | 54 |
| | 6 or more | 16 | 16 |
| | 20–30 | 10% | 13% |
| Age | 31–40 | 48 | 47 |
| | 41–50 | 32 | 29 |
| | 51–60 | 9 | 8 |
| | Over 60 | 1 | 3 |
| Sex | Men | 22% | 9% |
| | Women | 78 | 91 |
| Parental status | Have children under 12 | 91% | 92% |
| | Do not | 9 | 8 |
| Number of memberships in community organizations | 4 or more | 47% | 42% |
| | 2 or 3 | 44 | 40 |
| | Only the Foundation | 2 | 3 |
| | Not ascertained | 7 | 15 |
| Occupation; husband's occupation | Professionals and semi-professionals | 29% | 20% |
| | Business proprietors | 19 | 10 |
| | Business executives | 14 | 6 |
| | Clerical-sales employees | 22 | 25 |
| | Skilled, semi-skilled workers | 15 | 26 |
| | Other; not ascertained | 1 | 13 |
| Self-identification with social class* | Upper class | 6% | 2% |
| | Middle class | 72 | 65 |
| | Working class | 22 | 33 |
| | | 100% | 100% |
| | | (247) | (212) |

* In response to the question: "In general, do you consider yourself a member of . . . ?"

counties. In all, 129 Chapter Volunteers and 105 March of Dimes Volunteers were interviewed. A summary of the major characteristics of these Volunteers is included in Chapter I of the text; Table 35 describes other characteristics of the thirty-seven-county sample, and provides the detailed statistics upon which the statements made in Chapter I are based. Additional statistical data concerning these Volunteers is included in Appendix B; the thirty-seven communities are described in Appendix C.

### 3. THE RANK-AND-FILE MARCH OF DIMES VOLUNTEER SURVEY

A mail questionnaire survey of rank-and-file March of Dimes Volunteers was conducted by the Bureau of Applied Social Research in February 1954. The questionnaire instrument used is on file at the Bureau.

The four counties in which a survey of the general public was undertaken were selected for this survey. The names and addresses of all Volunteers—above the rank of Private on the Mothers' March on Polio—who took an active part in the 1954 March of Dimes were obtained from Campaign Directors and their deputies. Questionnaires were mailed to Volunteers whose addresses could be obtained. In the four counties, 888 questionnaires were mailed and 459 were returned, a return rate of 52 per cent.

Table 36 describes selected characteristics of the rank-and-file March of Dimes Volunteers who returned the mail questionnaire.

*appendix B*

# THE
# CONSTRUCTION
# OF INDICES

## I. General Public Surveys

### 1. SOCIO-ECONOMIC STATUS

*Nationwide survey.* The index was constructed from two items:

1. Family income
2. Education

<table>
<tr><td>The scoring:</td><td colspan="2">EDUCATIONAL LEVEL</td></tr>
<tr><td>Weekly family income</td><td>High school graduates</td><td>High school nongraduates</td></tr>
<tr><td>$77 and more</td><td>1</td><td>2</td></tr>
<tr><td>$39 – $76.50</td><td>3</td><td>4</td></tr>
<tr><td>$38.50 and less</td><td>5</td><td>6</td></tr>
</table>

Distribution of cases*

| | |
|---|---|
| High (score 1) | 411 |
| High middle (scores 2, 3) | 552 |
| Low middle (scores 4, 5) | 548 |
| Low (score 6) | 414 |
| Unclassified | 75 |
| N | (2000) |

\* When "high" and "low" socio-economic status are reported in the text, "high middle" is combined with "high" and "low middle" is combined with "low."

*Four-city survey.* The index was constructed from three items:

1. Occupation of head of household
2. Education
3. Interviewer rating of economic level

*The scoring:*

**OCCUPATION OF HEAD OF HOUSEHOLD**

| | Professional, semi-professional, managerial, executive, clerical-sales workers | | Skilled, semi-skilled, unskilled workers | |
|---|---|---|---|---|
| | **EDUCATIONAL LEVEL** | | | |
| Interviewer rating | High school graduates | High school nongraduates | High school graduates | High school nongraduates |
| A, B | 1 | 2 | 3 | 4 |
| C | 5 | 6 | 7 | 8 |
| D, E | 9 | 10 | 11 | 12 |

**DISTRIBUTION OF CASES\***

| | Eastern City | Central City | South City | Desert City | Four Cities |
|---|---|---|---|---|---|
| High (scores 1, 2) | 50 | 53 | 65 | 95 | 263 |
| High middle (scores 5, 6, 9, 10) | 75 | 68 | 42 | 145 | 330 |
| Low middle (scores 3, 4, 7, 8) | 128 | 131 | 94 | 93 | 446 |
| Low (scores 11, 12) | 40 | 64 | 95 | 86 | 285 |
| N | (293) | (316) | (296) | (419) | (1324) |

\* See footnote, p. 283.

## 2. KNOWLEDGE OF FOUNDATION ACTIVITIES
### (FOUR-CITY SURVEY ONLY)

The index was constructed from five questions:

*1.* Do you have any idea about what this Chapter does for victims of this disease in this county?

*2.* When was this (March of Dimes) campaign?

*3.* What were the main things stressed in the March of Dimes campaign this year?

*4.* As far as you know, is the organization that operates the March of Dimes a member of the Community Fund (Chest)?

*5.* Have you heard of any vaccine which has been developed for use against polio? What has been developed? What else has been developed?

*The scoring:*

| Question | Response | Points |
|---|---|---|
| (1) | If money, treatment, hospitalization, or equipment mentioned | 1 |
| (2) | If January or "last month" mentioned | 1 |
| (3) | If gamma globulin, vaccine, or research mentioned | 1 |
| (4) | If "no" | 1 |
| (5) | If vaccine or gamma globulin mentioned | 1 |
| | Total possible points | 5 |

**DISTRIBUTION OF CASES\***

| | Eastern City | Central City | South City | Desert City | Four cities |
|---|---|---|---|---|---|
| High (4 or 5 points) | 95 | 56 | 57 | 155 | 363 |
| High middle (3 points) | 64 | 70 | 63 | 85 | 282 |
| Low middle (2 points) | 69 | 85 | 66 | 83 | 303 |
| Low (0 or 1 points) | 65 | 105 | 110 | 96 | 376 |
| N | (293) | (316) | (296) | (419) | (1324) |

\* When "high" and "low" scores are reported in the text, "high middle" is combined with "high" and "low middle" is combined with "low."

«285»

### 3. FEAR OF POLIO (FOUR-CITY SURVEY ONLY)

The index was constructed from three questions:

*1.* Which disease or illness do you personally fear most?
*2.* Which (of these six diseases) is furthest from being licked?
*3.* Of these (six) diseases, which do you think is the most damaging to the person who has it?

*The scoring:*

|  | QUESTION 1 | | | |
|---|---|---|---|---|
|  | Polio mentioned | | Polio not mentioned | |
|  | QUESTION 2 | | | |
| QUESTION 3 | Polio mentioned | Polio not mentioned | Polio mentioned | Polio not mentioned |
| Polio mentioned | 3 | 2 | 2 | 1 |
| Polio not mentioned | 2 | 1 | 1 | 0 |

DISTRIBUTION OF CASES*

|  | Eastern City | Central City | South City | Desert City | Four cities |
|---|---|---|---|---|---|
| High (scores 2, 3) | 24 | 27 | 23 | 29 | 103 |
| Middle (score 1) | 104 | 109 | 84 | 132 | 429 |
| Low (score 0) | 165 | 180 | 189 | 258 | 792 |
| N | (293) | (316) | (296) | (419) | (1324) |

* When "high" and "low" scores are reported in the text, "middle" is combined with "low."

### 4. EMOTIONAL INVOLVEMENT (FOUR-CITY SURVEY ONLY)

The index was constructed from four questions, selected by means of a factor analysis:

*1.* Here is a list of six common diseases and illnesses. If you could give money to help control only one of these, which would you pick as Number One?
*2.* Of these (six) diseases, which have you heard most about in the last year or so?
*3.* Of these (six) diseases, which do you think is most damaging to the person who has it?
*4.* Which do you think are the most serious diseases or illnesses in this country today?

*The scoring:*

| Question | Response | Points† |
|---|---|---|
| (1) | Polio selected | 4 |
| (2) | Polio mentioned | 3 |
| (3) | Polio mentioned | 2 |
| (4) | Polio mentioned | 1 |
|  | Total possible points | 10 |

† The points were selected in order to give weight to the differential extent to which responses to the four questions are interrelated.

### DISTRIBUTION OF CASES*

|  | Eastern City | Central City | South City | Desert City | Four cities |
|---|---|---|---|---|---|
| High (7–10 points) | 113 | 130 | 96 | 147 | 486 |
| Middle (4–6 points) | 82 | 62 | 78 | 117 | 339 |
| Low (0–3 points) | 98 | 124 | 122 | 155 | 499 |
| N | (293) | (316) | (296) | (419) | (1324) |

* See footnote, p. 285.

## 5. CONTRIBUTIONS TO FUND-RAISING CAMPAIGNS

*Nationwide survey—March of Dimes contributors*

The index was constructed from three questions:

*1.* Did you or your husband (wife) contribute to the March of Dimes during the campaign last month?

*2.* How did you make your contribution—through the mail, in a coin box, to a solicitor at the door, attending a benefit, or how?

*3.* Have you ever heard of the March of Dimes? (If yes) What is the March of Dimes?

|  | QUESTIONS 1 AND 2 | |
|---|---|---|
| QUESTION 3 | Contributed—other than through payroll deduction | Did not contribute; contributed only through payroll deduction |
| Mentioned either polio, the Foundation, the Mothers' March, a pool in Georgia, or Warm Springs | 2 | 0 |
| Did not mention any of above | 1 | 0 |

### DISTRIBUTION OF CASES*

| Contributors (score 2) | 1379 |
|---|---|
| Doubtful contributors (score 1) | 253 |
| Noncontributors (score 0) | 368 |
| N | (2000) |

* In the text, "doubtful contributors" are treated as "noncontributors."

*Nationwide survey—contributors to other fund-raising campaigns*

The index was constructed from two questions:

*1.* In the last 12 months, did you or your husband (wife) happen to give money to this organization?

*2.* How did you make your contribution—through the mail, in a coin box, to a solicitor at the door, attending a benefit, or how?

*The scoring:*

|  | QUESTION 1 | |
|---|---|---|
| QUESTION 2 | Contributed | Did not contribute |
| Other than through payroll deduction | 2 | 0 |
| Only through payroll deduction | 1 | 0 |

| DISTRIBUTION OF CASES* | | | | | |
|---|---|---|---|---|---|
|  | Community Chest Campaign | Red Cross Drive | Christmas Seal Sale | Cancer Crusade | Heart Appeal |
| Contributors (score 2) | 724 | 1030 | 1183 | 636 | 582 |
| Payroll deduction contributors (score 1) | 220 | 137 | 51 | 49 | 38 |
| Noncontributors (score 0) | 1056 | 833 | 766 | 1315 | 1380 |
| N | (2000) | (2000) | (2000) | (2000) | (2000) |

\* In the text, "payroll deduction contributors" are treated as "noncontributors."

## Four-city survey—March of Dimes contributors

The index was constructed from three questions:

*1.* During the last March of Dimes or polio campaign, did you or your husband (wife) contribute?

*2.* How did you make your contribution—through the mail, in a coin box, to a personal solicitor at the door, attending a benefit, or how?

*3.* When was this campaign (March of Dimes)?

*The scoring:*

|  | QUESTIONS 1 AND 2 | |
|---|---|---|
| QUESTION 3 | Contributed—other than through payroll deduction | Did not contribute; contributed only through payroll deduction |
| Mentioned "last month" or "January" | 2 | 0 |
| Did not | 1 | 0 |

| DISTRIBUTION OF CASES* | | | | | |
|---|---|---|---|---|---|
|  | Eastern City | Central City | South City | Desert City | Four cities |
| Contributors (score 2) | 231 | 215 | 159 | 328 | 933 |
| Doubtful contributors (score 1) | 12 | 19 | 53 | 34 | 118 |
| Noncontributors (score 0) | 50 | 82 | 84 | 57 | 273 |
| N | (293) | (316) | (296) | (419) | (1324) |

\* In the text, "doubtful contributors" are treated as "noncontributors."

*Four-city survey—contributors to other fund-raising campaigns*

The index was constructed from two questions:

*1.* In the last year did you or your husband (wife) happen to give to this organization?

*2.* How did you make your contribution—through the mail, in a coin-box, to a personal solicitor at the door, attending a benefit, or how?

The scoring:

| | QUESTION 1 | |
|---|---|---|
| QUESTION 2 | Contributed | Did not contribute |
| Other than through payroll deduction | 2 | 0 |
| Only through payroll deduction | 1 | 0 |

| | DISTRIBUTION OF CASES* | | | | |
|---|---|---|---|---|---|
| | Eastern City | Central City | South City | Desert City | Four cities |
| **Community Chest campaign** | | | | | |
| Contributors (score 2) | 193 | 142 | 157 | 264 | 756 |
| Payroll deduction contributors (score 1) | 64 | 100 | 66 | 78 | 308 |
| Noncontributors (score 0) | 36 | 74 | 73 | 77 | 260 |
| **Red Cross Drive** | | | | | |
| Contributors (score 2) | 170 | 136 | 136 | 218 | 660 |
| Payroll deduction contributors (score 1) | 55 | 51 | 42 | 41 | 189 |
| Noncontributors (score 0) | 68 | 129 | 118 | 160 | 475 |
| **Christmas Seal Sale** | | | | | |
| Contributors (score 2) | 252 | 218 | 219 | 323 | 1012 |
| Payroll deduction contributors (score 1) | 1 | 11 | 7 | 11 | 30 |
| Noncontributors (score 0) | 40 | 87 | 70 | 85 | 282 |
| **Cancer Crusade** | | | | | |
| Contributors (score 2) | 132 | 107 | 118 | 218 | 575 |
| Payroll deduction contributors (score 1) | 14 | 21 | 15 | 9 | 59 |
| Noncontributors (score 0) | 147 | 188 | 163 | 192 | 690 |
| **Heart Appeal** | | | | | |
| Contributors (score 2) | 152 | 120 | 77 | 247 | 596 |
| Payroll deduction contributors (score 1) | 9 | 17 | 9 | 10 | 45 |
| Noncontributors (score 0) | 132 | 179 | 210 | 162 | 683 |
| N | (293) | (316) | (296) | (419) | (1324) |

* In the text, "payroll deduction contributors" are treated as "noncontributors."

## II.  Volunteer Survey*

### 1. PATIENT CARE INVOLVEMENT

The index was constructed from three items concerning the importance of the patient care program:

1. Activity of greatest interest
2. A "strong point" of the Foundation's program
3. The "key" to the Foundation's success in obtaining public support

*The scoring:*

| | |
|---|---|
| Positive scores on all three items | 3 |
| Positive scores on all items | 2 |
| Positive score on one item | 1 |
| No positive scores | 0 |

DISTRIBUTION OF CASES*

| Score | Chapter Volunteers | March of Dimes Volunteers |
|---|---|---|
| 3 | 25 | 0 |
| 2 | 45 | 32 |
| 1 | 35 | 42 |
| 0 | 24 | 31 |
| N | (129) | (105) |

\* Volunteers with scores of two or three are treated in the text as "highly involved."

### 2. SOCIAL CLASS

All Volunteers were rated by the interviewers as belonging to either the upper, the upper middle, the middle, or the lower middle class. This impressionistic judgment was based upon the interviewer's estimate of each Volunteer's standing in the community, his approximate income, his occupation, and his "style of life." An attempt was made to base these judgments upon the standards prevalent in each community, rather than upon nationwide or metropolitan standards. The social class composition of the Volunteers studied is given in Table 35, p. 280. For the purpose of characterizing Chapters according to their membership homogeneity, "upper" and "upper middle," and "middle" and "lower middle" were combined. Chapters were classified as "upper" if two-thirds or more of the Volunteers interviewed were rated as "upper"; as "middle" if two-thirds or more were rated as "middle"; and as "mixed" if neither group predominates. (See Chart 4, p. 295.)

### 3. POLITICAL PREFERENCE

Volunteers were asked which political party they preferred; "Democrats for Eisenhower" in 1952 were classified as Democrats. The political

---

* See Chapter 1 and Appendix A for descriptions of Volunteers other than those presented here. The data in this section refer to the Volunteers interviewed during the Columbia University thirty-seven-county survey, not to the eighty-five-county survey conducted by the American Institute of Public Opinion.

composition of the Volunteers interview is given in Table 35, p. 280. For the purpose of characterizing Chapters according to their membership homogeneity, Chapters in which two-thirds or more of the Volunteers interviewed are Democrats were rated as "Democratic"; Chapters in which two-thirds or more are Republicans were rated as "Republican"; and Chapters in which neither group predominates were rated as "mixed." (See Chart 4, p. 295.)

## 4. OCCUPATION

The occupations of the Volunteers (or the husbands of Volunteers) who were interviewed are given in Table 35, p. 280. For the purpose of characterizing Chapters according to their membership homogeneity, a different classification scheme than that given in Table 35 was used. Regardless of their occupation, Volunteers were classified as belonging to either the "business community" or the "professional-governmental" community. Chapters in which two-thirds or more of the Volunteers interviewed belong to the "business community" were classified as "business," and vice versa. Chapters in which neither group predominates were rated as "mixed." (See Chart 4, p. 295.)

## 5. FUNCTIONAL COHESIVENESS

Functional cohesiveness is an impressionistic rating of the degree to which Chapter Volunteers work together as a "team" on Foundation activities. "Low" functional cohesiveness is found in so-called "one-man" Chapters and in Chapters in which administration is decentralized. "High" functional cohesiveness is found in Chapters in which there is a great deal of group activity, and generally effective administration. "Medium" functional cohesiveness describes those Chapters in which neither of these extreme situations exists. (See Chart 4, p. 295.)

## 6. STATE REPRESENTATIVE RATING

In November, 1953, all State Representatives were asked by the Foundation's National Headquarters to classify all Chapters within their jurisdiction into three groups of equal size: above average (AA), average (A), and below average (BA). They were asked to base their judgment upon the overall performance of Chapter responsibilities; they were specifically asked, however, *not* to use March of Dimes per capita receipts as a criterion. The rating refers, accordingly, to such responsibilities as Chapter administration, conduct of the patient care program, and information-education activities. (See Chart 4, p. 295.)

## 7. MAIN SOURCE OF 1954 RECEIPTS

In order to ascertain the extent to which total March of Dimes contributions in the thirty-seven counties are based upon one major activity— the Mothers' March on Polio—an analysis was made of the sources of contributions to the 1954 March of Dimes, based upon the County Campaign Reports for each county. Chart 2, below, reports the two (or three) largest sources of contributions, and the percentage of all contributions from these sources. Only sources which represent more than 10 per cent of all receipts are included; in two counties, there was only one such source. The following code is used in Chart 4, p. 295.

| | | | |
|---|---|---|---|
| AF | Armed Forces | MM | Mothers' March |
| CC | Coin collectors | SE | Special events |
| DC | March of Dimes Cards | SC | Schools and colleges |
| EE | Employer-employee gifts | SG | Special gifts |

## III.  Community Characteristics

### 1. REGIONS OF THE UNITED STATES

There is no completely satisfactory method of grouping the forty-eight states and the District of Columbia by region. The methods used by the Bureau of the Census were not satisfactory for the purposes of this study, since they use classifications which are either too gross (the four-region system) or too refined (the nine-region system). Accordingly, a five-region system which varies only slightly from the Bureau of the Census four-region system was developed:

| East | South | Midwest | Southwest | West |
|---|---|---|---|---|
| Connecticut | Alabama | Illinois | Arizona | California |
| Delaware | Arkansas | Indiana | New Mexico | Colorado |
| District of Columbia | Florida | Iowa | Oklahoma | Idaho |
| Maine | Georgia | Kansas | Texas | Montana |
| Maryland | Kentucky | Michigan | | Nevada |
| Massachusetts | Louisiana | Minnesota | | Oregon |
| New Hampshire | Mississippi | Missouri | | Utah |
| New Jersey | North Carolina | Nebraska | | Washington |
| New York | South Carolina | North Dakota | | Wyoming |
| Pennsylvania | Tennessee | Ohio | | |
| Rhode Island | Virginia | South Dakota | | |
| Vermont | | West Virginia | | |
| | | Wisconsin | | |

### 2. MEDIAN FAMILY INCOME

All references in the text to median family income refer to the year 1949 (1950 Census). When the unit of analysis is the Foundation Chapter, the following cutting points are used, unless indicated otherwise.

| High | $2950–5600 |
|---|---|
| Medium | 1650–2949 |
| Low | 500–1649 |

When the unit of analysis is the individual respondent to the nationwide general public survey, i.e., when individuals are classified according to the

median family income of the county in which they live, the following
cutting points are used:

| | |
|---|---|
| High | $2950–5600 |
| Medium | 2350–2949 |
| Low | 500–2349 |

It was necessary to use different points in these tables since only 10 per
cent of the respondents in the nationwide survey live in counties having
a median family income of less than $1650 per year.

### 3. POLIO INCIDENCE

Polio incidence rates were used as variables in this research because of
their presumed effect upon behavior and attitudes; it was therefore necessary to make use of the rates for the years prior to the measurement of
behavior and attitudes. Since both behavior and attitudes are potentially
influenced not only by the rate during the previous year, but by the rates
during several previous years as well, it was necessary that the rates for
several years be taken into account. Since the rate for the most recent
year has more of an effect than that of more distant years, a three-year
weighted average was used.

A weighted average is one in which the components are not averaged
directly, but are averaged after having been multiplied by a weighting factor. The weighting formula used in this research is best described by demonstrating its use in a hypothetical example.

| Year | Polio rate for county | Weighting factor | Product |
|---|---|---|---|
| 1951 | 20 cases per 100,000 pop. | 2 | 40 |
| 1952 | 40  "    "    "    " | 3 | 120 |
| 1953 | 30  "    "    "    " | 5 | 150 |
| | Sum of weights: | 10 | |
| | Sum of products: | | 310 |

The sum of the products was then divided by the sum of the weights, giving
in this hypothetical example a 3-year weighted average of 31 cases per
100,000 population.

The use of this computation formula resulted in a three-year weighted
average for each county in the United States. In order to correlate these
rates with qualitative variables, such as region, as well as with other grouped
data, it was necessary that they be grouped in some way. The following
cutting points were used:*

| | |
|---|---|
| High | Over 44 cases per100,00 |
| High medium | 24–43 cases |
| Low medium | 11–23 cases |
| Low | Less than 11 cases |

* When high, medium, and low rates are reported in the text, high medium and low
medium are combined. When only high and low rates are reported, the two medium
groups are either excluded (Chapters IV and VI) or combined with high and low
(Appendix C).

# THE
# THIRTY-SEVEN
# COUNTIES AND
# CHAPTERS

THROUGHOUT THIS volume Volunteers are identified only by citing the Chapter or March of Dimes position which they hold and by noting the name of the county in which they serve—not directly, but by means of pseudonyms given each county. If one city or town dominates the county, the county is identified by a name given to that city or town; if the county contains several population centers, a name has been given to the county. In both cases, of course, the Chapter serves the entire county. So that the reader will have some familiarity with these communities, this Appendix describes their basic characteristics. Chart 2 locates the thirty-seven counties by region and population size; Chart 3 locates them according to their economy and their median family income; and Chart 4 describes six characteristics of the thirty-seven Chapters which are mentioned in Chapter I of the text.

## Chart 2—Regional Location and Population Size, 37 Counties

| | POPULATION SIZE* | | |
|---|---|---|---|
| Region | Metropolitan | Small City | Rural |
| East | Smoky City | Eastern City<br>Upstate City<br>Mountain County | Lumber City |
| South | South City<br>Greenback City<br>Friendly City<br>Steamboat City<br>Defense Town<br>Central City<br>Soybean City | Fabric Town<br>Milltown<br>Pulpwood City<br><br>University City | Payday Town |

293

## Chart 2—Regional Location and Population Size, 37 Counties (cont.)

POPULATION SIZE*

| Region | Metropolitan | Small City | Rural |
|---|---|---|---|
| Midwest | Power City<br>Glass City<br>Cattlefeed City<br>Corn City | College Town<br>Lakeside County | Dirtroad County |
| Southwest | Desert City<br>Oil City<br>Gas City | (none) | Hometown<br>Oldtown |
| West | Steel City<br>Harbor City<br>Valley City<br>Suburb County | Wheat County<br>Market Town | Upland County<br>Pinetree County |

* "Metropolitan" counties are those located in a Standard Metropolitan Area, as designated by the Bureau of the Census. "Small city" counties are those counties not located in a Standard Metropolitan Area but which have a population of at least 50,000 (1950 Census). "Rural" counties are those which have a population of less than 50,000.

## Chart 3—Economy and Median Family Income, 37 Counties

MEDIAN FAMILY INCOME LEVEL OF COUNTY*

| Economy† | High | Medium | Low |
|---|---|---|---|
| Agricultural | (none) | (none) | Upland County<br>Dirtroad County<br>Hometown<br>Oldtown |
| Manufacturing | Smoky City<br>Power City<br>College Town<br>Steamboat City<br>Soybean City<br>Upstate City | Lakeside County<br>Steel City<br>Friendly City<br>Greenback City<br>Glass City | Fabric Town<br>Milltown<br>Defense Town<br>South City |
| Agricultural-<br>manufacturing | Wheat County | Mountain County<br>Lumber City<br>University City<br>Eastern City<br>Pinetree County | Payday Town<br>Pulpwood City |
| Trade | Valley City<br>Harbor City<br>Corn City<br>Desert City<br>Suburb City | Central City<br>Market Town<br>Oil City<br>Gas City<br>Cattlefeed City | (none) |

* Median family income data are for 1949 (1950 Census). The following cutting points were used:

| High | $3300 and over |
|---|---|
| Medium | $2700 to 3299 |
| Low | Less than $2700 |

† The economy of the county was determined as follows. Using the 1950 Census, the percentage of the labor force engaged in agriculture, manufacturing, trade and other industry groups was computed. The country was then classified according to the industry group to which a plurality of the labor force belongs. In the case of "manufacturing" countries, if more than 10 per cent of the labor force is engaged in agriculture the county was classified as "agricultural-manufacturing."

## Chart 4—Selected Characteristics, 37 Chapters*

| Chapter | Social class composition | Political composition | Occupational composition | Functional cohesiveness | State Representative rating | Main source of 1954 receipts |
|---|---|---|---|---|---|---|
| Cattlefeed City | Middle | Dem. | Mixed | Low | AA | MM 49%, SG 21% |
| Central City | Middle | Rep. | Mixed | High | AA | MM 42%, DC 12%, SC 12% |
| College Town | Upper | Rep. | Bus. | Medium | AA | MM 28%, DC 16% |
| Corn City | Upper | Rep. | Mixed | High | A | MM 29%, DC 20% |
| Defense Town | Middle | Dem. | Mixed | Low | AA | Not reported in detail |
| Desert City | Middle | Rep. | Bus. | High | AA | SE 28%, MM 21% |
| Dirtroad County | Mixed | Mixed | Mixed | Low | A | DC 36%, MM 14% |
| Eastern City | Mixed | Rep. | Bus. | High | AA | MM 23%, SE 49% |
| Fabric Town | Mixed | Dem. | Mixed | Low | AA | MM 24%, EE 23% |
| Friendly City | Upper | Rep. | Bus. | High | AA | MM 54%, DC 16% |
| Gas City | Upper | Mixed | Bus. | High | AA | MM 40%, SG 25% |
| Glass City | Middle | Dem. | Mixed | Low | AA | MM 25% |
| Greenback City | Upper | Dem. | Bus. | Medium | AA | EE 18%, SG 17% |
| Harbor City | Upper | Rep. | Bus. | High | A | DC 42%, MM 22% |
| Hometown | Middle | Dem. | Bus. | Low | BA | CC 75%, MM 25% |
| Lakeside County | Middle | Mixed | Prof. | High | AA | SG 23%, EE 20% |
| Lumber City | Middle | Rep. | Bus. | High | AA | Not reported in detail |
| Market Town | Middle | Mixed | Bus. | Low | AA | SE 22%, MM 19% |
| Milltown | Middle | Dem. | Prof. | Low | BA | MM 20% |
| Mountain County | Middle | Mixed | Prof. | Low | AA | MM 38%, EE 14% |
| Oil City | Mixed | Dem. | Bus. | Low | AA | MM 69% |
| Oldtown | Upper | Dem. | Bus. | Low | BA | SE 47%, MM 24% |
| Payday Town | Middle | Dem. | Bus. | Low | BA | EE 47%, MM 18% |
| Pinetree County | Mixed | Rep. | Bus. | High | A | DC 42%, MM 16% |
| Power City | Middle | Rep. | Mixed | High | BA | MM 49%, DC 26% |
| Pulpwood City | Middle | Dem. | Bus. | Low | AA | EE 44%, MM 20% |
| Smoky City | Mixed | Mixed | Mixed | Low | A | MM 52%, EE 17% |
| South City | Upper | Mixed | Bus. | High | AA | AF 44%, SE 28% |
| Soybean City | Mixed | Rep. | Mixed | High | AA | DC 32%, MM 18% |
| Steamboat City | Middle | Dem. | Mixed | High | AA | EE 40%, MM 15% |
| Steel City | Mixed | Dem. | Bus. | High | AA | MM 34%, SE 23% |
| Suburb County | Mixed | Dem. | Mixed | High | AA | MM 23%, DC 22% |
| University City | Middle | Mixed | Bus. | Medium | AA | DC 28%, MM 20% |
| Upland County | Upper | Mixed | Bus. | High | AA | MM 34%, DC 24% |
| Upstate City | Middle | Rep. | Mixed | Medium | BA | MM 30%, EE 19% |
| Valley City | Mixed | Rep. | Prof. | Low | A | MM 26%, DC 22% |
| Wheat County | Middle | Mixed | Prof. | Medium | BA | MM 28%, AF 12% |

* See Appendix B for a description of these characteristics and an explanation of the abbreviations used in this Chart.

# REFERENCES

## Preface

1. Alexis de Tocqueville, *Democracy in America*, Vol. 1 (New York: Vintage Books, 1954), p. 198. This book was first published in 1835.

2. James Bryce, *The American Commonwealth*, Vol. 2 (New York: Macmillan Co., 1891), p. 269.

3. See Herbert Goldhamer, "Voluntary Associations in the United States," in Paul K. Hatt and Albert J. Reiss, Jr. (eds.), *Reader in Urban Sociology* (Glencoe, Ill.: Free Press, 1951), pp. 505–506.

4. *Fortune*, with the collaboration of Russell W. Davenport, *U.S.A. The Permanent Revolution* (New York: Prentice-Hall, 1951), p. 128.

5. See Robert K. Merton, *Social Theory and Social Structure* (Glencoe, Ill.: Free Press, 1949), pp. 194–95; Seymour M. Lipset, Martin A. Trow, and James S. Coleman, *Union Democracy* (Glencoe, Ill.: Free Press, 1956), pp. 417–18; and Patricia Kendall and Katherine M. Wolf, "The Analysis of Deviant Cases in Communications Research," in Paul F. Lazarsfeld and Frank Stanton (eds.), *Communications Research* 1948–1949 (New York: Harper and Brothers, 1949), pp. 152–79.

6. Lipset, Trow, and Coleman, *op. cit.*, p. ix.

7. Philip Selznick, "An Approach to a Theory of Bureaucracy," *American Sociological Review*, 8 (1943), p. 49.

## Introduction

1. Chester I. Barnard, *The Functions of the Executive* (Cambridge: Harvard University Press, 1938), p. 79.

2. Philip Selznick, *TVA and the Grass Roots* (Berkeley and Los Angeles: University of California Press, 1949), p. 251.

3. *Ibid.*

4. See Kenneth E. Boulding, *The Organizational Revolution* (New York: Harper and Brothers, 1953).

5. See Sherwood D. Fox, "Voluntary Associations and Social Structure," unpublished Ph.D. thesis, Harvard University, 1953.

6. Arnold M. Rose, *Sociology* (New York: Alfred A. Knopf, 1956), p. 311*n*.

7. See, for example, Max Weber, *The Theory of Social and Economic Organization*. Translated by A. M. Henderson and Talcott Parsons; edited by Talcott Parsons (New York: Oxford University Press, 1947), pp. 329–41.

8. Most exceptions to this statement are studies of trade unions. See Seymour M. Lipset, Martin A. Trow, and James S. Coleman, *Union Democracy* (Glencoe, Ill.: Free Press, 1956), for the most comprehensive sociological analysis of a trade union yet undertaken. Other important sociological analyses of individual voluntary associations are Oliver Garceau, *The Political Life of the American Medical Association* (Cambridge: Harvard University Press, 1941); Sheldon L Messinger, "Organizational Transformation: A Case Study of a Declining Social Movement," *American Sociological Review*, 20 (1955), pp. 3–10, a study of the Townsend Organization; Joseph R. Gusfield, "Social Structure and Moral Reform: A Study of the Woman's Christian Temperance Union," *American Journal of Sociology*, LXI (1955), pp. 221–32; and Donald D. Stewart, "Local Board: A Study of the Place of Volunteer Participation in a Bureaucratic Organization," unpublished Ph.D. thesis, Columbia University, 1950, a study of the World War II volunteer Selective Service Boards.

9. Wayne McMillen, *Community Or-*

ganization for Social Welfare (Chicago: University of Chicago Press, 1945), pp. 587–91.

10. Adult Leadership, 2, 8 (1954), p. 11.

11. Ruth Wessels and Margaret Wingert, "Please Pass the Questionnaires," Adult Leadership, 2, 8 (1954), pp. 19–20.

12. See, for example, Garceau, op. cit., and Lipset, Trow, and Coleman, op. cit.

13. Seymour M. Lipset, "The Political Process in Trade Unions: A Theoretical Statement," in Morroe Berger, Theodore Abel, and Charles H. Page (eds.), Freedom and Control in Modern Society (New York: D. Van Nostrand Co., 1954), p. 105.

14. Ibid., p. 106.

15. Ray E. Johns, The Co-operative Process Among National Social Agencies (New York: Association Press, 1946), p. 199.

16. David B. Truman, The Governmental Process (New York: Alfred A. Knopf, 1951), p. 118.

17. Ibid., pp. 116–17.

18. McMillen, op. cit., p. 587.

19. Adult Leadership, 2, 8 (1954), p. 11.

20. Lipset, op. cit., p. 105.

21. Johns, op. cit., p. 193.

22. Truman, op. cit., p. 120.

23. See, for example, the definitions employed in two standard reference books in the field of voluntary health associations: Selskar M. Gunn, and Philip S. Platt, Voluntary Health Agencies (New York: Ronald Press, 1945) and Harold Cavins, National Health Agencies (Washington: Public Affairs Press, 1945).

24. National Tuberculosis Association, Annual Report on the Occasion of the Fiftieth Anniversary, 1954, p. 19.

25. American Heart Association, 1953 Annual Report, p. 31.

26. United Cerebral Palsy, Answering Questions About Cerebral Palsy; United Cerebral Palsy, Fourth Annual Report, 1953, p. 7.

27. National Society for Crippled Children and Adults, 1954 Annual Report, p. 8.

28. New York Times, September 23, 1937, p. 3.

29. Alvin W. Gouldner, Patterns of Industrial Bureaucracy (Glencoe, Ill.: Free Press, 1954), p. 164.

30. Philip Selznick, "Foundations of the Theory of Organization," American Sociological Review, 13 (1948), pp. 28–35.

31. See Philip Selznick, "An Approach to a Theory of Bureaucracy," American Sociological Review, 8 (1943), pp. 47–48; Leonard Broom and Philip Selznick, Sociology (Evanston, Ill. and White Plains, N.Y.: Row, Peterson and Co., 1955), pp. 213–16.

32. See Barnard, op. cit., pp. 122–23.

33. See Robert K. Merton, Social Theory and Social Structure (Glencoe, Ill.: Free Press, 1949), p. 51.

34. Herbert A. Simon, Administrative Behavior (New York: Macmillan Co., 1947), p. 3.

35. Bernard R. Berelson, Paul F. Lazarsfeld, and William N. McPhee, Voting (Chicago: University of Chicago Press, 1954), pp. 327–47.

36. See Lipset, Trow, and Coleman, op. cit., pp. 427–32; Hanan C. Selvin, "A Critique of Tests of Significance in Survey Research," American Sociological Review, 22 (1957), in press; and Robert K. Merton, George R. Reader and Patricia L. Kendall (eds.), The Student-Physician (Cambridge; Harvard University Press, 1957), pp. 301–305 for statements of this position.

## CHAPTER I

### Maintaining Membership Interest

1. See, for example the description of voluntary associations in Japanese farming and fishing communities contained in John F. Embree, Suye Mura: A Japanese Village (Chicago: University of Chicago Press, 1939), pp. 163–70 and Arthur F. Raper, Tamie Tsuchiyama, Herbert Passin, and David L. Sills, The Japanese Village in Transition (Tokyo: General Headquarters, Supreme Commander for the Allied Powers, 1950), pp. 198–99 and 231–36. See also S. N. Eisenstadt, "The Social Conditions of the Development of Voluntary Association—A Case Study of Israel," in Eliezer Kaplan School of Economics and Social Sciences, Scripta Hierosolymitana, Vol. III (Jerusalem: He-

brew University, 1955), pp. 104–25, for a brief review of the emergence of voluntary associations in a society undergoing rapid change.

2. For a description and discussion of the relative paucity of voluntary associations in France, see Arnold M. Rose, *Theory and Method in the Social Sciences* (Minneapolis: University of Minnesota Press, 1954), pp. 72–115.

3. For a list of studies bearing upon this point, see Arnold M. Rose, *Sociology* (New York: Alfred A. Knopf, 1956), p. 312*n*, and Bernard Barber, "Participation and Mass Apathy in Associations," in Alvin W. Gouldner (ed.), *Studies in Leadership* (New York: Harper and Brothers, 1950), pp. 481–84.

4. James Bryce, *Modern Democracies*, Vol. II (New York: Macmillan Co., 1921), p. 542.

5. Philip Selznick, *The Organizational Weapon* (New York: McGraw-Hill Book Co., 1952), p. 96.

6. Barber, *op. cit.*, pp. 484–86.

7. Leonard Broom and Philip Selznick, *Sociology* (Evanston, Ill. and White Plains, N.Y.: Row, Peterson and Co., 1955), pp. 440–41. An important exception to this generalization is the International Typographical Union, in which membership attendance at meetings is much more frequent. See Seymour M. Lipset, Martin A. Trow, and James S. Coleman, *Union Democracy* (Glencoe, Ill.: Free Press, 1956), pp. 261–66.

8. David Riesman and Nathan Glazer, "Criteria for Political Apathy," in Gouldner (ed.), *op. cit.*, p. 505.

9. See, for example, an editorial on the subject of membership nonparticipation in the affairs of the New York Automobile Association in the *New York Times*, December 22, 1955, p. 22.

10. Seymour M. Lipset, "The Political Process in Trade Unions: A Theoretical Statement," in Morroe Berger, Theodore Abel, and Charles H. Page (eds.), *Freedom and Control in Modern Society* (New York: D. Van Nostrand Co., 1954), p. 118.

11. National Foundation for Infantile Paralysis, *By-laws of the National Foundation for Infantile Paralysis, Inc. as of June 1, 1952*, p. 2. Although the Membership of the Corporation and the Board of Trustees have an identical membership, they are officially two distinct groups which meet either as Members or as Trustees.

12. National Foundation for Infantile Paralysis, *Manual for Chapters*, 1949 ed. p. 7.

13. National Foundation for Infantile Paralysis, "Orientation Manual for State Reperesentatives," mimeo., p. E.D. (B–1).

14. National Foundation for Infantile Paralysis, *Chapter Reference Book: Chapter Organization*, p. 11.

15. National Foundation for Infantile Paralysis, *Reference Book for Chapters*, p. 54.

16. American Cancer Society, *1954 Annual Report*, pp. 13 and 69.

17. National Multiple Sclerosis Society, *Chapter Handbook, passim; 1954 Annual Report*, p. 1.

18. Rose, *Theory and Method in the Social Sciences*, p. 52.

19. *Adult Leadership*, 3, 5 (1954), p. 13.

20. Selskar M. Gunn and Philip S. Platt, *Voluntary Health Agencies* (New York: Ronald Press, 1945), p. 259.

21. National Foundation for Infantile Paralysis, *Chapter Reference Book: Chapter Organization*, p. 11.

22. National Foundation for Infantile Paralysis, *Manual for Chapters*, 1949 ed., p. 20.

23. *Ibid.*, p. 22.

24. National Foundation for Infantile Paralysis, *Reference Book for Chapters*, p. 19.

25. *Ibid.*, p. 16.

26. See Rose, *Sociology*, p. 314*n*.

27. National Foundation for Infantile Paralysis, *Manual for Chapters*, 1949 ed., p. 13; "Orientation Manual for State Representatives," mimeo., pp. F.D.R., 2–3.

28. Foster R. Dulles, *The American Red Cross: A History* (New York: Harper and Brothers, 1950), pp. 68 and 535.

29. Robert Michels, *Political Parties* (Glencoe, Ill.: Free Press, 1949), p. 32. Italics supplied. This book was first published in Germany in 1911.

30. *Ibid.*, p. 400. No attempt is made here to provide a thorough critique of Michels' pioneering analysis. See C. W. Cassinelli, "The Law of Oligarchy," *American Political Science Review*, 47 (1953), pp. 773–84; Lipset, *op. cit.*, pp. 82–124; Reinhard Bendix, "Bureaucracy: The Problem and Its Setting," *American Sociological Review*, 12 (1947), pp. 493–507; Peter M. Blau, *Bureaucracy in Modern Society* (New York: Random House, 1956), pp. 93–96; Lipset, Trow, and Coleman, *op. cit.*, pp. 3–16; and Philip

Selznick, "The Iron Law of Bureaucracy," *Modern Review,* January, 1950, pp. 157–65 for more extended comments on the "iron law of oligarchy."

31. Michels, *op. cit.,* p. 26. See also Cassinelli, *op. cit.,* pp. 782–83.

32. David B. Truman, *The Governmental Process* (New York: Alfred A. Knopf, 1951), p. 141.

33. John E. Tsouderos, "Organizational Change in Terms of a Series of Selected Variables," *American Sociological Review,* 20 (1955), p. 209. See also F. Stuart Chapin and John E. Tsouderos, "The Formalization Process in Voluntary Associations," *Social Forces,* 34, 4 (1956), pp. 342–44.

34. Barber, *op. cit.,* p. 487.

35. Tsouderos, *op. cit.,* p. 209.

36. Oliver Garceau, *The Political Life of the American Medical Association* (Cambridge: Harvard University Press, 1941), p. 54.

37. Philip Selznick, "An Approach to a Theory of Bureaucracy," *American Sociological Review,* 8 (1943), p. 52.

38. Truman, *op. cit.,* pp. 142–43.

39. Selznick, *The Organizational Weapon,* p. 308.

40. Bendix, *op. cit.,* p. 494.

41. Bernard Barber, " 'Mass Apathy' and Voluntary Social Participation in the United States," unpublished Ph.D. thesis, Harvard University, 1948, pp. 258–59.

42. Herbert A. Simon, *Administrative Behavior* (New York: Macmillan Co., 1947), p. 114.

43. Truman, *op. cit.,* p. 153.

44. Gunnar Myrdal, for example, in a chapter entitled, "The American Pattern of Individual Leadership and Mass Passivity," places part of the blame for membership nonparticipation upon "the relative inertia and inarticulateness of the masses in America." Gunnar Myrdal, *An American Dilemma* (New York: Harper and Brothers, 1944), p. 712. Michels also cites the existence of an "indifferent and apathetic mass" as one of the "psychological" sources of minority rule. Michels, *op. cit.,* p. 52.

45. Barber, "Participation and Mass Apathy in Associations," p. 486.

46. Kenneth E. Boulding, *The Organizational Revolution* (New York: Harper and Brothers, 1953), p. 11; Truman, *op. cit.,* pp. 157–67.

47. See Martin Kriesberg, "Cross-Pressures and Attitudes: A Study of the Influence of Conflicting Propaganda on Opinions Regarding American-Soviet Relations," *Public Opinion Quarterly,* 13 (1949), pp. 5–16. For examples of withdrawal from political participation as a result of cross-pressures, see Lazarsfeld, Berelson and Gaudet, *op. cit.,* pp. 56–64 and Berelson, Lazarsfeld and McPhee, *op. cit.,* pp. 27–28.

48. Barber, "Participation and Mass Apathy in Associations," p. 486.

49. National Foundation for Infantile Paralysis, *Chapter Reference Book: Chapter Organization,* pp. 12–14.

50. See Maurice Dobb, "Bolshevism," in *Encyclopedia of the Social Sciences,* Vol. II (New York: Macmillan Co., 1937), p. 625 for a description of this controversy.

51. See Georgia Warm Springs Foundation, "Statement of Receipts from Organization to December 31st, 1932." Source: Franklin D. Roosevelt Library, Group 14, Financial Papers, Georgia Warm Springs Foundation, 1924–35.

52. Letter from Roosevelt to O'Connor, December 8, 1931. Source: Georgia Warm Springs Foundation Office, Box 1516, folder 1.

53. "A History of Georgia Hall," mimeo., August 28, 1940. Source: Franklin D. Roosevelt Library, President's Personal Files 76, Box 2.

54. Arthur Carpenter in the *Asheville* (N.C.) *Citizen-Times,* January 17, 1937, Section A, p. 5.

55. Turnley Walker, *Roosevelt and the Warm Springs Story,* (New York: A. A. Wyn, 1953), p. 224.

56. National Foundation for Infantile Paralysis, Turnley Walker Collection, Typescript account of O'Connor (n.d.).

57. National Foundation for Infantile Paralysis, *1940 Annual Report,* p. 47.

58. Franklin D. Roosevelt, "Informal Remarks on Reception of Fund Raised by Birthday Ball in Behalf of Crippled Children, May 9, 1934," in *The Public Papers and Addresses of Franklin D. Roosevelt,* Vol. 3 (New York: Random House, 1938), p. 227.

59. Franklin D. Roosevelt, "Wanted— Enlistment for a Crusade," front page editorial in *The Polio Chronicle,* July, 1931 (published by the Georgia Warm Springs Foundation at Warm Springs, Ga.).

60. Georgia Warm Springs Foundation, *Certificate of Amendment of Certificate of Incorporation,* September 12, 1934.

61. National Foundation for Infantile

Paralysis, *1940 Annual Report,* p. 47.

62. Letter from Roosevelt to O'Connor, October 18, 1937. Source: National Foundation for Infantile Paralysis, Turnley Walker Collection. Press release for November 8, 1937.

63. Letter from O'Connor to Roosevelt, October 26, 1937. Source: Georgia Warm Springs Foundation Office, Box 1717, folder 4.

64. National Foundation for Infantile Paraylsis, Turnley Walker Collection. Press release for November 8, 1937.

65. See National Tuberculosis Association, *Annual Report on the Occasion of the Fiftieth Anniversary,* 1954, pp. 6–10, for a brief historical account of this organization. An account of the President's Birthday Ball Commission for Infantile Paralysis Research will be included in the forthcoming history of the Foundation.

66. For a sample of these protests, see the collection of letters, telegrams, and excerpts in Georgia Warm Springs Foundation Office, Box 1717, folder 4, beginning in November, 1937.

67. National Foundation for Infantile Paralysis, *Minutes of the Board of Trustees,* November 10, 1938. "Report of the President to the Board of Trustees on Local Situations."

68. National Foundation for Infantile Paralysis, *Minutes of the Board of Trustees,* November 10, 1938.

69. National Foundation for Infantile Paralysis, *Expansion of Plans to Meet Local Needs, Speech of Basil O'Connor, President of the Foundation, over Mutual Network, November 10, 1938,* p. 5.

70. National Foundation for Infantile Paralysis, *Reference Book for Chapters,* p. 9.

71. *Ibid.,* p. 17.

72. *Ibid.,* pp. 16–17.

73. National Tuberculosis Association, *op. cit.,* p. 9.

74. American Heart Association, *1953 Annual Report,* p. 5. American Cancer Society, *1954 Annual Report,* pp. 11–12.

75. National Foundation for Infantile Paralysis, *Reference Book for Chapters,* p. 45.

76. National Foundation for Infantile Paralysis, *Chapter Reference Book: Chapter Organization,* p. 15.

77. In States which have either many counties or a large population there are two or more State Representatives.

78. National Foundation for Infantile Paralysis, *Chapter Reference Book: Chapter Organization,* p. 31.

79. National Foundation for Infantile Paralysis, *Certificate of Incorporation of the National Foundation for Infantile Paralysis, Inc., Pursuant to the Membership Corporation Law,* filed January 3, 1938.

80. F. Emerson Andrews, *Philanthropic Giving* (New York: Russell Sage Foundation, 1950), p. 138.

81. *Ibid.,* p. 142.

82. Community Chests and Councils of America, Inc., *United Community Campaigns: 1955 Facts Book,* p. 4.

83. Community Chests and Councils of America, Inc., *1955 Experience in United Funds and Extended Federation Campaigns,* p. ii.

84. National Foundation for Infantile Paralysis, *Manual for Chapters,* 1939 ed., p. 16.

85. National Foundation for Infantile Paralysis, *Manual for Chapters,* 1949 ed., p. 13.

86. See National Foundation for Infantile Paralysis, *Publication No. 49,* December, 1955, and "Why a Separate March of Dimes?," mimeo. See also the statements of Basil O'Connor quoted in the *New York Times,* July 12, 1954, p. 14.

87. Community Chests and Councils of America, Inc., *United Community Campaigns . . . 1955: What, When and Where,* p. 2.

88. National Foundation for Infantile Paralysis, "Why a Separate March of Dimes?," mimeo.

89. John W. McConnell, "Welfare," in J. Frederic Dewhurst and Associates, *America's Needs and Resources: A New Survey* (New York: Twentieth Century Fund, 1955), p. 439.

90. See American Cancer Society, *1954 Annual Report,* pp. 56–57, and the *New York Times,* July 12, 1954, p. 14; November 4, 1955, p. 17; and December 15, 1955, p. 49.

91. Elihu Katz and Paul F. Lazarsfeld, *Personal Influence* (Glencoe, Ill.: Free Press, 1955), pp. 62–65.

92. National Foundation for Infantile Paralysis, *Chapter Reference Book: Chapter Organization,* p. 13.

93. *Ibid.,* p. 12.

94. National Foundation for Infantile Paralysis, *Reference Book for Chapters,* p. 10.

95. *Ibid.,* p. 11.

96. *Ibid.,* p. 87.

CHAPTER II

*Preserving Organizational Goals*

1. Philip Selznick, "An Approach to a Theory of Bureaucracy," *American Sociological Review*, 8 (1943), p. 49.

2. Robert Michels, *Political Parties* (Glencoe, Ill.: Free Press, 1949), p. 373. Michels' analysis, however, was directed primarily toward organizations in which authority and functions are delegated upward by the members to the leaders, particularly the German Social-Democratic Party.

3. Walter R. Sharp, *The French Civil Service* (New York: Macmillan Co., 1931), p. 446.

4. Alvin W. Gouldner, *Patterns of Industrial Bureaucracy* (Glencoe, Ill.: Free Press, 1954), pp. 220–21.

5. Robert K. Merton, *Social Theory and Social Structure* (Glencoe, Ill.: Free Press, 1949), p. 155.

6. Arthur K. Davis, "Bureaucratic Patterns in the Navy Officers Corps," in Robert K. Merton, Ailsa P. Gray, Barbara Hockey, and Hanan C. Selvin (eds.), *Reader in Bureaucracy* (Glencoe, Ill.: Free Press, 1952), pp. 389–90.

7. S. D. Clark, *Church and Sect in Canada* (Toronto: University of Toronto Press, 1948), pp. 425–31.

8. Selznick, *op. cit.*, p. 48.

9. *Ibid.*, pp. 51–54.

10. Max Weber, *The Theory of Social and Economic Organization*. Translated by A. M. Henderson and Talcott Parsons; edited by Talcott Parsons (New York: Oxford University Press, 1947), pp. 333–34.

11. Selznick, *op. cit.*, p. 52.

12. Seymour M. Lipset, "The Political Process in Trade Unions: A Theoretical Statement," in Morroe Berger, Theodore Abel, and Charles H. Page (eds.), *Freedom and Control in Modern Society* (New York: D. Van Nostrand Co., 1954), p. 121.

13. *Ibid.*, p. 96.

14. Weber, *op. cit.*, p. 328.

15. Efficiency is of course only one of the functions served by organizational rules. See Gouldner, *op. cit.*, pp. 157–80, for an extensive discussion of other functions which rules may serve.

16. Merton, *op. cit.*, pp. 154–55.

17. Peter M. Blau, *The Dynamics of Bureaucracy* (Chicago: University of Chicago Press, 1955), pp. 191–93.

18. Merton, *op. cit.*, p. 157.

19. Davis, *op. cit.*, p. 392.

20. Marshall E. Dimock, "Bureaucracy Self-Examined," in Merton, Gray, Hockey and Selvin, *op. cit.*, p. 401.

21. Selznick, *op. cit.*, p. 50.

22. See Leonard Broom and Philip Selznick, *Sociology* (Evanston, Ill. and White Plains, N.Y.: Row, Peterson and Co., 1955), p. 143.

23. Philip Selznick, *TVA and the Grass Roots* (Berkeley and Los Angeles: University of California Press, 1949), pp. 251–52.

24. F. J. Roethlisberger and William J. Dickson, *Management and the Worker* (Cambridge: Harvard University Press, 1943), pp. 379–548.

25. Merton, *op. cit.*, p. 156.

26. Davis, *op. cit.*, p. 392.

27. Selznick, *TVA and the Grass Roots*, pp. 217–46.

28. Merton, *op. cit.*, p. 158.

29. Weber, *op. cit.*, p. 330.

30. Max Weber, *Essays in Sociology*. Translated and edited by H. H. Gerth and C. W. Mills (New York: Oxford University Press, 1946), p. 216

31. Merton, *op. cit.*, pp. 157–58.

32. Blau, *op. cit.*, pp. 191–92.

33. National Foundation for Infantile Paralysis, *Manual for Chapters*, 1949 ed., p. 32.

34. National Foundation for Infantile Paralysis, *Chapter Reference Book: Chapter Patient Care Program.*

35. National Foundation for Infantile Paralysis, *Reference Book for Chapters*, pp. 202–203.

36. See the *Annual Reports* of the National Tuberculosis Association, the National Society for Crippled Children and Adults, the American Cancer Society, the American Heart Association, United Cerebral Palsy, and the National Multiple Sclerosis Association.

37. Turnley Walker, "Warm Springs," *Holiday*, 15 (February 1954), p. 84. See also Turnley Walker, *Roosevelt and the Warm Springs Story* (New York: A. A. Wyn, 1953) for a vivid account of the informal atmosphere which prevails at Georgia Warm Springs.

CHAPTER III

## Recruiting Volunteers

1. See, for example, the November, 1952 issue of *Adult Leadership*, which is entirely devoted to the problem of "Getting and Keeping Members," and National Multiple Sclerosis Society, *Volunteers and Their Work*, Service Bulletin No. 3, a manual which discusses the problem of recruiting volunteer workers in some detail. Since this Society was not founded until 1946, and is still in a period of growth, the recruitment of volunteers constitutes a major problem. The Foundation, however, devotes relatively little space to this problem in its various manuals. Three pages in its guide to Chapter activities are devoted to membership, but largely to the special problem of obtaining broad community representation. See National Foundation for Infantile Paralysis, *Reference Book for Chapters*, pp. 9–11.

2. Sherwood D. Fox, "Voluntary Associations and Social Structure," unpublished Ph. D. thesis, Harvard University, 1953, pp. 59–68.

3. See David B. Truman, *The Governmental Process* (New York: Alfred A. Knopf, 1951), pp. 39–43.

4. Bernard Barber, " 'Mass Apathy' and Voluntary Social Participation in the United States," unpublished Ph. D. thesis, Harvard University, 1948, p.179.

5. National Foundation for Infantile Paralysis, "Orientation Manual for State Representatives," mimeo., p. C.D. (E-1).

6. American Cancer Society, *Publication No. 21*, p. 1.

7. American Heart Association, *What is the American Heart Association*, 1954, p. 2.

8. American National Red Cross, *This is the Red Cross*, 1955, p. 1.

9. Community Chests and Councils of America, Inc., Advisory Committee on Citizen Participation, *To Have and To Hold Volunteers in Community Services*, 1950, p. 6.

10. Community Chests and Councils of America, Inc., *A Volunteer Bureau Handbook*, Bulletin No. 168, September, 1952, p. 1.

11. Community Chests and Councils of America, Inc., Advisory Committee on Citizen Participation, *How to Say Thank You, Volunteers!*, p. 1.

12. Philip Selznick, *TVA and the Grass Roots* (Berkeley and Los Angeles: University of California Press, 1949), pp. 59–64.

13. Robin M. Williams, *American Society* (New York: Alfred A. Knopf, 1952), pp. 386–440.

14. Cora Du Bois, "The Dominant Value Profile of American Culture," *American Anthropologist*, 57 (1955), pp. 1232–39. Interestingly, Du Bois does not mention "humanitarianism" as a dominant American value.

15. Arthur Kornhauser and Paul F. Lazarsfeld, "The Analysis of Consumer Actions," in Paul F. Lazarsfeld and Morris Rosenberg (eds.), *The Language of Social Research* (Glencoe, Ill.: Free Press, 1955), p. 393.

16. *Ibid.*, p. 396.

17. Elihu Katz and Paul F. Lazarsfeld, *Personal Influence* (Glencoe, Ill.: Free Press, 1955), p. 189.

18. See, for example, National Multible Sclerosis Society, *1954 Annual Report*, p. 6 and United Cerebral Palsy, *1954 Annual Report*, p. 1. The Board of Trustees of the American Foundation for the Blind, to cite another example, contains twenty-seven members. Of these, eight are blind themselves and another nine are officers in various organizations established to assist blind people. See American Foundation for the Blind, *Help for the Deaf-Blind*, p. 4.

19. Clyde Kluckhohn and Florence R. Kluckhohn, "American Culture: Generalized Orientations and Class Patterns," in Lyman Bryson, Louis Finkelstein and R. M. MacIver (eds.), *Conflicts of Power in Modern Culture* (New York: Harper and Brothers, 1947), p. 116.

20. Williams, *op. cit.*, p. 471.

21. John P. Marquand, *Sincerely, Willis Wayde* (Boston: Little, Brown and Co., 1955), p. 295.

22. See Morris Janowitz, *The Community Press in an Urban Setting* (Glencoe, Ill.: Free Press, 1952) and Floyd Dotson, "Patterns of Voluntary Association Among Working-Class Families," *American Sociological Review*, 16 (1951), pp. 687–93 for evidence which contradicts the traditional view that urban life is necessarily impersonal in nature; see Katz

and Lazarsfeld, *op. cit.*, for an impressive statement of the importance of primary group relationships in decision-making.

23. Clyde Kluckhohn, *Mirror for Man* (New York: Whittlesey House, 1949), pp. 249–50.

24. Robert C. Angell, *The Integration of American Society* (New York: McGraw-Hill Book Co., 1941), p. 119.

25. Herbert Goldhamer, "Some Factors Affecting Participation in Voluntary Associations," unpublished Ph. D. thesis, University of Chicago, 1943, pp. 4–5.

26. Sherwood D. Fox, "Voluntary Associations and Social Structure," unpublished Ph. D. thesis, Harvard University, 1953, p. 29.

27. Williams, *op. cit.*, p. 470.

28. Allen H. Barton, "The Concept of Property-Space in Social Research," in Lazarsfeld and Rosenberg, *op. cit.*, pp. 45–50. This article contains both a detailed description of the reduction of attribute space and examples of its application to a variety of analysis problems.

29. Peter H. Rossi, "Why Families Move," in Lazarsfeld and Rosenberg, *op. cit.*, pp. 461–62.

30. Kornhauser and Lazarsfeld, *op. cit.*, p. 397.

31. Philip H. Ennis, "They Changed to Tea: A Study in the Dynamics of Consumer Behavior," unpublished research report of the Bureau of Applied Social Research, Columbia University, 1954, p. III–2.

32. Hazel Gaudet, "A Model for Assessing Changes in Voting Intention," in Lazarsfeld and Rosenberg, *op. cit.*, p. 432.

33. J. Stannard Baker, "A Framework for Assessment of Causes of Automobile Accidents," in Lazarsfeld and Rosenberg, *op. cit.*, p. 445.

34. Katz and Lazarsfeld, *op. cit.*, p. 190.

35. Kornhauser and Lazarsfeld, *op. cit.*, p. 393.

36. See Baker, *op. cit.*, for a discussion of the methodological problems involved in determing the reasons for auto accidents.

37. Talcott Parsons and others, "Some Fundamental Categories of the Theory of Action: A General Statement," in Talcott Parsons and Edward A. Shils (eds.), *Toward a General Theory of Action* (Cambridge: Harvard University Press, 1951), p. 19.

38. Talcott Parsons, Edward A. Shils with the assistance of James Olds, "Values, Motives, and Systems of Action," in Parsons and Shils (eds.), *op. cit.*, p. 144.

39. See, for example, Katz and Lazarsfeld, *op. cit.*, and Bernard R. Berelson, Paul F. Lazarsfeld, and William N. McPhee, *Voting* (Chicago: University of Chicago Press, 1954).

## CHAPTER IV

## *Assisting Polio Victims*

1. National Foundation for Infantile Paralysis, *Polio Facts for Speakers and Writers*, p. 23; *1954 Speakers Handbook*, p. 107.

2. National Foundation for Infantile Paralysis, *1955 Annual Report*, p. 39.

3. Based upon responses to the following questions:

*Serious*
"Which do you think are the most serious diseases or illnesses in this country today?"
*Most serious*
"Which one of these do you think is *most* serious?"
*Most widespread*
"Of these diseases (list handed to respondent), which do you think affects the most people in America?" (Data for four cities only.)
*Most fear-inspiring*
"Which *one* disease or illness do you personally fear most?"

4. See Survey Research Center, University of Michigan, "The American Public Discuss Cancer and the American Cancer Society," mimeo., 1948, for a discussion of some reasons underlying the widespread concern over cancer in America today.

5. In response to the question, "Generally, of these diseases (list handed to respondent), which have you heard most about in the last year or so?"

6. Based upon the following items: (1) knowledge of what the local Chapter

does; (2) knowledge of when the March of Dimes campaign took place; (3) knowledge that research was stressed in the 1954 March of Dimes campaign; (4) knowledge that the March of Dimes does not belong to the Community Chest; (5) knowledge of gamma globulin and the new Salk vaccine. See Appendix B for a description of the Knowledge of Foundation Activities Index.

7. See Jerome Ellison, "Who Gets Your Charity Dollars?," *Saturday Evening Post*, 226, 52 (June 26, 1954), p. 125, for an example of lay criticism.

8. See, for example, Herbert H. Hyman and Paul B. Sheatsley, "Some Reasons Why Information Campaigns Fail," in Guy E. Swanson and others (eds.), *Readings in Social Psychology*, Revised edition (New York: Henry Holt and Co., 1952), pp. 86–95.

9. James H. S. Gear, "Poliomyelitis in the Under-developed Areas of the World," in World Health Organization, *Poliomyelitis*, Monograph No. 26 (Geneva: World Health Organization, 1955), p. 44.

10. Matthieu Freyche and Johannes Nielsen, "Incidence of Poliomyelitis Since 1920," in *World Health Organization, op. cit.*, p. 60.

11. In some countries, e.g., Japan, polio seems still to be largely an endemic disease. See John R. Paul, "Poliomyelitis Attack Rates in American Troops in 1940–48," *American Journal of Hygiene*, 50 (1949), pp. 57–62.

12. Source: United States Public Health Service. See National Foundation for Infantile Paralysis, *Poliomyelitis 1955: Annual Statistical Review*, Table 2.

13. *Ibid.*, p. 7.

14. John R. Paul, "Epidemiology of Poliomyelitis," in World Health Organization, *op. cit.*, p. 19.

15. See W. S. Robinson, "Ecological Correlations and the Behavior of Individuals," *American Sociological Review*, 15 (1950), pp. 351–57; Herbert Menzel, "Comment on Robinson's 'Ecological Correlations and the Behavior of Individuals'," *American Sociological Review*, 15 (1950), p. 674; and especially Hanan C. Selvin, "The Effects of Leadership Climate on the Nonduty Behavior of Army Trainees," unpublished Ph. D. thesis, Columbia University, 1956, *passim*, for discussions of the problems involved in establishing correlations between ecological and individual variables.

16. See footnote 3, above. Data concerning "most widespread" could not be used in this table, since this question was not asked of the nationwide sample.

17. National Foundation for Infantile Paralysis, *Poliomyelitis 1955: Annual Statistical Review*, p. 4.

18. In response to the question: "Which do you think are the most serious diseases or illnesses facing the *children* of this country today? Which *one* is the *most* serious?"

19. National Foundation for Infantile Paralysis, *Poliomyelitis 1955: Annual Statistical Review*, Table 3.

20. National Foundation for Infantile Paralysis, *Facts and Figures About Infantile Paralysis*, 1947, p. 29. The findings of this study do not necessarily apply to the country at large, since the percentage of all cases which are paralytic in nature varies greatly from community to community, and from year to year. See Albert B. Sabin, "Epidemiologic Patterns of Poliomyelitis in Different Parts of the World," in International Poliomyelitis Conference, *Poliomyelitis* (Philadelphia: J. B. Lippincott Co., 1949), pp. 3–4.

21. Rolla A. Dyer, "United States," in International Poliomyelitis Conference, *op. cit.*, p. 352.

22. In response to the question: "Do you know someone personally who has had any of these diseases or illnesses?" (List handed to respondent.)

23. Dyer, *op. cit.*, p. 352.

24. See Sabin, *op. cit.*; Freyche and Nielson, *op. cit.*, and Paul, "Epidemiology of Poliomyelitis" for discussions of the environmental correlates of polio incidence.

25. National Foundation for Infantile Paralysis, *The Polio Vaccine: What You Should Know About It*, Publication No. 19, February 1956, p. 8.

26. Source: National Foundation for Infantile Paralysis, *1951–1955 Annual Reports; Poliomyelitis 1955: Annual Statistical Review*, Table 2.

27. Polio incidence data obtained from unpublished data on file at the National Foundation for Infantile Paralysis, based upon reports of the United States Public Health Service. Patient care data obtained from the Chapter Treasurer's Reports of the thirty-seven Chapters.

28. National Foundation for Infantile Paralysis, *1954 Annual Report*, pp. 58–61; *1955 Annual Report*, pp. 55–57.

29. National Foundation for Infantile

Paralysis, *Chapter Reference Book: Chapter Patient Care Program*, pp. 18–19.

30. *Ibid.*, p. 4.

31. *Ibid.*, p. 7.

32. *Ibid.*, pp. 17–18.

33. *Ibid.*, p. 4.

34. *Ibid.*, p. 2.

35. *Ibid.*, p. 1.

36. See National Foundation for Infantile Paralysis, *Reference Book* for Chapters, pp. 161–72 and *1955 Annual Report*, p. 38.

37. Computed from data published in National Foundation for Infantile Paralysis, *1951–1955 Annual Reports*.

38. National Foundation for Infantile Paralysis, *Reference Book for Chapters*, p. 162.

39. See, for example, the maps of the United States published in each recent Foundation *Annual Report*, showing the state-to state variation in polio incidence during the year.

40. National Foundation for Infantile Paralysis, *Reference Book for Chapters*, p. 5.

41. National Foundation for Infantile Paralysis, *Chapter Reference Book: Chapter Patient Care Program*, pp. 57–58.

## CHAPTER V

### *Raising Funds*

1. Donald Young, "Foreword," in F. Emerson Andrews, *Philanthropic Giving* (New York: Russell Sage Foundation, 1950), p. 5.

2. See Andrews, *op. cit.*, pp. 73–74. See also Edward C. Jenkins, *Philanthropy in America* (New York: Association Press, 1950); Arnaud C. Marts, *Philanthropy's Role in Civilization* (New York: Harper and Brothers, 1953); and John R. Seeley and others, *Community Chest: A Case Study in Philanthropy* (Toronto: University of Toronto Press, 1957) for discussions of the role played by philanthropy in American society.

3. National Foundation for Infantile Paralysis, *Chapter Reference Book: Chapter Organization*, p. 23.

4. Source: National Foundation for Infantile Paralysis, *March of Dimes Guide for 1955*, p. 7.

5. National Foundation for Infantile Paralysis, *Manual for Chapters*, 1949 ed., p. 13.

6. Per capita receipts from the 1953 campaign. Source: National Foundation for Infantile Paralysis, *1954 Campaign Guide*.

7. See Max Weber, *The Theory of Social and Economic Organization*. Translated by A. M. Henderson and Talcott Parsons; edited by Talcott parsons (New York: Oxford University Press, 1947), pp. 124–32.

8. See Robert K. Merton, *Social Theory and Structure* (Glencoe, Ill.: Free Press, 1949), pp. 179–95 for a discussion of the sociological relevance of this theorem. See also Seymour M. Lipset and Natalie Rogoff, "Class and Opportunity in Europe and the U.S.," *Commentary*, 18 (December, 1954), pp. 562–68.

9. See Melvin A. Glasser, "M-Day for Polio," *Adult Leadership*, 3, 3 (1954), pp. 5–7 for an account of Volunteer participation in the vaccine field trials.

## CHAPTER VI

### *Giving to the March of Dimes*

1. See, for example, Community Chests and Councils of America, Inc., *1955 Experience in United Funds and Extended Federation Campaigns*, p. 1.

2. Sources: Community Chests and Councils of America, Inc., *United Community Campaigns: 1955 Facts Book* and the *1954 Annual Reports* of the five

independent associations. The National Tuberculosis Association total, however, is for the 1952 Christmas Seal Sale.

3. See F. Emerson Andrews, *Philanthropic Giving* (New York: Russell Sage Foundation, 1950), p. 73.

4. See Community Chests and Councils of America, Inc., *1955 Experience in*

*United Funds and Extended Federation Campaigns*, p. 5.

5. Median family income data are for the year 1949 (1950 Census). See Appendix B for a description of the criteria used to establish cutting points. Since counties located in the East, Midwest, and West generally have a higher median family income than counties in the South or Southwest, it was necessary to examine this relationship separately in each region of the country. The same relationship obtains, however, when the data in Table 19 are controlled by region.

6. Source: National Foundation for Infantile Paralysis, *1954 Campaign Guide*.

7. Source: National Foundation for Infantile Paralysis, County Campaign Reports for 1954.

8. In response to the question: "If someone in your family got polio and you needed financial help, where do you think you might turn?" When asked specifically, "Do you know of any organization which might help you?" another 8 per cent mentioned the Foundation. However, since the Foundation had already been mentioned at this point in the interview, it is very possible that responses to this specific question were influenced by what the respondent has "learned" during the interview.

9. Herbert H. Hyman, "The Value Systems of Different Classes: A Social Psychological Contribution to the Analysis of Stratification," in Reinhard Bendix and Seymour M. Lipset (eds.), *Class, Status and Power* (Glencoe, Ill.: Free Press, 1953), pp. 426–42.

10. Paul F. Lazarsfeld, "The American Soldier: An Expository Review," *Public Opinion Quarterly*, 13, 3 (1949), pp. 377–404. See also Genevieve Knupfer, "Portrait of the Underdog," in Bendix and Lipset (eds.), *op. cit.*, pp. 255–63 for illustrations of unawareness on the part of low status people of opportunities which could serve to improve their status or in other ways benefit them personally.

11. Paul F. Lazarsfeld, *Jugend und Beruf* (Jena: Fischer, 1931), p. 19. Quoted in Knupfer, *op. cit.*, p. 263.

12. Items scored as follows:

*Patient care program*
Respondents received a high score if they mentioned treatment or patient care in response to the question: "Can you tell me anything about what this organization does with the money it collects through the March of Dimes?" All others received a low score.

*President Roosevelt*
Respondents received a high score if they mentioned President Roosevelt in response to the question: "Do you happen to know who founded this organization? Who was it?" All others received a low score.

*Chapter in the county*
Respondents received a high score if they replied positively to the question: "As far as you know, is there a Chapter of the National Foundation for Infantile Paralysis in this county? All others received a low score. Data for four cities only.

*Chapter patient care program*
Respondents received a high score if they mentioned either the Foundation or the Chapter in response to the question: "If someone in your family got polio and you needed financial assistance, where might you turn?" All others received a low score.

*Research theme*
Respondents received a high score if they mentioned gamma globulin, vaccine, or research in response to the question: "What were the main things stressed in the March of Dimes campaign this year?" All others received a low score. Data for four cities only.

*Sponsorship of March of Dimes*
Respondents received a high score if they mentioned the Foundation in response to the question: "Do you happpen to know the name of the organization that puts on the March of Dimes?" All others received a low score.

*Nonparticipation in Community Chest*
Respondents received a high score if they replied negatively to the question: "As far as you know, is the organization that operates the March of Dimes a member of the Community Fund [Chest]?" All others received a

low score. Data for four cities only.

13. See Norman Miller, "The Jewish Leadership of Lakeport," in Alvin W. Gouldner, (ed.), *Studies in Leadership* (New York: Harper and Brothers, 1950), p. 195.

14. Items scored as follows:

*News about polio*

Respondents received a high score if they selected polio in response to the question: "Of these diseases, which have you heard most about in the last year or so?" All others received a low score. Data for four cities only.

*Acquaintance with a victim*

Respondents received a high score if they mentioned knowing a polio victim in response to the question: "Do you know someone personally who has had any of these diseases or illnesses?" All others received a low score.

*Young children in family*

Respondents received a high score if they are under forty years of age and have children under twenty-one years of age. All others received a low score. The parental status of seventeen respondents was not ascertained.

*Acquaintance with a Chapter assisted victim*

Respondents received a high score if they replied positively to the question: "Do you know anyone who has been helped by the local Chapter?" All others received a low score. Data for four cities only.

*High polio incidence*

Respondents received a high score if they live in counties which had a 1951–1953 weighted polio incidence rate of forty-four cases per 100,000 population or higher: a low score if they live in counties with a rate of ten cases per 100,000 population or lower. Respondents living in areas of medium polio

incidence not included. See Appendix B for a description of this index.

15. See reference 14, above.

16. See reference 5, above.

17. Source: National Foundation for Infantile Paralysis, 1954 *Campaign Guide.*

18. Items scored as follows:

*Popularity*

Respondents received a high score if they selected "polio" or "crippled children" in response to the question: "Here is a list of seven diseases or illnesses. If you could give money to help fight *only one* of these, which would you pick as Number One?"

*Saliency*

Respondents received a high score if they spontaneously mentioned the March of Dimes in response to the question: "There are a number of organizations which hold campaigns to collect money to fight different diseases or illnesses. Which of these campaigns have you heard about?"

*Contribution*

Respondents received a high score if they contributed to the March of Dimes in the past year. See Appendix B for a description of the procedures followed to discriminate between contributors and noncontributors.

19. See Peter H. Rossi, *Why Families Move: A Study in the Social Psychology of Urban Residential Mobility* (Glencoe, Ill.: Free Press, 1955).

20. See, for example, Bernard R. Berelson, Paul F. Lazarsfeld and William N. McPhee, *Voting* (Chicago: University of Chicago Press, 1954).

21. Items scored as follows:

*Seriousness*

Respondents received a high score if they mentioned polio in response to the question: "Which do you think are the most serious diseases or illnesses in this country today?" All others received a low score.

*Crippling aftereffects*

Respondents received a high score if they mentioned polio in response to the question: "Which do you think are the most serious diseases or illnesses facing the children of this country today?" *and* who mentioned "crippling" in response to the question: "Why do you think it is most serious?" All others received a low score.

*Fear*

Respondents received a high score if they scored high on the Fear of Polio Index. Respondents received a low score if they scored low in this index. Respondents with medium scores not included. See Appendix B

for a description of this index. Data for four cities only.

*Emotional*
 *involvement*

Respondents received a high score if they scored high on the Index of Emotional Involvement. Respondents received a low score if they scored low on this index. Respondents with medium scores not included. See Appendix B for a description of this index. Data for four cities only.

22. Jerome Ellison, "Who Gets Your Charity Dollars?," *Saturday Evening Post*, 226, 52 (June 26, 1954), p. 125.

## CHAPTER VII

## *Volunteers and the Foundation*

1. Arnold M. Rose, *Union Solidarity* (Minneapolis: University of Minnnesota Press, 1952), pp. 52 and 61.

2. *New York Times*, May 20, 1956, p. 70.

3. Foster R. Dulles, *The American Red Cross: A History* (New York: Harper and Brothers, 1950), p. 509.

4. David Riesman, *Individualism Reconsidered and Other Essays*, (Glencoe, Ill.: Free Press, 1954), p. 232.

5. David B. Truman, *The Governmental Process* (New York: Alfred A. Knopf, 1951), p. 129.

6. See Seymour M. Lipset, "The Political Process in Trade Unions: A Theoretical Statement," in Morroe Berger, Theodore Abel, and Charles H. Page (eds.), *Freedom and Control in Modern Society* (New York: D. Van Nostrand Co., 1954), pp. 82–124 and Seymour M. Lipset, Martin A. Trow, and James S. Coleman, *Union Democracy* (Glencoe, Ill.: Free Press, 1956) for extensive discussions of the structural sources of minority rule in trade unions. *Union Democracy* is a case study of the International Typographical Union, a union selected by the authors for intensive analysis because of its unique status as a truly democratic national labor organization.

7. See Dulles, *op. cit.*, pp. 304–306, 526–27, and 535–38.

8. Peter M. Blau, *Bureaucracy in Modern Society* (New York: Random House, 1956), p. 69.

9. See Martin Scheerer, "Cognitive Theory," in Gardner Lindzey, (ed.), *Handbook of Social Psychology* (Cambridge: Addison-Wesley Publishing Co., 1954), pp. 91–142, for a comprehensive review of this phenomenon and an extensive bibliography.

10. David Krech and Richard S. Crutchfield, *Theory and Problems of Social Psychology* (New York: McGraw-Hill Book Co., 1948), p. 82.

11. *Ibid.*, p. 81.

12. See, for example, Theodore M. Newcomb, *Social Psychology* (New York: Dryden Press, 1950), pp. 90–96.

13. A. Lawrence Lowell, *Public Opinion in War and Peace* (Cambridge: Harvard University Press, 1923), p. 22.

14. Robert K. Merton, "Patterns of Influence: A Study of Interpersonal Influence and of Communications Behavior in a Local Community," in Paul F. Lazarsfeld and Frank N. Stanton, (eds.), *Communications Research: 1948–1949* (New York: Harper and Brothers, 1949), pp. 189–190.

15. *Ibid.*, p. 196.

16. *Ibid.*, p. 197.

17. National Foundation for Infantile Paralysis, *Manual for Chapters*, 1949 edition, p. 7.

18. National Foundation for Infantile Paralysis, *Reference Book for Chapters*, p. 54.

19. *Ibid.*, p. 6. Italics supplied.

20. *Ibid.*, p. 54. Italics supplied.

CHAPTER VIII

## The Rewards of Volunteering

1. Rudolf Heberle, "Ferdinand Tonnies' Contributions to the Sociology of Political Parties," *American Journal of Sociology,* 61 (1955), p. 217.

2. Henry D. Thoreau, *Walden* (New York: W. W. Norton and Co., 1951), p. 22.

3. Clyde Kluckhohn, *Mirror for Man* (New York: Whittlesey House, 1949), p. 249.

4. David Riesman, *The Lonely Crowd* (New Haven: Yale University Press, 1950).

5. See, for example, Herbert Blumer, "Collective Behavior," in Alfred M. Lee, (ed.), *Principles of Sociology* (New York: Barnes and Noble, 1955), p. 199 and Joyce O. Hertzler, *Society in Action* (New York: Dryden Press, 1954), pp. 362–63.

6. Louis I. Dublin, "Foreword," in Selskar M. Gunn and Philip S. Platt, *Voluntary Health Agencies* (New York: Ronald Press, 1945), p. v.

7. Arnold W. Green, *Sociology* (New York: McGraw-Hill Book Co., 1956), pp. 532–33.

8. Hadley Cantril, *The Psychology of Social Movements* (New York: John Wiley and Sons, 1941).

9. Talcott Parsons, *The Social System* (Glencoe, Ill.: Free Press, 1951), p. 521.

10. Blumer, *op. cit.,* p. 199.

11. Rudolf Heberle, "Observations on the Study of Social Movements," *American Sociological Review,* 14 (1949), p. 349.

12. C. Wendell King, *Social Movements in the United States* (New York: Random House, 1956), p. 27.

13. See Franklin D. Roosevelt, "Extemporaneous Remarks at Thanksgiving Day Party at Warm Springs, Georgia— an Informal History of the Institution, November 29, 1934," in *The Public Papers and Addresses of Franklin D. Roosevelt.* Vol. 3 (New York: Random House, 1938), pp. 485–90 for a first-hand account of these events.

14. See Ira R. T. Smith with Joe Alex Morris, *"Dear Mr. President . . ."* *The Story of Fifty Years in the White House Mail Room* (New York: Julian Messner, 1949), pp. 158–61.

15. Max Weber, *The Theory of Social and Economic Organization.* Translated by A. M. Henderson and Talcott Parsons; edited by Talcott Parsons (New York: Oxford University Press, 1947), pp. 358–59.

16. *Ibid.,* pp. 361–62.

17. *Ibid.,* p. 364.

18. For theoretical statements of this process, see Ernest Troeltsch, *Social Teachings of the Christian Churches* (New York: Macmillan Co., 1949), pp. 331–43; Blumer, *op. cit.,* pp. 202–14; King, *op. cit.,* pp. 39–57; and especially Weber, *op. cit.,* pp. 363–92.

19. Weber, *op. cit.,* p. 365.

20. Basil O'Connor, "His Bequest to the People," in Special Supplement, "Roosevelt: A First Appraisal by Those Who Knew Him," *New Republic,* 114 (April 15, 1946), p. 544.

21. National Foundation for Infantile Paralysis, *1953 Campaign Guide,* p. 5.

22. National Foundation for Infantile Paralysis, *1953 Annual Report,* p. 4.

23. *Ibid.*

24. National Foundation for Infantile Paralysis, *1953 Campaign Guide,* p. 5.

25. National Foundation for Infantile Paralysis, *1953 Annual Report,* p. 5.

26. National Foundation for Infantile Paralysis, *The Story of the National Foundation for Infantile Paralysis,* 1941, p. 6.

27. National Foundation for Infantile Paralysis, *1952 Annual Report,* p. 5.

28. National Foundation for Infantile Paralysis, *Reference Book for Chapters,* p. 6.

29. National Foundation for Infantile Paralysis, *1952 Annual Report,* p. 4.

30. American Cancer Society, *1954 Annual Report,* p. 27.

31. American Heart Association, *1954 Annual Report,* p. 25.

32. National Tuberculosis Association, *Annual Report on the Occasion of the Fiftieth Anniversary,* 1954, p. 4.

33. American National Red Cross, *This is the Red Cross,* 1955, p. 1.

34. See Philip Selznick, *TVA and the Grass Roots* (Berkeley and Los Angeles: University of California Press, 1949), p. 251.

CHAPTER IX

## The Future of the Foundation

1. *New York Times*, June 12, 1956, p. 37.

2. C. Wendell King, *Social Movements in the United States* (New York: Random House, 1956), p. 114.

3. Philip Selznick, *TVA and the Grass Roots* (Berkeley and Los Angeles: University of California Press, 1949), pp. 258–59.

4. Arnold M. Rose, *Theory and Method in the Social Sciences* (Minneapolis: University of Minnesota Press, 1954), p. 58.

5. Clyde Kluckhohn and Florence R. Kluckhohn, "American Culture: Generalized Orientations and Class Patterns," in Lyman Bryson, Louis Finkelstein, and R. M. MacIver (eds.), *Conflicts of Power in Modern Culture* (New York: Harper and Brothers, 1947), p. 116.

6. Peter M. Blau, *The Dynamics of Bureaucracy* (Chicago: University of Chicago Press, 1955), p. 195. See also Peter M. Blau, *Bureaucracy in Modern Society* (New York: Random House, 1956), pp. 95–96.

7. Blau, *The Dynamics of Bureaucracy*, p. 195.

8. Planned Parenthood Federation of America, *Birth Control U.S.A.: Highlights of the Program*, p. 8; *The Most Important Thing*, p. 3.

9. American Social Hygiene Association, *Social Hygiene News*, April, 1955.

10. Owen E. Pence, *The Y.M.C.A. and Social Need* (New York: Association Press, 1939).

11. *Ibid.*, p. 12.

12. *Ibid.*, p. 315.

13. *Ibid.*, p. 236.

14. Joseph R. Gusfield, "Social Structure and Moral Reform: A Study of the Woman's Christian Temperance Union," *American Journal of Sociology*, 61 (1955), pp. 221–32. The discussion in the text is based entirely upon this study.

15. *Ibid.*, p. 222.

16. *Ibid.*, p. 225.

17. *Ibid.*, p. 232.

18. *Ibid.*, p. 228.

19. *Ibid.*

20. Sheldon L. Messinger, "Organizational Transformation: A Case Study of a Declining Social Movement," *American Sociological Review*, 20 (1955), pp. 3–10. The discussion which follows is based largely upon this study. See Arnold W. Green, *Sociology* (New York: McGraw-Hill Book Co., 1956), pp. 547–55, for further details of the Townsend Movement.

21. Messinger, *op. cit.*, p. 4.

22. *Ibid.*, p. 10.

23. The discussion of the Red Cross in the text is based entirely upon Foster R. Dulles, *The American Red Cross: A History* (New York: Harper and Brothers, 1950).

24. Cited in Dulles, *op. cit.*, p. 16.

25. *Ibid.*, p. 218. Italics supplied.

26. *Ibid.*, p. 219.

27. *Ibid.*, pp. 276–94.

28. Cited in *Ibid.*, p. 521.

29. *Ibid.*, p. 527.

30. *Ibid.*

31. *Ibid.*, p. 528.

32. Blau, *Bureaucracy in Modern Society*, p. 95.

33. *Ibid.*, pp. 95–96.

34. Rose, *op. cit.*, p. 51

35. Seymour M. Lipset, Martin A. Trow and James S. Coleman, *Union Democracy* (Glencoe, Ill.: Free Press, 1956), pp. 76–77.

36. V. L. Allen, *Power in Trade Unions* (London: Longmans, Green and Co., 1954), p. 9.

37. Victor Cohn, *Four Billion Dimes* (No publisher; no date), p. 128. This book consists of reprints of a series of articles which first appeared in the *Minneapolis Star and Tribune* in April, 1955.

38. See, for example, the statements of Basil O'Connor quoted in the *New York Herald Tribune*, January 7, 1957, p. 2 and in *Time*, January 21, 1957, p. 62.

39. *New York Times*, January 13, 1957, p. E–11.

40. See National Foundation for Infantile Paralysis, *Annual Reports* for summaries of grants made and other support given to these activities.

# INDEX OF SUBJECTS

Volunteers (*cont.*)

image held of Foundation, 205, 207–209, 211, 214, 215, 228

comparisons with other organizations, 205

comparisons with Red Cross, 206–211, 249

perception of Foundation, 215–217, 220, 228, 265

identification with National Headquarters, 216–217

determinants of perception, 220–222, 224–225, 231–232

continued participation in program, 233

Volunteers (*cont.*)

participation in social movement, 243–252, 270–271

Woman's Christian Temperance Union, 258, 269

similarities to Y.M.C.A., 259–260

failure to adjust to changes in environment, 259–261

Young Men's Christian Association

organizational adaptation of, 258–259

similarities to W.C.T.U., 259–260

# INDEX OF NAMES